Faith
and
Fragility

OTHER BOOKS BY THE AUTHOR:

Churches and Immigrants (1961)
Race and Religion in New Zealand (1966)
The Breaking of Traditions (1968)
Christianity in Chains (1969)
Religion in Australia (1971)
Western Religion (editor, 1972)
Identity and the Sacred (1976)
Religion and Identity (editor, 1978)
Wholeness and Breakdown (1978)
The Fixed and the Fickle (1982)
The Firm and the Formless (1982)
Meaning and Place (1983)
The Faith of Australians (1985)
How God Hoodwinked Hitler (1985)

Faith and Fragility

Religion and Identity
in Canada

Hans Mol

TRINITY PRESS
Burlington, Ontario, Canada

Canadian Cataloguing in Publication Data

Mol, Hans, 1922-
   Faith and fragility : religion and identity
in Canada

Includes index.
ISBN 0-919649-73-4

1. Canada--Religion. 2. Christianity--
Canada. 3. Identification (Religion)
4. Religion and sociology--Canada.
I. Title.

BL2530.C3M64 1985   306'.6   C85-090039-5

ISBN 0 919649 73 4

© 1985 by Hans Mol

Trinity Press
960 Gateway
Burlington, Ontario
L7L 5K7 Canada

Printed in Canada

TABLE OF CONTENTS

ABOUT THE AUTHOR

Johannis (Hans) J. MOL was born in the Netherlands and is professor in Religious Studies at McMaster University. He obtained his Ph.D. in sociology at Columbia University, New York. He was lecturer in sociology at the University of Canterbury in New Zealand from 1961-1963 and fellow in sociology in the Institute of Advanced Studies of the Australian National University from 1963 until he came to McMaster in 1970.

He is the author of 13 books and monographs in the sociology of religion, and the editor of two more. The best known of these works are *Religion in Australia* (1971), *Western Religion* (1972), *Identity and The Sacred* (1976), and *Meaning and Place* (1983). He has also published close to 50 chapters in books and articles in refereed journals. In 1978 he was invited to give the Payne lecture at the University of Missouri and the opening address at the International Conference for the Sociology of Religion in Tokyo.

He has been very active in professional organizations. From 1963-1969 he was the secretary-treasurer of the sociological Association of Australia and New Zealand. From 1970-1978 he was first secretary and subsequently president of the Sociology of Religion Research Committee of the International Sociological Association.

INTRODUCTION

Originally this study was *not* intended to be a textbook on religion in Canada. However, several colleagues who appraised the book suggested that it could admirably serve that purpose. Partly, of course, it came into being because I felt that my classes at McMaster University needed a more systematic, social-scientific overview of religion in Canada than was provided by the existing texts. The latter often left out large areas of material (such as native religion), adopted perspectives alien to the social-scientific approach (such as theology or philosophy) and in all instances stressed some units of social organization (such as society) at the expense of others (such as family).

Yet the intention of the book has little do with filling a market need. For one, the market is too small to be of much interest to commercial publishers. For another, market considerations would have meant soft-pedalling an approach alien to a substantial section of colleagues teaching religion in Canadian courses. For a third, I intended to do much original research for the book and consult as many sources as were available (the bibliography contains over 500 items and even so is not exhaustive). Lastly, and chiefly, I wanted *Faith and Fragility* to be the third and last book of the *F & F* trilogy. Like its two predecessors (*The Fixed and the Fickle* on religion and identity in New Zealand and *The Firm and the Formless* on religion and identity in aboriginal Australia) it has the explicit aim of critical application, refinement and elaboration of the identity frame of reference for the study of religion as developed in my 1976 *Identity and the Sacred*. The title, as in the other two books, draws attention to the fact that from a social-scientific point of view, religion is constantly attempting to make whole (or render fixed, firm, faithworthy) that which may fragment (or be fickle, formless, fragile).

What is the identity model of religion? To put it in the simplest of terms: It treats society as a jostling configuration of cooperating, but also contending units of social organization ("identities", "systems"). In this tussle of individual, family, ethnic group, denomination, community, class, society, tribe, clan, sect, nation, etc., religion always *either* reinforces particular units, thereby augmenting the power of each, *or* reconciles the tension

1

between them (providing, for example, a perspective or belief transcending class, race, national or communal division) *or* redresses imbalances (defending the disprivileged, unemployed or underpaid against the powerful corporation) thereby changing the balance of power in accordance with its transcendental frame of reference.

Implied in this too short a summary is the conviction of the author that the best possible theory in the mid-eighties is neither functionalism (stressing the way society hangs together) nor conflict theory (stressing the power struggle between the components of a society), but a combination of both. Elsewhere (Mol, 1982c) I have called this approach dialectical. In this book I use functionalism when I stress the cohesion and the boundary defense of the various units of social organization. Yet I also make grateful use of the insights of the conflict school. The book not only describes the conflicts and prejudices between the various religious frames of references, but is also particularly interested in the way religion deals, or dealt, with tension and friction between the various units of social organizations, such as French and Irish ethnic groups, families and communities amongst the Hutterites, or personality and society on the frontier. This abiding interest in the stiffening and softening boundaries around social organizations continues a theme in many of my previous writings. Actually, these flexible boundaries form the heart of the identity model of religion which has been expounded in various books and articles (Mol 1974, Mol 1976, Mol 1978, Mol 1978a, Mol 1979, Mol 1979a, Mol 1979b, Mol 1983).

At first sight the model appears to underestimate change. Yet it stresses the pivotal function religion has for the transition from one identity to another (rites of passage). Many religions also advocate the kinds of change which lead to greater social justice, more wholesome family life, and a more humane treatment of individuals. However, the identity approach maintains that the ultimate goal of these and other religions is a better fit with particular blueprints of existence, and that these blueprints (or objectified frames of reference) side with order rather than with disrupting change. It therefore stresses a constant dialectic between forces which lead to identity consolidation and those which lead to identity fragmentation.

This dialectic operates even at the heart of the four mechanisms of sacralization which reinforce identities. The first, objectification, sometimes desacralizes some standards before it sacralizes others. Commitment or emotional anchoring often "de-commits" or "detaches" before actually reinforcing loyalties and allegiances. Conversion on the personal level and charisma on the social level always pass through a phase of distantiation from the evil, chaotic, anxiety-ridden past before fervent witnessing to present salvation or future hopes. Ritual (or sameness enacting) at times strips old patterns before welding new ones. Myths (dialectic dramatizations) contrast basic elements of existence, such as sin and salvation, light and darkness, good and evil, continuity and discontinuity, fragmentation and integrity, identity and change.

The theoretical perspective of this book is comprehensive in two ways.

It makes extensive use of anthropological, historical, psychological as well as sociological materials. It also offers an accounting scheme for all religious organizations and movements (whether primitive, sophisticated or secular). It is concerned with the fit between actual religious events and forms of existence and a logically consistent, comprehensive, social-scientific account of these events and forms.

Yet this very purpose also makes it less than comprehensive in that it does not move beyond questions of mutual effect. It does not want to treat a theological perspective of religion as somehow less real, relevant or true; on the contrary, it maintains that the identity (or dialectical) model is only *one* way of making anthropological, psychological or sociological sense of these materials. It assumes that religious utterances, writings, prescriptions and proscriptions have their own rationale, provided by beliefs rather than by their ultimate social effects, even if the latter appear to be necessary for survival.

A further note on comprehensiveness: Although the five parts of which this book consist cover the Canadian religious scene, within each of these parts many groups were left out. The reason for incorporating some religious organizations rather than others and for treating some of these groups in different ways will be discussed in the introductions to each of these parts. The latter will also explicate the theoretical intentions often unobtrusively presented in the chapters that follow. The unstated intention behind incorporation and selection of data is often my desire to find out whether or not the dialectical or identity model was relevant on a large variety of fronts (historical, statistical, theological, ethnographic, psychological, sociological).

Only one of the chapters (the first one) has been published before. I would like to thank the editor of *Studies in Religion* for permission to reproduce the article on traditional Eskimo religion from Volume 11, Number 2. I also would like to thank the colleagues who appraised this volume for the Canadian Federation for the Humanities. Their suggestions were often very apt and helped me substantially in the revision of the original manuscript. This book has been published with the help of a grant from the Canadian Federation for the Humanities, using funds provided by the Social Sciences and Humanities Research Council of Canada.

The great temptation of this study has been to make each chapter into a separate book through more primary research, participant observation, or detailed surveys. Going into greater depth was to me intrinsically more interesting than relying as much as I did on secondary accounts and description, of which I was sometimes rather sceptical. Yet my stubborn concern with the original goal (to deal with Canada as a whole), my fear of getting bogged down (with four or five other projects waiting in the wings) and my hope that eventually thesis writers might refine the identity model through more primary research, kept me on the original path.

Hamilton, Ontario,
January 1985
Hans Mol

PART I

THE RELIGION OF NATIVE PEOPLES

Usually sociologists deal with the contemporary western religious scene, while anthropologists handle native religions. Their methods, categories and distinctions tend to differ because their materials differ. We all assume that there is a deep gap between the modern and primitive world, and yet by acquiescing to the differences we deny ourselves the vantage point (supposedly intrinsic in science) from which these assumptions and ideologies can be scrutinized. The varying distinctions and categories take modern culture, whether scientific or religious, so much for granted that any common purpose or functioning shared by modern and primitive culture is obscured.

If the identity frame of reference holds water, then it must make encompassing sense of, must allow for crucial observations about, and must lead to valid generalizations regarding both native religions and Christianity in Canada. This means that it must strive for categories (such as the mechanisms of sacralization) which can be applied to both native religions and Christianity and which are organically and consistently linked to theory. Too often classifications within both the sociology and anthropology of religion hang in the air and seem to have been selected for no other reason than that they made sense to the researcher in his particular situation.

The first two chapters in Part I trace the effect of the entire complex of native beliefs in souls, spirits and deities, native myths, taboos, shamans, magic words and rites of passage on the physical and mental integrity of individuals, on their integration with the ecosystem and on tribal, clan, and family unity. As has been said before, the identity model of religion aspires to be all-encompassing. Applying it to non-western, native religions is a test of its comprehension. Therefore, the investigations concentrate on the traditional, original religious forms in order to maximize the differences with Christianity. During the research I came across an important set of beliefs and practices (such as animal spirits and rituals dealing with the remains of game) which could not naturally relate to units of social organization. They all had to do with the natural environment and they all seemed to strengthen the close interaction of natives and ecosystem. Of course,

7

behind this fit was the enhanced potential for physical survival: sensitive dealings with nature would guarantee a better share of its fruits. Yet, such beliefs and practices were clearly directed to a non-social system. Therefore the ecosystem was introduced as an additional unit in which religious strengthening operated.

In the first chapter the identity frame of reference is inferred rather than explicated. The reason for this is partly due to a wise warning from Robert K. Merton, the supervisor of my dissertation in the sociology department of Columbia University in New York more than twenty-five years ago. He said that the theoretical skeleton of the thesis was too obvious and that it was better not to let theory detract from good writing, style and readability. Just as important was the suggestion by some of my friends that the hard sell of the identity frame of reference (I tended to go into detailed clarification particularly when faced with uninterested, atheoretical, disbelieving audiences) was counterproductive. Well, chapter one became decidedly soft sell, although other chapters show the theoretical skeleton more clearly. At any rate, the balance between the plus of faith and the minus of fragility in Chapter 1 is just another way of saying that, in the dialectic between sameness and change, religion shores up the former more often than the latter, and that it attempts to absorb change back into the familiar frame of reference.

The second chapter deals with traditional Indian religion in all of Canada rather than within one or two tribes. Yet, the reinforcing effect of guiding spirits on individual integrity, the link between the immortal soul and social order, or between the mortal soul and physical well-being, the powerful effect of a totem on clan cohesion, the dramatizations of existential opposites in myths, the contributions taboos make to concrete delineations of conduct, the restoring quality of shamanic rites for personal and communal equilibrium, the enhancement of confidence through amulets, the retracing of tribal order through rites, the guidance by rites of passage from one identity to another, and the emotional unity brought about by dreams, are held in common by most, if not all, of the traditional Indian religions found in Canada.

The third chapter is probably the best example in the book of the ways religion deepens conflict between different races because it is totally bound up with the culture of the one rather than the other. And yet, once the cruel battle of culture conflict has been lost or won, religion also has the means to quicken reconciliation and integration. The process of adjustment runs smoothest on the more superficial level of changing addresses to guardian spirits into Christian prayers, taboos into Christian prescriptions and proscriptions, amulets into crucifixes. It runs much less smoothly when one considers the changeover from native to Christian meaning system as springboard for thought and action. Charismatic movements, with their fervent visions of the future, their anti-white sentiments, and their Christian legitimations, were, and are, only partially successful, and in Canada Indians continue to differ strongly from whites on social and economic indicators even when almost all of them nominally belong to Christian denominations.

As in my other books, conversion and charisma are treated essentially as mechanisms for incorporating, rather than annihilating, change. Both desacralize, or emotionally strip, a previous identity (for instance, an alcoholic, demoralized native, or a corrupt, dissolute Indian community) and sacralize, or emotionally weld, a new one (for instance, a sober, dynamic individual or a clan with clear purposes and certain hopes). Yet the new identity is built on an old, redirected one rather than on entirely new cultural foundations. The charismatic leaders which emerged and vanished all over Canada in all areas where Indian and western culture clashed identified with the strains and stresses of the native population, yet possessed firmly grounded intuitions and visions which were, in all instances, inspired by the Christian West. They welded their followers into purposeful bands of individuals who blended aboriginal and apocalyptic strains.

CHAPTER 1

TRADITIONAL INUIT RELIGION

In the middle of October, 1923, the Arctic explorer Knud Rasmussen made camp at Malerualik on the southern shore of King William Land. The approaching winter and the stormy weather had unsettled the group of Netsilik Inuit living in the area. All of a sudden a frightened woman appeared with the message that one of the local *angakoks* (shamans, or people gifted to communicate with the spirit world) was engaged in a bitter fight with four ghosts. Rasmussen (1931, 81) describes how the peaceful gathering of Inuit was instantly changed into a howling mob. They all "stormed down to their tents to protect their children against the evil spirits." Angry ghosts and spirits were closely associated in the Inuit mind with raging blizzards, elusive game and the disaster of famine and starvation. In those situations shamans would investigate what was at the bottom of the trouble and make amends by fighting or conciliating the spirits. They would locate the taboos which had been transgressed and fly through the air or dive to the bottom of the sea in order to appease the avenging forces.

Often the appeasement took place in a communal séance. Rasmussen describes such a séance amongst the Copper Inuit in Agiaq on the south shore of Coronation Gulf. It happened on January 25, 1924. Rasmussen had been stranded in the area during a violent snowstorm. The blizzard was so bad that his party of Inuit had to hold on to one another while bucking the icy slashing winds and pushing their way to the snow hut where the séance was being held.

The Inuit of the region believed that this kind of storm was caused by the anger of Narssuk, the baby son of a giant and his wife who had both been killed by another giant and his adopted human son. Narssuk had flown to the skies from where he continues to send bad weather to the wicked. When he is especially angry (for instance, when women keep their menses a secret and taboos are transgressed), he loosens the thongs of his caribou skin napkin "and lets it blow, rain or snow or drift" (Ibid. 230). Séances are then held and shamans go to his abode in the sky, to subdue him and to tie his napkin so that the weather can settle.

The Agiaq séance begins with a meal of dried salmon, blubber and frozen seal. Then the shaman in charge summons his helping spirits to increase his power over the evil forces tormenting and lashing the settlement. His audience bolsters his confidence by insisting that he is up to the formidable task of making hidden forces appear. Finally, in trance and possessed by a helping spirit, "he is no longer master of himself or his words" (Rasmussen, 1932, 58). He now describes a variety of spirits and the women start guessing who of the departed are meant, until they finally agree that the storm is caused by the evil spirits of a couple which died very recently.

The shaman now seizes another, older, shaman in the audience. Until now the latter has been quietly singing a song to the Mother of the Sea Beasts who lives at the bottom of the sea. Her name is Arnakaphaluk (Sedna to the Baffin Islanders and Nuliajuk to the Netsilik Inuit). She is the guardian of all taboos and rules all the sea animals. She rules through spirits: the good ones make animals easy to hunt and the bad ones make them disappear. She also rules the spirits which affect the weather.

In the middle of the song the younger shaman brutally flings his older colleague backwards and forwards, as though the old man harbours the evil spirit. Finally all life seems to have left him. Now he is revived through rubbing and stroking. This process of killing and reviving is repeated three times. The older shaman, who is now also thoroughly entranced, sees naked beings rushing through the air and raising blizzards and the helpless Narssuk shaking "the lungs of air with his weeping" (Ibid., 60). However, his helping spirit is going to stop them, the shaman announces, and will conquer all evil spirits. Then both shamans, joined by all the others, sing a hymn to Arnakaphaluk. Rasmussen observes that this appears to console the people. They feel reassured that the weather will be fine in the morning. They all return to their various snow huts and indeed the next morning they are greeted with dazzling sunshine!

At other séances Arnakaphaluk is coaxed by the shaman and the hymns of his audience to come to the surface through a hole in the ice. There she takes possession of the shaman who is hunched over the opening. He begins to writhe in pain and to moan incessantly. While the men of the audience hold and control him, Arnakaphaluk, through the shaman, announces in a deep voice that the bad hunting or the bad weather results from taboos being broken and from careless dealing with the ancestral traditions. Upon hearing this, men and women begin to confess all their sins until there is nothing left to confess. Then the shaman announces that Arnakaphaluk's lamp has been righted again (while the hunting is bad her lamp is said to be upside down) and that her hair is smooth and clean, "for as long as all sins are not confessed her hair is usually in the wildest disorder" (Ibid. 26).

The descriptions by Rasmussen apply to many other Inuit tribes in the Canadian North, Alaska and Greenland. Sometimes scholars point out that the beliefs help to extend and erroneously complete the knowledge about cause and effect in the snow bound world. Weyer (1969, 237) explains Inuit religion as a mixture of curiosity and ignorance: "(s)upernatural design is inferred where natural causation is not apparent." Others think that there is more to Eskimo religion than premature satisfaction of curiosity. They feel that religion focuses wishdreams for better health and hunting. Yet there are religious elements which do not readily fit the "curiosity" or "wishdream" explanations. One example is the special spirit sign mentioned by Rasmussen (1931, 241) when he gave a mug to a girl for whom it was a new and strange object. In this instance, the sign consisted of crossing the breast with a long snow knife, first down from the left shoulder obliquely to the right hip, then from the right to the left. The purpose of the sign was to ward off malevolent spirits. Offerings left at sacred sites or processions around the stranger's sledge to confuse invisible spirits similarly overtax explanations of this kind.

It may be wise to avoid the term "explanation" altogether. Explanation often becomes "explaining away." Usually the attempt hides the assumption that Western categories of thinking are vastly superior. It may be more sensible to confine oneself to answering the question: "What effect does this religious event or do these religious practices have on the individual or the community under consideration"?

By focussing on this question we usually (if not always) find that Inuit religion consolidates the unity of individual and nature, the wholeness (whether physical or mental) of self or society. Religion seems to be one way to deal with the numerous factors which can potentially or actually undermine stable existence, whether it be the blizzard, the unsuccessful seal hunt, birth, illness, death, culture contact (a stranger), or even a new mug.

With this in mind we can now look in greater detail at the various elements which make up Inuit religion: beliefs (souls and spirits, deities and myths); commitments (feelings evoked by taboos, shamans); rituals (magic words and rites of passage).

SOULS and SPIRITS

For the Inuit the entire world was peopled with souls, spirits and ghosts. Both the dangers and the benefits of existence were represented (objectified) by malevolent and well-disposed powers. The unfamiliar was to be treated with particular care: it had in the past done, and might again do, incalculable damage. And so when Rasmussen (Ibid., 36) arrived in an Inuit settlement near Shepherd Bay in May 1923, a procession of solemn, silent women paraded in a circle around his sledges and dogs. The procession over, gravity and formality gave place to joviality and cheer. The women (all of whom were particularly vulnerable because they had gone through childbirth) had cut a circle around the foreigners in order to confuse the spirits inside the ring of footprints and to prevent them from entering the settlement. Strangers are believed to trail all sorts of mysterious and invisible spirits in their wake and they have to be rendered harmless before they can do any damage.

The Inuit fear unfamiliar territory. When Mowat (1955, 236) decided to visit Angkuni, or Great Lake, his Ihalmiut guide Ohoto had very mixed emotions about the trip. No Inuit of his tribe had visited the area for more than thirty years and he was afraid of the shallow graves and the restless, unseen spirits of the area.

Yet the familiar too could not be taken for granted. It had to be treated with proper care and reverence. The Koksoakmiut on the south shore of Ungava Bay conciliate the spirits dwelling in the prominent features of the landscape, such as rocks, bays and islands, with offerings (Turner, 1894, 194). To the Netsilik, important fishing places as well as wading and crossing places of the caribou are holy. Specific parts of the caribou have to be offered at the precise spot where it was killed in order not to break the taboo of the place (Rasmussen, 1931, 67,179,180). The belief in spirits sacralize territorial integrity. Only the most alienated, and therefore feared, shaman of the Caribou Inuit, Kakumee, could disregard the territorial integrity of the Ihalmiut. When he returned from a five-month trip into foreign territory to the south, he came back a changed man who had not only acquired many treasures of the white man but had also learned to lie and steal. He was therefore treated as an outcast whose tents were situated apart from the rest of the people (Mowat, 1955, 202ff).

Yet territory was by no means the most important dwellingplace of souls and spirits. Existence was delineated not just by the familiar features of the landscape, but even more by its inhabitants, whether animal or human. Animals were vital for man's survival. They all had souls and great care was taken by the Inuit not to offend these souls. The Utkuhikjalingmiut at Lake Franklin always leave some skin around the anus of the caribou they have killed because they believe that its soul will be insulted if women touch that part. A small piece of salmon is laid under the platform skin of the snow hut where the Inuit who has caught it is sleeping (Rasmussen 1931, 504) in order to show respect for the soul of the salmon in question. The Copper Inuit companion of Jenness (1970, 103,169) solemnly knelt in the snow after he had shot a ptarmigan and chanted a prayer in order to appease its spirit. Later, when the same companion shot a bear and its young, he placed a needle-case beside the mother and a miniature bow and arrow beside the cub to accompany their souls to their spirit home. By scrupulous observation of the various taboos about animals, the Inuit believe that their souls will be well disposed and that they will prefer to be killed by the same hunter in future reincarnations. If, by contrast, the taboos are not observed, the souls of the animals will turn into evil spirits (*tornaits*) and seek revenge.

Human souls are also immortal and they too can turn into evil spirits if the proper death taboos are not observed. Reincarnation of human souls into animals is also possible. A Baffin Island Inuit recognized the soul of his mother in a fox he had just trapped. Another human soul of the same tribe had entered a huge polar bear in order to avenge wrongs done during her lifetime (Boas, 1907, 234, 252). The Padlimiut believe that evil men are often reincarnated as animals (Rasmussen, 1927, 86). Souls, whether animal or human, are therefore intricately intertwined with an entire system of structures (taboos) and social behaviour patterns (being well-behaved towards others). They are inextricably linked with the wholeness of nature and society and, as it were, complete the closure of both.

Yet humans are different from animals in that they also have a mortal as well as an immortal soul. The mortal soul represents the physical and mental integrity of the person in whom it dwells. Often sickness is thought to be a disorder of the soul, or an intrusion of an evil spirit. The angakok (shaman) will then be called in the same manner as a doctor is consulted in Western society. He will attempt to restore the soul by magic or drive out the tornaits (evil spirits). Jenness (1922, 173) relates how the angakoks (shamans) of the Copper Inuit restore health by removing foreign objects (pieces of bone, worms) which have been placed in the patient by an offended soul. At other times, the sickness of the soul is explained as a transgression of a taboo. Confession and penitence then restore the soul to its former vigour. At the death of the person, this mortal soul also dies.

Amulets and fetishes are other ways of dealing with the forces which might impair or strengthen a person's integrity. They are sometimes bought at a great price. Halo (an Ihalmiut of the Caribou Inuit tribe) bought a seal-tooth amulet at the price of a new kayak. Other amulets on his belt, such as a miniature parka, ensured him against accidental death from freezing or drowning (Mowat, 1955, 277). Yet the spirits which dwelt in these various objects do not just ward off bad luck, they also provide good fortune. "....(A)n old harpoon head placed on the piece of skin that the hunter stands on at the breathing hole makes the seals tame" (Rasmussen, 1931, 269). A woman often wears amulets to ensure that she will bear a son (if she does not have one yet), or when she does, that the son will be a good hunter of bears or caribous. Shamans have particularly powerful amulets: the latter may help them to have visions or to be transformed into a bird or a seal so that they can fly or dive to the dwellings of deities.

Another soul peculiar to humans only was the name soul. It stood for the power inherent in the name of a person who had recently died and who had certain attributes such as strength, uprightness or skill in hunting or sewing. A child who was given this name was supposed to inherit the characteristics of the former carrier of that name. The name soul is generally a helper or guardian of the individual. The Mackenzie Inuit (Stefansson, 1951, 400ff.) feel that this guardianship is particularly important when the child's soul is still undeveloped. The older a person becomes the less he is addressed (and treated!) as though he is the guardian. It may come as a shock to the adolescent to discover that his or her *nappan* (the soul acquired at birth) is now strong enough, and that the special privileges that come with having a particular *atka* (guardian spirit) have now disappeared. The *atka* represents both a personal and a social element: it is personal in that it strengthens the individual's management of his niche in nature and society; it is also social in that it perpetuates the communal link with the deceased person for it keeps the memory of his desirable qualities alive amongst the living.

DEITIES and MYTHS

Like souls and spirits, Inuit deities represent forces which round off, or close, existence. They are objectifications of whatever thwarts or sustains the integrity of the individual or the unity of community and its niche in nature. They improve mastery in that representation delineates the unpredictable and thereby constrains the intractable.

Yet deities also differ in at least two respects from souls and spirits. They are distinct entities in their own right. They are more than spirits being housed in an amulet or souls residing in a body. They tend to be more circumscribed, complex and personified, and their power extends over a wider range. The Mother of the Sea Beasts is almost human in her moods and in her concern with taboos and structure. One of Rasmussen's (1931, 500) informants describes her as a force which keeps mankind and the earth in balance. This could hardly be said of any of the large variety of spirits and souls peopling the Inuit world.

More importantly, deities are also often portrayed as guardians and managers of spirits. The Mother of the Beasts confines the beasts to her house at the bottom of the sea when she is angry or when she has been offended by humans. It is up to her to either lock them up or release them. In some areas (such as the Coronation Gulf) she can dispatch bad weather and drown individuals by breaking up the ice. She also has the power to gather the souls of the sewing materials and the tools of the men when people break taboos (Rasmussen 1932, 24).

The Mother of the Beasts is the major deity of the Canadian Inuit. However, the cult disappears in the most western areas: the Alaskan shamans make their journeys of appeasement to the Moon Spirit. The Labrador Inuit in the east appeal to a male divinity, Torngarsoak, if they hunt whales and seals. His wife, Superguksoak, is in charge of the land animals, especially the reindeer (Hawkes, 1970, 124). Further to the south, some of the Caribou Inuit, who live inland believe in a deity called Pinga, who lives somewhere out in space and keenly watches man's treatment of animals and the respect he pays to his daily food (Rasmussen 1927, 81f.)

In all other regions, the Mother of the Beasts is the central goddess. She lives beneath the ocean, and in some regions she has a father living with her while her dog husband guards the entrance. Her name and the details of the myth vary from tribe to tribe. Typical among her myths is the following one from Cumberland Sound (Weyer, 1969, 349ff.)

A girl by the name of Avilayoq is married to a dog, but their fantastic offspring (Inuit, white men and other creatures) are so noisy that she moves to an island so as not to annoy her father. One day she is seduced by a petrel who moves her to his village. The father takes her away, greatly upsetting the petrel husband who unleashes a raging gale. On the verge of drowning, the old man throws his daughter overboard. Yet she holds on to the sides, so that the father has to chop off the first joints of her fingers which become whales. When she still does not give up, he chops off the second joints as well. They become seals. Since she is still holding on with the stumps of her hand, he knocks out her left eye. Only then does she let go. The dog husband drowns, too, as does the father. Avilayoq becomes Sedna, the Mother of the Beasts (the latter being her own joints). She still has only one eye and she cannot walk, but slides along, one leg bent under, the other stretched out. Because her hands are stumps, shamans have to help comb and braid her hair when humans make it unruly through their sins.

The myth of the Mother of the Beasts is obviously more than a rational speculation about famine and frightful weather or an answer to the question: "What causes bad luck?" Scholars who look for the key of meaning along those lines, invariably have to fall back on the inferiority of the native mind. And then it is embarrassing for the fieldworker with these assumptions to discover that the same native in daily life is not any less logical than his western counterpart. Rasmussen tried to reason about the problem of irrationality in myths with Ikinilik, his clear-headed Utkuhikjalingmiut informant, who mixed up the tale of a girl Putilik being mated to her father's dog with the myth of Nuliajuk (the name for the Mother of the Beasts in the area). But Ikinilik made it plain that logic was not of the essence of the tale and myth. What to him was important was that "Nuliajuk....watches over all beasts, all the game of mankind, and that is enough for us. How she turned into such a dangerous and terrible spirit is surely immaterial" (Rasmussen 1931, 499). Dramatization is more essential to myth than logical sequence, he seems to say. The same is true for the mix-up of Narssuk (the sky deity) and the Mother of the Beasts (the ocean deity) in the Agiaq séance, both being held responsible for the blizzard. A divine division of labour seems to be secondary to the expression of chaos impinging on human order.

Dramatization is also more essential to myth and séance than the wish for good weather and the successful hunt. To be deprived of either is surely a serious matter. But more serious is to have no context in which to fit the raging blizzard and the elusive seal.

Seen then with Inuit eyes, as much as possible, the Mother of the Beasts appears to represent the precarious union of man and nature. She is a mother of both humans and animals and, as such, structures the world in which both depend on one another. She does this structuring by firmly insisting on rules and taboos. Even in her physical being she combines human origins and seal-like qualities (stumps and a sliding foot). She may be as ugly as Venus is beautiful, yet she too is "woman" who includes in her very being the intrusive "male." Whether this male is a dog or Mars is less important than that the intercourse tames aggression and chaos.

There are other minor deities and myths in Inuit society. We have already met Narssuk (Sila to the Netsilik), the giant baby who lives out in space and whom the angakoks (shamans) appease by tying his napkin. His penis is so large that four women can sit on it side by side (Rasmussen 1931, 230).

There is also the Moon Spirit who, according to the Inuit on the west coast of Hudson Bay, maintains fertility and helps barren women to become pregnant (Rasmussen 1929, 74). Women placate him in order to give birth to boys. This also means that those who do not want to become pregnant must avoid the moon. He represents, par excellence, the aggressive lustful male; he pursues even his own sister, the Sun Spirit.

According to the Moon myth a brother and sister murder their own mother. Being ashamed of their deed they wander the world and have many strange adventures. They also commit incest and now, being more ashamed than ever, they attempt to be born again into a new life. They decide on becoming sun and moon and light a torch of moss.

> (R)unning out of the passage, they ran round their snow
> hut, the sister in front and her brother behind, and there
> they were suddenly lifted up from the ground and raised
> into the air. But as they were being lifted from the ground
> the sister put out her brother's torch, and they rose and
> rose, and kept on rising, till they came right up to the sky
> and became sun and moon (Ibid., 236).

Taboos and moral prescriptions often form the backdrop in Inuit myths. Murder and incest are implicitly condemned. Orphans (in some of the myths, the Mother of the Beasts was originally a badly treated orphan; Narssuk's parents were slain) punish humans for their lack of compassion. Tolerance and kindness are usually rewarded in the same way as quarrelsomeness and lack of generosity are punished (Weyer 1969, 251). Yet, in the myths, morality as a force which binds individuals, communities and families together is not separated from the powers which binds all these to nature. The essence of Inuit religion from the social-scientific point of view is its dramatization of existence and the ever-present lurking potential for breakdown of wholeness, regardless whether that wholeness pertains to nature, society, individual or, more often, to all three at once.

TABOOS and SHAMANS

Wholeness in the abstract, however, was not the conscious source of Inuit meditation and speculation. It was expressed in the concrete lineaments of society sufficiently enough to make glittering generalities superfluous. Taboos concretized and structured the entire world of hunting and associating. Action was never artibrary but was always delineated in appropriate and inappropriate behaviour, united in an indissoluble, taken for granted, totality.

Often delineating, as such, seemed to be more important than the actual content of the delineation, or taboo. Sea and land animals were as strictly divided as the unclean and clean animals in Leviticus 11. And so in Labrador caribou could not be cooked together with seal. Yet in southeastern Baffin Island cooking them together was actually recommended, because it was thought to create friendship between the souls of animals (Boas 1907, 489).

Taboos also clarified the priorities of the Inuit world. Every time the proper taboos and sacrifices were observed, the spiritual forces whom they served were accorded their rightful place in the overall scheme of things. The souls of animals could easily be upset if the proper taboos regarding their hunting, killing and eating were not kept. Therefore dogs are often not allowed to gnaw bones. If it happened anyway, the Ungava natives (Turner 1894, 201) cut a piece of the animal's tail or ear to allow his blood to flow. In other words, blood sacrifice made up for the unwitting disrespect shown to souls. The act reinstated the subtle, precarious hierarchy of relations of which the entire Inuit world was composed.

Taboos minimized the arbitrariness or meaninglessness of acting and behaving. They did so by categorizing these acts into proper and improper ones. The evolutionary origin of our present-day analytical, differentiating facility may very well lie in this intricate construction of plus and minus, positive or negative, set of taboo relations. It is improper for the Iglulik Inuit (Rasmussen 1929, 194) to work on iron while caribou are being hunted with bows and arrows. On the other hand, it is proper for those who do not engage in such a hunt (such as the women) to sharpen the arrowheads for the men. Originally these taboos may, or may not, have drawn attention to the power and danger of iron. This brought about considerable change which taboos contained in their web of proscriptions and prescriptions. Whatever the origin of the taboo, however, it subsequently furnished the Inuit world with a more elaborate skeleton of rules which kept arbitrariness at bay and advanced the outline of the whole.

The structuring of existence as an ingenious technique was one thing. Just as, if not more, important was the emotional attachments to these structures of proper and improper behaviour. Awe and fear intermingled strongly with any and all taboos. It was not just that transgressing taboos made the transgressor suffer — it might hurt the entire community. The Cumberland Sound Inuit (Weyer 1969, 377) believed that a vapour surrounded transgressors and that it was this vapour which repelled the animals. The feeling of having done something wrong triggered the sensitive consciences of the natives and enveloped them in an undefinable, vapour-like cloud of unease. The taboos therefore cemented social sentiments via an aroused conscience.

Angakoks, or shamans, were the major force in Inuit society for healing broken structures. Confessions were an important antidote for making the vapours of taboo transgression disappear. The angakoks would invite these confessions in the séances and then restore communal or personal confidence after a clean breast had been made of all the sins.

The angakoks are the much appreciated, and even necessary, merchants of feelings. They turn fear into courage, despair into faith, sin into salvation, fragmentation into wholeness. They do this not as performers for a discriminating audience, but as guides of those who cry out for help. Through their chanting and eager expectations the members of his community help the angakok get into a trance. They are at one with him and he transports them out of apprehension and anxiety into a frenzy of confession climaxed with an exhausted sense of well- being. They are eagerly willing to be associated with their angakok in his dramatic struggle with evil forces, his pleading to, and appeasing of, the powers causing their predicament and the euphoria of being rescued by the helping spirits. The angakok, in turn, is finely attuned to what his community is ready to hear. Yet he is also different from them in that he alone, like charismatic leaders anywhere, provides the transforming point of reference, tearing a threadbare integrity and weaving a new one.

Being different is therefore an important prerequisite of being a successful angakok. Abnormal physique or unusual vision and dreams set a young Inuit apart from his community and make him an appropriate candidate for shamanism. Sometimes a child of a famous angakok follows in his father's footsteps, but in such instances he too has to go through an arduous process of training in magic practices, wrestling with spirits, fasting for long periods of time and exposing himself to long separations and extreme hardship.

Mowat (1955, 207ff.) tells the story of how Kakumee, son of a famous shaman of the Caribou Inuit, became an angakok. He went away from his camp, starving himself while seated in a half-shelter of snow on the ice. After several days his legs were so cramped that he fell and crashed through the ice when he tried to get up. In the green mist of the water he saw the head of a man without a body, whose arms and legs sprouted out of the head. The bearded face with the blue eyes floated around him, making horrible bubbling sounds in his ears. Kakumee struggled but fainted, and on recovery found himself frozen to the ice next to the hole. Struggling out of his stiff clothing he ran naked for a full day over the lake, but found that his power as a new born shaman prevented his freezing to death. After that, Kakumee was an obsessed man who was very much afraid of using the bodiless head of the white man as his helper. Later, when desperately afraid and lost in unknown, hostile, Indian country, he finally screamed out a summons to his helping spirit, he not only saw the aurora flicker with sudden violence, but actually found the head of his vision in an abandoned white man's cabin.

Kakumee's story is unusual in that his helper was a white man's head. The dying and rising experience in his training is not, however. To overcome death is the sign of becoming a great shaman (Weyer 1969, 433).

Angakoks both officiate at communal séances called at the occasion of general upset and act as medicine men and doctors for the sick or the barren. Only in the last two instances do they charge for their services. In the case of sickness or accident the angakok attempts to discover why the soul is listless or who has stolen it. If it is a malevolent spirit, the shaman exorcises him. If the soul is stolen, he restores it. If a foreign matter has entered the body, it is removed. In cases of barrenness on Baffin Island, cohabitation with the shaman is practised (Weyer 1969, 424). To sum up, Inuit shamans restore health, whether social or personal, most often by emotional stripping and welding.

MAGIC WORDS and RITES OF PASSAGE

In the same way as an ordinary strip of fur is different from the same strip when it is called "amulet", so the ordinary word differs from the magic word. It is the special power assigned to the latter which makes the difference. Like the amulet, the magic word provides the owner or utterer with the power to be more composed, a more successful hunter or to become well again in illness. Often these magic words are like prayers addressed to spirits or souls. They are secret and must be used sparingly, since they wear out from too much use. They often use ancient or obscure language. It is the otherness of the language which makes them especially effective. Rasmussen (1932, 113ff.) records some magic words which were sung. For instance, the following magic words would help the soul to stay in the person if he was in pain:

> That old woman's, your mother's breasts, whisper,
> Name them and wait! That old woman's drying rack
> let it drop down!
> The old woman's, your mother's breast become full.
> Go back to them, I return to you! What you must
> turn back for, turn back for it!
> If you turn back for it, you will arise!

Obviously the sufferer derives comfort both from the magic intention of the words and from the association with motherly love.

Rites of passage are rites which guide change resulting from marriage, birth or death. They strip an old identity (dependent child, childless or father-dominated family) and weld a new one (for instance, married woman, family with child or family without a father).

There is little evidence in Inuit society of ceremony at the occasion of marriage. Yet taboos and customs delineate the married from the unmarried state. Young girls of the Mission Inuit in Labrador wear pink ribbons, married women blue and widows white ones (Hawkes 1916, 115). The same author mentions how, in Labrador, the changeover from the noisy romping child to the shy, bashful eligible woman is affected by both a change in hairdo and in dress. She now also has her chin tattooed.

Taboos and customs surrounding childbirth are recorded in much greater detail and are also more elaborate. Amongst the Copper Inuit, the woman who has given birth must pull her hood up over her head for a few days. As soon as possible after the birth she must also make a fire under her cooking pot so that her child will walk early. Whenever she eats, she must cut off a small piece of meat, rub it over the child's mouth and throw it behind the lamp, so that the child will never be in want of food.

Sometimes, when the child has been eagerly expected, a magic song is sung over it, but this must be done before it has its first breast feed. Also, immediately after birth the father or grandmother must lift it up, pronounce a special prayer formula and name it after a deceased relative. The Copper Inuit also betroth their children at birth (Rasmussen 1932, 41ff.).

The Netsilik (a tribe of the Central Inuit) insist on removing the woman about to give birth to a separate, temporary snow hut. Only when the delivery is difficult do people attend to her, because anyone assisting her has to adhere to the same strict birth taboos. A woman giving birth is regarded as unclean and dangerous, especially to all hunters. Everything going well, the baby is born in a hole in the snow, to avoid making sleeping rugs unclean and unusable. During the birth an elderly woman is sometimes allowed to be present to name all the dead people of whom she can think. The baby is called by the name which is pronounced at the moment of birth. It is believed that if the baby cries too much, a malevolent spirit has entered; then a new name is given in order to drive the old one out.

The Netsilik also utter magic words over the infant before its first feed. After a few days the mother is removed to another, better-built, snow house, but here, too, she is separated from husband and family. Here she stays for a month, after which the settlement moves to another hunting place as the place where a child is born is regarded as unclean. If it becomes necessary to move before the month is up, mother and child must be taken out through a hole in the wall of the snow hut to confuse the spirits (Rasmussen 1931, 220, 258ff.).

Death rituals are very elaborate and differ from region to region. Yet, as all rites of passage, they can be fitted into three phases: (1) Identity stripping (2) Transition (3) Identity welding. We will take each of these phases in turn.

(1) Identity stripping. It is in this phase that the place of the deceased is eliminated from family and community. As soon as it is felt that death is at hand the dying person is prepared for burial by, for instance, dressing him in new clothes. Sometimes he or she is left alone to die, or even removed to another hastily built snow hut, as the Inuit believe that the place where someone has died must be abandoned. The Iglulik of Baffin Island and the Melville Peninsula are typical. When Captain Lyon (1970, 228ff.) of H.M.S. *Hecla* stayed with them in 1822 he was struck by what he called their "brutal insensibility." Leaving the dying blocked up in a snow hut without anyone caring one way or the other and then burying them in such a nonchalant manner that dogs later could undisturbedly eat the remains,

seemed to him utmost barbarism. Yet, not so far away, the Netsilik crowd around the dying and cry woefully when the ghost is given up (Rasmussen 1931, 263).

Lyon also describes how at other times the dead are removed, not through the entrance of the snow hut, but through a window, and how after three days of mourning the dwelling is abandoned. At the shallow grave, lightly covered with snow in winter or by a few stones in summer, the bodies are positioned according to age. "Infants have their feet placed towards the rising sun, or east; half-grown children, south-east; men and women in their prime, with their feet to the meridian sun; middle aged persons, to the southwest; and very old people, the reverse of children, or west" (Lyon 1970, 236). Some of their belongings (weapons, cookingpots, etc.) are placed at the grave. In many Inuit groups (for instance, the Labrador natives-Hawkes 1970, 120) these belongings are broken in order to liberate the soul and make it useful to their owner.

The Iglulik, as described by Captain Lyon, have two abodes for the souls of the dead. Those who are drowned at sea, starved to death, murdered, or killed by walruses or bears go to heaven in the sky. It is here that a variety of great and powerful spirits reign. Others, however, go to a world below which has four stages, the best and most happy of which is the last and lowest. Here it is continually summer and the sun never sets. There is plenty of game and fish and the souls occupy themselves with feasting, singing, dancing and sleeping.

It is the social part, or the immortal soul, which is the subject of the elaborate stripping measures. It has to be sent on its way in order to allow the remaining members of the family or community to repair its integrity. The removal of the body through a hole in the wall specially cut for the occasion, a widespread custom in many primitive societies, is one way of preventing the soul from finding its way back. Another way is observing the taboo on uttering the name of the deceased. The Iglulik (Rasmussen 1929, 106), for instance, are reluctant to mention the name of the deceased until it has been given to a newly born child.

The second, or transitional, phase is characterized by expressions of loss. Wailing is the most obvious way to display grief. It allows for the free flowing of sentiment and the expression of meaninglessness. The Labrador Inuit "sets up an unearthly wailing, the women tearing their hair and beating their breasts, and otherwise giving vent to excessive grief" (Hawkes 1916, 119). As too much grief is obviously dangerous for a viable community, Inuit hedge the period of mourning with numerous taboos. They structure and guide behaviour during this unsettling period and thereby modify dishevelment. Remaining indoors, cutting off some hair, not combing hair, not washing are typical of expected behaviours during the period of mourning. Other widespread taboos in Inuit society at this time deal with the avoidance of sharp instruments such as knives, picks and needles (Weyer 1969, 271). The natives explain this taboo as a means to prevent the souls of the departed from hurting themselves. Taboos are particularly strict during the three to five days that the soul is supposed to be still around, according to the local beliefs. In some areas the soul of women is thought to linger one day longer than that of men. In other areas (Boas 1888, 590) the soul is believed to leave the body immediately after death. During mourning respect for the departed is often shown through acts of self-denial such as eating particular foods. The Iglulik (Rasmussen 1929, 199ff.) and the Cumberland Sound Inuit (Boas 1907, 145) refrain from sexual intercourse during this period.

The third phase of rites for the dead can be called identity welding. It is at this stage that the integrity of family and community is re-established. The strict mourning taboos are relaxed, often according to the nearness of the relationship with the deceased. The practical problems as to how to fill the gap of caring, mending, hunting are resolved. At this time the Caribou Inuit in the neighbourhood of Chesterfield Inlet have a closing ceremony. Those who lived with the deceased face different directions in their hut, say the local word for "enough" and then ceremonially wash hand and face (Weyer 1969, 275). Other memorial ceremonies in other regions are held around the grave. Boas (1907, 145) describes such a ceremony in the Cumberland Sound (Baffin Island). The relatives reminisce about the deceased as though he is present and promise to name a child after him. They then have a meal around the grave and leave a portion for the dead. Other celebrations of this kind were observed in the Mackenzie Delta (Weyer 1969, 283).

SUMMARY

Birth and death, sickness, the visit of a stranger, the introduction of steel knives and guns, abundance and scarcity of game, abnormally good and unusually bad weather — in short, all change tended to upset the Inuit status quo. Changes were therefore incorporated into a stable frame of reference so that their effects could be contained. All religious expressions contributed to this containment. The souls and the spirits, the deities and the myths, the taboos and the shamans, the magic words and the rites of passage together built a world which made a stronger whole out of the various forms of endangered integrity. These forms might consist of the unity of nature and society, or of the community as such, or of one's body, but in all instances religion provided the plus which fitted in with the minus (or potential minus) of their fragility.

The ubiquity of taboos in Inuit society is particularly telling in this regard. Taboos provided structure and form (a plus) where otherwise chaos and meaninglessness (a minus) would reign. Both appropriate and inappropriate behaviour eliminated the possibility of meaningless behaviour. And yet taboos were not just props for tottering structures. They also took change as it came and tamed its noxiousness. The dead were removed through a special opening cut in the snow hut in the certain belief that the inevitability of death could be postponed by irreversible separation from life. However painful and traumatic, the minus of detrimental change would be resolved by the hard-worked plus of the spirit world. And in the cancelling-out process, a workable semblance of balance would enable the Inuit to carry on as usual. The souls of the dead were now politely, but firmly, sent on their way, leaving time to heal the wounds. With any luck, the minus of death could even be changed into the plus of a beneficial spirit, provided of course that the souls of the dead were properly treated.

Of course there were changes which ultimately destroyed the finely attuned religion and culture of the Inuit. But for the inroads made by western civilization we need a new chapter.

CHAPTER 2

TRADITIONAL INDIAN RELIGION

The Eastern Crees (an Indian tribe on the eastern shore of James Bay, Quebec) tell the story of a very old man who is abandoned during a famine. He is very slow on his feet and can only hobble around with the aid of a stick. He slows everyone down at the very time that one has to move about frequently in order to survive.

After his people leave, he tries to put a meal together, but there is nothing with which to make it. Ten days elapse and now, greatly weakened, the old man lies down to die. While waiting for the end he hears someone at the door of his tent. It is his mistabeo.

A mistabeo is a spirit guiding a particular individual. In the case of the old man the mistabeo had faithfully guided him most of his life, but had abandoned him when he had gotten very old. The Indian had protested against this faithlessness, particularly because the mistabeo had originally volunteered his services and had not been pressed into them as so often happened. Yet nothing could be done, and so the old man had asked only that the guiding spirit would return when he was starving.

And now the mistabeo has returned and says: "Why can't you walk? Look, there is a partridge outside your tent in a tree." The old Indian takes his gun and shoots the partridge. He plucks and cooks it and so gathers enough strength to shoot a few more. The mistabeo also shows him a porcupine in a tree and a lake with a herd of caribou. All these animals are killed, their meat dried. There is now enough food for the entire clan.

Mistabeos can also predict the future and so the old man learns that his people will return. Finally they arrive, exhausted and bedraggled, starving as ever. Their surprise knows no end when they see the old man not only alive but even prospering. He forgives their heartlessness and puts on a big feast. Until his death, his people never leave him again (story told by John Blackned to Richard J. Preston, 1975, 173ff.).

SPIRITS

Canadian Indians differ considerably in language and custom. Yet they all believe in guiding spirits such as the mistabeo. The Ojibwa (on the northern shore of Lake Superior) see them as specks of light and hear their low, singing voices in the tent where the conjuring or the summoning of spirits takes place.

Much further west (the interior of British Columbia) guiding spirits often appear to local Indians in animal guise. Young men fast and meditate in the woods for days in order to receive visions and to be visited by spirits. They feel that the latter will be particularly prone to offer their services if the Indians are humble and persistent enough in their search, and if their sorry state evokes the appropriate pity. The Plains Cree, too, are convinced that the longer they fast the more power the spirits will bestow (Mandelbaum 1979, 161).

Kwakiutl youth (on the coast of British Columbia) believe that in addition to fasting, cleanliness attracts guiding spirits, "because only the pure find favor with them, while they kill the impure" (Boas, 1970, 393). In this tribe as well as others on the west coast of Canada, spirits tend to become hereditary and serve successive generations of the same clan. In Labrador, too, the mistabeo is frequently regarded as the reincarnation of an ancestor (Speck 1977, 39).

Guiding spirits are a source of strength and confidence to the individual Indian. They can be relied upon in times of trouble and danger. Yet too much reliance can be bad. One should not wear out one's welcome with them (Landes 1971, 178). They also take a dislike to the overbearing and proud. Since they have superior knowledge of both the present and the future, it is good common sense to stay on their right side by deference and appeasement.

To the Naskapi (Labrador) the mistabeo also guards a man's conscience and will be more willing to help an individual if the latter is trustworthy, generous and kind. It is the mistabeo of the teacher "that makes him strong and wise, of the leader that gives him fertile schemes and influence over others, of the successful hunter who garners game for him, of the warrior who garners enemies for him" (Speck 1977, 38).

Guiding spirits reinforce individual integrity. They make the young men braver or, as in the mistabeo story of the Eastern Cree, help an old man to persevere. They toughen the individual and promote his (or her) sureness and sense of security. Yet they also clip his wings, if necessary, for the sake of a larger group or social integrity. They impose restricting taboos and abandon those who insist on anti-social autonomy or drain meagre resources. In other words, they bolster personal identity but not at the expense of family unity or clan survival.

Still, this is not always the case. The Naskapi feel that the mistabeo prompts desires for intoxicants, tobacco, gluttony, vengeance or sheer malevolence (Ibid., 43). The spirits tend to strike a balance between individual and social good, but occasionally they bolster self-expression, even when this obviously clashes with social harmony and leads to lethal infighting. Le Jeune (Hultkrantz 1953, 268) mentions how a shaman of the Algonquin (central Ontario) kills an antagonist by sending his guardian spirits after the latter's soul.

Another important domain in which the spirits operate is the ecosystem. Humans are not the only ones protected by spirits. The Algonkians (an umbrella term for all Indians in the eastern half of Canada speaking the same language) believed that animals, trees, rock formations, rivers, etc., have their own protectors. Some of these are thought to be rather harmless but others have to be placated. Indians passing the Chaudière Falls near Ottawa appease its spirit with gifts of tobacco. So do the Nathaway Indians when they travel past the Manitou Falls in northern Saskatchewan (Thompson 1971, 137).

Knowing the spirits of a particular territory gives the Indian the necessary confidence to enter the area. In the woodlands of eastern Canada, territory is a sacred trust to each band. Indians from other areas have to get permission to hunt or fish in the territory not their own and they will only do so when driven by famine. "Strangers had no rights whatever; all were considered as enemies, and any native might rob or kill an 'outsider' without fear of punishment" (E. Jenness 1966, 21)

On the west coast of Canada, the Kimsquit (part of the Bella Coola tribe) believe that the deity Alquntam has allotted and marked the property of each community. The area is dotted with spots where the power of creatures sent by Alquntam have become localized in stone and petrified. Some of these can be consulted and propitiated with meat, or eagle down (McIlwraith 1948, 131,594ff.).

Animal spirits are particularly important to the Canadian Indian. The Kwakiutl on the coast of British Columbia think of the environment as peopled with spirits one cannot take for granted. Boas (1966, 157) quotes the following prayer which is addressed to a young hemlock tree by a man who is about to cut it down for a trap:

> Thank you, friend, for letting me find you. I have come to hire you, friend, to work for me that you may be the deadfall of my trap for the landotter, who is intelligent when he is being trapped. Now only take care and call the landotter, that he may come and go under you. When you fall, fall behind his shoulder blades so that you will kill him.

Both the Kwakiutl Indian of the west coast addressing the spirit of the hemlock and the old Cree on the eastern shore of James Bay conversing with his mistabeo attempt to master nature and yet also defer to it, as though the ecosystem has its own requirements, rules and destiny.

Not all spirits are equally important. They often form a hierarchy within the ecosystem based upon the influence on humans. Bear spirits in the eastern woodlands are treated with particular respect: the hunter will explain to the bear why it is necessary for him to be killed. Then he takes care that bones and skull are put on a pole so that dogs can not reach them. On the west coast the Nootka treat the killed bear as an honoured guest. They make it sit up and give it a ceremonial hat to wear. They offer it food and beg it to eat. The Naskapi make sure to cast the eyes of a killed beaver into the water, so that it can return to life. A properly treated animal will feel grateful to the hunter and will seek him out at a later reincarnation. For the same reason of respect the Naskapi never break the backbone of the big lake trout. On the other hand, otters and birds are given less ritual attention (Speck 1977, 113, 120, 125).

SOULS

Souls and spirits are often used as synonyms for one another. The Montagnais-Naskapi (Labrador) use the word *atcak* for soul or shadow, but then the mistabeo, or guiding spirit, is not distinguishable from the way the soul actually operates in the life of the individual or the animal. The soul also guides, motivates and causes dreams; Speck (1977, 35) therefore compares both the soul and the mistabeo with ego. Or, to say it in the words of a young Mohawk Indian, *oulonta*, soul, "also means something that makes a person whole" (Waugh and Prithipaul 1979, 48).

Wherever Canadian Indians use the idea of the soul or spirit, the idea of the fit of person or animal in the social or ecological system is not far behind. Most souls (later we will mention an important exception) represent the part of existence which survives physical integrity. They objectify the forces operating harmfully or beneficially in society or nature; they are sectional distillations of the social and ecological system; they transcend the life of the individual and are therefore immortal. It is the immortality of spirits and souls which reinforces the continuity and orderliness of an otherwise discontinuous and dynamic configuration of systems.

It is particularly at death that the soul is seen as closely related to the place of an individual in family or clan. The loss is carefully and ritually repaired by sending the soul on its way, allowing the social system to reintegrate. Dreams (when the soul is thought to roam around) also have an integrating effect on the ego and its niche in the environment. These issues will be dealt with later at greater length.

The link between the immortal soul and the social order becomes rather clear when Indians explain insanity, or socially unacceptable conduct. They equate the disintegration of personality with the loss of the soul or the fighting of two souls. The Bella Coola (central coast of British Columbia) say of a person who has taken leave of his senses that his soul has departed. In such an event the shaman is called in. He searches for the departed soul and, if he can locate it, catches it in his cloak which is then placed around the madman. The Bella Coola also regard the soul of the infant which is not socialized as yet as embryonic and weak (McIlwraith 1948, I, 94ff.). Similarly the Ojibwa account for the anti-social conduct of a drunk as a temporary leave of his soul. Sometimes a death is explained as the result of the struggle of two souls within one person (Hultkrantz 1953, 214,28).

Not all souls are immortal or survive physical integrity. The Algonquins (Eastern Ontario) distinguish the immortal soul from the one which dies with the body and tends to be synonymous with health or physical wholeness. So do the Ojibwa: one soul dies at death and the other roams about and eventually goes to the Indian Elysium (Schoolcraft, 1969, 79).

However much evidence there is of belief in a unitary soul amongst Indians south of the Canadian border, Canadian tribes generally hold the view that there are at least two souls, one mortal, one immortal. Hultkrantz (1953, 145), who made the most thorough and detailed study of the soul concept amongst North American Indians, feels that the Christian view of the indivisibility of the soul is one reason for the rise of the unitary soul concept. Yet, the dual soul-conception, he says, offers "the best explanation of such general primitive phenomena of religious belief as the dream-wanderings, the states of soul-loss and the double-ganger." The problem with Hultkrantz's attempt to link religion to native intellectual curiosity and individual experiences (Ibid., 19) is that he overlooks the possibility that belief in souls reinforces various overlapping, and interdependent, but also separate and independent identities or systems such as the ecosystem, tribal and family identity, individual bodily wholeness.

If one takes this view of the function of the soul concept (and its function does not exhaustively explain either its emergence or its persistence) one can avoid both Tylor's and Hultkrantz's rationalistic and individualistic biasses for the explanation of the unitary soul. In this "system," or "identity," view of the soul, Indians believing in dual (or multiple) souls stress the independent or separate aspect of the system of which they were a part (body vs. social system), whereas Indians believing in a unitary soul stress the interdependence of these systems and the transcendental order straddling them all.

TOTEMS

The word totem (emblem) is of Ojibwa origin. Long, who traded in the territory of the Ojibwa in the second half of the eighteenth century is the first to introduce the term to the public at large. He says that the tribe uses the word for a favourite spirit watching over an individual and that therefore they "never kill, hunt or eat the animal whose form they think this 'totem' bears" (Hodge 1969, 464). Also, among the Salish (southern British Columbia), the totem is indistinguishable from a personal guardian spirit and bolsters the individual's integrity and confidence. They call it *scomeq* and believe that it both protects and instructs the individual (Hill-Tout 1978, 138ff.).

Yet, in contrast with guardian spirits, totems can also be collective and can represent the clan. In British Columbia these totems (generally in the shape of a bird or other animal) are carved on the totem poles and painted on the facade of dwellings. Boas (1916, 535) mentions how on the coffins of the Tsimshian Indian (central coast of British Columbia) the clan bird is represented as though it is flying out. Apparently the Tsimshian closely connect the immortal soul (and the now vanishing place of the deceased in the social system) with the totem.

On the other side of the continent, amongst the Iroquois of southern Ontario and northern New York, the powerful effect of a totem or emblem on clan cohesion is particularly obvious. Around 1570 five tribes, the Cayuga, the Mohawk, the Oneida, the Onondaga and the Seneca are welded into one powerful nation of Iroquois through the subdivision of each tribe into two moieties (exogamous halves). Each of these can only marry spouses of the other. They, in turn, are subdivided into four clans (1) Wolf, Bear, Beaver, Turtle; (2) Deer, Snipe, Heron, Hawk. "The Seneca Wolf felt himself to be closer to a Wolf from the Cayuga, Onondaga, Oneida or Mohawk tribes than to a member of the other clans of his own tribe; and this feeling of affinity welded the League into an indissoluble union "(Muller 1968, 180-1).

Other units of social organization, such as the family, are also reinforced through worship and sculptural representation of ancestors in animals or birds (MacLean 1896, 441).

DEITIES and MYTHS

Like spirits, deities tend to sum up and reinforce aspects of order. They are different from spirits in that they straddle less particular, more general, sections of that order. They also have more power and autonomy. It is this distinctiveness which tends to set the realm of order, as objectified in a deity, apart from the unpredictable realm of the mundane.

In Labrador the caribou, moose and beaver have their own chiefs who control the spirits of the individual animals. If these individuals are treated disrespectfully they complain to their ruler who may take all the game of the area away until such time as amends have been made. It is not the killing which upsets the animals (after all, they will be reincarnated), but the disorderly way of disposing of their remains (Speck 1977, 83ff.). On the other side of the continent, on the coast of British Columbia, the Kwakiutl similarly believe in animal hierarchy. To them the salmon is important and therefore their chief is ceremonially enticed to come ashore (Boas 1970, 475ff.).

The animal rulers generally have the same shape as their charges. In 1634 the French Jesuit Le Jeune (1972, 13) quoted his informers as saying that the chief of the beavers is as large as a cabin. Yet this ruler in turn has his own master, Messou, who is not only the chief of all animals, but also the restorer of the universe after it had been destroyed by a flood.

Belief in Messou is common in the entire area from Saskatchewan to Newfoundland, an area occupied by those Indians who speak the same Algonkian language. Yet the name differs from tribe to tribe. Some call him Gloskap, others Michabo or Wieska, but he is best known as Nanabozho, the Great Hare. He personifies life and renewal of life. "He is this life struggling with the many forms of want, misfortune and death that come to the bodies and beings of nature" (Hewitt in Hodge 1969, 331).

According to one Algonkian myth, Nanabozho is the oldest of four brothers, all born of a great primal being. The second son is much less gifted and is too gentle for his own good. His older brother has to constantly protect him until finally the evil spirits get the better of him. A third son is the white hare who gets to live in the North. The fourth brother, Chakekenapok (meaning flint or firestone), personifies the hardness of winter. He has cruelly caused his own mother's death and is deeply resented by Nanabozho. The latter pursues him all over the world until he finally catches up with him. In an epic fight various pieces are chipped from the body of this cruel brother, some of which become the Rocky Mountains. Finally Nanabozho kills and disembowels Chakekenapok, whose entrails become vines.

In the Indian myths Nanabozho is often portrayed as the fighter of evil. Ceremonies have an effect on his moods. During one of these ceremonies, when the sacred medicine bundles are cast on the ground, all his melancholy and anger vanishes to be replaced by feelings of affection and joy. In another myth Nanabozho is the chief of a large variety of animals floating on a raft and searching for firm land. After many attempts the muskrat dives deeply and comes up with a grain of sand. The Great Hare expands this into habitable earth. However, he is not very pleased with his creation and becomes distrustful of the other animals. Rumbles in the interior of the earth show that Nanabozho is still at work (Ibid., 334).

There are many variations on similar mythical themes. David Thompson (1971, 112ff.) who was a trader for the Hudson's Bay Company around the turn of the eighteenth century, records some beliefs of the Nahathaways in northern Manitoba and Saskatchewan. They believe in a Great Spirit (Kitchi Manitou) who makes man and animal but then leaves it to the trickster hero Weesaukejauk to teach them how to live. However, the latter is rather careless and condones vicious quarrels between his charges. Kitchi Manitou becomes very angry when he sees the ground red with blood. He washes the earth clean with a great flood. All men and animals are drowned except an otter, a beaver and a muskrat who happened to be on a raft with Weesaukejauk. As in the Nanabozho myth, the muskrat comes up with some earth and the trickster hero creates life from scratch.

There is a tendency in Indian myths to stress the concreteness of animal chiefs and deities. If there are beliefs in a more abstract supreme being who is omnipotent, omniscient and infallible, (as, for instance, amongst the eastern Crees of James Bay), they remain rather unarticulated. The Crees certainly don't dream about them and deal much more actively with their mistabeos, who have more modest power and knowledge (Preston 1975, 142).

Hallowell (1971, 6ff.), writing of Indians east of Lake Winnipeg, similarly describes beliefs in a supreme being whose name is seldom uttered. No one ever dreams of Kadabendjiget, he says, in contrast with the lesser spirits who actively mold man and his environment. This was also observed among natives in the Quebec area by Charles l'Allemant (1972, 4), superior of the Jesuit mission in New France, in a letter he wrote in 1626 to his general in Rome: "They believe in one who has created all; yet they don't give him any homage." Jenness (1976, 73) sums it up as follows:

> Most of them (Indians) thought that even the Great Spirit
> was too remote to trouble himself greatly about human
> affairs; and while they rendered him lip service, and occa-
> sionally approached him in prayer, they directed most of
> their thoughts to those lesser powers - the spirits of birds
> and animals, and of the sun, the winds and the thunder -
> that seemed to exert a more immediate influence on their
> daily lives.

Or, to say this differently: the vagueness of a transcendental order allows for the absorption of a wide variety of experiences. Yet the more concrete delineations of the various sytems of which the Indians feel themselves part secure their viability more effectively than the over-arching frame of reference.

The Iroquois in southern Ontario and northern New York differ from the Algonkians in language and custom. Yet they have rather similar myths. These too revolve around themes of good and evil, cruelty and kindness, destruction and restoration. A typical myth runs as follows:

The goddess Ataensic is thrown out of heaven by her husband. After she has fallen on earth she gives birth to two sons. One is the Great Spirit, Hawenneyu, who creates and protects man and all useful animals and plants. The other is the Evil Spirit, Hanegoategeh, who creates monsters, poisonous snakes and noxious weeds (Morgan 1972, 156ff.). He sows discord and multiplies calamities.

Both spirits have their assistants and emissaries. Heno, assistant to the Great Spirit, is in charge of thunder and rain; he also admonishes and avenges; and in some myths he dwells in a cave behind the Niagara Falls. The Iroquois think of themselves as his grandchildren. The Great Spirit also sends lesser spirits to the earth, for instance, the spirits of corn, beans and squashes. By contrast, Hanegoategeh sends spirits who bring pestilence and disease.

On the west coast of Canada the Kwakiutl believe in a variety of great spirits. The most formidable of them is Baxbakualanuxsiwae which means "Man Eater at the Mouth of the River." He is a cannibal who lives at the headwaters of the rivers at the North End of the world, the source of darkness, death and disease. His appetite for humans is insatiable and women provide him with bodies and victims. He also swallows potlatch (or wealth, given in exchange). His body is covered with mouths and his abode is visualized as being at the center or post of the world. He has many slaves and one of them (a raven) eats the eyes of the people whom his master has devoured while other birds live on the brains of his victims. Yet, he is easy to subdue and one of his many names is "wishing to be tamed."

The mouth and eating are central metaphors in Kwakiutl cosmology. They stand for destruction, bestiality and anti-social conduct, and they are tamed by elaborate etiquette: noblemen and noblewomen chew their food very deliberately, hardly opening their mouths, for they don't want to show their teeth. "Boxness," or the boundedness of containers, is a second important metaphor to the Kwakiutl. It represents the principles and units of social organization, kinship, self and other, cooperation and competition, and many other dialectic oppositions (Walens 1981, 14, 91, 46).

There are many variations on a common theme of the Man Eater being subjugated and killed. One of the myths (Boas 1970, 394ff., 457ff.) runs as follows: One day four mountain-goat hunters come to the Man Eater's house while he is away. A woman in the house helps them to trap the cannibal. At her instruction they dig a hole, the bottom of which they fill with red-hot stones and the top of which they cover. When Baxbakualanux-siwae comes home, he falls in the trap. The hunters quickly cover the hole with boards and so the Man Eater dies a gruesome death. The men then take the masks and whistles of the cannibal, and the woman (who reveals herself as being one of their daughters) teaches his sacred songs. When the father wants to take his daughter home, she proves to be rooted in the ground. The deeper the men dig, the thicker the root becomes, and so they decide to cut it. However, the daughter convinces them that this will mean her death and so they leave her behind. They promise to visit her occasionally and to give a winterdance in accordance with her instructions.

It is in this major winterdance ceremony that the Kwakiutl act out the main theme of the myth: the alternation of life and death, being killed and resurrected, or, as Goldman (1975, 109) has it: "For Kwakiutl all metaphysical issues of antagonism are resolved simply and neatly by the Hegelian trick of transformation of opposites: death turns to life, life to death." Locher (1932, 41) calls the winter ritual:

> an extensive rebirth rite, in which the powers of death and
> darkness come to the front, but ultimately are unable to
> hold their own against life and light. The secret of the
> ritual consists in the conception that life and light do not
> come into being without death and darkness, so that both
> these aspects not only may, but even must, be united.

TABOOS and SACRIFICE

Beliefs in spirits and deities have little integrating effect unless they are held strongly and consistently. Indians, therefore, take it for granted that everyone is fully committed to the beliefs and institutions and they expect that the coming generations will be just as loyal. Taboos are constant reminders of these commitments. They define existence. They are concrete rules of appropriate and inappropriate conduct in a comprehensive set of circumstances. And so Bella Coola women of the west coast cannot eat bear meat. As well, their husbands place the bear skull in a tree close to the scene of the kill, for otherwise they will be blinded (or so they think). On the other side of the continent the Naskapi of Labrador have a taboo against women stepping over the legs of a hunter or over his snowshoe tracks. If they do so anyway, his legs will become weak or sore.

To challenge them deliberately is treason to the Indian. Of course transgressions take place, but they are a serious matter, and so the Iroquois (Morgan 1972, 170) make public confessions of sins before their religious festivals. These disclosures are always followed by promises to make amends. Confessions are also common in other areas of eastern and northern Canada. In southern Ontario sins are cast on a pure white dog which is then strangled and burnt as a sacrifice (Jenness 1976, 74).

Sacrifices, like confessions, reinforce commitment to the Indian view of the world. They articulate and clarify priorities. And so morsels of meat or tobacco are offered to the spirits at appropriate times and places. Not giving the spirits their due makes an Indian feel guilty. Neglect, he feels, has a bad effect on his own destiny.

Fasting is another way to find favour with the spirit world. Young Indians, in particular, abstain from both food and water while searching for a guiding spirit. If they live on the plains and participate in the Sun Dance, they also refrain from sexual intercourse (Mandelbaum 1979, 194-5). At this dance severed finger joints are sometimes offered to the sun (MacLean 1896, 442). On the west coast the Kwakiutl (Boas 1970, 502) require sexual abstinence for participants in their Winter Dance and the Bella Coola (McIlwraith 1948, I, 116) practise ceremonial chastity to find favour with the supernatural beings.

SHAMANS

In all Indian communities in Canada, shamans are the experts on the spirit world. They exemplify the spiritual priorities and they are the brokers with the spirits. They are priests, prophets, doctors all rolled into one. Sometimes they conjure and act as witchdoctors, magicians and sorcerers (the favourite appellation of the early French missionaries), yet they always focus religious activity, and restore personal or social integrity. A conjurer "was an important instrument of morale in so far as he was able to establish confidence in the face of danger and at the same time to supply information that could be taken as the basis of action" (Hallowell 1971, 65).

It is not easy to become a shaman. If a child is a dreamer, or has fainting spells, parents begin to think of him (sometimes "her") as a possible shaman. Arduous periods of fasting, separation in the wilderness and instruction by other shamans follow.

The Kwakiutl initiate a new shaman in rites which are analogous to the death/resurrection rituals of their Winter Dance. "After initiation, shamans must be continent for a period varying from several months - in one case sixteen months - to four years. They are not allowed to sing love songs; they must not wail after the death of a relative....they are also not allowed to laugh" (Boas 1966, 136-7).

The best shaman is always a somewhat marginal figure, an intermediary between two worlds, and therefore not a full citizen of either. Sometimes he is an individual given up for dead and yet miraculously restored to life (Boas 1930, 32, 46, 54). At other times he is a visionary who can foretell the future or who has a sixth sense for the location of game. A shaman of the Haida (west coast) accompanies every war party in order to pinpoint the proper time and place for the attack (Corlett 1935, 94). Often he accentuates his difference from other mortals by never washing or combing his hair, by growing it long, or by wearing a long piece of bone in the perforated septum of the nose (Ibid., 92). One famous shaman of the Plains Cree was a transvestite (Mandelbaum 1979, 168).

Generally the most prestigious and effective shaman would be in two worlds (the spiritual and the human) simultaneously or, as Goldman (1975, 100) has it: "The shaman becomes established as a marginal person who straddles the boundaries between his own kind and the universe of spirits."

Yet the marginality of a shaman is relative. He is separate, but only in the sense in which spirits are separate. He is the eminent defender of the Indian system of meaning. In the seventeenth century the Jesuit missionaries from France often succeeded in Christianizing the common people; then the shaman would reassert the authority of the spirits and the missionaries had to start all over again. The shaman is the spokesman of the spirits and reminds the people of the consequences of their transgressions. He powerfully wields the forces of conformity (Cooper 1971, 86).

Most of the extensive literature on shamans deals with the cures they effect. Here, too, they are go-betweens. On the one hand is the individual whose physical or mental integrity is impaired and on the other the world of the spirits in which order and wholeness are objectified. They connect the one with the other through emotional welding techniques. Mandelbaum (1979, 162ff.) describes such a curing session for a patient belonging to the Plains Cree.

The shaman starts by invoking the help of his guiding spirits. After asking them to uphold their part of the pact with him, he performs a series of magical acts in which he reinforces the belief of patient and onlookers in the spirits. Then he blows over the body, placing his mouth over the affected area and sucking out the substance which has made the patient sick. (This is a widespread custom over the entire North American continent.) The substance will then be shown to all and sundry. It can be anything: a toad, a pebble, a thorn, a hair, a snail, a strange insect, a piece of flint, a bit of twig. The showing of this ill-making substance forms the climax of faith-healing and it frequently has the desired results. If a shaman fails too often, his reputation will be in jeopardy and his power will evaporate.

During the curing sessions the shaman attempts to discover the cause of the disease. Has the patient transgressed a taboo? Amongst the Bella Coola stepping on a dead salmon insults the spirit of the latter and makes the offender sick (McIlwraith 1948, I, 561-2). Or has his soul left him? In such a case the shaman may go on a long fast or on a long journey to retrieve the lost soul and catch it between the palms of his hand. Or is the delirium caused by the visitation of a spirit? Then the spirit will have to be diplomatically shown its way. A large variety of medical herbs and nauseating concoctions are other means to effect a cure.

Sometimes shamans are leaders of native ceremonies. This is particularly true for the west coast, where native social organization is more elaborate than in other parts of the country. The Kwakiutl chiefs, who have already acquired supernatural power as the incarnations of the ancestors, in addition become shamans during the Winter Dances. Together they form the Society of Sparrows which organizes the ceremony and manages the invitations, the seating and the order of the dances. They counter the Society of Seals to which they themselves have belonged in previous seasons and which consists of those natives who dramatize possession by the Man Eating spirits. The Sparrows act as the tamers of the Seals, restorers of normality. They guide the novices through their spiritual ordeal and secure the safety of their souls (Goldman 1975, 88ff.).

There were other societies in Canada (for instance, the Midewin of the Ojibwa) in which the shamans played a prominent part. They tended to be particularly concerned with ancestral origins, death and renewal. Yet whatever their differences in function, shamans everywhere were bridgebuilders with the world of the spirits. As such they constantly mended an impaired realm of integrity, whether physical or mental, personal, ecological, or social.

AMULETS

Amulets do for the individual what rites do for family, community or tribe. They both replenish and reenact wholeness. An individual feels his confidence and courage enhanced through carrying, touching or addressing his amulet. The community similarly feels drawn together through common dancing, singing and praying. Both amulets and rites draw boundaries around a person, a family, a clan or a tribe and fortify what is within those boundaries.

And so the Kwakiutl (Boas 1966, 363) place seagrass in the bottom of the cradle to ensure that the frail child will be strong when it grows up. The Naskapi hunter (Speck 1977, 235) wears a special charm of beads to enhance his prowess and skill. The Bella Coola shaman carries a life-stick, the life-giving end of which cures the patient (McIlwraith 1948, I, 559).

Occasionally the community as a whole possesses amulets. The prairie tribes collect charms for a "medicine bundle" protecting families and clans. The bundle is treated with great care. It is brought inside when the weather is bad. When the bundle is opened, each article (whether bird skull, piece of animal skin, an odd stone, a buffalo horn or a bear paw) must be separately addressed with prayers and songs.

Mandelbaum (1979, 172-3) describes such a bundle of the Plains Cree. It was called *oskitci*, or pipestembundle, and was originally given by the Great Manitou to Earth Man, the first human being. It contains a decorated, three-to four-feet-long pipestem, some sweetgrass, tobacco and a pipe tamp. It is a great honour to be chosen by the tribe as owner and guardian, yet it also carries responsibilities of fearlessness, liberality and equanimity. The pipestembundle always requires peaceful behaviour. In its presence quarrels and conflicts are to end and its owner must intervene in all intertribal disputes. Pipesmoking and passing the pipe around in native councils is often a solemn occasion, particularly for the Cree and the Ojibwa. It seals agreements and decisions, but it can also be the sacred, deeply moving communion of an entire clan, leaving everyone with the feeling that through the ceremony all powers of self, society and nature are united (Newbery 1979, 178).

Divining is another way to keep the world of arbitrariness away. Many tribes in middle and eastern Canada scorch the shoulder blades of an animal. Then they "read" the blemishes. Dark spots are areas where game can be found. Other marks stand for individual hunters. Death, famine or plenty can all be read on the scorched shoulder blade. In all instances divining bridles the open-endedness of existence.

RITES

In the section about spirits it has been shown how the prayers, addresses and rites reinforce the native niche in the ecosystem, thereby simultaneously treating and fortifying the latter. However, rites also strengthen a variety of units of social organization or moderate the relations between them.

The family is one of these units. At the beginning of the berry season each Plains Cree family has its own ritual. An old male member consecrates the cooked berries and thanks the Great Spirit for his gifts. Then the Sun is asked to ripen the berries, the Thunder to provide the rain and the Earth to bring forth its fruits.

On the west coast, individual families narrate the origins of their mythical ancestors at tribal ceremonies. These myths also legitimate the land rights of each family and are represented in the sculpture of the totem poles in front of their houses. At the top of such a pole one usually finds the bird or animal in the form of which the ancestor has come to earth. Lower down are the animal spirits which have assisted the ancestor. The glories of the ancestors are recounted or dramatized at dances and other social occasions. The family and its traditions are thereby placed within the larger, tribal whole.

Particularly where native social organization has become rather elaborate, as on the West Coast, ranks and hierarchies are strengthened through recognition in ritual. The ritual giving of presents (potlatch) establishes the place of a man in the tribal rank-order: the greater the gift, the higher the rank of the giver. Through a large gift a chief enhances the renown of his ancestors. The giving itself reinforces rank-order: the first and largest gift goes to the highest-ranking guest, and lesser gifts go to lower-ranking guests and so on down the line.

On the prairies food distribution and seating takes place accord ing to rank. In Labrador eating and seating at the bearfeast is in accordance with age and rank as hunter.

Generally rites strengthen tribal unity. We have already mentioned the Man-Eating ceremonies of the Kwakiutl which dramatize the interdependence of life and death, light and darkness. Cosmic symbolism is the hub of the Sun Dance on the prairies. It is held for several days around a large pole erected on the grounds of a lodge. The pole represents the world-tree, the channel of communication between man and the sun deity (Hultkrantz 1979, 141). At the top is the "thunderbird's nest" with gifts for the Great Manitou. The natives dance and sing around it after touching it reverently. Often the dedication of young braves is expressed through self-torture. They take skewers attached with rawhide lines to the top of the Sun Dance pole and drive them through their chest muscles. Then they dance, stretching the line until the skewers break the flesh and release them.

The Blackfoot in Alberta (Hellson 1979, 197) use the Sun Dance for the initiation of novices in their various societies. The Sun Dance is the center for the organization of these groups vis-a-vis one another. Mock battles between them enliven the scene.

RITES OR PASSAGE

These rites differ from others in that they guide the passing from one identity or phase to another. Birth, initiation, marriage and burial are typical rites of passage. They incorporate the new member (baby, bride, novice) into the family or community or they mend the change in the social fabric caused by death. Because these rites deal with change they often include a stripping, or desacralizing phase (detaching individuals from their previous niche) before the welding or sacralizing phase can take place.

Birth

Taboos relating to pregnancy set mother and baby apart in some Indian tribes. Bella Coola expectant mothers never eat salmon tails, as they do not want the infant born feet first. At the onset of labour pains women separate themselves and babies are generally born in the woods or other sheltered spots.

The Kwakiutl similarly have numerous taboos. The expectant mother is not supposed to eat whale meat or squid. Nor does she look at anything ugly, deformed or sick. Otherwise the baby may become ugly, deformed or sick, she thinks.

Once the child is born Indians have a naming ceremony, often accompanied by a feast. Mandelbaum (1979, 140-1) describes this rite for the Plains Cree of the prairies. The father asks a shaman to name the child. The latter lights a pipe, addresses the spirits and takes the baby in his arms. He then pronounces the new name which occurred to him in one of his visions. He then asks the guiding spirit to protect the child. After this the baby is passed around to all the guests, each of which addresses it now by its new name and makes a wish for its future happiness. The ceremony concludes with a common meal.

The Eastern Cree of Quebec have a similar naming ceremony, as do the Dene who speak the Athapascan language and live primarily in the Northwest Territories. A peculiarity of the Dene tribes is that the father of the child drops his own name and is now addressed as "the father of so-and-so."

Details vary in other parts of Canada. Soon after birth Kwakiutl babies have the septum of their nose pierced to keep sickness and ghosts away. Four days later the lobes of the ear are perforated as well. These babies first get a temporary name (after the place where it is born). The official naming takes place about ten months after birth. At this ceremony the child's hair is singed off and the whole head and face are painted with red ochre. Red ochre is also distributed to the invited guests. Towards the end of the ceremony the guests receive a handkerchief for tying around their heads. Then the baby too is covered with a handkerchief (Boas 1966, 359ff.).

Initiation

In some Canadian tribes a new name marks the coming of age. The Iroquois in southern Ontario attach a naming ceremony for youth of age fifteen or so to certain seasonal festivals. The youth keeps this name for the rest of his life.

The Plains Cree have elaborate initiation rites for girls as soon as their menstruation begins. She is secluded in a small tipi. After four days the women of the camp guide her back to her father's tipi. Here she steps over kindled sweetgrass smudges while two of the women pray for their guiding spirits. After this a meal is served, a pipe is offered to the spirits and gifts are distributed. On the west coast the Kwakiutl have both a naming and potlatch (present-giving) ceremony for a girl after her first period.

It is in the transitional phase of their lives that boys often go on "vision quests." They seclude themselves from the camps for praying and fasting and thereby become more prone to have dreams and visions. In this hallucinatory state they often see guiding spirits disguised as animals or birds who then become attached to them for life, teach them songs and help them in danger. The vision quests are common in large parts of Canada, from the Micmac in New Brunswick to the Crees in the prairie provinces.

On the west coast the noble families of the Kwakiutl initiate their children in the "Seals," one of the two major categories of participants in the Winter Ceremonial. Here the novices often have to impersonate one of the many Man-Eating spirits. This entails living in the woods for an extended period of time. In a state of emaciation they see and feel themselves being swallowed by the man-eating spirits dominant in Kwakiutl myths. On their return the initiates are restored to their humanity by the shamans of the Sparrows, the other category of actors in the Winter Ceremonial.

Marriage

The few wedding ceremonies in Indian society consist generally of a simple exchange of gifts between the families of bride and bridegroom. A Naskapi suitor, for instance, presents gifts to the parents of the prospective bride to seal his serious intentions. The Hurons (Ontario) go somewhat further. They organize wedding feasts with much dancing and eating. The parents of a Plains Cree couple exchange gifts, but the bridal family is also expected to make a new tipi for the pair. The highlight of the wedding here is the bridegroom's acceptance of a new pair of moccasins from the bride.

As always the west coast Indians go in for more ostentation and ritual according to the status of the families involved. Commoners go to little trouble, but chiefs make up for it. The families exchange many treasures and animal skins. The Bella Coola nobles celebrate marriages with large feasts, many speeches about ancestral myths, much dancing and marriage songs made for the occasion. The Kwakiutl include in their ceremony the "immovable rooting" of the bride to the floor of her father's house. Through the display of treasures (natural and supernatural, such as songs), chiefs acting for the groom gradually shake her loose from her footing (Goldman 1975, 82).

Death

As in other primitive communities burial rites are more elaborate than other rites of passage, possibly because death demands greater adjustments for family and community than birth and marriage. The phases of emotional detachment from the deceased, sense of loss and meaninglessness, and emotional attachment to the changed familial or communal identity are overlapping and yet clearly represented in all Indian funerals.

In the separation phase the deceased is buried or cremated, sometimes together with the belongings with which he or she is most clearly associated. To emphasize the separation, the Blood Indians (southern Alberta) tear down the dwelling in which the individual has died, or they move camp altogether. Other tribes treat the spirits of the dead as dangerous and possibly hostile even though everyone might have felt very close to the person before he or she died. In 1636 Jean de Brébeuf (129) described how the Hurons (southern Ontario) bury their dead decked out in valuable robes, stockings, shoes and belts. The Kootenay (southeastern British Columbia) sometimes kill the horse of the deceased to accompany him. The Naskapi in Labrador do the same with a beloved dog. The Thompson River natives in the west go even further for a very prominent person: they kill or bury alive one of his slaves to serve him in the hereafter. The Ojibwa deposit bows and arrows, a knife, dish, spoon, blankets and other articles for use on the journey to the "Land of the Sleeping Sun" (the West). The Bella Coola burn clothing and other personal belongings on the grave.

Much of the ritual deals with sending the soul on its way. The Plains Cree have a ceremony on the fourth day after death. First a pipe is smoked, then the Great Spirit is addressed while the pipestem is pointed to the North where the spirit dwells who directs a wandering soul, and where lives the spirit which keeps the soul from looking back on its journey. Then the pipestem is directed to the South where the spirit dwells who keeps the soul in the Green Grass world. Subsequently, all present at the ceremony puff at the pipe, after which food is offered and eaten (the final or consolidating phase).

In eastern Canada the belief is widespread, regarding the place where souls go, that they pass over a constantly moving log spanning a swift stream to the village of the ancestors situated on a large meadow. Only the just, however, get there safely. The vicious souls cannot navigate the log, fall in the stream and are lost for good. The Iroquois believed that only Indians could go to this heaven, George Washington being the only exception, as he had protected Indian rights (Morgan 1972, 178).

Separation from the deceased is sometimes accentuated through taboos covering those who have handled the body in some way. For instance, the Loucheux (Yukon) will not allow those who buried the dead to eat fresh meat for a certain period.

There is ample room in Indian tribes for the expression of the "meaninglessness" phase in death rituals. It is a dangerous phase, for the sense of loss of the nearest relatives may put the values and behaviour patterns of the ongoing community into jeopardy. For this reason full allowance is made for emotional release while, at the same time, its expression is fully structured by custom. When a Bella Coola Indian is critically ill all friends and relatives gather at his house to wail and weep. After his death the female relations tear out tufts of hair. The Plains Cree have a custom whereby mourners gash forearms and legs. The Kootenay mourners cut off hair which is then buried with the body. In other places of the west (MacLean 1896, 194), mourners are supposed to appear dishevelled and unkempt while the closest relative sometimes cuts off one finger at the first joint. On the West coast the spouse of the deceased is expected to sit motionless for four days with the knees drawn up to the chin. He or she is not supposed to associate with other people for four months and leaves the house through a separately cut door. Relatives of the dead belonging to the Salish in southern British Columbia abstain from fresh food. Here a widow abandons the customary bed and a young widower refrains from sexual intercourse for a full year after his wife has died (Hill-Tout 1907, 204).

The final, consolidating phase of death rituals consists invariably of a communal meal. Here the fellowship of the survivors can reassert itself as independently viable. The Iroquois in southern Ontario hold a feast of "re-associating with the public" ten days after the death of one of its members. At this occasion his property is divided amongst heirs and friends. From now on his or her name is not to be mentioned again. After a funeral Kootenay attendants take a thorn bush, dip it into a kettle of water and sprinkle the doors of all lodges. The bush is then broken to pieces and thrown into a kettle of water which is drunk by all the mourners. The Loucheux have a large mortuary feast to finish the funeral rites. They ritually smoke a pipe (always a powerfully integrative occasion) and make speeches about the good qualities of the deceased. The Bella Coola too provide a meal to all participants at which ancestral myths are recited and presents are given. Several months after the funeral a memorial potlatch may be given for important chiefs.

The largest feast of all was given by the Hurons every ten years or so in the Feast of the Dead. De Brébeuf (131ff.) gave a graphic description of such a feast in 1636. All the bones of the Hurons departed in the preceding decade are dug up, cleaned and decorated by each family. They are then wrapped in furs of lesser or greater value according to the wealth of the family and the rank of the deceased. Speeches are made about each of the deceased, food is distributed and the bones reburied in a large common grave, lined with furs. The ceremony ends with an exchange of presents, divisions of furs and a funeral chant.

DREAMS

Dreams integrate personality. They structure and anchor emotionally disparate, or unconnected, experiences. Like taboos, they take the sting out of arbitrariness. Like spirits, they allow for a vision beyond the disjointed and the incongruous. They mitigate anxiety and provide incipient, emotionally soothing, unity. Like transcendental meaning systems, for which (to judge by Australian aboriginal religion) the dream might very well have been the prototype, they can be a platform from which action can be confidently undertaken. Dreams functioned both ways amongst the Canadian Indians. In 1693, Francis du Peron, a Jesuit missionary in New France, summed up the importance of dreams for the Indians as follows:

> All their actions are dictated to them directly by the devil who speaks to them, now in the form of a crow or some similar bird, now in the form of a flame or a ghost, and all this in dreams, to which they show great deference, - so great that, if they are asked to express their sentiments upon any subject, they say: "wait until we have consulted the dream." For better results they fast beforehand. They consider the dream as the master of their lives, it is the God of the country; it is this which dictates to them their feasts, their hunting, their fishing, their war, their trade with the French, their remedies, their dances, their games, their songs; to see them in these actions, you would think they were lost souls (372-3).

The missionaries looked upon Indian dreams as a prime obstacle for conversion. To them it was "devilry" because dreams went to the firm core of an unshakeable belief competing with their own faith. Later manifestations of Indian religion may well have been affected by the world view of the white man and it is therefore important to quote from the earliest sources. In this letter of Francis du Peron to his brother we have such an early source. It suggests that to Indians the dream or vision had both a crystallizing quality (it is their god) and a cathartic one (it is the basis for decision and change).

On dream as crystallization: the Plains Cree allowed only those who were good at dreaming to paint designs on tipis. On the west Coast, where body and face paintings were common, designs were often derived from dreams and visions. Dreams often represented culturally anchored archetypes or invisible core meanings, and visionaries who could represent these images in designs or in myths were in great demand. Dreams and visions allowed disparate patterns and experiences of the individual to congeal, or as Muller (1968, 171) writes with regard to North American Indians: "Dreams set the seal on tradition, legality and authority."

On dream as catharsis: the Canadian Indian believed that guardian spirits did their guiding primarily in dreams. The dream mediated between the beyond and appropriate action, whether this was hunting, attacking, defending, curing, or performing rites. It is through the dream that the Canadian Indian believed that the guardian spirits transmitted their advice, their encouragement, but also their warnings. A Kimsquit native (British Columbia coast) saw the side of his canoe being shattered in a dream. As he had long observed ceremonial chastity (making for reliable vision) he and his friends were extra careful the next day. Normally they would not have left the canoe when they encountered treacherous ice, but this time they did and indeed saw their canoe shattered soon afterwards. Yet, they remained

safe. (McIlwraith 1948, I, 614-5). Stories of this kind abound in the literature. They all come down to the same native conviction that the frame of
reference provided by the dream is the safest guide for appropriate action in
a whimsical world.

SUMMARY

Indian tribes in Canada differed considerably from one another. The
hunting and gathering tribes of the northern woodlands differed from the
corn-growing Iroquois to the south. Even greater was the distinction between those living east of the Rockies and the affluent, highly organized
tribes on the Pacific coast of British Columbia. All these differences had an
effect on religion and the kinds of problems with which it dealt.

Yet the similarities were even greater than the differences. All Canadian
Indians believed in spirits occupying both inanimate and animate objects.
Through interaction with these spirits Indians strengthened their personal
niche in the social and physical environment. Yet their beliefs, commitments, rites and myths also strengthened collectivity and the ecosystem
vis-à-vis the individual. Religion was the prime mediator between the
various Indian identities, whether ecological, social or personal.

These identities were fragile not only because they occasionally con-
flicted with one another, but also, and more significantly, because change of
any kind impaired integrity. Shamans and rites of passage formed the prime
forces in the Indian arsenal for the defense of personal, family and clan
wholeness. The shamans cured individual sickness, guarded communal
taboos, reinforced morale, guided the chase. They did all this through
recapturing souls, pursuing evil spirits or more generally through mediating
between the spiritual and the mundane world. Rites of passage stripped
obsolete identities and welded new ones. They guided the transitions neces-
sitated by birth, growing up, marriage, but, above all in Indian society,
death.

Myths and dreams were other antidotes to the ever-present potential for
disintegration. They summed up and dramatized the lineaments of tribal
and personal realities. Myths and mythical heroes acted out major themes of
hardship and cruelty struggling with prosperity and kindness. Death and
life, destruction and restoration, evil and good, darkness and light, all were
very familiar motifs in Indian stories and legends. Dreams and visions, for
their part, anchored emotionally disparate experiences for they hinted at an
objectified order, a system of core meanings. Dreams and visions were the
source of warnings and encouragements, they also upheld ancestral traditions and their unifying inpulse provided a platform for confidence in
decisions.

CHAPTER 3

THE CHRISTIANIZATION OF THE CANADIAN NATIVES

Religion and culture always closely intertwine, and in primitive societies they are often indistinguishable. By contrast, in advanced and differentiated societies a dialectical relationship takes the place of a close meshing of religion and culture. In Canada, when native and European cultures met and clashed, it took both parties some time to realize how profound the differences were and how these differences were most visible in the beliefs and rituals of each. There followed a time of mutual recriminations and ridicule. Each accused the other of making no sense, of possessing no reason. This period of hostility (the first subheading of this chapter) was followed by a period of adjustment by the natives (the second subheading) in which religious adaptation followed economic and political accommodation. Yet economic adjustments are easier to make than religious ones, if only because the latter are closely bound to a time-honoured way of life. All over Canada, therefore, charismatic movements (the third subheading) expressed the profound upheaval of an embattled native identity and the attempt to compensate for insecurity through the erection of boundaries (anti-white sentiments), through selective mixing of both native and Christian traditions and through concrete delineation of the future (the second coming of Jesus and other millenarian visions).

HOSTILITY

Contact between diverse cultures is usually a severe threat to the identity of both. It erodes boundaries around systems of meaning and customary ways of thinking, acting and reacting. Both cultures suffer in this process, yet an advanced one suffers less. The primitive society, wishing to improve its mastery over nature, attempts to adapt comprehensively in order to reap the superior benefits of the advanced culture. Adaptation results not only in change but also in a projection of hostility onto the identity-subverting agency. Since it plays so important a part in identity preservation on both sides of the culture conflict, religion, rather than technological or economic change, becomes the butt of mutual hostility.

Until the seventeenth century Canadian Indians hardly felt the full impact of European culture. In the 1500s Jacques Cartier had his scraps with the natives, but contacts were intermittent and furtive as were those of the Basque fishermen and the fur trading *coureurs de bois*. Yet even these meetings occasionally had their lasting consequences. The Algonkian belief in Jesus as the sun god probably goes back to such sporadic encounters (Le Jeune 1626, 4).

Much greater impact had the French missionaries who, at their own peril, began to live amongst the natives. Most of the missionaries, dedicated and ready for hardships, were impressive representatives of their own culture and French Catholicism. They went to remarkable trouble to learn the native languages, produced dictionaries and translations and made every effort to facilitate communication. They were supported in all this by the religious fervency of the Counter- Reformation in seventeenth-century France. The sufferings and martyrdom they underwent were widely published, making them heroes at home. Confidence in their God-given mission and their strong desire to dispel vast ignorance and gross superstition (as they thought) made them immune to the influence of native religion. However much they relativized native beliefs, these beliefs had little relativizing effect on their own vision of the world. If anything, their proselytizing strengthened rather than weakened their own convictions.

By contrast, the natives were less immune and more vulnerable. Even those very early contacts with Europeans had introduced profound changes into their mode of living (trapping and trading, for instance). Although they thought that they could at least hold on to their culture and religion, their shamans soon discovered that these, too, were endangered and stood on the ramparts even when other natives were more easily persuaded. In January 1616, when the Recollect father Joseph Le Caron accompanied Champlain on a visit to the Petuns, or Tobacco Nation, south of what is now the Georgian Bay in Ontario, his life was made miserable by shamans who felt threatened by Christian teachings and used every opportunity to deride them. Ten years later a similar fate befell father Joseph De La Roche Dallion who, at the instigation of the shamans, was robbed and threatened with death by the Neutrals in southern Ontario.

Father Paul Le Jeune had his share of acrimonious encounters with shamans whom he persistently called "sorcerers." He silently suffered their jeers and taunts to the great merriment of the bystanders. The natives felt that a man who had learned to speak their language should have more sense and be less ignorant. Le Jeune spoke of open warfare with the shamans at Tadoussac who manipulated his audiences so effectively that he was reduced to a laughingstock. Yet, when the "sorcerers" were absent, the Jesuit father had comparatively smooth sailing with the natives (Le Jeune 1634, 17-18, 56-7).

The shamans commonly blamed the missionaries for whatever disaster had befallen the natives, whether famine, disease, or drought. In 1636 the Jesuits were accused of causing the prevailing drought by the cross which they had erected at their dwelling in Ihonatiria (Huronia). Father de Brébeuf, who tried to persuade them that a cross was not an instrument of vengeance, accommodated them by repainting the symbol. However, he also suggested that the natives should appeal to his God. A procession was formed and de Brébeuf said nine masses. A deluge of rain followed which considerably enhanced the priest's standing vis-à-vis his adversaries (de Brébeuf 1636, 83-4).

The natives were accustomed to magical contests: superior priests had better magic, so they thought. Although de Brébeuf had impressed the people, memories were short, and shamans had the advantage of astute crowd-manipulation. A year later, in 1637 (twelve years before his actual martyrdom), de Brébeuf wrote a farewell letter from Ossossane (on the Georgian Bay). A hunchbacked, ogre-like shaman had stirred up the natives who then condemned the missionaries to death for causing an epidemic. On that occasion massacre was avoided because of a farewell feast to which the executioners were invited and at which de Brébeuf made a most persuasive speech. Shortly afterwards, the nephew of an important Huron chief was converted, soon followed by the rest of his family. This was a breakthrough. Up to this time the converts had come from those Indians who were marginal to their own society: the sick, the dying, the captives and others who were either unpopular or ostracized. The success of the Jesuit mission was assured from this point onwards, and the very village of Ossossane, which had made life for the Jesuits so difficult in 1637, ten years later contained more Christians than pagans (Parkman 1963, 449).

However, dark clouds soon began to gather over the mission to the Hurons. Christianity might now be a serious contender for the entire network of Huron religiosity, but the identification with one carefully selected tribe (the Hurons were deemed to be more gentle and sedentary than others) precluded its identification with its traditional enemies, the Iroquois. The latter associated Christianity with the French and the anti-Iroquois alliance. In the configuration of tribes in eastern Canada the Iroquois were the most aggressive and had the strongest sense of identity, and, consequently, they had been ruled out as likely candidates for conversion. By contrast, the milder and weaker Hurons were perceived as riper prospects.

The dark clouds began to burst towards the end of the 1640s. On the 16th of March, 1649, the villages of St. Ignace and St. Louis were destroyed by the Iroquois; the two priests living there, Jean de Brébeuf and Gabriel Lalemant, were put to death after savage torture. De Brébeuf was 'baptized' with boiling water, then around his naked shoulders were hung red-hot axes and a belt of pitch and resin around his body was set on fire. With this martyrdom and that of several other priests, and the subsequent occupation of large parts of Huronia by the Iroquois, the central mission post at Ste. Marie among the Hurons was abandoned.

The French Jesuits, however, did not have exclusive rights on martyrdom. In 1752 John Christian Erhardt and six other Moravians from Hernhutt in Saxony, who had established a mission near Nain in Labrador, were massacred by the Inuit. In spite of this, the Moravians did not give up. A dozen years later Jens Haven re-established the mission. Few converts were made in the eighteenth century in spite of the self-denial, hard work, linguistic intelligence and sensitivity of the Brethren and their families. They prevented alcohol abuse and the economic exploitation of the natives by insisting the Inuit take full title to 100,000 acres around their stations and manage their own trading posts. In this way they successfully helped the Inuit to enter the modern age without the degeneracy caused elsewhere.

In the first decade of the nineteenth century the Brethren converted an Inuit shaman at the Hopedale mission. According to their records, he changed from "a monster of iniquity" to a mild and gentle Christian (Gosling, 282). Other conversions soon followed and at the end of the century (Grenfell 1922, 223) the majority of the Inuit population of Labrador had become Christianized, even though the outside influences through fishermen, traders and the Hudson's Bay Company had increased.

The story repeats itself in western Canada. The Methodist missionary E. Ryerson Young writes how, with the exception of a shaman or two, the Cree in Manitoba were receptive to his message and that he felt greatly rewarded for his labours when several of the "conjurers" were converted and one of them publicly burned his medicine-bag (Young 1893, 228; 1894, 118-121).

Yet conversion did not always resolve conflicts. Some baptized shamans continued to pine away for their old friends, the spirits. Alualuk (an Inuit shaman east of the Mackenzie Delta) pitied the loneliness of the spirits and made extra sure to say his prayers and to keep the Christian commandments to obviate the anger of his rejected erstwhile friends (Stefansson 1951, 373).

Conflicts existed not only between natives and whites, but, as one can expect in differentiated societies, also within the white community. This confused the Indians, who took the indissoluble unity of religion and society for granted. Now they were forced to distinguish between the self-denying altruism of the missionary, the ruthless greed of the trader and the land-grabbing exploits of settlers and government. This lack of white integrity impeded missionary success. An Ojibwa chief (MacLean 1896, 176) reasoned that Christianity had been accompanied by fatal diseases. Why should he become a Christian when so many whites were just as wicked and habitually drunk as he was?

Some missionaries, therefore, attempted to separate Indian and white society. In western Canada where both the Catholic Oblate Fathers and the Anglican Church Missionary Society pioneered the mission field, William Duncan, an Anglican lay missionary removed his community of converted Tsimshians from Port Simpson on the B.C. coast to Metlakatla. By separating them from whites, Duncan felt that he could help the natives to better come to terms with Western technology and life-styles. In British Columbia the Oblate bishop Paul Durieu similarly attempted to synthesize traditional culture with Christianity by creating missionary buffers between natives and whites (Patterson 1972, 16, 154). The root of the conflict between fur traders (Hudson's Bay Company, for instance) and missionaries lay, above all, in diverging policies. While the missionaries, who functioned best in terms of their past experiences as guardians of communal identities, wanted settled congregations similar to the French and English farm villages, the fur traders wanted a scattered population of hardworking trappers (Crowe 1974, 143).

Once the native had made crucial distinctions among the diverging interests and values of the whites and had invested their trust accordingly, they had to further differentiate among competing denominations. In western and northern Canada the Anglicans and Catholics were often at loggerheads with one another. Chamberlin (1975, 66) mentions how the latter were not above snatching Protestant babies for baptism. Lurie (1971, 432) used the term "denominational colonialism" for this competition and observes that "(w)herever possible, the first mission in power jealously guards its prerogatives against competing religions and even against secular agencies concerned with Indian Affairs."

To the natives, however, the similarities between the competing denominations were much more obvious than the differences. However true this was for beliefs, it was a fact that the policy of the Church Missionary Society and the Methodist (later United) Church to train native clergy for the indigenous church differed substantially from the Catholic tendency to keep foreign clergy while allowing for local adaptations and innovations (Patterson 1972, 170).

ADJUSTMENT

Sometimes conflict resolves itself in obliteration, and the Canadian native population came close to that resolution. War and disease (measles, smallpox, influenza and tuberculosis) wiped out entire clans; the apathy of those who survived was occasionally worse than death. Many could countenance the loss of pride and dignity only in the alcoholic stupor or other momentary means for forgetting.

Yet the offspring of the survivors began to accommodate themselves to the increasing hordes of white people flooding the country. Cultural bridges were built and compromises made. An increasing birthrate began to show greater confidence in the future, even if most natives remained on the periphery of white society.

Particularly in earlier days the complicated world of the white man was not always understood. In an essay about the American War of Independence a native child wrote: "It was no wonder that the Americans got angry at the English, for the English were so mean that they put tacks in the tea they sold to the Americans" (Stefansson 1951, 414). To some Inuit a sermon on the death of Christ was thought to upbraid them for former murder (Hawkes 1970, 13).

Generally, however, the translation from one meaning system to another was effective. Addresses to the guardian spirits became Christian prayers. The Inuit Stefansson met on his journey in 1908 had high regard for the Christian prayers for caribou, even though such prayers tended to lose their efficacy with age, they said. However, the Inuit persisted in using their own whaling charms as they produced better results.

Christian prescriptions and proscriptions were readily absorbed in the elaborate system of native taboos. In an Inuit discussion about the lack of the white man's intelligence a native said: "Did the wisest of us ever think of the fact that a day might be taboo?" The Inuit had no trouble keeping the sabbath with all its corres ponding rules (they were and are better chur- chgoers than the whites, for instance) even to the extent of refusing to take advantage on a Sunday of a fair wind or a golden opportunity for hunting. The sabbath was kept with the same seriousness as eating potatoes with a fork or bathing on Saturday nights (Stefansson 1951, 25, 37, 81, 89, 374-5, 412). This was as true for the Inuit in the Mackenzie Delta as it was for the Tsimshian Indians further south who, in spite of the storming and swearing of their employers, refused to work as packers in the mines on Sunday (Withrow 1895, 180).

Deities and their functions were also adjusted to Christian doctrine. To the Micmacs in New Brunswick, the "second coming of Christ became the second coming of Gloscap to free his people from the troubles and oppres- sions that bore down upon them" (Upton 1979, 154). Native eschatology began to accommodate the idea of retribution in the hereafter, the presence of the Supreme Being in the land of the dead and the dualism between God and devil (Hultkrantz 1980, 174-5). Nanabozho, who survived the cosmic flood and began the world again from scratch, became Noah of the Old Testament. Nanabozho's turning bits of his own flesh into racoons for food became associated with the wafer turning into the body of Christ (Leland 1884, 338).

The alternation between Christian and native beliefs is well described by Fred Bodsworth in his novel *The Sparrow's Fall*. Jacob Atook of the Atihk-anishini (a tribe living close to where the Severn enters Hudson's Bay in northern Ontario) accepts the beliefs of Father Webber of the Canadian Arctic Evangelical Mission. Contrary to the tribal practice of arranged marriages he marries Nimawassa Niska, who has been promised to someone else. As a result, the couple has to escape the vengeance of the spurned fiancé. On the verge of starvation, far from other natives, Jacob slowly returns to the old beliefs in forest and animal spirits.

> " I'm sure Father Webber's God is the most powerful
> spirit," Jacob went on, "but he's far way in the place called

heaven, and the forest spirits are many and near. And
maybe many weak spirits close by could have more power
than one stronger spirit far away" (p.20).

He is particularly perturbed by God's love for even a miserable sparrow
(hence the title of the book). Famine, however, drives him to deny the
beauty or love in nature and he kills the caribou against what he feels is
Manitou's (God's) will. Yet at the end of the book he again accepts his wife's
argument that only God could have kept the unborn baby in her womb alive
in spite of her extreme emaciation.

Indian dreams began to incorporate Christian images, and the Jesuits,
who had originally regarded dreams as obstacles to conversion, now began
to encourage them (Bailey 1969, 137). A Huron dreamed about meeting a
young Frenchman in the splendour of paradise. He had known the Frenchman before his recent death, but now, because he was not baptized, could
not accompany him in heaven. The Huron therefore had his wife and
children baptized and intended to follow the Jesuits' example. Another
native of the same tribe had a nightmare about the flames and demons of
hell. Such dreams increased the desire of many to become Catholic, if only
to avoid a terrible fate in the afterlife.

Dreams about visits to heaven were not confined to a few eccentric
Indians. Inuit in every community, says Stefansson (1951, 429 ff.), are in
the habit of visiting with Saint Peter and Christ in the same way that they
used to have discussions with the man in the moon. St. Peter would teach
them hymns and chants; Christ taught arts and crafts, reading and writing.
Yet these present-day visions and revelations were kept secret, as the Inuit
felt that the missionaries did not approve.

The missionaries' refusal to engage in easy, free-flowing communications with, and visits to, heaven was a decided liability to the natives. They
were used to their shaman making heavenly journeys. The popularity of
sectarian movements (for instance, Pentecostalism) amongst Inuit and Indians in Canada indicates that religious informality and experiential witness
fill a need which most missionaries were not able to meet. In other respects,
however, (confession, healing, comforting, religious socialization) the natives had no trouble transferring their shamanic expectations to the Christian leaders.

Rites of passage were also mutually adjusted. When the son of a Huron
shaman died, the Jesuit fathers buried him in holy ground even after his
parents, against Christian practice, had painted the body and dressed it in
furs. "This greatly pleases these Barbarians, and often influences them to
allow their children to be made Christians," comments Le Jeune (*Jesuit
Relations*, Vol. 8, 1636, 259).

Other rules were also accommodated to Indian circumstances. In 1688,
after a winter of famine at Fort Joseph on the southern end of Lake Huron,
the Jesuit Father Claude Aveneau dispensed with the rule of a meatless Lent
(Lahontan, 1970, Vol. I, xx). Other rules, however, were strictly enforced.
Both Catholic and Protestant clergy continued to insist on monogamy and

chastity before marriage.

Amulets and fetishes had been adamantly opposed by the missionaries, but, as they were easy to hide, converts sometimes continued to use them. More often they substituted crucifixes, rings, figures of the saints, Christ and the Virgin Mary and used them for the same purposes, such as good luck in the hunt, good health and bravery. The Rev. Jean Enjalran wrote in 1676 that he had to keep a constant supply of medals, crosses, rings and rosaries for his converts. He expressed regret not to have an independent income as "I would with only a hundred francs make many conversions" (*Jesuit Relations*, 60, 137-9). Protestant missionaries were at a disadvantage as they had little with which to replace native amulets and charms.

CHARISMATIC MOVEMENTS

It was one thing to substitute Christian proscriptions, deities and crosses for native taboos, culture heroes and amulets. It was quite another to adopt an entire Christian system of meaning as the springboard for thought and action. To their distress the missionaries found that many converts paid only lipservice to Christian theology and ritual, while actually being motivated by the native traditions. To their even greater distress the astute observers amongst them discovered that converts often found themselves in a meaningless limbo where the old beliefs and practices had lost their power and where the new ones had not yet taken sufficient root. They discovered that natives were masters at simulation but incapable of coordinating thought and action in the Western manner. To the less sensitive missionaries this was proof of the congenital inferiority of the race. To the more sensitive it was disquieting, to say the least, that natives and whites would continue to be foreigners to one another. Christ was obviously not the bridge he was thought to be.

The natives were the losers in this ongoing exchange. Their old way of life had become obsolete and the new vision was propagated by the very race which had destroyed the old certainties. As is often the case with native cultures in similar situations, there arose a variety of charismatic leaders who courageously stripped the attachments to an irredeemable past and welded their people to a new vision in which a golden future figured prominently. In most instances this vision incorporated both native and Christian elements, drew sharp boundaries around Indian identity through militantly anti-white beliefs, clarified priorities through ascetic behaviour or sacrifice and concretized the future so that it could be a springboard for thought and action.

Some of these charismatic leaders became well-known, but others had only local impact and were soon forgotten. At one time or another all areas of Canada were affected by them even if their influence did not endure.

Handsome Lake was the first of the well-known prophets. He belonged to the Iroquois in southern Ontario and northern New York and, like his people, went through prolonged periods of defeatism and alcoholism. The fierce Iroquois had been redoubtable opponents in the seventeenth century, but had gradually come under the sway of the Christian missions. The Jesuit Father Isaac Jogues had begun a mission amongst the Mohawk (one of the five tribes making up the Iroquois) in 1642, but was murdered by them four years later. However, towards the end of the eighteenth century (in 1788) Christianity had advanced far enough for the first Protestant (Anglican) church in Upper Canada to be erected on Iroquois territory near Brantford. The native captain Joseph Brant had been a prime instigator of the plans for this church.

Yet the Iroquois had supported the losing side in the American Revolution and had become demoralized as a result. It was Ganeodiyo, or Handsome Lake (1735-1815), who lifted them out of a morass of decadence. Late in life (1799) and thought to be on his deathbed, Handsome Lake had a vision of three celestial visitors sent by the Great Spirit. They restored him to health and made him prophet to the Iroquois. This mission he carried out tirelessly and with remarkable enthusiasm until death. The message centered around both moral and spiritual regeneration, the one supporting the other. Sobriety and industry were to take the place of drunkenness, gambling and idleness, not because these values were good in themselves, but because the omnipotent, omniscient, creator god, the Great Spirit, or Hawenneyu, demanded it. All Iroquois had sinned against the Great Spirit and it was their sins which had barred the ancestors from entrance into heaven. Instead, they were roasting with wife-beaters, quarrelers and thieves in hell, where they were dumped alternately into cauldrons of boiling and freezing liquids. The good natives, on the other hand, went to a lush heaven where the white man could not enter. Good natives also heeded the stream of advice which Handsome Lake passed on from the Great Spirit, instructions containing extensive details about appropriate agricultural pursuits and family ethics (Morgan 1972, 237, 257).

Handsome Lake's anti-white, anti-Christian faith galvanized large sections of his people into an effective tribal force which has continued into the present day. The welding was often accomplished by a variety of old, reinstated rites, the most important of which was the feather dance dedicated to Hawenneyu, "the good brother and the first half of the day; .... the so-called social dance, including the war dance were dedicated to the evil brother, Haninseono and to the declining half of the day" (Muller, 1968, 187).

Another major prophet was Louis Riel (1844-1885). He was a Métis (half-breed of French and Indian origin) born in St. Boniface in what is now Manitoba. As all other Métis of the area he was raised Catholic and was very active in his religion. He led two Métis rebellions against the new settlers who were encroaching on their area and he formed two provisional governments, one in Manitoba in 1870 and another one in Saskatchewan in 1885. Although both proved to be forerunners of provincial governments, Riel was hanged for treason.

Riel inspired his followers with visions which he continually received and communicated. He called himself "Prophet of the New World," "Infallible Pontiff" and the midpoint of history. He referred to his people in biblical terms as the chosen people and believed that the Indians were descendants of the Hebrews. He also believed that a persecuted papacy would flee to the Métis in Manitoba in 2333 A.D. and remain there until 4209 A.D. when Christ would return to the earth. Because the Mosaic laws of the Hebrews were significant in his religious scheme, Riel wanted to re-introduce circumcision, the Saturday sabbath and polygamy. With many other millenarians Riel found the Book of Daniel and the Book of Revelation to be central parts of Scripture. He prophesied that Rome would be buried and that London and Liverpool would sink to the bottom of the sea while the entire world was being purified. He raged against the liberalism and self-indulgence of the age and identified himself with the knight on the white horse of the Apocalypse (Flanagan 1979, 84ff., 95). Riel's strong beliefs in a clearly delineated future had a contagious effect on his followers and heightened for them what Klassen (1977, 279) calls "the importance of regional units, particularly of clear ethnic identity."

In addition to Riel and Handsome Lake, many lesser known prophets have emerged from time to time amongst the natives and Métis. They were all bridgebuilders in combining native and Christian beliefs, and they spoke with great conviction and passion to fellow natives wallowing in lethargy. They usually condemned the use of alcohol, thereby improving communal and family stability, and nearly always stressed the imminent return of Jesus or claimed themselves to be the Messiah.

These charismatic movements could be found in many places at diverse times: Home Bay on Baffin Island in 1922, the Belcher Islands in 1941, Fort Chipeweyan in 1812, Fond du Lac in 1969 (Crowe 1974, 150-1). In the second half of the eighteenth century a Micmac by the name of Marten convinced a whole village that he was God and allowed the people to kiss his feet (Upton 1979, 154). In the next century, also in the Maritimes, a variety of other Micmac messiahs arose (Bailey 1969, 147). More recently Bock (1979, 146ff.) described a small zealous Bible-group among the Micmacs of the Restigouche Reserve in New Brunswick which had strong anti-clerical, anti-establishment and anti-drinking views and had adopted Jewish instead of Christian holidays.

On the west coast a Kaska shaman by the name of Old Kean prophesied the complete destruction of the white man in the Second World War (Muller, 1968, 155). Other examples of native charismatic leaders in the West were John Slocum and Uzakle in British Columbia and Wowoka on the Plains (Patterson, 1972, 18).

An extensive discussion of these minor prophets in Canada is contained in John Webster Grant's (1980, 125ff.) description of messiahs in the Northwest. In the middle of the nineteenth century, on the Hudson Bay coast, two natives who presented themselves as Wasetek (Light) and Jesus Christ predicted the arrival of a mansion from heaven with space only for

Indians. They wanted all dogs sacrificed and destroyed. Their dreams and visions formed the basis of the authority they possessed, as had traditionally been the case with the shamans.

In 1859 further west among the Swampy Crees of Ile à la Crosse, the son of chief Bear Foot, originally very active in the local mission, claimed to be the Son of God. He rejected the whites and proclaimed the Montagnais to be his chosen people. He wanted his large following to give away all their worldly possessions, to burn all their tents and to kill all their dogs. His central doctrine was that eternal life stemmed from both earth and sun and he painted glorious pictures of a lush heaven in which there was no place for whites. The movement petered out after a number of years and was absorbed back in the Catholic Church.

In the last quarter of the twentieth century movements have arisen which resemble the charismatic activities of a previous era. They similarly deal with native consolidation and anti-white sentiments, but tend to derive their emotional unity more from a variety of secular, strongly believed in causes than from visions of heaven and the return of Jesus. The leaders of these movements are rather well-educated, articulate Indians who know how to take astute advantage of white indeterminacy and legal traditions. The causes around which they rally their people vary from area to area. In Alberta they may centre around the sale of oil and gas on the land of native bands; in the Northwest Territories they may deal with proposals for a pipeline; in Quebec they may involve the $225 million compensation from the mammoth James Bay hydroelectric project.

This does not mean that traditional religion is altogether neglected. Some leaders, such as Harold Cardinal, are aware that causes as such are not sufficient to arouse people from apathy and chronic fatigue. Like the prophets of old, Cardinal speaks about "rebirth," but the return to old religious principles and rituals ordered under worship of the Great Spirit has a vague and rather secular ring. The crusade for native rebirth is anti-white and anti- Christian. According to Cardinal (1969, 80ff.), the missionaries have poisoned and killed the Great Spirit, but now the churches themselves are dis credited and therefore new opportunities have arrived. "In this rebirth, Indian people will undergo a process of de-brainwashing themselves from the stultifying, century-long hold that the so-called Christian denominations have imposed on them" (Cardinal 1977, 222). Yet the Great Spirit as described by Cardinal is remarkably similar to the Christian God and rather unlike the ancient native spirits and deities. He is the Creator who did provide the Indians with their laws and it is in His image that children must be raised. More importantly, Indians and Christians even now have much in common: thanksgiving, shared suffering, self-torture, virgin birth, the flood, brotherly love and prophecy (Cardinal 1969, 80-1).

THE PRESENT TENSE

In modern secular Canada, native groups are under much less pressure
to conform to Western culture demands, whether Christian or not. The
situation is the reverse from the periods of conflict and adjustment described in the previous sections. Our culture seems to put a premium on
native separateness as though the whites themselves project on the native
races their own nostalgia for pockets of meaningful belonging. Certainly the
idea that there is a redemptive quality in segments of our society which
preserve quaint traditions and a time-honoured system of meaning is widespread. It is in this climate that there are ample opportunities for sectarian
movements of dedicated individuals. This is reflected to some extent in the
vigour of Pentecostalism amongst the Eastern Cree near James Bay, the
natives in the McKenzie Delta and the Kwakiutl in British Columbia,
where Rohner and Rohner (1971, 127) observed that "relatively more
villagers attend Pentecostal services than Anglican," even if it was the
Church of England which had begun the mission there as early as 1878
(Codere 1969, 502).

Although the census figures cannot show anything about actual beliefs
and the zeal with which they are held, they indicate convincingly that
denominational representation amongst the Canadian natives is a function
of early missionary activities. However, before going into this, something
should be said about the present "fit" of the native population in Canadian
society.

The Canadian natives are hardly typical of Canada as a whole. Their
alcoholism and crime rates are considerably higher. The average income of
natives 15 years and over, ($8,600), according to the 1981 census, is about
two-thirds of the non-native average ($13,100). The percentage of native
men over 15 without income (15%) is twice as high as the percentage of
non-native men (7%). Their educational attainment is much lower: according to the 1981 census 41.4% had less than grade 9 education as
compared with 22% of the non-native population. On the other hand, native
population has been increasing at about twice the rate of the Canadian
population during the period 1951 - 1971. In the 1981 census the average
number of children born to never-married native women was 3.8; to non-
natives, 2.5. Of all the natives enumerated by the 1981 census 62.4%
reported English as the first language they learned as children, 28.7%
mentioned a native language and 4.6% French. The natives are also much
more rural. Just four in ten were classified by the 1981 census as living in
urban areas as compared with eight in ten for other Canadians. Although
only 28.7% of the general Canadian population lives in British Columbia
and the Prairie provinces, 58% of all natives do so.

In spite of all these differences only a negligible percentage of Indians
and Inuit (4.0%) mentioned any other than the common Western religious
sects and denominations when they were asked to state their religion, as
table 3.1 shows.

TABLE 3.1

Percentage distribution of the religions of natives and the total population in Canada, according to the 1981 census

	Natives (413,380)	Total Population (24,083,495)
Anglican	20.3	10.1
Baptist	1.3	2.9
Lutheran	.4	2.9
Pentecostal	3.3	1.4
Presbyterian	1.1	3.4
Roman Catholic	53.0	47.3
United Church	8.6	15.6
Other	6.0	9.1
No religion	6.0	7.3
	100.0	100.0

In the same way as figures of the total population generally reflect the ethnic origins of the nation, so the native figures reflect the early missionary work amongst Indians and Inuit. The overrepresentation of both the Roman Catholic and the Anglican churches goes back to the various Catholic orders and the Church Missionary Society of England who both pioneered missionary activity in many parts of the dominion long before the arrival of other denominations. In the 1951 census where close to 80% of the Inuit in the Northwest Territories proved to be Anglicans and close to 80% of the Indians in Alberta, Catholic, the reasons were to be found in the zealous missionary activities of the original denominations in those areas. On the prairies where the French Jesuits in the first half of the eighteenth century and the Oblates in the latter half of the nineteenth (Hodge 1969, 298) had started very active proselytizing, Catholic missions were a full century ahead of the others.

As said before, however, the original missionary activities do not necessarily reflect present religious motivation. To discover more about this we need a more sensitive device than the Canadian Census.

SUMMARY

Wherever the early missionaries went, they clashed with the defenders of native beliefs and ritual. More often than not, these defenders of the faith were shamans who felt deeply that not just their own shamanic role but the entire ethnic, clan and tribal integrity was at stake. Their fears were justified. Lives were lost, but the invisible damage to a time-honoured system of meaning was even more devastating in the long run.

The damage was almost entirely inflicted on the native race. If anything, the missionaries and the churches behind them gained from the encounter. Witnessing for the faith and suffering for the Christian cause were important ways of strengthening that faith and cause. By contrast, the native way of life was mortally wounded, its vitality sapped.

The generations which survived the cultural wounds and the crippling diseases had only one choice open: accommodation. And so Christian norms and injunctions replaced native rules and taboos: worship of Christ and the Virgin Mary was substituted for prayers and sacrifices to guardian spirits and deities; crosses and rosaries took the place of amulets and fetishes; ministers and priests superseded shamans and witchdoctors; Christian theology and Bible stories of Creation, the Flood, and the sacrifice of Jesus on the cross supplanted the many myths which often dealt with similar themes.

Yet replacement differed from revitalization: in the changeover something vital had escaped. Rather than vitality and purpose, lethargy and anomie tended to predominate after Christianization, and in order to recover the lost element and to revitalize the native races, various charismatic movements arose. Whether led by Handsome Lake, Riel or dozens of lesser-known prophets, these movements always strongly delineated native or Métis identity from white culture. They did so by means of bold anti-white sentiments even when many elements of Christianity were absorbed in the message. They also concretized the future in such a way that it galvanized meaningful action. Finally, they clarified priorities through ascetic behaviour or sacrifice of goods and animals to which one was strongly attached.

Many of these movements have left no trace. So far, secular "rebirth" movements have not been very successful in moving native groups from a peripheral, welfare-oriented, protest-prone position to a more dignified organic place in Canadian society. Without the Christian missions the natives often would not have survived, even on the periphery of Canadian culture. In spite of their humanizing effect, however, these missions could not undo the incisive, destructive effect of culture conflict. Nor is it possible, as many native idealists seem to think, to go back to pre-conflict beliefs and rituals, for the effects of destruction cannot be cancelled. All one can hope for is re-construction. Yet apathy and defeatism are formidable obstacles in the welding of a new identity. Historically only the charismatic movements managed to overcome these obstacles, but, as the example of the Inuit and Indians in Canada shows, their effect has been limited.

PART II

RELIGION AND ETHNIC GROUPS

Wherever migrants settled in the new world, their religion functioned as anchors of the past or as shelters from culture conflict. Canada is not an exception. Here the denominations and sects introduced by the settlers maintained the old country beliefs and practices. Services were sometimes held in the old language long after the members had adopted English (and occasionally French) as their mother tongue. This led to controversy with the younger generations which had become thoroughly Anglicized.

Chapter 4 looks at both the history and the most recent census data of seven of the largest ethnic groups in Canada. It suggests that old-country religion reinforced ethnicity all the more when the immigrant group and its members were marginal to Canadian culture. It also provides evidence that, in a number of instances, the major Canadian denominations tended to attract the Anglicized members of those groups, thereby reinforcing national identity and leaving the strenghtening of ethnic identity to the churches brought over from the Old World.

The conflict between ethnic and national identity in Canada has usually been muted. Yet, particularly during the First and Second World Wars, this conflict in many instances came to a head. Congregations often suspended their foreign language services in order to show that loyalties lay with the nation than with the old country. Even so, Canadians eyed many of the ethnic enclaves with suspicion. Catholicism in particular needed all the diplomacy of its bishops to cushion the claims of its many ethnic parishes for greater autonomy and more resources at the expense of the national and international functions of the Church. Only in two instances (the breakaway Polish National Catholic Church and the Ukrainian Greek Catholic Church, which became independent of other dioceses) did the Catholic Church not manage to heal the rift between ethnic and national identity.

The large immigration waves after World War II revived the perennial strain between cultures. Parishes which had become thoroughly Canadianized reverted to services in the old world language in order to accommodate the nostalgia of the newcomers. Yet, in the 1980s, hildren of these immigrants frequent English services, and the ethnic loyalties which the older generation took for granted now has to be taught to the younger ones.

Chapters 5 and 6 look at three groups of immigrants who came from the old country to escape religious harassment rather than poverty. Religion was, and is, even now to a varying degree, the cement binding these groups together against the inroads of a secular society. Yet, however strong the boundaries of separation, both external and internal threats proved to be more than equal in piercing them.

The Mennonites have undergone the ravages of anglicization, urbanization and affluence. Internally they have suffered from splits and divisions facilitated by the absence of hierarchical control over theological disputes and factional conflicts. The Hutterites have succeeded in separating themselves geographically and can therefore minimize culture contact. Even so, the schoolhouse on colony grounds, the lures of urban luxury, the struggle for power between family and community, the occasional incompetent leader, the tension between individual self-will and communal responsibility, all have taken their toll. Doukhobor identity has suffered even more. In spite of nude demonstrations, communal arson, and other, more religious means of protecting communities, the communitarian ideals have crumbled altogether. The fissioning and fusing of personal, family and community identities had already begun in Russia and continued in Canada. The anarchical bent of their religious beliefs and practices was no match for identity erosion.

CHAPTER 4

ETHNIC GROUPS

Canada is no exception to the finding that religion often consolidates ethnic roots. Soon after arrival immigrants discover that the way of life they have taken for granted is now at risk. To their dismay they realize that better economic opportunities come at the price of adjusting to new ways, foreign practices and strange norms. The natural roots for personal or group identity have been torn and a strong urge develops to restore and nourish them. Religion becomes a much appreciated ally in this recovery process.

The degree of identity dislocation depends on approximately five factors (Mol 1961, 58; Mol 1979a, 32). Identity disruption is maximized when immigrants are older (after forty it becomes increasingly more difficult to adopt a new language and to shed a matrix of familiar habits and customs), when they have arrived recently (time heals wounds and facilitates adjustments), when the native culture diverges strongly from the culture of the new country (great differences in language structure, ways of acting and reacting), when the immigrants are widely dispersed (opportunities for ethnic gatherings are minimal), and when changes have been inadequately visualized (accurate anticipation of differences aids adjustment). In some countries or periods of history a sixth factor operates: the degree of latitude or constraint on foreign organizations (freedom to assemble facilitates the formation of ethnic enclaves). The sacralizing effect of religion varies with the configuration (negative accumulation, cancellation and positive accumulation) of these factors. The more negative for acculturation the sum of these factors is, the more religion will be invoked to protect the old ethnic roots.

In Canada all religious organizations originally arrived with the new settlers. French Catholicism consolidated French identity when New France was colonized; the Church of England maintained and reinforced what the English settlers and soldiers thought their culture was all about. Subsequent immigrant groups from other countries found the cultural vacuum largely filled by the French and British; still, there was room enough for all, and economic expansion was more important to the charter races than cultural and religious compatibility. And so presently, according to the 1981 census, 27% of the Canadian population is of French origin, 40% British (25% English, 5% Irish and 6% Scottish), 5% German, 3% Italian, 2% Ukrainian, 2% Dutch, 1% Scandinavian, 1% Polish and 1% Jewish. Other groups also with more than 100,000 members are the Hungarians, Greeks, Chinese and Yugoslavians.

None of the smaller ethnic groups spoke English or French and their religion almost always proved to be the strongest preserver of each particular foreign language and culture. If the culture diverged considerably from the British or French one and the newcomers could settle together on the Canadian frontier (as was the case with the Ukrainians in the prairie provinces at the beginning of this century), this preservation process could go unhindered for several generations. However, once Canadian culture, through schools, government administration and political participation, began to infiltrate these cultural enclaves and the younger generations began to feel the lure of better economic opportunities in industry, these religious organizations tended to lose their hold on the acculturated. This was and is the case with the Ukrainians.

Other scenarios present themselves. A considerable number of immigrants came from Catholic countries such as Italy, Poland, Lithuania, Portugal or from countries with vast Catholic regions, such as Germany, Holland and Hungary. Here the native Catholic churches preserved culture and language, but, because they were under tutelage of the local diocese and bishop, subtle (or sometimes not so subtle) pressures could be applied to move with an increasingly acculturated membership. These pressures were often resented, but, with one exception (the Ukrainian Catholic Church), the Catholic Church managed to maintain a geographical rather than an ethnic base for its diocesan system.

Protestant immigrants usually brought religious organizations with them in which ethnic autonomy was stronger than Canadian or international authority. And so the Norwegian, Swedish, Finnish, Icelandic and German Lutherans all established their churches in Canada, usually with the help of American sister organizations. Within these churches tension often developed between the younger acculturated generations and the older ones for whom the native language and culture was a major pillar of security. Or, as happened after World War II, a new wave of unacculturated immigrants arrived, reverting the Lutheran churches' gradual movement towards Canadianization.

Again a different scenario is presented by the Christian Reformed Church which a large minority of Dutch immigrants brought with them. Here the doctrines and church orders of the native *Gereformeerde Kerk* were sternly preserved in Canada, but, on the basis of experiences in other countries, the Christian Reformed Church insisted on staying ahead of the acculturation process by inaugurating English services when its membership was barely ready for them.

The major denominations in Canada (corresponding with the original religious organizations of the charter races, the French and the British) have been actively, yet subtly and diplomatically involved in conflict moderation between foreign-language minorities and a burgeoning, gradually expanding Canadian culture. The Catholic Church (the religion of almost half the population) has allowed the proliferation of a large variety of ethnic parishes, all reinforcing specific ethnic identities. Yet it has successfully kept them under the wings of the hierarchy ever ready to advance the ultramontane (international) or national vision of its task. The United Church (with 15.6% of the Canadian population) has, particularly in the first half of this century, thought of Canada as the Kingdom of God in Anglo-Saxon terms and as an active agent of assimilation of foreigners (Clifford 1977; Hutchinson 1978, 137). How well it has succeeded is shown by the large percentages of Canadians of foreign origin who now claim to be United Church (German 13%, Ukrainian 13%, Dutch 15%, Scandinavian 24%, Polish 6%), even though this church was not represented in the countries of origin. The Anglican Church (with 10% of the Canadian population) has similarly drawn substantial portions of the foreign segments of the Canadian population into its fold.

With this outline in mind we can now discuss the effect which religion had on the ethnic identity of the major non-English-speaking immigrant groups on the Canadian scene.

THE GERMANS

According to the 1981 census, 1,142,365 Canadians claimed to be of German origin. Germans therefore formed the largest foreign ethnic group. In 1971 as much as 68% traced their origins back to those Germans who arrived before World War II, and 32% reported they came after 1946, often as displaced persons from the eastern regions of the German Reich. There is considerable difference between these two categories.

Much of the earlier migration was caused by poverty in some of the German states and the prospect of fertile, cheap land in the prairies. It is therefore not accidental that 44% of German- Canadians live in the Prairie provinces, compared with only 17% of the total Canadian population. Many of the new settlers came to Canada via the United States and therefore had become sufficiently anglicized to start on their own. They had enough confidence in their own ability to forego the security of the all-German settlement, and this partially accounts for the fact that in the 1971 census as much as 20% (as against 7% of the post-World War II immigrants) belong to a typical Canadian religious organization, the United Church. Protestant settlers, in particular, would often be too far away from a German Lutheran or Reformed Church and would join the local United Church with which they had much in common anyway, as in a number of German states (for instance, Prussia) the major protestant denominations had also united. In addition the United Church (or the Methodist and Presbyterian churches before 1925) were genuinely concerned with the welfare of immigrants and welcomed them with open arms.

Yet other Germans would settle together, often at the instigation of the Catholic Church. In these settlements (for instance, St. Peter's and St. Joseph's in Saskatchewan) the church played a vital role in community life. It preserved German culture and language and resisted the secular invasions from outside the colony. Here it reinforced ethnic identity, often at the expense of a sense of national or international loyalty. This was, of course, also true for Catholics of a different national origin. When, in 1926, a French priest in a mixed parish of St. Peter's colony was replaced by a German one, French attendance dropped and many neglected to pay church dues (Dawson 1936, 318-23). Of German-Canadians at the time of the 1981 census, 25% claimed to be Catholic. Originally these settlers had mainly come from the Catholic south and west of Germany.

An equal percentage of Germans (25%) belonged to the Lutheran church which prevailed in the north and east of Germany. Some of the ancestors of this group were German soldiers belonging to the English troops which had captured the French fortress at Louisburg in 1748 and again in 1758. Others, from Wurtemberg and Saxony, were with Sir Edward Cornwallis when Halifax was built in 1749 and in 1755 they, together with 300 later arrivals from Germany, established the first Lutheran Church in Canada, St. George's. They had no ordained Lutheran minister, but read sermons from the Prussian Book of Homilies and sang Lutheran hymns twice every Sunday. Occasionally the Church of England minister from St. Paul's would administer the Lord's Supper, but the officers were set on keeping the Lutheran Confession and the German language. In 1783 when a Lutheran clergyman, the Rev. Bernard Michael Houseal, finally came to Halifax with the United Empire Loyalists, he proved to be thoroughly anglicized and, with the younger generation becoming less and less fluent in German, St. George's became Anglican. (Cronmiller 1961, 38-44). For many years, however, hymns were still sung in German.

About the same time (1753) hundreds of German immigrants established Lunenburg in Nova Scotia. Three-quarters of them were either killed by Indians or died from smallpox and other diseases, but the remainder made a go of the settlement (it helped that 60 head of cat tle from the Basin of Minas were left behind by the French Canadians expelled in 1756 [Eylands 1945, 34]). They met in private houses for sermon-reading, praying and singing until, in 1767, they obtained the services of the Rev. Paul Bryselius who was of Swedish- origin and ordained first as a Lutheran and later as a Church of England clergyman. Not caring much for the Anglican bent, the congregation soon reverted back to their lay services in German. In 1770 they began to build a church (Zion Lutheran) which has managed to remain Lutheran until the present day. Many more German immigrants came to Nova Scotia and the area which was later called New Brunswick, but if numbers enabled them to build a Lutheran church, as in Clementsport near the Annapolis Valley, it often became Church of England in the next generation. The result is that, at present, Nova Scotia Lutheranism is almost entirely confined to Lunenburg County (Cronmiller 1961, 54-5).

Germans (mainly from the Palatinate) came to Canada with the United Empire Loyalists, and in the first half of the nineteenth century a steady flow of tradesmen and farmers settled in various parts of Upper Canada (particularly the counties of Brant, Bruce, Waterloo and Welland). Where the numbers were sufficient and the settlements close together, German Lutherans usually began religious services in their homes; but it proved to be hard to attract ordained clergy. As in the Church of England, budding congregations had the choice between what Cronmiller (1961, 130) calls clerical imposters and tramps, or no pastor at all. Hard-working German Protestants who had made a success of their enterprise and had become acculturated often became caught up in Methodist and other enthusiastic frontier religions. Where Lutheran congregations were established, the language issue (whether to change from German to English) sooner or later arose. Usually (as was the case with St. Paul's Lutheran in Hamilton, Ontario, Ibid., 181) expansion came to a halt when the older generation continued to insist on the exclusive use of German. In 1896 a special English district of the Canada Synod was formed to better serve the needs of those Lutheran parishes which had moved beyond ethnic boundaries (Ibid., 193). Both World Wars put strong pressure on the ethnic loyalties of the Germans. During World War I, the pastor of First Lutheran Church in Toronto resolved the crisis in his congregation by holding all services in English. Only in the second half of 1918 did his parishioners feel safe enough to reintroduce a German service on the second Sunday of every month. His successor, Dr. Albert Grunwald, had similar problems during World War II. He visited the federal and and provincial authorities and the heads of the United and Presbyterian Churches to satisfy them that all his members were loyal and law-abiding Canadian citizens. Again all German language services were suspended for the duration of the War (Barbier 1976, 25 and 1978, 74).

German Lutherans also took vigorous part in the settlement of the West which took place around and after the beginning of this century. They were often aided by the financing and manpower of the mission boards of various American Lutheran organizations which had become more prosperous by that time. One of these organizations (the Missouri Synod) established its first church in 1895 in Stoney Plain, west of Edmonton, Alberta, amongst Lutherans of Austrian origin. The congregation built a school teaching Bible history, German and English, but it was closed during World War I because of anti-German feelings (Eylands 1945, 323). As recently as 1945 (Ibid., 23) the majority of the Lutheran congregations in the West were bilingual, in contrast to the East, where English had by now begun to predominate.

After World War II the situation changed again when large numbers of German refugees were re-settled in Canada. They exerted pressure "for a more German-oriented worship life at a time when most of the Lutheran churches in Canada were at the point of discontinuing German-language services" (Threinen 1977, 16).

THE ITALIANS

The second largest ethnic group in Canada, according to the 1981 census, consists of 747,970 Italians. Less than 25% of this group traced their origins back to Italians who arrived before World War II. The bulk came after 1946, attracted by the economic opportunities of Canada and their corresponding lack in the home country.

Although it was an Italian (Giovanni Caboto, or John Cabot) who discovered Canada and on the 24th of June, 1497, planted the royal flag of King Henry VII on Newfoundland or Cape Breton Island (which at the time he thought was part of Asia), few Italians took part in the early colonization. In the first decade of this century they began to arrive in greater numbers to work on the railways or in heavy construction only to disappear again as soon as they had earned enough to alleviate some of the poverty at home. Yet in Toronto and particularly in Montreal, "little Italies" of less transient types started to appear. Because most Italian immigrants were Catholic, the Church commenced to take suitable interest even though their mobility proved to make this work rather hazard. The first Italian parish to be established in Montreal (in 1905) was Madonna del Carmine, and, as the archbishop himself (Paul Bruchesi) belonged to an old Montreal Italian family, the work was undertaken with commendable speed. Toronto was not so fortunate, and the Italians there "had to appeal directly to the Vicar Apostolic, the Papacy's representative in Ottawa, for help in convincing the Irish clergy that there should be an Italian parish" (Harney 1978, 19). This parish, also named Madonna del Carmine, was established in 1908.

Patriotic feelings ran high in the Italian ethnic communities. Before arriving in Canada the immigrants thought of themselves primarily in regional or local terms (being from Calabria or Bologna, for instance), but the foreignness of the new environment (in which they were lumped to-gether indiscriminately) gave them a sense of common Italian brotherhood. And so the feast days of local patron saints and madonna cults tended to fade into the background and be replaced by ceremonies in which all could participate, such as the Columbus Day celebrations established by the Order of the Sons of Italy of Ontario. Orders and lodges of this kind protected Italian settlers against death and misfortune through the payment of benefits. Some of them (such as the Grand Lodge of Quebec) became rather controversial when in 1926 they mixed patriotism and promotion of Fascism (Spada 1969, 102-3). It was the existence of fascist organizations in the Italian ethnic groups which led during World War II to internment of a small number of Italians (one-half of a percent).

Large waves of Italian immigrants began rolling in during the 1950s.

The Catholic Church established a goodly number of Italian parishes all over the nation to provide the newcomers with a home away from home and to help them become acclimatized to a new language and a new way of life. Presently the tendency is for the older generations to frequent these parishes even if the family has moved away to different areas of the town or city. By contrast, the younger generations, who went to Canadian schools and became integrated in the economic and cultural life of the nation tend to join the local, English-speaking parishes. In 1971 as much as 72% of Italian Canadians from the large post-World War II immigrant wave still spoke Italian at home. This percentage was only 9% for those who traced their origins back to earlier migrations. With the exception of the small percentage of Italians who have and will become assimilated into a Francophone environment, the more recent bulk of immigrants is likely to progressively leave the Italian parishes for local, English- speaking congregations. As compared with all other Canadian denominations the Catholic Church has the advantage of extensive representation throughout the nation, the changeover from ethnic to Canadianized communities can take place with a minimum of friction. This changeover is much more difficult for those smaller, foreign churches which somehow have to accommodate both acculturated and non-assimilated immigrants.

THE UKRAINIANS

In the 1981 census 529,615 Canadians claimed to be of Ukrainian origin. In 1971 as much as 83% traced these origins back to Ukrainian stock which had arrived before and after the First World War and settled in the Prairie provinces, while 17% came from Ukrainians who were displaced during World War II.

The earlier immigrant waves came primarily from the western Ukraine (Galicia, Transcarpathia, Ruthenia), which had been under domination by Catholic nations, primarily Poland. They belonged to the Uniat, or Ukrainian Catholic, Church which had come into being by the Act of Union between Catholicism and Orthodoxy at Brest-Litovsk in 1596. It was also called the Greek Catholic church because it maintained the Byzantine, or Eastern, rites of Greek Orthodoxy which had been the religion of the region since A.D. 988. Yet it had accepted Roman Catholic dogma and was therefore removed from the influence of centres of Eastern Orthodoxy. Its unique place within Roman Catholicism was further stressed by the right of priests to marry before ordination, as was the case in Greek Orthodoxy.

Soon after their arrival in Canada at the end of the nineteenth century, the Ukrainians began to congregate on Sundays and feast days for the reading of Scripture and the Psalter. They began to build modest churches, sometimes together with other Ukrainians who were Orthodox. As yet the prospect for the settlement of Uniat priests was slim. When priests and missionaries (Basilians and Sisters Servants of Mary Immaculate) finally

began to arrive, various controversies developed with the Roman Catholic
bishops who "did not sense the group's determination to safeguard its
ethnicity (and) did not realize that .... the traditional Ukranian church was
absolutely essential if they were to retain their identity" (Woycenko 1967,
78). This was particularly true in Winnipeg where Bishop Langevin objected to the newly established Ruthenian Greek-Catholic Church of St.
Nicholas (Marunchak 1970, 102). The bishops were particularly against
having married priests in the Ukrainian parishes. Yet it was very difficult to
find the celibate priest or widower in the old country who could be persuaded to move to Canada.

The issue seemed resolved in 1912 when Nykyta Budka became the first
Ukrainian Greek Catholic bishop in Canada and established what was later
called the Ukrainian Greek Catholic Church, independent of any other
Catholic diocese. However, Budka upset some of the lay intelligentsia by
unduly extending his control over Ukrainian institutions and church properties. He also issued a pastoral letter on July 27, 1914, calling for loyal
support of the Hapsburg emperor, thereby antagonizing Canadian authorities who began to consider Ukrainians as hostile to the Allies
(Woycenko 1967, 85).

In 1918 a substantial minority of dissenters established the Ukrainian
Greek Orthodox Church of Canada as independent of both Rome and
Moscow while maintaining the Eastern rites common throughout the Ukraine. They were joined by immigrants from the eastern Ukraine and
Bucovina who had retained their links with Orthodoxy and also by those
who favoured the use of the modern Ukrainian language rather than the Old
Church Slavic. The new church repudiated the 1596 union with Rome
which, it was felt, had been forced on the Ukraine and insisted on Ukranian
clergy alone in contrast with the Ukrainian Greek Catholic Church, where
many priests from other nations served parishes. The new church determined that individual congregations could hire and fire their priests, had
title to the church property and that bishops were to be chosen by a general
convention (Marunchak 1970, 113).

At the end of the second decade of the century, as much as 90% of all
Ukrainians in Canada belonged to the two warring factions (Marunchak
1970, 460); but, with the decline in ethnic consciousness, the percentage
dropped from 82.6% in the 1931 census to 79.0% in 1941, 69.8% in 1951,
58.5% in 1961, 52.2% in 1971 and 48% in 1981. Both the Ukrainian Greek
Catholic and the Ukrainian Greek Orthodox Churches kept the fires of
Ukrainian national sentiment burning and were very active in keeping the
membership aware of the Soviet repression of religion and Ukrainian identity in the homeland. The Ukrainian Greek Catholic Church (always the
largest) suffered a greater decline (from 58.0% in 1931 to 30.0% in 1981)
than the Ukrainian Greek Orthodox Church (from 24.6% in 1931 to 18.0%
in 1981 [Darcovich and Yuzik 1980, 175]).

The considerable decline of Ukrainian interest in the traditional Ukrainian denominations is partly caused by their singularly close association

with ethnic identity. The fading boundaries around Ukrainian identity had an inevitable effect on the loss of influence of both the Ukrainian Catholic and Ukrainian Orthodox churches. The native churches and the first-generation immigrants fought tooth and nail during the First World War when, in 1916, the teaching of Ukrainian was forbidden in the public schools of the prairie provinces where the vast majority had settled. By contrast, the younger generations of Canadian-born Ukrainians have now lost their interest in the native language, so much so that, according to the 1971 census, only 23.8% of the third generation have retained the language as compared with 83.6% of the first and 58.9% of the second generation. Yet the retention percentages of the second and third generation Ukrainians who belonged to the Ukrainian Catholic Church remained much higher (77.2% and 44.0%, respectively). This was also true for the Ukrainian Orthodox Church where the corresponding percentages were 73.4% and 46.6%. By contrast, the percentage of third-generation Ukrainians who belong to non-native denominations and who have retained the native language has dropped even further: 12.0% for Roman Catholics, 7.9% for United Church and 7.4% for Anglicans (Kalbach and Richard, 1980, 90).

The loosening of Ukrainian identity and the gradual absorption of Ukrainians into the national fabric is also shown in the increasing percentage of those who now belong to other denominations. From 1931 to 1981, those belonging to the Roman Catholic Church increased from 11.5 to 17.5%, those belonging to the United Church from 1.6% to 13.4%, those belonging to the Anglican Church from 0.3% to 3.8%. Paralleling this move away from the traditional Ukrainian denominations is the move to the cities in general and to Ontario and British Columbia in particular. In 1931 only 10.9% of Ukrainians resided in Ontario. By 1981 this percentage had risen to 25.3%. Corresponding figures for British Columbia were 1.1% and 12.0%. By contrast, the percentages for Manitoba dropped from 32.7% to 18.8%, and those for Saskatchewan from 28.2% to 14.5%. In 1931 as many as 70.5% of Ukrainians lived in rural areas, but by 1971 this percentage had dropped to 25.0%. For the population at large the corresponding percentages are 39.3% and 23.8 (Petryshyn 1978, 82). All this means that many Canadians of Ukrainian stock now live in areas where their native churches are often not represented. It also means that the intermarriage rate with non-Ukrainians has increased considerably. In 1921, 87.5% of Ukrainian marriages were endogamous; by 1971 this percentage had dropped to 38.7%. This has the inevitable effect of decreasing identification with the Ukrainians in general and their Catholic and Orthodox Churches in particular.

Although the native churches serve a steadily diminishing number of those for whom Ukrainian language and identity is salient, they are very hesitant to cater wholeheartedly to the younger, assimilated generation. In some churches it is still not very common to have a service in English and all the church organizations stress the learning of Ukrainian, reinforce the old-world customs of choral-singing and dancing, and celebrate Easter and

Christmas in typical Ukrainian ways. Yet even for the younger, Canadianized generations the religious reminders of their roots adds meaning to life which often escapes them in the bustling metropolis. Compared with the first half of this century, the pressures of social conformity are less severe, and therefore many secularized Ukrainians will maintain some customs such as gifts of an Easter *pysanka* (the decorated Easter egg), symbol of wholeness and resurrection, life out of death.

THE DUTCH

The fourth largest ethnic group in Canada, according to the 1981 census, consists of 408,235 Dutch people. Although most of them came with the post-World War II wave of immigrants, a fairly large percentage (about 40%) had arrived much earlier.

The earlier segment of the Dutch ethnic group is overrepresented in the Prairie provinces (55% here are of the old stock) and underrepresented in Ontario (the corresponding percentage here is 26%), according to the 1971 census. Like so many other immigrants from the European mainland, they were attracted by the excellent farming opportunities of the West. In 1912 some of the Dutch established Neerlandia ninety miles northwest of Edmonton which, in one generation, "became a model farming center, the largest and most thoroughly Dutch community in Canada" (Lucas 1955, 464). Soon after their arrival the settlers started a Christian Reformed Church. Another thriving colony was founded at Nieuw Nijverdal in the Lethbridge area of Alberta. This community soon split into three parts, each with their own Christian Reformed Church. Dutch Catholics went mainly to the eastern provinces where they were absorbed into Catholic parishes, sometimes so speedily that in a very short time they "lost practically all of their Dutch characteristics" (Lucas, 1955, 467). Yet, of the old Dutch stock, only a very small percentage (2%, 1971 census) is Christian Reformed; and, although the corresponding Catholic percentage (14%) is higher, this percentage is also considerably below the Catholic proportion of the population of the Netherlands (28.5% in 1947 - the percentage of the Christian Reformed was 10% at the time). The bulk of the older Dutch segment of the Canadian population has been completely absorbed into the culture. Only 3% of this group still speak Dutch in their own homes and as much as 40% belong to the major Canadian churches (29% United, 11% Anglican, according to the 1971 census). Another 20% of those claiming to be originally of Dutch stock are Mennonites. Their ancestors, followers of Menno Simons, a persecuted Dutch priest who turned anabaptist, left the Netherlands at least four centuries ago and speak German rather than Dutch. Petersen (1955, 182) claims that some Mennonites changed their national origin to Dutch as a result of the anti-German feeling of World War I. Yet Epp (1974, 335) argues that the Dutch origin is based on fact.

Most of the Dutch in Canada have arrived since World War II. They differ considerably from the old ethnic stock. They tended to settle in areas of industrial expansion (southern Ontario) rather than the West. Having arrived more recently, a larger percentage (12% as compared with 3% of the old stock, 1971 census) still speak Dutch at home. Yet, this percentage is far below the comparable percentages for all other ethnic groups, Scandinavians excepted. However, according to the 1971 census, it is their religious composition which differs considerably from that of the old ethnic stock. As much as 28% (as over against 2%) belong to the Christian Reformed census category; 29% are Catholic (as over against 14%). By contrast, only 15% (3% Anglican and 12% United) belong to the mainline Canadian churches as compared with 40% of the older group. The reasons for the divergence between the old and new ethnic groups are not hard to find. Pre-World War II immigration often took place via the United States and was generally determined by laws of supply and demand. Post-World War II immigration was directed by, and hinged on, a sponsorship system, under which the highly organized Catholic and Christian Reformed Churches sponsored the lion's share of the immigrants. There were other sponsoring agencies for the Dutch (a non-denominational, governmental one and one belonging to the former state church - the Reformed Church, which linked with the Reformed Church of America and the United Church), but the Catholic and the Christian Reformed Churches were particularly active on the Canadian scene.

The Catholic Church employed Dutch-speaking chaplains who helped the sponsored immigrants to settle in suitable jobs. They also assisted with finding appropriate accommodation and eased their charges into the existing parish structure. This task was facilitated by the insistence of all sponsoring agencies that the immigrants learn English before departure from the Netherlands (if they did not know it already). The result of this careful preparation was that the Catholic Dutch seemed to be less in need of ethnic parishes as way stations towards integration into Canadian society than other European Catholics. In addition, Catholics in the Netherlands had for centuries occupied a lower, minority status and therefore valued their Catholic identity more than their national one. Also, Dutch migrants have proved to be generally more marginal in their community of origin (Frijda 1960, 88-91) than those who remained. This double marginality (weak ties with both nation and community) facilitated for many assimilation into Canadian Catholicism.

The Christian Reformed Church (also a distinct minority in Dutch culture) similarly shepherded the immigrants into jobs and housing with a minimum of commotion. It, too, put suitable stress on the learning of English, so much so that the Christian Reformed congregations in Canada (although of Dutch origin) are rather loath to call ministers from the Netherlands as they cannot preach too well in English and tend to be schismatic (Norel, as quoted by Petersen, 1955, 190). Instead, they usually employ ministers from the mother church in the USA. Yet they want assimilation to go only so far and insist on protecting the membership from both the secular aspects of Canadian culture, and, what they call "religious flabbiness" of the Canadian churches. The historical reason for this stance is that the Christian Reformed Church (in the Netherlands, "Gereformeerde Kerken") came into being in the nineteenth century as a protest against the liberalism of the Dutch Reformed (state) Church. They established a number of colonies in the USA in order to shore up their calvinist orthodoxy.

The orthodox tradition and the suspicion of secularism is still very much part of the Christian Reformed Churches. Consequently researchers (such as Petersen and Ishwaran) write about their "religious clannishness" and their "cultural ghettoism." They indeed separate themselves from society at large, but on doctrinal and religious, rather than ethnic, grounds. For this reason they have more in common with sects than with those immigrant groups for whom religion relates above all to old country traditions and memories.

Although the Christian Reformed do not sacralize Dutch identity, they methodically sacralize other forms. Family life is strongly reinforced by the rituals of prayers and Bible reading at mealtimes. Plaques in the home referring to Christ as Head of the house, strong beliefs in the sacredness of marriage (and the corresponding rejection of divorce), the scriptural legitimation of the role of father and mother, are ever so many ways to buttress the family against secular onslaughts (Ishwaran, 1971, 299). The local congregation is also very much a moral community, the identity of which is constantly strengthened by sermons, mutually agreed-upon norms, and the insistence that sins be confessed (sometimes openly) before communion. According to the Christian Reformed, it is the local congregation which guards the purity of its members and makes up for the lapses of the individual. Yet it is above all personal identity (or personal salvation) which is articulated by the church, as individuals are not only the vehicles of God's and the community's moral purposes, but also valuable in their own right. The Christian Reformed believe that the highest form of personal integrity is achieved through faith in God's predestined (and therefore solidly secure) order.

THE SCANDINAVIANS

The 1981 Canadian census groups the Danish (with 57,940 or 20.5%), the Icelanders (with 22,755 or 8.1%), the Norwegians (with 102,735 or 36.3%), the Swedes (with 78,360 or 27.7%) and the Scandinavians (no other designation with 21,005 or 7.4%) together under the heading Scandinavian (282,795 individuals). There is some justification for this common classification: all Scandinavians speak similar languages and all have (or used to have) a Lutheran state church to which almost everyone belongs. Yet, when they arrived in Canada (usually via the United States and mainly in the West - 82% live in the Prairie provinces and British Columbia) nationality was important enough for them to establish their separate Danish, Icelandic,

Norwegian and Swedish Lutheran churches. With the rapid Canadianization of the Scandinavians (according to 1971 information, not even 1% of the old stock [305,400 individuals] used the native language at home; for the new stock [79,400] the corresponding percentage was only 7%), these national churches were amalgamated, but but not until a fair number of Scandinavians had joined the mainline Protestant churches, United and Anglican. Of the old stock, 30% put down "Lutheran" on the 1971 census form, 30% United and 9% Anglican. For the new stock the corresponding percentages are 45, 15 and 7, showing that even for the more recent arrivals there is a tendency to deviate considerably from the Scandinavian Lutheran pattern.

How important national identity was to some of the earliest immigrants is illustrated by the controversy surrounding the 1876 call of the Rev. Paul Thorlaksson to the first Icelandic congregation in Canada, in Gimli, Manitoba (west of Lake Winnipeg). Although Thorlaksson was an ordained Lutheran minister, had been born in Iceland and preached in Icelandic, he was suspect because he was trained at Concordia Seminary in St. Louis and represented a "foreign" (Norwegian) Lutheran synod. Nevertheless he was called. Yet a number of settlers, although they could hardly afford a minister's stipend (they were destitute and poor, they had arrived in the wilderness the year before and had been decimated by privation and smallpox during the winter) called the Rev. Jon Bjarnason because he had had his seminary training in Iceland and was more "broadminded" theologically. Bjarnason became the patriarch of the Icelandic Synod.

The Danes were involved in similar controversies. One of the oldest Danish colonies in Canada had been established in 1872 at Salmonhurst in New Brunswick. The settlers had managed to obtain the services of a Lutheran pastor, but when he left, the work was taken over by the Anglican Church. This was not to the liking of everyone, and in 1905 some of the Danes withdrew and again formed a Danish Lutheran Church (Cronmiller 1961, 245).

The Swedes also had their own churches and up to the 1920s used Swedish alone for their services. However, the younger generation began to lose knowledge of the language with the result that, for the sake of organizational survival, parishes began to back away from the old policy of reinforcing Swedish identity. In the twenties the Augustana Synod (in which all Swedish churches in Canada were united) began to lose communicants, pastors and even entire congregations. It then began to introduce English in the Sunday Schools and the youth organizations, and by 1936 only one out of more than forty was using Swedish only (Eylands 1945, 297).

The Norwegian Lutheran Church was the largest of all. Wherever the Norwegians settled a Lutheran congregation would soon be organized, because to them it was *both* "the primary and prominent organization of their identity also in Canada" (Loken 126, 1980) *and* the place where literacy and learning (schools were usually attached to the Scandinavian churches) were fostered. In 1920 it had as many as 140 congregations and preaching places in the Prairie provinces, but a quarter of a century later this number had been reduced by half. Drought and depression drove many settlers away; but, in addition, "the emphasis on nationality and language continued to the point that English speaking descendants of immigrants left the church of their fathers" (Evenson 1974, 91).

As with the Icelandic churches, the Norwegian parishes were both ethnically and doctrinally divided, for beliefs can separate as effectively as language. In the Norwegian case, many immigrants had been affected by the evangelical revival of Hans Nielsen Hauge who opposed the ecclesiastical elite and fostered personal commitment. These immigrants established their own Lutheran Free Church which in 1945 had 27 congregations and missions (Eylands 1945, 305). In 1963 they joined the moderate American Lutheran Conference which by then was comprised of a large variety of previously ethnic churches which had become anglicized and had scratched out the ethnic boundaries.

THE POLISH

Another large ethnic group in Canada is formed by those of Polish descent. In 1981 there were 254,480 residents claiming to be of Polish stock, about 60% of pre-World War II origin and 40% of post- World War II origin. These two groups differ considerably from one another. The first consisted originally of poor, landless immigrants, the second of refugees often ex-servicemen, professionals and urban dwellers. According to the 1971 census, only 9% of this first group spoke primarily Polish at home, while 36% of the second group did. The first group was heavily overrepresented in the Prairie provinces (46%, whereas only 16% of the Canadian population lived there); of the second group, as much as 60% resided in Ontario. Of the first group, only 64% were still Catholic, of the second the percentage was 82. Of the first group, 17% now belonged to such un-Polish denominations as the United Church (12%) and Anglican church (5%), of the second group, only 5% belonged to both of these denominations combined.

The earliest immigrants from Poland were the Kashubs who settled in the Renfrew area of Ontario in 1858. They left their native country partly because they feared the Germanizing pressures from Protestant Prussia, partly because they were poverty-stricken. They were deeply religious and on Sundays walked for miles to the nearest Catholic Church served by an Irish priest. But they could not understand English and complained about the lack of concern with Polish customs. Finally, in 1875, a Polish priest arrived. A chapel was built in Wilno, and from that time onwards the children were instructed in the Polish language and catechism (Radecki and Heydenkorn 1976, 21-2, 91).

In the nineteenth century a few more landless peasants from Poland trickled into Canada, mainly into the West. The trek began in earnest in the first decade of this century when close to 67,000 Poles arrived. They had come from a country where the Catholic Church, the main pillar of national unity had been oppressed by Orthodox Russia to the east and Protestant Prussia to the west. Wherever they went they established Polish Catholic churches which, as in the homeland, began to function as agencies of cultural preservation. Winnipeg became a major centre. Here, Bishop Langevin did not like the zealous proselyting of the Protestants amongst his flock and obtained the services of two Oblate fathers. One of them established the Holy Ghost parish with both a Polish school and a Fraternal Aid Society which provided aid for families at times of sickness or death (Radecki 1979, 48).

To some members of the Holy Ghost parish, the Polonization of the church did not go fast enough (they had to share the building originally with Germans, Ukrainians, Hungarians, Slovaks and other Catholics), and so they established a separate Polish National Catholic parish in 1904 which was outside the jurisdiction of the Catholic bishop. They linked up with the Polish National Catholic Church in the USA, which had begun in the 1890s as a protest against the "attempts by the American Bishops to assimilate the Polish immigrants by opposing Polish schools and other distinct culture manifestations" (Radecki 1979, 106). This group now has ten parishes in Canada.

Generally, however, the Catholic bishops were helpful and diplomatic enough not to let this happen. They encouraged the building of churches and chapels, which often began as log structures, and provided the people with Polish priests whenever possible. The priests, in turn, paid suitable attention to the typical national festivals. Foremost among them were *Oplatek* (the Wafer), the breaking of the Holy Bread before the Christmas Eve supper (the *Wigilia*, the highlight of the Christmas celebration) and *Swiecone* (the Blessed Food, breakfast shared by the family on Easter Sunday). These ceremonies reinforced family cohesion, particularly the Christmas Eve bread-breaking, which obliged members to forgive family squabbles and conflicts (Radecki and Heydenkorn 1976, 162). The church is the link with these family festivals: attendance at the midnight Mass traditionally follows the *Wigilia*, and the Easter food has been blessed in the church on the preceding Saturday. The Polish Catholic Church has built a Polish altar at the Martyr's Shrine in Midland, Ontario. Many pilgrims from all over Canada go there in August. The pilgrimage coincides with the celebrations of the Madonna at Czestochowa, the most sacred monastery in Poland (Radecki 1979, 152-3).

The Polish Catholic Church has also been involved in Polish national holidays. Polish Constitution Day (established on May 3, 1791) and Independence Day (November 11, 1918) are often celebrated by solemn Masses and with marches by veterans and boyscouts, following the services (Radecki 1979, 153). During World War I and World War II the Catholic parishes in Canada collected funds for the homeless and other war victims in Poland. Even at this great distance, the Polish Catholic Church regards it as a patriotic duty to commemmorate national losses and successes.

Since the depression of the 1930s, the situation of the Polish Catholic congregations in western Canada has changed drastically. As was to be expected, the Canadian-born generations felt much less attached to the country of origin. In addition, many rural settlers of Polish origin moved to the cities.

> The number of Polish parishes and missions in the west continued to increase to over 200 by 1930, but since that time there was a decline in their number, and in their Polish character. By 1973, only about 30 remaining parishes had Polish priests serving all residents of an area, and none of them could be termed exclusively Polish (Radecki 1979, 55).

Another important reason for the changing situation was the flow of 64,000 Polish refugees and ex-servicemen after World War II to Ontario rather than the Prairie provinces. This meant that the transitional function of the ethnic parish (from foreign enclave to amalgamation with primarily English-speaking Catholicism) had to be fulfilled by a different set of congregations. Yet, as in the West, with the ceasing of large-scale immigration of Polish citizens, the population to be served by these parishes becomes progressively older. For the increasingly larger percentage of Canadian-born persons of Polish stock, the Polish parish does not serve anymore as a nostalgic device and it feels just as comfortable in the local, English-speaking church. The bishops are not altogether joyless about this chain of events. After all, it means that the pressures for special considerations, special education and special services are gradually diminishing.

Of course the bishops are less happy about the fact that more and more young people of Polish descent do marry non-Polish, often Protestant partners. This partly explains the percentage of all people of Polish extraction now belonging to the United Church (6.1% in 1981 as compared with 1.1% in 1941) and the decrease of those belonging to the Catholic church (80.0% in 1941 as compared with 75.3% in 1981).

THE JEWS

The last of the major Canadian ethnic groups to be considered here is formed by the Jews. In 1981 there were 264,020 residents claiming to be of Jewish stock, about 60% of pre-World War II origins and 40% who came after that war. As recently as 1881 there were only 1,333 Jews in all of Canada. In the following two decades, and particularly in the first two decades of this century, this figure rose rapidly to 6,501 (0.1% of the population) in 1891, to 16,493 (0.3%) in 1901, to 74,760 (1.0%) in 1911 and to 125,445 (1.4%) in 1921. Presently Jews comprise 1.1% of the population. Very few of them (10.2%) live outside Ontario (50.0%), Quebec (34.5%)

and Manitoba (5.3%); and, even in those three provinces, they live predominantly in the capital cities. They are by far the most urban of all ethnic groups. In 1981 only 1.5% lived in rural areas even though 24.4% of the total Canadian population lives there, and even though in the heyday of immigration various Jewish farm settlements such as Moosomin, Wapella, Sonnenfeldt, Edenbridge, Hirsch and Lipton were established in Saskatchewan. Jews are also overrepresented in the upper social- economic strata of the population. In the 1971 census 6.6% had managerial occupations (compared with, for instance, 3.4% of Anglicans and 2.0% of Catholics). Although at that time only 2.6% of the population earned more than $15,000, 10.6% of Jews did so. The average income of Jews, fifteen years old and over was $7,703,-, of the population at large $5,033,-. They also have more education than the average Canadian: in 1971, 13.22% of all Jews had a university degree in contrast with 4.65% of the population at large.

Although the Jews had been without a homeland from A.D. 70 when the Romans destroyed the temple in Jerusalem until 1948 when the state of Israel came into being, they have been remarkably resistant to amalgamation by other nations. Against all odds they defended their separate ethnic identity against the homogenizing intentions of state and community. Without Judaism this feat could have never been accomplished. The sense of being a nation with which God had a special covenant, the religious delineation of dietary and other laws, the constant reiteration of their sacred history, and the expectation of reward at the end of days when the Messiah would return them to the promised land kept them intact, in spite of pogroms (a Russian word for organized massacres and mass persecutions) and other, more subtle, forms of discrimination.

Most of the Jewish settlers in Canada were the direct victims of persecution in their country of origin. This is particularly true for those who have arrived since 1880. The few who arrived earlier came on a more voluntary basis. Aaron Hart, a commissioned officer in the British army marched on Montreal in 1760 and settled in Trois Rivières where he became the city's commercial lynchpin. When he died in 1800, "he was reputed to be the wealthiest man in the British Empire outside of the British Isles" (Sack 1965, 48). The Oppenheimer brothers came to the U.S.A. in 1848, but were attracted to the goldfields in British Columbia; in 1885 they set up the first wholesale grocery business in Vancouver. One of them (David) became its mayor (Rosenberg 1970, 70).

The bulk of those who came after 1880 had been oppressed in Eastern Europe. When, in 1881, Csar Alexander II was assassinated by revolutionaries (some of which had been Jews), many Jewish settlements were attacked and their inhabitants expelled. Some of these found their way to Winnipeg, suddenly adding 340 immigrants to the eight Jewish families already there (Belkin 1966, 30). In the first two decades of the twentieth century thousands of Jews also arrived from Rumania and Poland; as well as from Russia and the Ukraine where other pogroms occurred in 1903 and 1905. They were usually assisted from funds made available by Baron de

Hirsch to the institute which carried his name. The pattern of Jews fleeing oppression and escaping to the more promising shores of the American continent repeats itself for the Nazi holocaust and the post World War II ravages in Europe.

Ethnic separation of the Jews has never been total. Yiddish, the Jewish folk-language, is based on German mixed with Hebrew, Roman and Slavic elements. After their arrival in Canada, Jews often grouped together in terms of a common country of origin rather than in terms of a common ethnic stock. And so, in Hamilton, Ontario, Polish Jews founded the Adas Israel, Rumanians the Agudas Achim and Lithuanian- Polish immigrants the Ohav Zedek congregations (Rosenberg 1970, 99).

Presently, however, the main divisions within the Jewish ethnic group do not reflect so much the European origin as the various degrees of adjustment to Canadian culture: Orthodoxy (least integrated), Conservative (modifying many of the strict Jewish practices) and Reform (most integrated). These divisions are not only typical for Canada, but can be found wherever Jews settled and established synagogues in more recent times. For Canada, or more specifically, Toronto, Kallen (1977, 52), expresses the situation most succinctly when she says: "From Orthodox through Conservative to Reform the emphasis on acculturation increases and the emphasis on distinctive ethnic socialization decreases."

Orthodoxy demands (and usually gets) strict adherence to the many dietary (Kosher) food laws. To eat pork or shellfish, or to mix certain foods (such as milk and meat) is an abomination to the Orthodox Jew as both the Hebrew Bible (the Old Testament to Christians) and the Talmud (which extends, interprets and applies the laws of the Torah, the first five books of the Hebrew Bible) contend. The Orthodox also believe that the laws of the Sabbath (from sunset on Friday to sunset on Saturday) are divine decrees and therefore refuse to work, travel or carry money on that day. All these laws and rules (as many as 613) structure the entire life of the Orthodox Jew. They keep him separate from Canadian culture and remind him constantly of his Jewish identity. The Reichmann brothers, who are "the world's largest developers with international assets estimated at more than $7 billion growing at nearly a billion dollars every six months" (Newman, 1981, 199) are also ultra orthodox. They live close to one another in North Toronto, but refuse to worship in a nearby synagogue because it uses electricity on Saturdays and instead worship at the more austere Beth Jacob synagogue on Overbrook Place (Ibid., 203).

Some of the Orthodox are more scrupulous than others. The Chassidim stand out because of their full beards, earlocks, long black topcoats and broad-brimmed felt hats. In contrast with other Orthodox Jews, they pattern their lives on a Rebbe, a charismatic figure to whom they attribute extraordinary powers of perception and wisdom. In Montreal, the Lubavitcher Chassidim also stand out from other Jews through their witnessing to non-observing Jews whom they assist and exhort to "reorganize their lives around Yiddishkayt" [Orthodox Judaism], (Shaffir 1974, 60). In

Canada there are far more Orthodox (174 in 1960) than Conservative (25) and Reform congregations (7). However, as Rosenberg (1971, 66), who supplies these figures, points out, the Orthodox synagogues are much smaller, often no more than a prayer-hall without rabbis (comparable to ministers and priests in Christianity). The Conservative and Reform congregations, on the other hand, generally have an extensive membership and impressive educational and social facilities, as well as a sanctuary for worship Conservative Judaism follows a more adaptive policy. Canadian Jews who belong to Conservative congregations often come from Orthodox homes. Yet the emphasis on education and economic success in the latter inevitably resulted in a closer fit with the cultural expectations of the host society. And so the Conservative Jew is a typical, mainstream, middle-class Canadian who confines his Judaism to the home. Yet even here, the dietary and Sabbath laws are only selectively observed. The Jewish traditions are still important to him, but on the Sabbath he drives to the synagogue in his car (his Orthodox friend walks), and, when he arrives, he sits together with his wife and family (his Orthodox friend insists on separating the sexes). He is also less inclined to think about the Jewish laws as divinely ordained, although he sends his children, often protesting, to the classes in the synagogue which train them in Yiddish, Hebrew or Jewish lore. Conservative parents tend "to delegate to the congregational school the distinctive ethnic socialization of their young, [but, at present this] appears to have done more to alienate Conservative youth from Judaism and Jewishness than to gain their commitment" (Kallen, 1977, 104-5). By contrast, most of the Jewish children of Kallen's Toronto sample which came from Orthodox homes were, "like their parents, clearly dedicated to maintenance of Jewish ethnic distinctiveness through everyday observance of Judaic tradition" (Ibid., 110).

The Reform Jews are sufficiently integrated into Canadian culture to be impatient with an ethnic system of prescriptions and proscriptions. They usually don't hesitate to eat non-Kosher foods, pork, shellfish. They happily eat milk products and meat from the same dish, because, to them, these rituals are a function of time rather than of divine revelation. English has replaced Yiddish in the home; secular learning has been substituted for the study of Hebrew and the sacred scriptures. Yet the Reform Jews have a sufficient emotional attachment to their ethnic origins to oppose intermarriage of their children. In her Toronto sample, Kallen (Ibid., 91) found some Reform parents "moved back into the ghetto" when their teenagers began to date non-Jews. Presently Reform congregations in Canada seem to have more respect for specific Jewish traditions than in earlier days as in 1853 when the first Reform congregation in Canada (Anshe Sholom) was founded in Hamilton, Ontario, and when the exuberant spirit of enlightened liberalism and utopian views of the brotherhood of men seemed all-pervasive. The creation of Israel in 1948 and the Six-Day War in 1967 increased Jewish solidarity everywhere and have replaced an earlier universalism. The majority of Reform Jews are now Zionist, and contribute financially and otherwise to the preservation of the Jewish homeland (Israel). In the final quarter of the twentieth century, pluralistic tolerance in Canada has given new respect to ethnic separateness. Therefore, the original traditions become a more attractive option to those who find it difficult to contend with lack of structure and meaning in the national mosaic.

Anti-semitism and discrimination have had their separate effects on the consolidation of Jewish identity in Canada. The religious differences between Jews and Christians exacerbated the distinction between Jewish ethnic and Canadian social identity and have tended to increase among Jews a sense of belonging together. The identity conflicts, in turn, have made the Jews a ready-made scapegoat for national or regional disjunctions. During the depression in the 1930s, "there were many instances of anti-[S]emitic flare-ups and frequent discrimination in housing, property and civil rights" (Rosenberg 1970, 185). Earlier, in 1807, Ezekiel Hart (1770-1843, a son of Aaron) was elected to the Legislative Assembly of Lower Canada to represent Trois Rivières in Quebec. However, he was not allowed to take his seat mainly because he was a Jew, partly because the antiSemitic stance of the French was a good cover for their anti-English sentiments. It was not until 1831 that Parliament granted Jews the same rights and privileges as other citizens of the province (Sack, 1965, 104). However, that was not the end of anti-Semitism. In the Dominion House of Commons, in 1906, Henri Bourassa called the Jews "the most undesirable class of people any country can have .... vampires on a community instead of being contributors to the general welfare of the people" (Rosenberg 1970, 180). Later Bourassa became much less vituperative. However, in 1935, Adrien Arcand, Minister of Labour in the Union Nationale government of Maurice Duplessis, stirred up an even more militant anti-Semitism. He wore Hitler's swastika and gave the Nazi salute. He was interned in 1940 for subversion of the democratic process.

The Judaic tradition strongly strengthens the family. The home is regarded as a religious sanctuary. The *mezuzah* (scroll proclaiming the love of God) is fastened to the doorpost, suggesting that God guards the home. The mother lights the Sabbath candles on Friday evenings and the father blesses his children at the Sabbath table. Kertzer (1974, 64) calls Judaism "essentially a family religion." To protect the family, the Jewish religion prohibits adultery, incest, homosexuality (Leviticus 20 and the Talmud). Yet divorce could be relatively simple: a legal document given by the husband to the wife would send her on her way, according to Deuteronomy 24:1. In actual fact, divorce is regarded as morally reprehensible (Steinsaltz, 1977, 133). Intermarriage is strictly forbidden and even the most assimilated of Jews will still frown on his children marrying outside the fold. Although increasing, the intermarriage rate for Jews is the lowest in the country. Driedger (1980, 78) found that Jewish university students in Winnipeg ranked highest among all other major ethnic groups on endogamy (91.3%).

Rites of passage ensure a minimum of disturbance in family and community relations. Circumcision (the removal of the foreskin of the penis) is universally practised and seals the covenant between Abraham, the father of the race, and Jehovah. By implication, it also signifies the entrance of the infant (generally eight days old) into the Jewish community. Marriage rites take place under a *chupah* (canopy) to underline the separation of the new couple and their entitlement to privacy. They also sip from a single cup of wine to symbolize their unity. Even in the most secular Jewish homes *bar mitzvah* (the ceremony at which a 13-year-old Jewish boy becomes an adult member of the Jewish community by reading from the *Torah*) is commonly held and is functionally not different from other initiation ceremonies. In less orthodox families a *bat mitzvah* (corresponding ceremony for girls) is sometimes added. At death the simple funeral service is reminiscent of Christian burial in that appropriate psalms (such as 15, 23 and 90) are usually read and "dust is returned to dust." Mourning is religiously structured by prayers three times a day for seven days (*shiva*) while neighbours bring the first meal to the sorrowing family.

To sum up: in Jewish communities religion is the most formidable force for strengthening a separate identity. The inroads of Canadian secular culture can be best measured by the progressive absence from synagogue attendance: in a sample of Jews in Toronto, more than half of the Orthodox did attend regularly, but less than a quarter of the Conservatives and Reform did so (Kallen, 1977, 80). Ethnic separation is best achieved amongst those (Orthodox) Jews who adhere to all Judaic prescriptions and proscriptions and least amongst those (Reform) Jews whose interest in religious ritual is minimal or altogether absent.

CHAPTER 5

MENNONITES AND HUTTERITES

Mennonite sectarianism finds its origin in the growing differentiation between political and religious organization in the early sixteenth century. It went further than Lutheranism, which severed the close tie between empire and Catholicism but settled as the state religion of some German states and all of Scandinavia; it also went further than Calvinism and Zwinglianism, which similarly severed Catholic alliances but settled as the civil religion of Geneva and Zurich. By contrast, Mennonitism took the early Christian Church as its model and renounced all links with political/geographical boundaries. Instead, it drew the boundary around an exclusively religious principle: the community of believers. Within the boundary were those who believed in rebaptism (or Anabaptism), those who, in accordance with the common New Testament practice, accepted adult baptism as a seal of their confession of faith. Also within were those who refused to swear an oath (according to Matthew 5:34) or to resist violence (Matthew 5:39). Without were those who accepted infant baptism as a portal into society at large and who did not object to swearing an oath or bearing arms.

Yet, because the entire weight of Mennonite organization was on the local congregation, and because other loyalties to supra-local political or religious bodies were usually pale by comparison, internal splits and divisions could take place relatively unimpeded. There was no external check on, and arbitration of, conflicts. It was easy for those who, for some reason or other, could not fit into the local pattern of authority and discipline to leave and start a splinter group with modified doctrines and practices. After all, individual responsibility and personal faith were the cornerstones of Anabaptism, and individuals could therefore justify their disagreements on theological grounds. In addition, splintering was advanced by the pull of the social environment in the direction of greater acculturation and accommodation.

In Canada the 1971 census counted 168,150 Mennonites: 60% resided in the Prairie provinces (primarily Manitoba with 35%), 24% in Ontario and 16% in British Columbia. The Mennonite Yearbook counted only 85,907 members spread over eighteen denominations in 1972, but these were only the baptized adults and did not include children and adolescents. The Prairie Mennonites mostly belonged to the Dutch branch, which had originated in Frisia, Flanders and Saxony in the sixteenth century. Menno Simons (1496-1561), a Dutch Catholic priest from Witmarsum who had joined the movement in 1536, had become their most outstanding leader, and gradually the Anabaptists, who by that time had also declared themselves against oath-taking and military resistance, were named after him. They were outlawed in the Holy Roman Empire and many re-settled in the Vistula Delta in and around Gdansk (formerly Danzig). When militarization of the region increased, Catherine the Great of Russia found many willing to settle in the fertile regions north of the Black Sea which had just been seized from the Turks. They established a large colony at Chortutza on the Dnieper and later (in 1803) another one, 100 miles to the east at Molotschna (Epp, 1974, 49). In the same way as the Dutch language in the Vistula region had kept them separate from the local population, so the use of German reinforced their Russian enclave. This did not sit too well with the Russian authorities. They appreciated the hard-working, well-disciplined, sober and intelligent settlers, but were less than happy about the absence of linguistic and other loyalties to Russia. The resulting friction induced thousands of Mennonites to migrate to North America and from 1874 to 1876 more than 6000 arrived in Canada where the large majority settled on the East Reserve (thirty miles southeast of Winnipeg) and the West Reserve (on the U.S., border to the southwest of Winnipeg). Many thousands more arrived in the 1920s when the Russian colonies suffered severely from the Bolshevik upheavals.

There was another branch of Mennonites which had originated in Switzerland and the south of Germany. In Zurich a monk, George Blaurock, and two well-educated, prominent young men, Conrad Grebel and Felix Manz, felt that the Zwinglian reforms of the 1520s did not go far enough in that they still condoned infant baptism and looked to the city council as a theological court of appeal. By the end of the decade (1530) Blaurock had been burned at the stake, Grebel had died of the plague and Manz had been forcibly drowned. Yet the movement spread over the region as far as the Netherlands. It continued to suffer persecution; therefore the Mennonites tended to gravitate to isolated valleys and areas, such as the Palatinate, which were relatively tolerant. In the first half of the eighteenth century several thousands migrated to Pennsylvania where both religious freedom and good land promised relief from constant insecurity. In the later half of that century the War of Independence created new pressures for unqualified loyalty to the new republic. As there was good land available in Upper Canada, many Mennonites from Pennsylvania began to settle in Welland, York, and particularly in Waterloo counties. Most of the Ontario

Mennonites trace their origins to this migration from the United States at the end of the eighteenth and the beginning of the nineteenth Century.

Among those who came during that period were the Amish, one of the strictest of Mennonite sects. They had split off from mainstream Anabaptism at the end of the seventeenth century because they felt that group boundaries were too loose. They insisted on stricter rules of excommunication of sinners: the latter should be totally shunned by all the faithful, including members of the family. They also introduced biannual communion with foot-washing and began to require untrimmed beards for men and conservative clothing fastened by hooks and eyes rather than buttons. They were named after their leader, Jacob Ammann, a native of Switzerland who had also lived, at one stage, in Alsace and Wurttemberg. Partly because of persecution, partly because of military upheavals, partly because the formation of separated colonies in Europe was very difficult, many members migrated to Pennsylvania in the eighteenth, but primarily the nineteenth century. After 1825 they also began to come in a steady stream (Gingerich 1972, 30) to Ontario, primarily settling in the area west of Waterloo. By 1875 there were five Amish settlements (Ibid., 40), which continued to be strongly influenced by the much more numerous Amish in the U.S.A. (they disappeared altogether in Europe). Presently there are almost 1000 Mennonites of the Amish persuasion in Canada (mainly in Ontario). They are divided into the Old Order Amish (650 baptized adults, according to the 1973 Mennonite Yearbook, Kauffman and Harder, 1975, 21) who continue to insist on eighteenth century European clothing and do not permit their members to own tractors or cars. By contrast, the Beachy Amish (named after a more progressive bishop in Pennsylvania) have 320 members, who have not only accepted modern farm machinery but also telephones and automobiles. Both groups still use German rather than English in their worship services.

Apart from the fast-growing Hutterites, who have all property in common and to whom a special section will be devoted, the three largest Mennonite denominations in Canada are the General Conference Mennonites (with 20,553 baptized members in 1972), the Mennonite Brethren Church (with 17,982 baptized members in the same year) and the Mennonite Church (8,984 members). The latter consists almost exclusively of Swiss Mennonites, although their home language is actually the German dialect of the Palatinate where many had found refuge. In Canada the great majority of their congregations are in Ontario. They are sticklers for tradition and adhere to the Mennonite Confession of Faith adopted at Dordrecht (the Netherlands) in 1632. They are therefore often called the "Old" Mennonites. They refused to conform to the world by insisting on simple dress and worship, were usually against divorce, smoking, drinking and did not participate in politics. However, at present, a substantial proportion (56% of the North American sample of Kauffman and Harder, 1975, 161) feels that one should vote, although in fact 60% did not do so. The other denominations are much more positive in this respect. Only 14% of the

General Conference Mennonites and 21% of the Mennonite Brethren had not voted in recent elections. Resistance to drinking and smoking has also diminished: only 56% and 66%, respectively, of the members of the Mennonite Church regard these activities as "always wrong" as compared with 35% and 50% of General Conference Mennonites and 51% and 76% of the Mennonite Brethren.

General Conference Mennonites separated from the Old Mennonites in the middle of the nineteenth century in the United States. They were in favour of more openness to other Christians and of greater adaptation to the American environment. This openness is still more characteristic of the General Conference Mennonites than others: the Kauffman and Harder study (p. 255) has 30% of them scoring "high" on a ecumenism scale as compared with 16% each for the Mennonite Church and the Mennonite Brethren. Yet, on such typically Mennonite issues as pacifism, there were almost as many (56%) General Conference Mennonites who scored "high" as members of the Mennonite Church (64%). Both groups differed rather strongly from the Mennonite Brethren, only 26% of whom could be classified in the top category.

The Mennonite Brethren are particularly strong in the Prairie provinces. Their denomination arose in the Molotschna Colony in Russia about the same time (1860) as the Conference Mennonites in the United States. In Russia, too, it was the influence of non-Mennonite culture which pushed towards separation. More specifically, it was the dynamic preaching of a Lutheran priest (Eduard Wust) in a nearby German settlement which moved many to become converted. This led to arguments with the more conventional Mennonites who submitted the dispute to the civil authorities of the colony. The Brethren, as the converted Mennonites were called by now, were ostracized and began baptism by immersion in contrast with the others who insisted on baptism by sprinkling. They came to Canada in large numbers in the 1920s. The emphasis on conversion still distinguishes the Mennonite Brethren. Peter Hamm (1978, 232) who separately analyzed the Canadian segment of the Kauffman/Harder study found that as many as 95% of the Canadian Mennonite Brethren had had a conversion experience as compared with 80% of the Church Mennonites and 65% of the General Conference Mennonites. Hamm applied the identity model of religion to his analysis of the Mennonite Brethren and came to the conclusion (Ibid., 562) that the sacralizing components (specific beliefs, Christian socialization, regular worship, conversion experiences, charismatic leadership, the centripetal effect of ecclesiastical conferences) more than stemmed the tide of the secularizing elements (public education, urbanization, economic ascendancy, occupational change, cultural assimilation). He therefore made a powerful case for the viability of Mennonite sectarianism in Canadian society.

Mennonites in Canada, like all other ethnic and sectarian groups, have seen the boundaries around their peoplehood at times subtly weakened and at other times forcefully strengthened. As long as they remained separate rural colonies, survival was never at stake. Yet Anglo-Saxon culture inevitably gained a foothold as soon as self-sufficiency diminished. As recently as World War II German was their language, particularly of the more recent immigrants, but during and after the war English became more and more the language of even those settlers.

Anglicization was dodged much more firmly in the early history of the Mennonite settlements in Manitoba. Contact with all Canadian authorities was kept at a minimum. Appeals "to the courts or other authorities of the country [were] declared a grave sin" (Francis 1955, 85). Instead, social control was maintained by excommunication. In the West Reserve such matters as sending one's "children to a public school, seeking employment with Anglo-Saxons, selling land to outsiders (even to Mennonites of other churches), mortgaging one's property....adopting such novelties as bicycles, buggies, musical boxes or sleigh bells" (Ibid., 89) were punished with excommunication. In these earlier days schools were attached to each church and "almost any male who had some schooling in the Old Country (Russia) and was not fit for homesteading, was called upon to serve as schoolmaster" (Ibid., 164). However, in the Manitoba School Act of 1897 "English was made the official language and Anglo-Saxon culture the basis of the public school system" (Ibid., 170), although ethnic minorities still had considerable autonomy. The demand for higher teaching standards and particularly the patriotism of World War I with its antagonism towards Germany resulted in the Manitoba School Attendance Act of 1916, whereby English was made the sole language of instruction and all children between seven and fourteen were compelled to attend school. The Mennonites thereupon changed many of their schools back to private institutions, as they were allowed under the law, but in 1918 these schools were condemned as inadequate and parents who out of protest refused to send their children to a recognized school were fined and sometimes even jailed (Ibid., 185). And so there was no escape from the intrusion of Canadian culture (each school had to fly the Union Jack) and the inculcation of patriotic sentiments. As Francis (Ibid., 186) has it: "....the school figured prominently as the most effective means to wean the children of immigrants away from the traditions of their group and to indoctrinate them with the ideals and values of the dominant majority."

In Ontario, too, Mennonite identity was under attack during World War I. Both loyalty to the German tongue and nonresistance stood in the way of militant patriotism. And so the town which was originally named after a Mennonite bishop (Ebytown) and subsequently renamed Berlin became Kitchener in 1916. The voluntary teaching of German in the schools faded altogether (Epp, 1974, 357). Yet Mennonites were, as in the past, specifically excepted from the Military Service Act of 1917. As a token of both gratitude and loyalty, Mennonites from all of Canada contributed generously to a variety of relief funds for war victims, the Red Cross, Victory Loan campaigns and, in Ontario, the Non-Resistant Relief Organization.

World War II again threatened a now recovered and vigorous Mennonite identity. In the 1920s some 20,000 German-speaking fellow believers
from Russia had arrived. The pan-Germanism of the Third Reich also
helped to resist "anglicization in Canada as russification had been resisted in
Russia" (Epp, 1978, 30). During the war the inevitable accusations were
made that the Mennonites were shirkers and wartime profiteers, but the
government continued to recognize the right of those who had arrived in
pre-World War I days to refuse military service. It did not recognize the
same rights for those who had arrived in the 1920s, as there was a general
feeling that the more recent arrivals were less loyal to Canada and more
inclined to defend Germany. They therefore had to prove that they were
bona fide conscientious objectors (Francis, 1955, 237). Those who obtained
conscientious objector status had to perform alternative service in lumber
camps, hospitals and farms. Yet there were several thousands of young
Mennonites who served in the armed forces, usually as volunteers. As in
World War I, Canadian Mennonites united in extensive relief work.

Although the inroads of Canadian culture have definitely changed Mennonitism (so much so that various Mennonite groups in this century decided
to migrate to South America where they felt less impeded), there are many
factors which have worked towards a maintenance of their identity. Specific
religious beliefs, the inculcation of loyalty as measured by church attendance, the successful prevention of mixed marriages and the religious
upbringing of children have all strengthened Mennonite boundaries.
Driedger and Peters (1973b) found that in Manitoba Mennonite students,
more than other students of German extraction, felt attached to their
in-group. They also participated more in Mennonite institutions than other
Germans did in theirs. The Kauffman/Harder survey found astoundingly
high church attendance patterns (but then, of course, it was based on a
sample of congregations, not of people who think of themselves as Mennonites): 94% of the Church Mennonites, 86% of the General Conference
Mennonites and 98% of the Canadian Mennonite Brethren went to church
more than twice a month (Hamm, 1978, 276). According to the same
survey, less than 6% of all Mennonites were married to a spouse belonging
to a different denomination (Ibid., 212). Mennonites believe in the indissolubility of marriage, have very few divorces, regard pre-marital and extramarital sex as "always wrong" and commonly practice family worship,
factors which tend to tie individuals, families and churches together.

In spite of changes in Mennonite identity through anglicization, urbanization and increasing affluence (although the average income of Mennonites
and Hutterites, age fifteen and over, in the 1971 census, was still only
$4,101 as compared with $5,033 for the population at large), at present they
seem to successfully stem the tide of secularization. Its strength lies with the
local community of believers rather than with the denominational hierarchy. Mennonites often think of themselves as suffering from *Tauferkran-
kheit* (Anabaptist illness) which means that they are embarrassed by inter-
minable tendencies for denominational conflicts and splinterings. Yet this

"illness" is the inevitable outcome of the historical decision to stress individual faith (adult baptism) and to recognize no civil (or indeed, interdenominational) authority as a theological court of appeal. This undiluted differentation will continue to make Mennonites vulnerable to abuse and bereft of mundane clout. Yet in modern, loosely structured, democratic societies, non-resistance movements have often shown remarkable strength in spite of firmly entrenched Macchiavellian ideologies.

THE HUTTERITES

The traditional link between religion and territorial identity was already severed in ancient Judaism. The covenant between Jahweh and his people proved to be firm even when the Israelites were slaves in Egypt or exiles in Assyria. Ever since then, ethnic and/or religious minorities (whether Jewish, Christian or Moslem) have justified their isolation within a larger society by theological precedent.

The Hutterites are a good example of a sect which constantly reaffirms its separate autonomy and cultural marginality on biblical grounds. It sprang up during the Reformation, but it never grew very fast because it insisted on following Christian injunctions to the letter. Pacifism (Isaiah 2:4 prophesied the beating of swords into plowshares) and Communalism (Acts 2:44 described how the first Christians had everything in common) went against the basic values of a viable national state with a capitalist economy. Like all other Anabaptist sects, it insisted that only believers should be baptized (Acts 8:37 sealed a confession of faith with baptism) and this, too, earned the Hutterites the hatred of emperor and Church alike.

The sect began in the early 1530s when a heterogeneous collection of craftsmen from Tyrol, Switzerland, Hesse, Bavaria and Wurttemberg, who had anabaptist and communal leanings, fled to relatively tolerant Moravia. One of them, Jacob Hutter, a hat-maker from Tyrol, had impressive talents as charismatic leader and welded the groups together into tightly knit communities of believers. However, the local Moravian nobility could not always protect the Hutterites (as they were now called after their leader) against the emperor, and in 1536 Hutter was caught in Austria, placed bound and gagged in freezing water and then set aflame after being doused in brandy (Hostetler, 1975, 23). In spite of periodic persecutions the Hutterian communities in Moravia continued to flourish, particularly under the leadership of Peter Rideman (1506-56), a Silesian cobbler who wrote the Hutterite confession of faith in prison in Hesse. This is still used today.

In 1622, during the Thirty Years' War, the Hutterites were finally expelled from Moravia and fled to Hungary where both the Hapsburgs and the Catholic Church were less powerful. However, after the war imperial authority reasserted itself and the Brethren were either exterminated or absorbed in the Catholic Church (Peters, 1967, 25ff.). A few escaped to

Transsylvania and Wallachia, and in 1770 a group of about sixty Brethren were allowed to settle on a private estate in Wischenka, north of Kiev in the Ukraine. A century later, however, a policy of russification and the introduction of compulsory military service made also the Ukraine too hot under the Hutterite feet and they migrated to South Dakota in the U.S.A. During World War I the issue of military service rose again. When two Hutterites died in a military prison, most of the colonies bought land in Alberta and Manitoba and migrated to Canada.

As in the Ukraine and South Dakota, conflict with the communities and provinces soon followed successful settlement. On the one hand states and provinces welcomed the newcomers as they needed the industry, competence, frugality and moral strength of the Hutterites for regional development. On the other hand, as usual, the 165 colonies (84 in Alberta, 53 in Manitoba and 28 in Saskatchewan) which had been established in Canada by 1974 insisted on outright separation and segregation in order to preserve the heavenly mandate of communism and pacifism. Although diversity and tolerance are of the essence of a pluralistic society, and in Canada sects, cults, ethnic and other groups are free to bolster their separateness from society at large, there is a point where too much autonomy can weaken national and communal identity. At various times and places local and other authorities felt that the Hutterites had reached that point.

Generally countries of large-scale immigration, such as Canada, can successfully absorb ethnic and other enclaves. Their cultural tentacles can reach into the remotest corners through schools, various levels of government, language, law and the mass media. The tentacles of Canadian culture have been, and are, powerful enough to erode the autonomy of many sects and ethnic groups. Several foreign cultures in Canada have disappeared because the old immigrant defenders gradually died and their children and grandchildren were socialized by the Canadian environment.

If the Hutterites have now for 450 years avoided such a fate, it is because they have successfully defended and strengthened the boundaries around their identity. Religion has been pivotal in this battle for autonomy. To understand how this came about, we should look first at the various external threats to the colonies and then to the internal problems which endangered their cohesion. Under each of these headings we can then analyze the part which religion played.

EXTERNAL THREATS TO HUTTERITE IDENTITY

During extensive periods of Hutterite history the pressures of state and church were too strong for survival. Refusal to bear arms was an affront to the state, which depended on military might for survival. Anabaptism and common ownership of goods was a heresy to the churches. By 1622 there were no colonies left in Moravia, by 1686 they were stamped out in Hungary and in 1695 the last "Bruderhof" in Transsylvania disappeared. Members either became Catholic or escaped, but there were very few places left in Europe where they could exist as part of a colony of fellow believers. Thousands were martyred and the details of the events leading up to their death were faithfully recorded in two histories, the major one of which ends in 1665 and contains a special "Martyr's Register." Another one continues the events in subsequent centuries and was finally published from manuscripts in 1947 (Peters, 1967, 122). It is the constant reference to a long tradition of ancestors who died for the faith which encourages present-day Hutterites to also resist the inroads of the outside world into their communes.

Yet more important than history is the strong conviction that only Hutterites perpetuate the small body of the elect. They alone are the true Christians; other so-called Christians have been corrupted by the world and must be avoided. Jesus' words in John 15:19 is the pivot and the prooftext for these convictions: "If ye were of the world, the world would love his own: but because ye are not of the world, but I have chosen you out of the world, therefore the world hateth you." Consequently the inroads of the world are diligently watched and firmly rejected.

One rather important inroad is the school. During their long history Hutterites established an enviable reputation for literacy and learning. However, they regard the basic secular philosophy of the Canadian schools with profound suspicion. They pay education taxes, but refuse to send their children to centralized schools. Most often they provide a schoolhouse on colony grounds to which the public school system appoints a teacher. As the Hutterite birthrate is the highest in Canada, there is usually no problem with filling the schools. The problem is rather that modern educational techniques do not exactly accord with Hutterite views of childraising. They sometimes prefer poor teachers (alcoholics, for instance) to effective ones, and they have been known to insist on firing teachers who were too lenient. It is therefore not surprising that the 1959 Alberta Report of the Hutterite Investigation Committee complains that the Hutterites have no loyalty to the country in which they live, do not vote or hold public office and consider flagraising or the singing of the national anthem in school idolatrous (Flint 1975, 58ff.). However, this is not necessarily true for all colonies. In Manitoba, Peters (1967, 150) reports the queen smiling benignly on her Hutterite subjects in the colony schools and the children lustily singing 'O Canada'.

Suspicion of the Canadian school system, however, is not enough for meeting the persistent threat of the world. Hutterites therefore counter the English school where they learn mathematics, reading and science with their own German school held on Saturdays and Sunday afternoons, and before and after normal school hours. It is in this school that all children learn the Hutterite ways and memorize catechism, Bible stories, prayers, hymns and Hutterite history. They also learn to read and write German script.

The external threat to Hutterite autonomy ebbs and flows as it did in other countries, such as the Ukraine and the U.S.A. which had both welcomed and persecuted the sect. In Canada, too, during the Second World War Hutterites came under pressure because of their pacifism. The United Farmers of Alberta wanted to repeal the federal guarantee of military exemption for Hutterites. They did not succeed, however, and Hutterite youth were allowed to take alternative service in labour camps for road and forestry work. In 1944 Hutterites were also prevented from buying or leasing land in Alberta. Yet during the depression of the thirties, colonies were welcomed with open arms in certain regions as they could buy out those farmers who were unable to meet their mortgage payments. After the Second World War Hutterites were allowed to buy land again, provided that the new colonies were at least forty miles from the others and would not be larger than 6400 acres (Flint, 1975, 109-11).

The inroads of Canadian culture, however, are not confined to schools and laws regarding land and military service. Through the *National Geographic* magazine or the *Reader's Digest* (to which the council does not object), the outside world enters into Hutterite consciousness. Radio, television and record players are not allowed, but are sometimes secretly listened to or watched in the teacher's house. Youngsters sometimes sneak into neighbouring towns to buy sweets and trinkets with money made from trapping (Hostetler and Huntington, 1967, 101). Yet they all feel guilty about these escapades, because the elect are supposed to be immune to the lures of the world.

INTERNAL THREATS TO HUTTERITE IDENTITY

It would be a fallacy to think that in its long history the Hutterite colonies succumbed only to the hostile forces of church and state. On the contrary. During long periods (for instance from 1819 to 1859 in the Ukraine) the principle of a community of goods was surrendered because of internal divisions within the colony. If anything, says Hostetler (1975, 117), it was the absence of persecution which "tended to maximize internal problems" during that period. The Hutterites themselves, however, blame the spirit of private property and individualism for the abandonment of communal living. The colony had prospered, and the various crafts (weaving, spinning, carpentry, shoemaking, blacksmithing, tailoring, etc.) had especially found a ready market for their goods in neighbouring towns. This had led to internal divisions according to income (not all of which was apparently handed over to the commune) and these divisions were aggravated by the antagonism between the preacher and his assistant. The solution would have been division into smaller colonies (thereby separating the contending parties) located further away from towns (thereby making separate access to markets difficult) and concentrated exclusively on farming (thereby increasing economic integration), but their "early experiences had made the Brethren fearful of innovating or branching out" (Ibid., 103).

After forty years (in 1859) the principle of a community of goods was re-established. Michael Waldner, a blacksmith and preacher known for his trances, inspired the return to the old Hutterite tradition. While in a deep coma he had a vision of an angel showing him heaven and hell. He himself was apparently destined for the latter, as the angel made it clear that only those who belonged to the saving ark or the saving remnant practising communism could enter the former. With his followers Waldner thereupon established a new community of goods, knitting it together with his visionary preaching.

Leadership and Hierarchy

Leadership can have an important effect on colony cohesion. Colonies sometimes disintegrate because of ineffective preachers who cannot stop competition and bickering between families or who drink too much (Ibid., 271). Leaders, however, are carefully chosen. Flint (1975, 32) describes elections at the Pincher Creek Colony in Alberta. Complete unanimity is required, he says, as each baptized member has knowledge of God and therefore no dissenting voice can be ignored. The minister is chosen by lot from those colony members who have received at least five votes.

Apart from the preacher, who is the main leader of the colony and presides at colony meetings, the colony steward (the economic boss), the field manager, often the German teacher and one or two foremen make up the council which makes all day-to-day decisions. Delinquents can be removed from office through appeal to an extra-colony council of ministers, but this proves to be rarely necessary. The hierarchy within each colony is constantly endorsed by the seating in the (usually) daily church services. The council members always sit in front facing the congregation. The leadership position of the preacher is acknowledged by his eating apart from all others. He uses this separation for individual discussions with members or guests.

The worshipping congregation is the vital instrument for mitigating tension and strengthening colony bonds. If the minister is a competent leader, he will not hesitate to censure individuals who breach the rules and cause tension by requesting that he or she stands during the church service, confess guilt or sit with the children. In more serious cases, such as instigating discord, members can be temporarily barred from church membership, are not allowed to shake hands with others and have to eat alone. Only in extreme cases is a person shunned or declared dead. This means that no one can communicate with him (Flint 1975, 22). Yet a competent minister will avoid censure as much as possible and will assure himself of complete community backing before disciplining fellow members. Resentment for unfair treatment can easily undermine the divinely ordained fellowship. To assure that no discontentment lingers, the community of saints is exhorted in the confession of faith (Rideman, 1950, 44) to forgive "here and in eternity" and to seal this promise with a handshake. By both observing the rules and insisting on the complete pardon leaders maximize the viability of their community.

Family Versus Communal Identity

Poor leadership and increase in family solidarity often go together in Hutterite society. When the communal fabric is weak families tend to fill the gap through stronger internal loyalties. More clearly defined boundaries between families seem to emerge naturally in such a situation. Even at the best of times brothers tend to support one another's recommendations to the council or to favour a father over a neighbour for a coveted position of authority. Or families take sides as to whether a new dining hall or a new barn should be constructed (Bennett 1967, 121). A cohesive commune has sufficient resources to counter such a trend, but a weak one has less resistance to nepotism or a power game between families.

Apart from poor leadership, dwindling opportunities for advancement within the Hutterite authority structure and fewer openings through lack of branching can contribute to family cohesion at the expense of the colony. Hostetler (1975, 272-3) observes: "Family loyalties tend to become stronger than colony loyalties when a colony is unable to satisfy the job aspirations of the younger male members of all families." This is all the more true if, as Bennett (1967, 118) notices, the family "sets up a barrier between the individual and his solidarity with the whole group."

The potential threat of family solidarity to Hutterite identity is countered by their extraordinary efforts to socialize and control the young and old separate from the family. From the age of two-and-a-half onwards, children learn, play, eat and worship separately from their parents. The parents themselves work, eat and worship separately from one another and from their children. In communal dininghalls, seating is according to age and sex. In the church services, men sit on the left and women on the right. The smallest children sit in the front, the older ones in the middle and the baptized members in the back. If someone is ill, his place remains open, indicating that the community rather than the family is incomplete. In Hutterite colonies, raising children is regarded as a communal responsibility, and, consequently ,family privacy is nonexistent. Nobody knocks on the door when visiting, and any adult will reprimand any child, if necessary.

In Hutterite history, periods in which communal cohesion was strong and family identity was weak alternated with periods in which family identity prevailed over the community of goods. Peter (1976, 339) detects five such alternating periods. From 1535 to 1685 the community of goods dominates the family; then, until 1761, the family dominates; following that time, the community of goods prevails until 1819, when a period of family supremacy follows. From 1860 until the present day, the practice of the first Christians to have everything in common is again followed to the letter.

Karl Peter associates periods of family domination with religious de-cline. This is hardly accurate. At all times Hutterite theology has sacralized both colony and family identity. Rideman, in his sixteenth century confes-sion of faith, uses as much space to prove the Christian foundation for a community of goods as he does to discuss Christian marriage. The latter, he says (p.98), is given from God. As a matter of fact, it even "instructeth and leadeth men to God"; and, to emphasize its God-given permanence, he underlines the sentence which occurs in all Christian wedding ceremonies: "What therefore God hath joined together, man should not sever."

Actual wedding ceremonies in Hutterite communities have many similarities with those of other Christians. Everywhere they detach bride and groom from existing family ties (the bride comes from another colony) and sacralize the new family unit. Hutterites have two ceremonies: one in the bride's colony and another one a few days later in the groom's church on a Sunday morning. The importance of the community is again shown in that the groom needs both the permission of the bride's parents and of her colony. Once permission has been granted, the engagement is announced in a church ceremony where vows are exchanged. The groom promises to be "a mirror and an example of honesty" so that both can live together as Christians. He also vows to sustain the bride "in health and in sickness, in love and in sorrow, never to leave her, until the Lord separates them through death." The bride makes the same promise and, in addition, vows to obey the husband (Hostetler 1975, 339-40). After this, the couple tours the colony and are toasted by every family. The bride is presented with many household goods and furnishings which she takes with her to the husband's colony.

A few days later, similar vows are exchanged in the groom's church. Here, the groom also promises not to insist that his wife must follow him if ever he leaves the community and the church. After the ceremony there is much feasting with a wedding cake, homemade wine and beer. The couple is then given a room in the parental apartment. Often this is the brideg-room's room from which the brothers have now been removed.

Although the separate wedding ceremony reinforces the family as an institution, the commune impinges by insisting that only baptized members can marry and by requiring community approval for the union. After the wedding there are no further rituals binding the family together: all rites are directed at the community, even though such popular pastimes as singing (no instruments!) can be done in the family context.

Personal Versus Communal Identity

Hutterites commonly see the threat to their colony cohesion coming less from the family than from the individual. All men have a tendency toward evil and pleasure in sin (Rideman, 1950, 57). Humans do not naturally seek God. They are deceitful and aggressive. They love what they should hate and hate what they ought to love. Only repentance, remorse and forgiveness can possibly save them from their sorry state (Ibid., 58-9). All this means that the community of believers would have been impossible if it had not been for Christ, who dwells in the believer's heart. Through this indwelling, every anxious, fearful, broken and contrite heart can find peace and comfort and participate in the fellowship of those who hear and observe the gospel and have all things in common (Ibid., 61, 43).

In actual practice, Hutterites load the dice against the individual in favour of the community. If the individual is saved, it is not his own doing, but Christ's who dwells in him and has gathered his disciples in the fellowship of the redeemed. The entire socialization process is geared to breaking the individual's self-will and controlling his impulses. This starts at a very early age (two and one-half to three years), when children begin to attend kindergarten for as long as eight to eleven hours daily. In the home, the child has been cuddled and coddled, but now the serious business of learning to obey and to fit in with others begins. Envy, vanity and self-assertion must be minimized, and, for the rest of the child's life, altruism, cooperation and congeniality are to be maximized. In all colonies, straps, willow branches or ladles are used for corporal punishment of the obstinate and disobedient.

Growing up in a Hutterite colony is synonymous with learning to accept discipline, so that finally, as full-fledged (baptized) members, they can "wait until God draweth them out and chooseth them" (Ibid., 80). Waiting for the Lord has two important advantages for the commune. The first one is that all members are attuned to a collective rather than a personal will. The second one is that those who may be elected for office (and Rideman is speaking about elections in the quoted passage) learn to accept responsibility without manipulating the inherent power for their personal aggrandisement. The theme of the individual part being welded into a close-knit fellowship also runs strongly in Rideman's section on the Lord's Supper (pp. 86-7). The body of Christ is represented by the loaf baked from many scattered and divided grains, and the blood of Christ is the wine made from many grapes all dissolved into one drink. This sixteenth century theme is taken up and elaborated by later Hutterite leaders, such as Ehrenpreis in the seventeenth century (Peters 1967, 24).

The high point of the long socialization process for the Hutterite is baptism. There are other milestones, such as the fifteenth birthday, when the individual joins the adults in the workforce and the eating hall; but voting, participation in the assembly and marriage are reserved only for those who are baptized. To be ready for baptism (girls are about nineteen and boys in their early twenties when they request it), candidates have to memorize the Apostles' Creed, hundreds of Bible verses and the answers to the many questions in the catechism. Even when a candidate for baptism is technically ready, the preacher may advise postponement. This happens particularly when the community feels that he or she is not sufficiently devoid of self-will. At the actual ceremony, usually on Palm Sunday, the individual consecrates, gives and sacrifices himself or herself to God, repents his sins, accepts brotherly punishment and admonition and promises to be obedient to Christ and his church. He is then sprinkled with water by the minister and his assistant.

Baptism is a watershed for the local community of believers. It unconditionally and solemnly seals the collective will in the minds and hearts of the members. Escapades into town, listening to the transistor radio and even temporary defections can be forgiven as sowing one's oats in adolescence. After baptism, however, transgressions of this kind are much more serious. Then defection becomes apostasy, and an individual is regarded to be irretrievably lost, as there is no hope of heaven outside the church.

Defection, to the Hutterite, is the severest threat to internal cohesion. It is a slap in the face, an open rejection of a carefully nurtured and diligently maintained unity. It is a tear in the social fabric, in that self-will proves to have triumphed over self-denial, the cornerstone of their communal existence. The colonies have a theological defense against the defections, which tend to be rare in healthy colonies. They point to the constant watchfulness which Christians have to maintain to keep the devil from infiltrating. Leaving the colony is a surrender to sin. Yet sin is man's normal condition, and therefore the faithful must be all the more grateful that God's grace has protected them so far. In actual fact, however, individual aberration is an overly simple explanation of apostasy. Hostetler (1975, 273) adduces good evidence that the defection rate is strongly associated with (a) dying, or declining, colonies in which there are unresolved leadership problems and bitter disputes with minister or manager, and (b) unequal access to position of authority through nepotism. Individuals can change little about either situation. If anything, lesser defection in the more cohesive colonies shows that strongly knit collective units have a remarkable viability even in those advanced countries which idolize the opposite: rational individualism and self-realization.

Apostasy is like death to the Hutterite. In both cases, a valued member has departed and the community feels incomplete. The important difference is that the baptized defector denies himself entrance into heaven, whereas the faithful departed will join the "more perfect communal living in heaven" (Ibid., 251).

Funeral services are very simple. A plain wooden coffin is usually made by the colony carpenter. The deceased is dressed in a white shirt (for men) or a plain black or blue dress (for women). In the olden days, graves used to be unmarked, to emphasize the lack of importance of the earthly resting place as compared with the eternal abode in paradise. Nowadays, however, each colony usually has its own cemetery and provides each grave with a tombstone. The period of mourning, the burial service and the meal afterwards all assist the community to slowly come to terms with the gap in its midst and to gradually regain its erstwhile viability. In life, as well as death, communal identity must persevere over personal identity.

Because self-expression, personal initiative, anger, and hostility have to be repressed for the sake of communal unity, psychologists and other mental health experts assume that there must be persistent personality disorders in Hutterite communities. To some of them it has come as a surprise that abnormalities are less frequent than in a normal population. Hutterites have proved to have far fewer symptoms of psychosis and schizophrenia. Yet there is a disease which the communities call *Anfechtung* (German for temptation). Its symptoms are a strong sense of having sinned, a powerful feeling of guilt and a tendency to withdraw. As articulation of sin and instilling of guilt feelings are prerequisites for group maintenance, Anfechtung can be expected. The problem, apparently, is that the compensating joy of God's grace and forgiveness is not experienced, and Hutterite preachers relieve this manic-depressive condition through private counselling and praying. Sometimes an appropriate sermon is read at a service for the restoration of health. Kaplan and Plaut (1956, 104), who investigated the mental health of Hutterites in South Dakota, therefore drew the firm conclusion that social harmony and conformity was "not paralleled by a similar harmony at the level of personality."

SUMMARY

The Hutterite colonies in Canada are an almost perfect example of a well-bounded group successfully warding off the inroads of other forms of identity. Their theology and strong commitment to biblical antecedents (pacifism, adult baptism, communism) sacralize the community, which thinks of itself as the elect remnant in an evil world. Sin and evil do not just reside in the enveloping Canadian culture, with all its idolatries, uncongenial laws, watered down, yet respectable, Christianity, the titillating tidbits of the mass media and hedonism gone berserk; they also exist right at the heart of the colony, in the hearts of the individual, for whom greed, self-will, aggression and lust come more naturally than altruism, self-denial, submission and discipline. The only safeguard which the elect have, therefore, is the actual working of Christ and the Holy Spirit within the community so that the evil from both without and within can be rendered innocuous.

The community goes to extraordinary lengths to maximize the impact of the theological variable through a process of life-long socialization culminating in baptism. Contriteness of heart and the surrender of the self to Christ and the community He rules are thereby made into a prerequisite for marriage. This, in turn, disciplines the ever-present potential of the family to become a strong competitor for the basic loyalties of the colony members. Yet, both in the 450-year history of the Hutterite community and in the present, family solidarity proves, and has proved, to be a ready alternative to the community of goods.

CHAPTER 6

THE DOUKHOBORS

In contrast with the Hutterites, the Doukhobors have less successfully battled the external and internal threats to their corporate existence. Their history has been one of many splits and much factional strife. Yet, like the Hutterites, they have again and again drawn on the resources of their theological traditions for a remarkable resurgence of sectarian vitality. Against considerable odds, and in spite of exile and martyrdom, the strongly held religious views of Doukhobor remnants endured. Often, corporate cohesion actually improved when adversity reached a climax.

The origins of Doukhobor religion are shrouded in mystery. The first generations of Doukhobors consisted of illiterate Russian peasants who were more interested in expressing their dislike of the ornate, priest-ruled, liturgical state religion of Orthodoxy than in writing history.

All through Russian history there had been protests of the Doukhobor kind. In 1654 Patriarch Nikon carried out liturgical reforms, against which the Old Believers protested. The Doukhobors, however, were much more radical. They rejected almost everything Orthodoxy stood for: the historical Christ, the Bible, the Church. Instead, they made God's dwelling in the heart central. They have more in common with a pious hermit and mystic, Danelo Filipovitch, who lived around the turn of the sixteenth century. It was he who threw the Scriptures and church liturgies into the Volga and declared that henceforth the source of truth lay in the Living Book, the Holy Spirit. (Doukhobors, to this day, use the term Living Book and apply it to the recitation of memorized portions of hymns, psalms and traditional lore.) Danelo Filipovitch subsequently declared himself to be God and nominated Ivan Souslof to be his son, Christ (Maude 1970, 99). Doukhobors have similarly tended to divinize their leaders.

The name Doukhobor ("spirit wrestler") first emerged around the turn of the seventeenth century when the Russian Orthodox Church began to use the word for those whom it contemptuously thought to be "wrestlers against

the Spirit." Ever since then, the sect has adopted the term for itself, turning
its meaning around to "those who fight with the Spirit of Truth." The first
recognizable leader was Sylvan Kolesnikof, who lived in the southern parts
of the Ukraine in the third quarter of the eighteenth century and taught his
followers to "bow to the God in one another," as each represented an image
of God on earth (Ibid., 114). Another leader later in the eighteenth century
was Ilarion Pobirohin. He claimed to be Christ and composed hymns with
anarchistic and pacifistic themes for the Living Book. He taught that God
had created man in order to provide His Spirit with a body. After his exile to
Siberia, Savely Kapustin took over the leadership and proved to be as
eloquent as he was charismatic. He is remembered in the Doukhobor oral
tradition as the lawgiver who established the principle of hereditary leadership. He, too, was regarded as Christ, as were those who followed him after
his death. Under the enlightened rule of Czar Alexander I, the Doukhobors
were allowed to settle in a fertile frontier region north of the Crimea.

During the first quarter of the nineteenth century the Doukhobor
villages prospered. Their inhabitants were industrious, drank sparingly and
were exempt from military service. They had everything in common and
made all decisions in the *sobranya*, a meeting in which all adults (men and
women) took part. The sobranya would begin with the chanting of hymns
around a table carrying the symbols of life: water, bread and salt. This
would set the stage for the business meeting. Everyone was allowed to speak
(each possessing the divine spark) and unanimity was required (God's Spirit
could not be divided). It was therefore important that a deep sense of
Christian fellowship and goodwill be established as a preliminary to decision
making (Woodcock and Avakumovic 1977, 43).

Soon, however, things began to deteriorate. Already in 1816 there was
little left of the communist experiment. The best land had been allotted to
Kapustin's relatives and other powerful families, and Kapustin's successors
proved to be drunkards and degenerates. Beginning in 1841, the
Doukhobor colonies were exiled to a new frontier in Transcaucasia, danger-
ously close to hostile Moslem Tartars. Yet, exile, pilgrimages and new
beginnings seemed to fit the Doukhobor way of life. They prospered again
in their new mountainous environment.

In 1886 a bitter dispute arose over leadership. Peter Vaselivich Verigin
had been the choice of the poor, the pious and the young, but he was exiled
by the czarist authorities who backed a much smaller party of well-to-do
Doukhobors. In his place of exile in northern Russia, Verigin met a number
of Tolstoy's disciples and began to read Tolstoy's works. This, together
with his reflections on the New Testament and Doukhobor tradition,
resulted in a steady stream of directives to the followers in Transcaucasia.
They were to return to Christian communism (which some of the settlements did), they were to refrain from eating meat (as it was wrong not only
to kill humans but animals as well), they were to give up drinking and
smoking; later, he also advised them to refrain from sexual intercourse for
the duration of the troubles with the authorities.

There was no letup of troubles, for, in 1894, Czar Nicholas II demanded the oath of allegiance, which Verigin and his followers refused to take. Things went from bad to worse when the Doukhobors also began to reject military service much more firmly. In 1895 they burned all weapons in huge bonfires. This led to further persecution, exile and the widespread atrocities still vividly remembered in the opening hymn of present-day sobranyas, "Sleep on, you brave fighting eagles," which "has inspired many a latter-day Doukhobor to choose a path of rebellion and imprisonment" (Ibid., 103). Yet the Doukhobors suffered their ordeal stoically, for, as Kapustin's hymn in the Living Book reminded them constantly, martyrdom was the sign of the end of the age when Christ would be restored to full kingship and they would be vindicated. From his new place of exile in northern Siberia, Verigin reinforced their determination by sending a message that under no circumstance were they to obey the earthly rulers. They had to suffer with Christ. However much their bodies were crushed, their spirits were invulnerable.

For many of them, these sufferings came to an end in 1899 when, through the intervention of Tolstoy and the English Quakers, 7,427 Doukhobors arrived in Saskatchewan and settled there. At least 12,000 were still left behind in Russia, but these were generally people who had made their peace with the government, or had refused to follow some or all of the Verigin directives. Those who came were warmly welcomed by the Canadian government, which was keen to settle the uninhabited frontier with industrious farmers. They were expressly exempt from military service.

EXTERNAL THREATS

In the first few years of settlement in what subsequently became Saskatchewan, administrative and cultural threats seemed to be miniscule. The Doukhobors were on their own in virgin territory. They built fifty-seven villages, naming them after the Russian communities they had left behind. Thirteen of these were in the North Colony and thirty-four in the South Colony, both close to what is now the central east border of Saskatchewan. There was another colony, 300 miles further west, near Prince Albert, where ten villages were established. This proved to be the wealthiest, as its inhabitants had been least persecuted in Russia and had been able to bring some capital with them. Yet all settlements eked out a precarious existence in that first year. Loghouses were built, but some of them housed as many as fourteen families, one large bunk for each. The ploughing began soon after arrival. Reminiscent of the Caucasian custom of twenty-four virgins hitching themselves to the plough and cutting a single furrow around the community at midnight to keep evil away, so here, twenty-four women dragged the plough through prairie's virgin land (Ibid., 162).

Everything was held in common, but already some of Verigin's proscriptions (he himself was still in exile in Siberia) began to be abandoned.

The North Colony began to liberalize the vegetarian rules by using the fish abundantly available in the adjoining Swan River. Many Doukhobors also began to earn money by working on farms and on the Canadian Northern Railway, and this led to intracolony jealousies, one village accusing the other of not pulling its weight sufficiently. This problem was resolved by allowing the village rather than the colony to become the commune. The ban on sexual relations was also lifted and the population began to increase rapidly.

Land Registration and Naturalization

After a few years, prosperity began to reign; but, simultaneously, pressures increased to swear an oath of allegiance to the king, in order that individual title could be given to the land. The Prince Albert Doukhobors had no qualms with these pressures. Most of them had already begun to farm their land independently, anyway. Those who had not given up communism were invited, in 1906, to join the South Colony. Here, and in the North Colony, the resentment against government regulations began to rise. The settlers felt that swearing an oath and individual landownership clashed with Christian principles. They were also afraid that naturalization would lead to conscription, to which they were even more opposed. From 1909 onwards, thousands left Saskatchewan for the Kootenay Valley in the south-eastern part of British Columbia, where their leader, Peter Vaselivich Verigin (who had been freed from his Siberian exile in 1902), had bought extensive landholdings.

The teachings of the Living Book, reinforced by the sobranyas, strengthened Doukhobor resolve to oppose Canadian regulations. A small radical section, the *Svobodniki*, or Sons of Freedom, had been foremost in the refusal to register their land, and they began to gain more influence during the crisis. Setting off on a pilgrimage to meet Christ, they travelled all the way to Fort William on Lake Superior, where they paraded in the nude on New Year's Day, confirming their disdain for all material possessions. Via a number of prisons, they eventually returned to the colonies. For several generations, the Doukhobors, in general, and the Sons of Freedom, in particular, continued to think of the Soviet Union rather than Canada as their home, and several schemes for return migration were considered. They all came to naught, partly because the communists persecuted their fellow believers. At present, even Sons of Freedom have title to their own blocks of land, on which they often build substantial houses.

Education

Land registration and naturalization were not the only areas where Doukhobors felt threatened. British Columbia required children between

the ages of seven and fourteen to attend school. Doukhobors were traditionally illiterate and felt learning to be both unnecessary and detrimental to the
faith. To them it was sufficient that, from an early age, children memorized
the hymns, psalms and catechism of the Living Book. In the catechism
(Herbison 1968, 554) the question was put: "Why do you not go to English
school and learn?"; the answer: "Your school teaches children to participate
in war and kill one another."

The Doukhobors did cooperate on the school issue originally, but when,
in 1912, four of their members were sentenced to prison for failing to
register a death, a special sobranya was convened which decided to withdraw their hundreds of children from the schools in Brilliant and Grand
Forks. A reconciliation of sorts was achieved, but tension about education
and registration continued to simmer. In 1923, as many as ten schools were
burned in the Brilliant district (Woodcock and Avakumovic 1977, 255).
Later in the decade, most Doukhobors began to cooperate fully with the
school authorities, but the radical Sons of Freedom thought otherwise.
They felt ever more strongly that Christ's return was at hand and that if they
were to be found unblemished by their Lord, the satanic teaching of the
government schools had to be eradicated. They began to forcibly remove
their children from the schools and responded with nude marches when the
police tried to make arrests.

Burning schools or withdrawing children from school became more rare
in subsequent decades. Yet, in 1953, there was a new rash of nude pilgrimages and fires in response to both a toughening stand of the authorities and
internal disputes amongst the Sons of Freedom. One hundred and forty-
eight adults were sentenced to three years in jail, and their children were
made wards of the state and housed in an unused sanatorium in New
Denver. Until the end of the decade their numbers were augmented by
other children of the Sons of Freedom who refused to go to school and were
caught in dawn raids or tracked in the woods where they were hidden. The
parents made several pilgrimages to New Denver, singing psalms in front of
the tall wire fences. They continued this practice until 1959 when they
promised to send their children to school if they were released. This indeed
happened, and in the next decade the children at Krestova (the major Sons
of Freedom village) had "a record of school attendance better than that of
the non-Doukhobor children in the neighbourhood" (Ibid., 355). In actual
fact, through the schools and higher education, Canadian culture has now
successfully penetrated Doukhobor culture. Through cultural assimilation
of the offspring of even the most radical Sons of Freedom and through the
lure of post-war affluence, Doukhobor identity has diminished considerably.

Pacifism

Closest to the Doukhobor heart was pacifism. It had been the express
exemption from military service which had attracted them to Canada in

1898. The promise was honoured during World War I, although there were local incidents with zealous magistrates imprisoning Doukhobors for not presenting themselves for military service. After angry marches and Doukhobor threats to burn their own possessions and crops, Ottawa intervened, and the prisoners were released. At the end of the war, when resentment against war profiteers was at its height, returned soldiers in the Kootenays demanded deportation of the Doukhobors to Russia and disposal of their land to the Soldier's Settlement Board. Since material possessions were not that precious to the Doukhobors anyway, Verigin at first inclined to dispose of the land, but the federal government declared that the Board had no right to carry out expropriations.

During World War II, pressures again increased on Doukhobor pacifism. Registration for military service was compulsory, and the Selective Service Act could direct the employment of all residents. Some politicians, such as John Diefenbaker whose constituency was at Prince Albert in Saskatchewan, insisted on revoking Doukhobor exemption from military service, but the government of the day again honoured its 1898 promise. A number of Sons of Freedom were jailed for refusing to register, but most Doukhobors consented to the compulsory registration. They balked, however, when it came to alternate service required of conscientious objectors. Gathering at Brilliant, B.C., on December 12, 1943, 3500 members were even more determined not to cooperate with the Selective Services Act. They gave a thunderous "No" to the official who presented an ultimatum compelling employment according to war-time priorities. The Sons of Freedom, always acting as the radical Doukhobor conscience, reinforced the determination by burning that same night the jam factory, once the pride of sectarian industry. And this was only the beginning of their religious disdain for anything to do with man's government and his miserable possessions. Nearby at Krestova, women's clothing and jewellery were burnt. John J. Verigin's house was put to the torch, two schools were destroyed and the Canadian Pacific Railway station at Appledale was reduced to a heap of rubble. Yet all this action was as much a counter to prevailing prosperity due to Doukhobor industry as it was an affirmation of pacifist principles. In contrast with the Doukhobor remnants in the Soviet Union who serve in the Red Army, the brethren in Canada have been accorded conscientious objector status up to the present day.

INTERNAL THREATS

Since the Doukhobors' arrival in Canada, their communitarian ideal has suffered probably more than that of any other group. In the beginning, everything was held in common. In the 1950s, only a tiny group of Sons of Freedom, led by a distant relative of the Verigins, Michael Orekoff, practised communism in Hilliers, not far from Qualicum Beach on Vancouver Island. The group, like their prophet, (now called Michael the Archangel) who died in 1951, believed that the Second Coming was near at hand and that Hilliers was the New Jerusalem where the 144,000 of the elect would gather at the end of time (Ibid., 325).

To some extent, the threat to communitarian ideals came from the Canadian culture, which took individual ownership of land for granted as the only form of ownership. Yet within the year of arrival in Canada, and before land registration became a serious issue, approximately one-third of the settlers farmed their sections on an individual basis. To work for the survival and betterment of oneself and one's family was a stronger motive than to labour for the common good. In the past, strong leadership had kept natural selfishness at bay, and also in Canada, leadership proved to be crucial for the maintenance of Doukhobor integrity.

Leadership

Deification of leaders and formation of dynasties has always been the Doukhobor response to the anarchic implications of their social and religious convictions. In a situation where one is against any government interference and religious formalism and one relies on the guidance of the Holy Spirit alone, integrity is considerably enhanced if that Spirit is concretely represented in a person. This is all the more true when the sect consists of illiterate peasants for whom western forms of rational individualism are totally foreign.

Peter Vaselivich Verigin (1859-1924) had carried the mantle of divine leadership long before the arrival of the Doukhobors in Canada. His suggestions had been law. He was a tall, good-looking man with a commanding personality, and, as his predecessors had been, he was looked upon as the Christ. When in 1902 he was allowed to join his fellow believers in Canada, he soon united the quarrelling followers. He made triumphal visits to the villages, accompanied by the choir of virgins who were being trained in the large headquarters, and the villagers greeted him with psalms and vegetarian repasts. He reinforced communal living, but relaxed the rules about animals not being used for labour. Soon he began to push for extensive farm mechanization, the capital for which came from the income of the more than 1,000 Doukhobors building the railway. The women, children and older men were left to run the farms. The outside income went to each village according to the number of railway workers. Community decisions were made in the sobranya, an elder assuming the responsibility of carrying them out, taking the contributions to the general fund and getting supplies from the general store in return. Waking time in the villages was about 5 a.m., when a choir "singing in the street would take the place of a waking bell, and at night the same choir would sing the equivalent of a vesper hymn to mark the day's end" (Ibid., 199).

The idyll of self-contained village life supported by a charismatic leader overseeing it all did not last long, if it ever existed. Apart from the land registration and naturalization issues mentioned already, Verigin's policies had their own, hidden, identity-destroying consequences. Both mechanization and working away from the village tend to bring the outside world within the boundary of a precarious commune. Values and norms about individual pay for individual achievement, about the desirability of creature comforts, and about competition rather than cooperation infiltrate rather easily through increasing contacts with a virile, confident frontier culture. In the long run, neither the sobranyas and other religious meetings nor charismatic leadership could stand up to the threat of an alien culture. If the Hutterites, through long experience and many setbacks managed to do so, it was partly with the aid of rural exclusivity. But Verigin (the Lordly, as he was now generally called) could not halt the slide into independence of a considerable number of Doukhobors, even if he succeeded in moving the commune-oriented ones to the Kootenays in British Columbia. The religiously motivated pilgrimages and migrations certainly had a retarding effect on the disintegration of the communal ideals, but in the new settlements they, too, ultimately failed.

In 1913, Verigin cut off all intercourse with the Independents in Saskatchewan, as he was afraid that their ideas might catch on in British Columbia; but the rot had set in. When Peter the Lordly was killed under mysterious circumstances in a train explosion in 1924, the Sons of Freedom were prominent suspects. Peter the Lordly was succeeded by his son Peter Petrovich Verigin (1880-1939), who was still in the Soviet Union at the time. The son, like his father, had considerable charismatic and management gifts, but had an unfortunate penchant for drinking and gambling which got him into much trouble with the law, even though the Doukhobors tended to overlook any flaws in their Christ.

It was during the regime of Peter Petrovich Verigin (or the Purger, as he was also called) that the ideal of communal ownership began to erode. First came a system of assessments whereby each family (all Doukhobors were divided into eighty "families," each with about 100 men, women and children) had to pay a certain amount of money to the central organization. This meant that now men who worked outside could keep whatever they earned over and above the assessment. Also, it was the family which was responsible for collecting the assessed amounts and for selling crops and other products to the central organization. In Saskatchewan and Alberta this assessment was based on acreage. During the Depression, the central organization, managed by the whimsy and extravagance of Peter the Purger, became insolvent, in spite of the large amounts borrowed from the savings of individual Doukhobors. Unemployment, diminishing income and assessments, the destruction of saw and flour mills by the radical Sons of Freedom all contributed to the bankruptcy of 1938. In order to prevent eviction, the British Columbia government took over all Doukhobor lands and buildings in that state and charged the occupants a nominal rent, reducing them to tenants. After World War II, these properties were offered back for sale.

When Peter the Purger died of cancer in 1939, his son Peter Iastrebov (the Hawk) Verigin, born in 1904, was chosen as his successor. However, he never reached Canada, but died in the Stalinist camps. A grandson of Peter Petrovich, assuming the name of John J. Verigin, took over some of the leadership responsibilities, but never, even after his formal recognition in 1960, did he acquire both the status and stature of his ancestors. Doukhobor cohesion and leadership crumbled together.

The Sons of Freedom by now had their own leader, Stefan Sorokin, who had fled Russia in 1929 and had belonged to a large variety of sects before becoming attracted to the Doukhobors. In the early 1950s, he became the dominant influence among the Sons of Freedom, who accepted him as the lost Peter Iastrebov; however, this influence was dissipated when he stayed in Uruguay, where he had gone to start a new colony.

Factions and Families

Whenever leadership was absent or weak, Doukhobor society tended to splinter. While Peter Vaselivich Verigin was exiled in northern Russia and ruled the Doukhobors by messages, his followers split into the Fasters (those who adhered to his command to abstain from alcohol and tobacco) and the Butchers, who were less inclined to deny themselves some pleasures in life. They were also called the Mad and the Bad Doukhobors. Further splits occurred when Verigin ordered a halt to sexual intercourse. And then there was the small party which had not accepted Verigin's leadership from the very beginning. Soon after arrival in Canada, the Doukhobors split into Independents and Communitarians, according to whether or not they ran their farms individually or communally. Within five years of arrival, the most radical Doukhobors began to form the Svobodniki, or Sons of Freedom.

Splintering was made all the easier when there were no communal restraints on the inevitable bickering and envy of neighbours and families. Already in Russia, unequal power and wealth had riven communities and bolstered family cohesion at the expense of the community. This oscillation of fissioning and fusing in personal, family and communal identities continued in Canada. Yet the common faith and the constant reminders of the ancestral martyrs countered at least some of these internal threats to cohesion. The sobranya (generally, "assembly," but Doukhobors mix business with the singing of psalms and hymns around the tables with the symbols of life) commonly begins with a song about the cruel tortures in the Siberian plains, the heavenly rewards gained by the martyrs "sleeping in the arms of the Lord," the resolve to follow in the footsteps of those who suffered "so we could journey ahead," and to overcome all temptation and "follow Christ and His word." The sobranya concludes with a song stressing the calm and the peace of the participants now going home with the good lessons of the meeting in their hearts.

Similar themes of unity in the face of an evil world pervades the *molenye* (Sunday morning worship service). Singing the Living Book is an important part of these services. One of the main anthems (Hawthorn 1955, 258) reminds the congregation that it has broken away from the old world of creeds and laws to follow only the crucified King. Doukhobors do not need mansions or thrones or prisons. They only want to forge cannons into plowshares and swords into hoes and wait for the world of deceit and corruption to come to an end. Heaven is for those who are pure and suffer faithfully and not for the wicked, who are greedy and jealous.

Yet the impressive unity of faith was often not enough to prevent that very greed and jealousy from creeping into day-to-day communal relations. With the exception of a few traditions, such as pacifism, and the rejection of a corrupt world, most other beliefs (for instance regarding communalism, vegetarianism, government relations) tended to become relativized by the all-pervasive anarchic strain. The latter facilitated a floating adjustability to prevailing power constellations. Wealthier families and diplomatic individuals could bend the consensus in the direction of their own preferences, expectations and goals.

Seating arrangements at Doukhobor meetings express the importance of families. In religious assemblies the sexes are separated, but kin tends to cluster. Whenever the sexes are not segregated, as, for instance, at festivals, families sit and participate together. At these occasions, each settlement region has its own place, but within each there is a specific permanent place for each family relative to all the rest (Mealing 1980, 185).

Rites of passage, as all other formalisms, are frowned upon. And yet they have always existed and have become more elaborate in latter days. They generally consolidate existing or new families. Birthrites consist of a simple naming of the child after birth. Doukhobors believe (Ibid., 186) that the baby has no soul until it has absorbed the Living Book and that the soul enters during this period of learning from the sixth to the fifteenth year. Baptizing a child is unbecoming for a Christian, Doukhobors believe. An adult baptizes himself with the word of truth (Novitsky in Maude 1970, 17).

Marriage ceremonies must be avoided, according to Doukhobor faith. Sacraments and ceremonies are offensive to God, and therefore it must be sufficient for the couple to be united in love, to have the consent of the parents and to make an "inward" vow before all-seeing God to remain faithful and inseparable to the end of days (Ibid.). In actual fact, even in the older, simpler days, Doukhobor marriage was a genuine rite of passage, clearly involving the stripping of a previous identity and the sacralization of a new one. At the wedding the groom's parents visit those of the bride and ask if there are objections to the marriage. If there are none, they place bread and salt on the table where the hosts have already put a jug of water, symbolizing the gathering of the symbols of life from two distinct sources. Both groups of parents then ask the couple whether they love one another, after which the couple, replying in the affirmative, ask for the benediction. After the blessing the partners kiss one another and bow to the feet of both parents (Dixon 1955, 190). With progressive Canadianization, Doukhobor weddings have become more elaborate with toasts, gift-giving, dancing and drinking, white gowns, and the cutting of the wedding cake in a large community hall rather than the home (Lewis in Hawthorn 1955, 278; Mealing 1980, 188-90).

Death is another threat to both communal and family integrity. Wakes and funerals in any society repair the tear in the social fabric and restore family and community to its normal operation. Doukhobor society is no exception. After death the body is prepared and put in a simple coffin. While visitors stream in, there is much chanting and weeping around the ceremonial table with the symbols of life. There is an abundance of food and prayers and chants are said in between the courses (Lewis in Hawthorn 1955, 267). The entire community is present at the burial. The coffin is respectfully lowered into the grave in the unkept graveyard. A few simple words and Bible verses (e.g., "Dust we are made of, we go back to dust") are spoken by the elder, then the grave is filled while the women sing. Afterwards there is some more fellowship around the table, helping the bereaved family to feel carried by the sympathies of the community.

More recently (Mealing 1980, 192ff.) the body tends to be taken to the community hall, where all-night vigils, psalm-singing, and entertaining of visitors takes place. Also, in contrast with the past, an undertaker is employed to make all the arrangements. A number of sittings of an elaborate meal are served after the funeral. It is an age-old Doukhobor custom to have a commemoration service at the grave six weeks after death, for Doukhobors believe that it takes the soul about forty days (the time between the resurrection and ascension of Jesus) to depart and arrive in Heaven. There is another formal meal after the commemoration service.

For a long time Doukhobors refused to register births, marriages and deaths with the authorities. Here, too, accommodation has taken place and the simple Doukhobor marriages are now recognized as fulfilling the requirements of the various provincial laws.

Individualism

Corporate identity remains fragile unless the membership is prepared to sacrifice a hefty dose of personal self-determination. There are both theological and economic justifications for individual autonomy in the Doukhobor society. The Russian scholar Orest Novitsky, who wrote a dissertation on the Doukhobor beliefs in Kiev in 1832, explained that, to Doukhobors, only the Christ within is the true priest. "In whomever Christ lives, he is Christ's heir, and is himself a priest unto himself" (Maude 1970, 16). And this means rejection of any external authority, including the church as the community of believers. One's own experience is superior to any other authority (Herbison 1968, 540).

Theoretically this makes any group effort perilous and unstable. Yet

Doukhobors are quite capable of corporate action (communal arson, nude demonstrations, pilgrimages). They run farmers' cooperatives and acknowledge charismatic leadership of elders. This inconsistency is sometimes attributed to Doukhobor illiteracy and irrationality. In actual fact, theology and action are consistent. The indwelling Christ represents an important social component which makes the individual constantly sensitive to peer pressures. Christ is one and the Christ within others is the same as the Christ of ego. This belief is central to the smooth functioning of the sobranya and to the unanimous decisions reached at the meetings. Individualism is not asserted, but surrendered. Herbison (1968 546), as a Quaker, innately understands this process:

> The effectiveness of the *sobranya* lies not in a building, which is unnecessary; not in ritual, which is minimal; not in preaching, which is incidental; not in personal communications and prayers, for which there is no provision; and not in the heightened sensitivity of mind and heart reaching for truth, because this is not characteristic. The *sobranya* is a settling-down into the past, an immersion of self into the group. The singing at a *sobranya* is monotonous, persistent, inescapable; it is vocal magic which takes the place of other forms and determinants of unity.

The uncritical immersion of self in the group runs closely parallel to the uncritical acceptance of verdicts, prescriptions and proscriptions of the leadership. It was in the leader that the Doukhobor saw the same Christ who dwelt in his own heart, and the unworthiness, perversion, or immorality of the leaders could therefore in no way unsettle a deeply felt trust and faith. The Christ within each and the more pronounced Christ in the leaders was, after all, only an extension of the Christ of the Living Book and the tradition. The gradual accommodation to Canadian society and the corresponding secularization of Doukhoborism has of necessity eroded the divinity of the leadership. It has also made the individual less submissive and passive and more spontaneous and aggressive. Consequently, defections from the Doukhobor fold are now easier, and these, in turn, erode the corporate identity still further. Yet the increasing search for havens of group security in Canadian society, together with the prevailing nostalgia for traditions of the past, counter the erosion.

The economic justification for individual autonomy is strong and powerful. Already two years after the arrival in Canada, prosperity became visible everywhere. The 1901 harvest had been very good and outside income had improved greatly. Yet this also led to greater pressure on the communal system, and in 1902 zealots began to urge a return to the sacrifices which Verigin demanded. All animal labour was renounced, everything made of leather and metal objects was burned or discarded. A pilgrimage was begun and aborted, but not after villages had been deserted and possessions (shoes, socks, shirts) had been discarded. Presently, most

Doukhobors work in local industry and trade where individual effort and skill are differentially rewarded. Again and again friction arose within the sect because individual members were not happy to part with the money they earned on the outside or because they refused to pay the annual assessments (Tarasoff 1969, 32-3). The lure of comfort and consumer goods in both the Russian and Canadian period of existence was a forceful counterpull to the ascetic principles central to Doukhobor identity. The nude demonstrations, the burning of possessions, the civil disobedience were ever so many attempts to deny the importance of earthly goods and power; yet they were also naive. Individuals working outside the fold inevitably compared themselves with other workers and began to adopt standards of comparison other than those prevailing in the sectarian community. Doukhobors never sufficiently understood that negative anarchism was an insufficient shield against the corruption of the world. They brought a tradition of rural self-sufficiency and a belief in the mystical role of land with them from Russia (Jamieson 1955, 45). Yet they gave this up, partly because in the early beginnings cash was needed desparately for becoming established, partly because Peter Vaselivich Verigin needed capital for his mechanization and industrial schemes. And so the intertwining of a forceful, individualistic, comfort-craving Canadian culture and an otherworldly, communal, comfort-denying Russian sect perilously threatened the survival of the latter. Still, the dominant culture has undergone its own metamorphosis and is presently much less sure of itself than in the beginning of this century. There is therefore no reason to think that, in the future, elaborate Doukhobor plans for a gradual return to communal living, such as the ones drawn up in 1961-1963 must be doomed. The number of burnings, nude demonstrations, and hunger strikes in prison was decisively smaller in the seventies as compared with the sixties (Woodcock and Avakumovic 1977, xii). Yet, in a free and pluralistic Canadian society, the possibility of an anti-material resurgence can never be dismissed out of hand.

SUMMARY

If one can rely on the census figures, the Doukhobors population in Canada reached its peak in 1941 with 16,878 members. The figures have dropped ever since. The latest available figures (from the 1981 census) show that, at that time, only 6,700 inhabitants of Canada thought of themselves as Doukhobors. The figure was 9,170 in 1971. The drop is caused by a number of factors. Education has propelled grandchildren and great-grandchildren of the original 7,427 settlers up the ladder of mobility and away from the peasant way of life. City life and mixed marriages have further weakened the ties with a sect the very existence of which presupposes that the civilized world is a den of iniquity. By moving away from its rural, self-sufficient shelter, and by making itself dependent upon income from the very culture it was supposed to despise, Doukhoborism allowed itself to be perverted by the values and material goals of its archenemies, the state, the governmental authorities, and consumer society. It was led like a lamb to the slaughter.

Most of the principles (pacifism being a notable exception) the Doukhobors possessed when they fled their country of origin and persecution have been surrendered: having all goods in common, vegetarianism, teetotalism, non-smoking. Instead of rebelling against the wicked world and evil authorities (they liked to compare themselves with a *plakoon trava*, a weed which flows against the current), they began to flow with the current. For several generations a militant minority, the *Svobodniki*, or Sons of Freedom, attempted to halt the process. At times of backsliding, compromise with authorities, and accommodation with an independent membership, they were ready to cast off all possessions and to shake the dust off their feet, as Jesus had clearly advised his disciples to do. The move to British Columbia succeeded, but many other marches came to nothing and the nude pilgrims usually landed in prison rather than in the promised land.

The boundaries around Doukhobor identity have been slowly eroded, even though their mystical, anti-church, anti-Bible, anti-creed form of Christianity kept them in as decent repair as it could. And yet Doukhobor anti-materialism had much in common with the large anti-material segments of Canadian youth. What is more, an anomic Western culture seems to cry out for strong havens of meaning and belonging which can halt its slide into collapse and begin revitalization from within. So far, however, Doukhoborism in Canada does not seem to have grasped the new opportunities as the older generation, at least, is too attached to the Russian peasant heritage and language.

PART III

SECTS AND NEW RELIGIONS

With few exceptions, sects and new religious movements erect strong boundaries around themselves. They dig the deepest possible moat between themselves and other units of social organization. This is not true for all of them, however. A number of new religious movements, such as Transcendental Meditation, The Institute of Applied Metaphysics (IAM), Mind Awareness and People Searching Inside (PSI), are essentially self-help organizations and fit in with the modern stress on self-realization and self-affirmation. In other words, they concentrate on "sacralizing" the self and so accord with important segments of Western culture. Actually it makes good sense not to use "sects" for these groups and to reserve the word for those which stand over against society.

By contrast, the great majority of sects and new religious movements regard society, the self, and similar competitors for strong loyalty (such as the family and other religious bodies), with deep suspicion. They insist on being what sociologists call "total" organizations, that is to say, organizations with a totally committed membership. Their uncompromising stance makes them loath to fit with the other "systems" in a society. And yet they often defend the very values of thrift, decency, responsibility and reliability so important for the smooth functioning of that society. They particularly appeal to those for whom society at large is uncongenial, in contrast with churches and denominations which are essentially congruous with and congenial to the social whole.

Because the status quo is uncongenial to the sects, they soak up some of the protest, anomie, and meaninglessness of the societies in which they emerge. Through crystallization of this protest they can subsequently become catalysts for change. Their tragedy is that transformation is, as the word implies, a temporary interlude. It is particularly in mobile societies that "one can most clearly observe the relevance of sects for the forging of a new identity, and the relevance of denominations and churches for maintaining this identity, once it was formed" (Mol 1976, 172).

Chapter 7, 8, and 9 illustrate these notions. Chapter 7 stresses the metabolizing functions of the Newlight Movement in the Maritimes at the end of the eighteenth century and of Methodism, further west, in the beginning of the nineteenth. The Baptists became the main heirs and consolidators of Newlightism, while in Upper Canada, Methodism soon became the religion of prosperous citizens. Towards the end of the nineteenth century, the Salvation Army began its mission among the flotsam of the burgeoning Canadian cities, but, later, in the twentieth century, its message of transformation became safely encapsulated in an extensive network of social services. In the West, the charismatic leadership of Bill Aberhart in Alberta welded a new Alberta. As with the other sectarian movements, his organization changed much personal and family dissoluteness into purposeful, concerted action.

Chapter 8 takes the two fastest-growing sectarian movements in Canada and attempts to establish a link between their obvious success and social dislocation. The Jehovah's Witnesses continue to provide the counterfoil of faith and indelible structure when much of existence proves to be frail, fragile and transient. The section on Pentecostalism goes more deeply into the link between its views of salvation and various levels of identity, whether personal, family, group, social or denominational. Its charismatic theology translates into greater organizational exuberance, and this, in turn, attracts many of the urban lonely.

Chapter 9 looks at some of the religious movements which have emerged since World War II. They, too, mop up pockets of alienation and usually shower affection and love on the new converts. They contrast the ugly, cold, world outside by stressing the warmth within their fold and, in the process, alienate the rest of society. Some families of recent converts have not taken the estrangement of their children well and have gone to much trouble to "deprogramme" or "decommit" them from their newly found source of communal salvation. Scientology is treated in greater detail because it combines, incongruously, a concern for individual wholeness with total and ruthless dedication to the organization. The conflict between sacralization of personality and the sacralization of the collectivity is well-illustrated by the notoriety Scientology acquired through many court actions and decisions.

CHAPTER 7

SECTS AND THE CANADIAN FRONTIER

HENRY ALLINE AND THE FRONTIER IN NOVA SCOTIA

On March 26th, 1775, Henry Alline, a twenty-six-year-old farmer of
Falmouth, Nova Scotia, had an intense conversion experience. All his
confusion, guilt, and darkness, he wrote, were expelled, and instead his
"whole soul, that was a few minutes ago groaning under mountains of
death, wading through storms of sorrow, racked with distressing fears, and
crying to an unknown God for help, was now filled with immortal love,
soaring on the wings of faith, freed from the chains of death and darkness,
and crying out "My Lord, and My God" (Alline 1806, 35). Up till then he
had been a young man with a more than average sense of fun, and a
well-developed ability for leading other unattached males of the village in
what he called "carnal mirth." Yet after his conversion he threw himself
recklessly into evangelizing so much so that he wore himself out and died of
tuberculosis on the 2nd of February, 1784, at age thirty-five. His last words
were: "Now I rejoice in the Lord Jesus."

During the nine years of his ministry, Alline radically changed the
religious scene of Nova Scotia. He preached fervent sermons wherever and
whenever he could find an audience. He composed as many as 488 hymns in
the actual language of the frontier. Most of these dealt with man's fallen
state, salvation, new birth and the triumph of Christianity. He also wrote
two theological works which challenged ecclesiastical formality and death-
dealing tradition and underscored the mystical union of Christ and the
believer. Man was made in the image of God, a spirit, simultaneously male
and female, but he fell because he shared God's freedom of choice and began
to admire his own grandeur. Since the fall, nothing short of a new birth is
able to restore man's inner union and restore his soul to God (Armstrong
1948, 89ff.).

Almost all the settlers who fell under the spell of Alline's charisma had been recent arrivals in Nova Scotia. Most of them (such as Alline's parents) had arrived in the early 1760s from New England to take advantage of Governor Lawrence's distribution of forfeited Acadian land. They were generally poor, property-less people, escaping the social divisions of the New England colonies (Mackinnon 1930, 40). Among them were those whom the well-to-do citizens of Halifax called "the scum of the Colonies .... not only useless but burdensome .... persons from gaols, hospitals and work-houses" (Armstrong 1948, 152). In other words, they had been on the periphery of their places of origin. As Clark (1968 152) has it: "It was the restless, adventurous, and often the thriftless and irresponsible who sought their fortune in new lands." Frequently they had poor work habits, could not pay their debts and lacked the frugality and perseverance of the successful farmers and tradesmen. In addition, they drank and gambled and sometimes left their families (if they had any) destitute. Yet now for the first time they had land of their own, and this tended to enhance a sense of discipline. Cooperation with neighbours - labour was hard to get and pay for - began to take the place of hard- headed individualism. Family cohesion (all working together on the farm) took the place of irresponsibility.

Yet in the early 1770s, a few years before Alline's conversion, many of the newcomers were unable to meet the conditions of their landgrant "to cultivate, improve, or inclose one third part of their land within the space of ten years," leading to forfeiture and forced sale of properties. This demoralized the population and put a strain on the upkeep of the Congregational Churches to which almost all the New England settlers belonged. Partly because of this, five of the ten churches were vacant by the end of 1771. In addition, the fishing villages began to suffer from the privateering and confiscations which followed the outbreak of the War of Independence in 1776.

A second, much smaller category of Nova Scotia inhabitants at the time consisted of Presbyterians from Ulster who settled in the north of the Peninsula (Truro, Londonderry, Onslow). They too had been attracted by the land grants. Many of them had fled the old country because of the oppression by English landlords and the Church of England - Presbyterians had to pay tithes to the Anglican clergy, were excluded from offices until 1779 and could not be legally married by their own clergy until 1782 (Mackinnon 1930, 29). (By contrast, not far away in Cumberland, a settlement of over a thousand Methodists from Yorkshire proved to be somewhat more loyal to the British Crown in Halifax.)

A third important category of inhabitants of Nova Scotia at the beginning of Alline's revival consisted of sailors, soldiers and settlers from England, found mainly in and around the garrisons such as Halifax. This group belonged to the Church of England, which was the established church of the colony for all intents and purposes. Alline referred to the inhabitants of Halifax as being "almost as dark and vile as in Sodom" (Stewart and Rawlyk 1972, 187), and apparently this opinion was shared by many who lived outside the capital.

The category of pro-English settlers was swelled enormously by the arrival of approximately 36,000 Loyalists displaced by the War of Independence in the American colonies. In 1783 alone they doubled the population of Nova Scotia. The minority consisted of aristocrats, professionals and owners of large landholdings in the South. Much larger was the group of small farmers, tradesmen, disbanded soldiers and labourers. They were all offered landgrants on favourable terms (Armstrong 1948, 108-12), yet they suffered, like the earlier settlers, from the vagaries and the hardships of frontier life. In fact, they actually suffered more in that they also had to cope with their nostalgia for the good life and their decline in social status. In contrast, most of the earlier settlers had lost nothing and actually gained a more favourable set of opportunities.

It was in this fertile soil of rapid change, frontier hardship and economic decline that Alline's charisma and fervent message of sin and salvation found an enthusiastic reception. He attracted a large following, many becoming converted and openly confessing their sins in the emotion-laden meetings. Others, like Alline, began to preach, making up with zeal and fervour what they lacked in education. Yet this lack of learning seemed to upset only the clergy, whose professional exclusiveness and status expectations reminded the parishioners of the social divisions in New England villages from which they had just escaped. The egalitarian mood of the frontier brooked no distinctions between educated and uneducated, proprietors and non-proprietors during the early communal consolidations. As a result, the major church in Nova Scotia (Congregationalist) was practically eradicated by the time of Alline's death, although he himself was raised in the Congregational Church and showed all the ascetic tendencies of his Puritan upbringing. The New Lights (as Alline and his followers were called) shook the inherited hierarchy of the typical New England village without actually changing the basic values which sustained it. Alline complained in his journal (p.20) about the deadly formality, externals, duties and commands of the Congregational Church, and yet he only transferred the authority concerning the same values of altruism, sobriety, purity, and humility from the concrete church to his Living Lord, for Whom he did all these things with a glad and joyous heart as a token of his faith and utter loyalty.

It was this change-over from the relatively encrusted village system of New England to the new communal identity of the recently established villages in Nova Scotia which the Congregational Church delayed and the New Light facilitated. The Living Lord rather than an ecclesiastical institution (inevitably intertwined with traditions of the past) allowed for new crystallizations of social relations, which everyone experienced as liberating. Or, as S.D. Clark (1948, 36) has it: "....the Newlight movement, through the flexibility of its organization and the attraction of its evangelical appeal, was able to make religion a powerful social reorganizing influence in the community..."

Yet this re-organization did not take place only on the communal level.

It also occurred on the levels of personal, family and regional identity. Sin, to Alline's hearers, was closely linked with their own state of marginality, irresponsibility and carnality. Sin, to them, summed up their personal past. Their drunken brawls, prodigality, and infidelity haunted them in spite of a facade of bluster. Guilt had been deeply and inevitably installed in their New England upbringing. Now a fellow sinner, not a self-righteous, never-straying clique of ministers and elders showed them, on solid scriptural grounds, that a new birth and a new integrity would put a definitive stroke through the entire bungled past. Salvation was concrete, not abstract; experientially, not academically, available. Provided they accepted Jesus as their authority and saviour, the new identity was there for the grasping. By tearful prostration in the assembly of fellow converts, they indeed felt born all over again.

The fervent exhorting and preaching of Alline and others affected not only communal and personal identity but also family cohesion. For those who had been converted, the living authority and infinite love of Christ pervaded all relationships with others. It was not enough, the New Lights said, to feel forgiven. One had to ask forgiveness from all those whom one had hurt in the past, foremost among whom were parents, spouses and children. Actual reconciliation often took place after confessions of unjust dealings, impetuous anger, irresponsible behaviour, and serious infidelity. Past tensions and bitterness tended, at least initially, to be replaced by a new sense of family integrity, and this increased the capacity for pulling together and freed energy for coping with the difficult and uncertain times.

The conversions which the revivals brought about were always expressed in individualistic terms. By turning to the Saviour a person changed and became more "whole" as the jargon had it. Yet hidden behind this very personal process was a less obvious, equally powerful social change. Jesus, the new source of personalized order, the authority for individual re-organization, summed up in His Being the very values (love, humility, consideration, self-denial) which encouraged greater family solidarity and discouraged the aggressiveness of the self-affirming rebel who had been at the bottom of the village hierarchy before his departure for the frontier. The revivals, therefore, modified the tensions existing between individual, family and community through the exclusive spotlighting of the living Saviour (whole-maker) who demonstrated, par excellence, that conflict and break-down (sin) in His own person had become transformed into light and love (salvation).

Another feature of Alline's revival was the sense of regional identity he evoked in his hearers. Their migration from the war and strife in the South, he said, was part of God's plan to establish His Kingdom in the North. The war was God's visitation on the ungodly, the so-called Christians, as punishment for the sin of being lukewarm. Not that his hearers were any better, he said, but the revival was a sign of God's miraculous intervention. "They were special members of the New England community who had been 'called' to Nova Scotia to serve as a saving remnant while New England abrogated her mission to lead the Protestant cause "(Stewart and Rawlyk 1972, 172). Plundering, burning, and enforced enlistment (well-described in Raddall 1977) were a few of the many means to purify the chosen race. God was readying them for His own historical purpose. This notion appealed both to the immigrants from New England and to the Yorkshire Methodists (Stewart and Rawlyk 1972, 186). Alline facilitated the detachment of the new settlers from their countries of departure and increased their loyalty to Nova Scotia. The revival movement therefore contributed to the formation of a new identity on at least the levels of person, family, community and region, in contrast with the churches, for which the maintenance of the old forms of integrity was the implicit task.

METHODISM AND THE FRONTIER

The division of labour between sect and church (the former assisting the creation, the latter the maintenance of identity) perpetuated itself wherever and whenever lands were opened up for settlement in Canada. Frequently, however, the settlers from Europe would bring their own churches with them and these then began to function as "agents of cultural preservation....not of cultural reorganization," as S.D. Clark (1948, 83) described them. The Church of England was such an agent for the English, the Presbyterian Church for the Scottish, the Catholic Church for the French, the Irish and the Poles, and later Ukrainian Orthodoxy for the Ukrainians, Lutheranism for the Danes, Norwegians, Swedes and Finns. Yet even the ethnic churches on the Canadian frontier could not always successfully compete with the fervent sectarian movements. This was particularly true, as we have seen, for the Congregational Churches in Nova Scotia which the New England settlers had brought with them and true to a lesser extent for the Presbyterian churches of the Ulstermen and the Church of England of the English newcomers.

One reason for the only limited success of the ethnic churches on the Canadian frontier was the gradual fading of old-world culture in the face of new communal and cultural demands. Another one was the lack of fit of a learned and often expensive ministry in egalitarian pioneer communities. A third, very practical, reason was the smallness and the impecuniousness of the ethnic enclaves. The most important reason, however, was the adroit ability of the sectarian movements for emotional detachment of threadbare identities (past sins, fragmentations, divisions) and the welding of new ones (salvation and wholeness of individuals and families).

Methodism in particular proved to be more and more successful the further west it moved along the Canadian frontier. In New Brunswick, predominantly settled by the Loyalist refugees from the south, Methodist revivals made many converts in the Saint John Valley at the beginning of the nineteenth century. In Upper Canada there were as many as twenty-one

Methodist preachers operating in 1811 (Clark 1948, 94). They were generally circuitriders, travelling from settlement to settlement, usually not very
well-educated, but full of zeal for the Lord. These men were generally single
and required little more than an occasional meal and a bed to sleep in. More
importantly, local laymen took up the task of evangelism in the absence of
the circuitriders and kept the fires burning. This was in strong contrast with
the Anglican and Presbyterian ministers whose special position in the
community the layman could not usurp.

Methodism, however, did not have a monopoly on revivals. At the
beginning of the nineteenth century, Presbyterian missionaries from the
United States evangelized the Niagara Peninsula. In the first quarter of that
century scores of Baptist churches sprung up, both in Upper and Lower
Canada, and all of them were the result of revival preaching. To the settlers,
however, organizational affiliation was less important than rebirth and
conversion. The movement of the spirit was salient, not the form into which
it was poured. Therefore spiritual fellowship across denominational and
class lines was stressed, rather than mere belonging. Speaking about Upper
Canada, S.D. Clark (1948, 102) observed: "The religious sect emerged to
take the place of the church .... Growth of revivalist influence led particularly to a serious weakening in the position of the Church of England." In
the latter church, ministry was a career, and, as such, the backwoods were
in no way enticing, particularly not to the British clergymen, for whom the
old country remained the apex of culture and civilization. In sharp contrast
were the Methodist circuitriders, who were often farmers, schoolteachers,
blacksmiths or carpenters. All felt "called" (Ibid., 147), and therefore
remuneration, housing and certainly standard of living and status were of
little consideration. They became the undisputed leaders of the frontier if
only because their ascetic and frugal habits fitted the value matrix of
responsibility, reliability and prudency, the hallmark of the successful
pioneer.

Yet the very sects which had so successfully attacked the formality and
the accommodation of the churches soon became the preservers of the
identities they had helped to bring about. The Baptist Churches, which had
been the main heirs of Newlightism, soon began to represent the successful
citizenry. The Methodist Churches in Upper Canada began to prosper and
develop a well-paid ministry. A now respectable membership was guided by
eminent preachers such as the Ryersons brothers, who tended to favour the
Tories as against radical politicians (Ibid., 269). Everywhere imposing
Methodist churches began to appear, and in these, zealous, but uneducated,
local preachers were less welcome than professional orators.

In the meantime, a new urban frontier of marginal migrants began to
emerge from Upper Canada to the Atlantic seaboard. Through industry the
cities began to attract newcomers in ever-greater numbers. Slums began to
be well-populated, but the erstwhile sectarian movements had now become
respectable denominations and unwittingly estranged the disprivileged and
poor. And so new movements more in tune with the urban proletariat began

to arise. They emerged often within the denominations (for instance Methodism), but generally organized themselves separately after a lapse of time.

A good example is the revival begun in Montreal by a charismatic Methodist minister Ralph Horner. He was converted in a camp meeting in 1872 but showed so much palpable disdain for Methodist authority and organization that the church had little choice but to expel him in 1895. This did not particularly worry Horner. He had gathered large numbers of followers for whom the power of the Spirit greatly outweighed denominational loyalties. Wherever he went, he felt compelled to witness to the pentecostal flame. His meetings became so large that tents had to be rented. To an outsider, the revivals resembled bedlam, with scores of converts falling to the ground and many others speaking in tongues. But to the insider, who often came from the lowest strata of society, the Holy Spirit had actually descended and miraculously saved him from sin and perdition. The Holiness Movement, as the Horner Movement began to be called, grew rapidly, particularly after the break with Methodism (Horner n.d.; Clark 1948, 368ff.).

THE SALVATION ARMY AND THE URBAN FRONTIER

Another dissenter within the increasingly respectable Methodist fold was William Booth in England whose evangelical message was addressed to the urban poor rather than to the marginal settlers on the frontier. The Booth revivals came to Canada with English immigrants who had been converted in the old country and began to spontaneously evangelize.

In May 1882, Jack Addie, an eighteen-year old drapery salesman, together with another young English immigrant, Joe Ludgate, began to hold rousing open-air meetings in Victoria Park, London, Ontario. Soon Addie found himself in court for beating drums and marching the streets.

> When the magistrate took his place on the bench the courtroom was filled to overflowing. Addie pleaded his own case. He impressed upon the court that he was a law-abiding citizen, and that the Army was not a law-breaking organization; and that what the law could not do, God had sent The Army to accomplish, and that drunkards, thieves and bad men had all been converted. At this juncture a converted drunkard jumped to his feet and shouted, "Yes, here's one right here"; and another convert shouted, "And here's another!" Soon all the converts were testifying while the irritated judge demanded order, and shouted loudly, "This is not a camp meeting" (Brown 1952, 15).

On this occasion Addie was fined five dollars or ten days in jail, but the sentence was never served.

About the same time an immigrant blacksmith, William Freer, and his wife had begun meetings in Toronto. They too made converts; and before long commissioned officers from the New York headquarters of The Salvation Army began to assist in the building of the Canada section of the organization. In spite of, or often actually because of, strenuous opposition to the open-air bands and witnesses, the Salvation Army began to increase by leaps and bounds. In 1884, 62 Corps and 175 Officers had spread over Ontario, and by the end of the decade the Salvation Army was well-represented in every part of the Dominion from St. John's, Newfoundland, to Vancouver, British Columbia.

In 1885 revivals took place in Saint John, New Brunswick, and soon Moncton and Fredericton followed. The Salvation Army began to make converts in Winnipeg in the winter of 1886/7, and a year later it "assaulted the wickedness of Vancouver" which resulted in many conversions (Brown 1952, 62).

After a rather inauspicious beginning (there were some ugly mob scenes), The Army became particularly well-entrenched in Newfoundland, where much of the fishing population was destitute. In some outports it was the only religious organization, and, if this were the case, "practically the whole population joined the Army" (Moyles 1977, 84). As Newfoundland had a denominational system of education whereby each denomination built its own schools and appointed its own teachers, a Salvationist network of schoolbuildings soon covered the island. According to the 1981 census, 8.0% of the Newfoundland population belonged to the Salvation Army. For the rest of Canada this percentage is only 0.5%. This means that although only 2.3% of the Canadian population lives in Newfoundland, as many as 36.1% of all Canadian Salvationists live there.

At the 1891 census, 14,131 residents of Canada filled in "Salvation Army" as their religion. Yet this growth had not taken place without much controversy and persecution. Particularly in Montreal and Quebec, the opposition was fierce. In 1887 the Salvation meeting hall in Montreal was set on fire. In the same year a homemade bomb went off during a prayer meeting in the Quebec Citadel. Twenty-one Salvationists were seriously injured in a mob attack during a procession through town. Later that year 600 university students and a mob of 5,000 smashed all windows of the Salvation Army Barracks. The Salvationists were forbidden to march. Yet during this period many conversions were made.

The success of The Army in those early, heady days was a combination of many factors. There was first of all the miracle element. Someone whom everyone knew as the town drunk or the wife-beater had turned over a new leaf and openly confessed his miserable sins to all and sundry in meetings and on street corners. To feel washed clean in the Blood of the Lamb was obviously a genuine experience - there was no inkling of hypocrisy in the testimonies. The joy of salvation was authentic and the audiences usually responded sympathetically. A second element was the contagious vigour of the gospel-singing with its stirring trumpet and tambourine accompaniments. Generally the meetings were brought into a receptive mood for testimonies by catchy songs and the lusty singing of young soldiers of either sex. The image of vigour was in no way diminished by the military precision, the uniforms and the army terminology pervading the entire organization. There was no escaping the impression that the crusade against evil and sin was relentless, and that only whole-hearted dedication could snatch victory from the clutches of defeat.

A third element was the consummate spectator attractions of the Salvation Army. Nothing was hidden or hushed in meditative corners. Even prayers were full of spectacular imagery: fire, blood, the fangs of Satan. Services were noisy, happy and full of zest, as though not Satan but dullness was the greatest enemy. Even if the bands were not up to standard, they still stirred the soul. In the early beginnings, before regular uniforms were introduced, anything that was out of the ordinary was worn. Jack Addie and Joe Ludgate began the Salvation Army work in Canada wearing the uniform of English bobbies, including the helmet. The beautiful Evangeline Booth, daughter of William and territorial commander of Canada from 1896 to 1904, dressed in an unorthodox uniform and red wig, "would majestically lead a parade to the Toronto Temple, riding a pure-white horse" (Moyles 1977, 17). A further factor was the adroit use made of converts. They were promptly put to work, so much so that there was little time for anything else. They helped out in the bands (anyone could beat a tambourine), carried a flag, sold the Salvation Army paper (*The War Cry*), attended meetings and rallies, taught Sunday-school, and, above all, were made to witness in the very pubs where they had been habitually drunk or the factories where they still worked. Their new role was forcefully impressed on the very environment where it had meaning, so that the miracle of their conversion had maximum exposure.

Yet, deep down, these factors for the success of the Salvation Army in the early days were less important than the fit of revivals and conversions with the dislocation of the times. The uprooted human beings whom it reached were often close to the physical and mental breaking point. Diseased bodies, social condemnation, family breakup, slum violence, criminal injustice, robberies and murders were all too familiar to the newcomers in the expanding cities. The Salvation Army was not afraid (it actually relished) to go to the disintegrating heart of personal, communal, family and social identities because it was here that it found Satan and sin in their raw, naked form. All its formidable, youthful energy was directed at the healing of the exact point of breakdown. Its vision of salvation was concretely directed at individual wrecks. Yet in actual fact it reinforced the very values (altruism, generosity, helpfulness, love, responsibility for others) which reconciled these individuals to the requirements of viable family life and communal vitality. An ostensible, exclusive stress on individual salvation encompassed a great deal of social salvation and it did not take long for the latter to be also articulated.

This became obvious the further the Salvation Army moved from its vigorous revival beginnings. It soon realized how inadequate social institutions were on the expanding urban frontier. The converted prostitute might now be reconciled with Jesus and might have the right mental set of attitudes for right living according to prevailing social standards, but she still had to find a job. The released prisoner needed a place to live. The battered wife, the skid-row drunk, the neglected orphan had to have homes from which they could set out to face the demands of a harsh society. And so a battery of social organizations arose, dealing with care for the destitute and those in need.

One of the first of these institutions was the Toronto Home for Fallen Women (1886), soon followed by two cottages for female drunks and dissolute women (The Inebriates' and Outcasts' Homes). In 1890 a Prison Gate Home for Men was established, populated by inmates who had served their sentences and had been picked up by the "Red Maria," a horse-drawn vehicle which would pull up at the same hour every day at the local jail. They would be lodged and given work (Brown, 1952, 86). Soon, all over the Dominion, a string of hospitals as well as homes for children and the aged were erected. There also was a Salvation Farm for those without work and for sick officers and a ship for meetings with Newfoundland fishermen. All these enterprises and institutions advanced the social integration of those who were on the periphery of Canadian society, who suffered rejection by that society and were a potential threat to its stability.

To a much larger extent than The Army realized, the same integration was accomplished by its evangelical arm. The revivals and the conversions made responsible citizens out of ruffians and derelicts. Yet Canadian culture separated "salvation" and "soup." The immaterial was considered irrelevant to the material. Canadian society certainly began to identify The Army with its charitable network and extensively supported its labours amongst the needy and its extensive auxiliary services during World War II; by contrast, it regarded The Army's evangelical work as vaguely irrespectable and out of line with expectations of reserve and emotional restraint. Presently, the Canadian population is largely unaware of how the evangelical services and The Army itself have strongly modified and traditionalized its exuberant appeals of the 1880s.

The hankering for a respectable niche within Canadian society had already begun before the turn of the century. Of course it had always been there: salvation is a deeply conservative notion, however irrespectable sin may be. Yet, in its early days, The Army somehow conveyed the impression that only those who had deeply experienced the intolerable burden of sin could truly be saved. When the next generation of Salvationists came along, this deep sense of sin seemed somewhat contrived as many of the younger members had been reared in decent Salvationist homes where it would be difficult to manufacture a realistic sense of dereliction and destitution. As a result, the emotional exuberance of salvation was of necessity blunted.

Just as important was the organizational necessity for consolidation. Only an efficient organization, it was felt in Salvation Army circles (and the military vocabulary and mode of operation contributed to this feeling), could bring about God's Kingdom. Yet this meant not only internal regimentation of loyalty, but also external support for the proliferating activities. Financial contributions depended on the legitimacy of The Salvation Army in Canadian society. In the same way as the various forms of personal, family and social identity were brought in line with one another through evangelism and social work, so Salvation Army identity was brought in line with the cultural expectations regarding religious organizations.

William Booth (The Founder, always spelled in capital letters by an adoring membership) was a formidable ally in this maneuvering for the respectable niche. His charisma had earned him universal respect, and the loyalty of the entire Salvation Army hierarchy to its leader was total. This meant that wherever he went (and he visited Canada a number of times) he was treated as saint and undisputed leader of a dynamic organization totally dedicated to the good of society. During his last visit, in 1907, he stayed with the Governor-General in Ottawa. On the evening of his departure there, he caused some consternation during a large dinner-party by insisting on praying. Everyone knelt at his or her chair while the waiters in scarlet stood with dishes in their hands. When it was all over, Earl Gray, the Governor-General, "exclaimed with the greatest enthusiasm and with immense earnestness: 'Wasn't that a beautiful prayer? I think that was the most beautiful prayer I ever listened to'"(Brown 1952, 116). There is no record as to whether or not William Booth was altogether happy about his prayer being treated as an aesthetic specimen, but there was no doubt that the Booth family had become somewhat impatient with the lingering sect, anti-establishment characteristics of the Salvation Army.

This had become obvious during Herbert Booth's (William's son) term of office as territorial commander in Canada from 1892 to 1896, at which time he was succeeded by Evangeline Booth. In a brief about the transfer of office to his sister, he suggested that the Canadian organization needed "a policy which will lift the tone of the Army, and bring it into better repute" (Moyles 1977, 123).

It was on account of this accommodative policy that a serious split occurred at the Salvation Army Headquarters in Toronto. Brigadier Peter Philpott, like a fair number of other Canadian officers, had become disillusioned with the dominance of the Booth family, their downplaying of evangelization, their un-Canadian intrusions and the high headquarter salaries. When Philpott was demoted by Herbert Booth in 1892, almost sixty officers and more than four hundred soldiers resigned with him. Philpott with some of his erstwhile colleagues established the Christian Worker's churches in Toronto and also founded the Philpott Tabernacle in Hamilton (Ibid., 127).

Yet the inexorable process of identity consolidation or organizational tuning was not to be stopped. Presently Philpott's Tabernacle in Hamilton is no way less in tune with middle-class Canadian society than the Salvation

Army citadels in the same city. This does not mean that the evangelical, or "church" arm of The Army has stopped growing. In the 1971 census the Salvation Army (with 119,665 adherents) had grown by 30% in the preceding decade, as compared with 18% of the population at large. Yet in the seventies it grew by only 5% (to 125,085) compared with 12% for the population at large (1981 census). Its origin in British culture still showed - in 1981, 85.0% of Salvationists claimed to be of British origin, as compared with 40.2% of the population at large. On the other hand, its urban predominance had now changed to a slightly rural overrepresentation (26.5% of Salvationists lived in rural areas as compared with 24.3% of all Canadians).

ABERHART AND THE FRONTIER IN ALBERTA

Also in the West, sectarian forms of religion had a crystallizing effect on various forms of identity. In Alberta it was the charisma and teaching of William Aberhart (1878-1943) which produced some of these effects. He was born on a farm near Egmondsville, Ontario, the fourth of eight children. His father was of German descent (the name was originally Eberhardt), but his mother was English (Johnson and MacNutt 1970, 16). He was very good at athletics and had a phenomenal memory. He became a school principal in Brantford in 1905 and in 1910 accepted the principalship of a high school in Calgary, Alberta.

Since his youth, Aberhart had been a very active member of the Presbyterian Young People's Society, and in Calgary he continued to teach his well-attended Bible classes in a variety of churches. He was particularly interested in prophecy and in Scofield's ideas on dispensation (God's blueprint for the future), and in 1918 he established the Calgary Prophetic Bible Conference. Under the aegis of this organization, the famous Sunday-afternoon lectures in the Palace Theatre were started. They attracted thousands of hearers; when they were broadcasted in 1925, audiences were counted in the hundreds of thousands (Mann 1955, 120). "One man reported walking fifteen blocks to visit his girlfriend on a warm afternoon in Calgary and claimed not to have missed one word of Aberhart's broadcast. People were sitting on the porches of their homes with their radios on" (Hiller 1972, 341). Aberhart had a commanding personality and was a very forceful speaker. The future to him was full of meaning: Christ was on the verge of returning to earth to remove the real Christians to the safety of heaven. He was so convinced of this coming event, called the Rapture, that "he slept with the blinds open at night hoping to be the first one to see Christ appear at the Rapture" (Elliott 1980, 326).

Aberhart believed that the Antichrist, assisted by the False Prophet leading the Christian denominations, would reign over a world of chaos and confusion after The Rapture and would brand all his followers with the mark of the beast (Revelation 13:17). Aberhart, assisted by his successor

Ernest C. Manning, wrote a play about this event called *The Branding Irons of the Antichrist* (Appendix D in Johnson and MacNutt 1970, 231 ff.). After seven years of utter disorder, called the Tribulation, Christ would return with the saved Christians, defeat the Antichrist in the Battle of Armageddon, and establish the Millennium. Much of Aberhart's preaching was an appeal for rebirth so that the Tribulation could be avoided.

The times were ready for Aberhart's religious messages. The first quarter of the century saw an increase in the Alberta population from 73,022 in 1901 to 607,599 in 1926. Immigrants had been attracted by the availability of good and cheap land. The prairie frontier had become a heterogeneous mixture of ethnic enclaves, each reinforced by its own religious organization. By 1931, 53% of Alberta was of English, 10% of German, 8% of Scandinavian, 7% of Ukrainian, 5% of French origin. Those settlers who were of English origin were represented by a variety of denominations: Anglican, Methodist, Catholic, Presbyterian (and later United Church), Baptists, and sectarian groups such as the Salvation Army, Mormons and Adventists. The Germans and the Scandinavians were generally Lutheran, the Ukranians Orthodox, the French Catholic. However, the longer their stay in Alberta, the more assimilated these groups became, and ethnic identity became less and less the only frame of reference. It was the forceful Aberhart messages which transcended ethnic and denominational boundaries and facilitated a provincial sense of solidarity. Aberhart felt that God was "superintending the affairs of this province .... and that Alberta was the initial location for the supernatural drama among men on earth" (Hiller 1972, 381).

The sense of a special destiny for Alberta was strongly advanced during the depression of the 1930s. Everyone suffered from the economic downturn. Unemployment rose dramatically and prices for farm products decreased correspondingly. There was much poverty and even greater social disorganization, and the future looked endlessly bleak for the majority of the population. Aberhart, excellent as he was in sensing people's predicaments, struck a chord with his message of the coming chaos and God's final victory. His hundreds of thousands of listeners took comfort from the weekly radio message that there was meaning in history in spite of untold misery. God's structure stood over against what seemed to be the endless powers of destruction. This message fitted with the Christianity of the various denominations, and yet it rose above the divisions in that it was both palpably non-institutional (Aberhart purposely hired theatres to minimize ecclesiastical associations) and supremely relevant to the perplexing times.

Aberhart's deep concern with relevance and his populist resonance had another consequence. Again and again he denounced the unscrupulous money-lenders and the eastern financial interests on which his hearers depended for their livelihood. His reading of Major C.H. Douglas' books on Social Credit persuaded him that this dependence was immoral, and that through the money-lender's restriction of credit, ordinary citizens were

denied their legitimate share in the cultural heritage and production potential. This legitimate share was the Social Credit, and Aberhart proposed that
social dividends, or purchasing power directly issued to the consumer,
would remedy the economic injustice.

Aberhart's charismatic personality, his enormous Alberta-wide radio
audience, his persuasive religious zeal, his powerful restoration of meaning
to people who suffered from meaninglessness, his crusade for greater
economic justice: all combined to give his new Social Credit party a resounding victory at the 1935 provincial elections. He was certainly assisted
by the scandals of the opposing United Farmers of Alberta, but the gaining
of 56 out of 63 seats was primarily due to the fact that Aberhart was known
and deeply trusted by the majority of Albertans, who had become disillusioned with big capital, self-serving politicians and wealthy churches. In
1940 Social Credit gained another, though reduced, majority (36 out of 56
seats) and Aberhart remained the premier of the province until his death in
1943.

Aberhart's charisma welded a new Alberta. Yet his forthright and plain
speaking about the morals of the day also invigorated many individuals who
had lost confidence in themselves and in their society. He took a hardline
stand on discipline, frivolity and temperance, and this, together with his
clear exposition of God's future action, seemed to infuse iron in many weak
spines. He insisted on conversion as the only way to salvation; he was
convinced that only regenerate followers of Jesus would be taken away at the
time of the Rapture and that even the sincere but unconverted churchgoers
had to suffer the persecutions and tortures of the Tribulation. It was this
theological and moral decisiveness which attracted those people whom time
and circumstance had demoralized. He very effectively used the biblical
stories of the Good Samaritan and of Christ washing the feet of his disciples
to impart lessons of social responsibility and personal humility. Entire
families felt cemented in their common resolve after hearing Aberhart's
stirring broadcasts.

SUMMARY

On the Canadian frontier (rural and urban) sectarian movements added
considerably to the shaping of practicable communities, closeknit families,
personal integrity and provincial identity. They did this in a variety of ways.
They browbeat their listeners into accepting and confessing their rebelli-
ousness and sins by contrasting them starkly with the saving power of
Christ. They dramatized and expressed the sin/salvation dialectic again and
again through the witness of converts and through other attention-
demanding techniques, whether Salvation Army bugles or soul-stirring
broadcasts. Through new institutions, rituals, sermons and renewed commitments, they reinforced the new identities they had helped to shape. In
spite of their advocacy of radical change in both individuals and social

institutions, they almost always refurbished the old time-honoured values of reliability, responsibility, consideration, altruism, kindness, decency, humility, discipline, self-denial, and austerity which had proved to be such vital supports of viable family and community life. They broke through the old divisions of class and status hierarchies and yet established similar structures, be it with different personnel. They were agents of social re-organization and yet also conservers of the new organizations they had helped to bring into being.

CHAPTER 8

JEHOVAH'S WITNESSES AND PENTECOSTALS

The Jehovah's Witnesses were the fastest-growing sect in Canada in the sixties. Their number increased from 101 in the 1901 census to 938 in 1911, 6,689 in 1921, 13,582 in 1931, 7,007 in 1941, 34,596 in 1951, 68,018 in 1961 and 174,810 in 1971. This means that they grew by 157% from 1961 to 1971, although the population increased by only 18% over the same period. Yet by 1981 they had decreased to 143,485 (82% of the 1971 figure), probably because of internal dissension. (The population increased by 12% during the same period.) The Witnesses are not equally distributed over the population. Whereas 22% of them live in British Columbia, only 11% of the general population resides there (1981 census). Yet, although as much as 26% of the population lived in Quebec in 1981, only 14% of the Jehovah's Witnesses did so. According to the 1981 census only 12.3% of the Witnesses, as compared with 26.7% in the population, are of French descent.

The figures the Jehovah's Witnesses themselves keep are much less dramatic. In 1973 they reported 52,773 members, only 30% of the 1971 census figures (Penton 1976, 228). There are a number of good reasons for the large discrepancy. The census figures include children who grow up in a Jehovah's Witness home. Those who occasionally attend a service, or used to do so, may continue to think of themselves as Jehovah's Witnesses and fill in the census form accordingly. By contrast, the Witnesses themselves have a much more rigorous view of what constitutes a member. To them only 'publishers' (a term based on the biblical description of the first Christians who published or spread the Word of the Lord throughout the world) qualify as bona fide members. These publishers must have dedicated themselves to Jehovah (the Old Testament word for God) through the act of baptism, after an extensive training programme. They must regularly attend the numerous meetings of the local Kingdom Hall and usually spend a minimum of ten hours each month in house-to-house canvassing (Stevenson

1968, 19). Anyone falling short of these expectations is not numbered amongst those who will be saved at the pending Armageddon, although of late the rules about the amount of witnessing from door to door have been relaxed. Another minor reason for the higher 1971 census figures is that the latter include the Witnesses in the Yukon and Newfoundland which do not belong to the Canadian Branch of the Watch Tower Society.

The increase in numbers of publishers in Canada has been much less dramatic: from an average of 38,382 in 1960 their number grew to 46,808 in 1970 (an increase of 22%) and to 66,395 in 1980 (an increase of 42%). The much smaller increase in numbers of publishers as compared with individuals who regarded themselves as Jehovah's Witnesses at the time of the 1971 census suggests that, at the time, the sect had a growing number of inactive members. Beckford (1975, 66) interprets the world-wide figures (for instance, 163,123 baptisms for 1972 as compared with an increase of only 86,197 publishers) to mean "that it is becoming increasingly common for Jehovah's Witnesses to remain active for only a short time and then to "retire" into a form of "associate" or "peripheral" membership, thereby forming a penumbra around each congregation which is activated only occasionally." This may have been true for Canada in the sixties, but in the seventies the gap between active and inactive members narrowed.

The census figures show three other events and characteristics peculiar to the Jehovah's Witnesses. First, their origin. There were so few in the early beginnings that the census did not even count them separately until 1901, when there were 101. The sect started inconspicuously in the U.S.A. in the last quarter of the nineteenth century. Charles Taze Russell (1852-1916), a Pittsburgh clothing store owner, together with some friends began a Bible class to learn more about Christ's Second Coming. The Bible Students, as they called themselves, grew in number, and by around 1880, as many as thirty congregations had been established. They soon extended their influence to Canada where similarly small congregations were formed by local businessmen, artisans and farmers. The cause was consolidated by Russell's visit to Toronto in 1891. Around that time William Peters Flewwelling, a worker at British Columbia Steel in Vancouver, organized the first Bible Student meetings in the West. In the last few years of the nineteenth century, Arthur N. Marchant established congregations in the Maritime provinces (Penton 1976, 9,35ff.). In the first decade of the century, Russell, by now president of the flourishing Watch Tower Society and its publishing ventures, made numerous visits to centres in Ontario, the Maritimes and Western Canada. Being a spellbinder and a patriarchal, charismatic figure, he left a stamp of urgency and mission wherever he went.

The second event reflected in the census figures relates to the militantly pacifist stance of the Bible Students (named Jehovah's Witnesses after 1931). Between 1931 and 1941 their numbers had dropped from 13,582 to 7,007. Already during World War I the Watch Tower Society had declared that any war was the devil's work; in 1916, a few months before he died,

Russell had been taken from a train in Gretna, Manitoba, and forced to return to the United States because he and his followers were deemed to be disloyal to the war effort. Russell's successor, J.F. (Judge) Rutherford (1869-1942), took an even stronger anti-war and anti-state stand. Watch Tower literature was banned in Canada, and during July and August, 1918 the banned literature was confiscated in a raid on the homes of Bible Students.

On July 4, 1940, during World War II, the Jehovah's Witnesses were declared a subversive movement and therefore illegal. Prime Minister William Lyon Mackenzie King stated that their refusal to salute the flag and their anti-war literature undermined "the ordinary responsibility of citizens, particularly in time of war" (Ibid., 135). The Witnesses went underground, hiding their literature in false closets, haystacks and coal mines and meeting under the guise of family parties and picnics. Those who were caught were sentenced to jail for an average of six months. Witness children continued to refuse to salute the flag and sing the national anthem at their schools. For this the Hamilton Board of Education suspended twenty-seven children, thereby compelling the parents to form a private "Kingdom School." Yet the Witnesses continued to canvass homes. They avoided arrest by witnessing not from the outlawed Watch Tower literature but from the Bible alone. In 1943 they were deleted from the Canadian list of subversive organizations (Ibid., 155) and the number of publishers rose from 6,081 in 1940 to 10,345 in 1944.

The third event reflected in the census figures is the strong opposition to the Witnesses in Quebec. Compared with other provinces, Quebec has only half the number of individuals who put "Jehovah's Witness" on the census form. The reason is not difficult to find. The Catholic Church in Quebec has adamantly opposed the strongly anti-clerical and anti-Catholic Watch Tower literature. In the 1920s and 1930s many Bible Students were arrested and jailed for canvassing without license. In 1945 people attending public lectures by the Witnesses in Lachine and Chateauguay were kicked and beaten. Catholic priests denounced the Witnesses as apostles of heresy and houseowners discouraged them with brooms, pokers and kettles filled with hot water (Ibid., 185). All this only encouraged the Witnesses. To them martyrdom and suffering for the cause was and is tangible evidence of Satan's power. They think of themselves as the vanguard of God's army and therefore the thick of battle is the place to be, and Quebec became their principal battlefield in North America (Hébert 1963, 265). With the Quiet Revolution of the 1960s and the weakening bond between church and province, bitter attacks on the Jehovah's Witnesses have ceased in Quebec. This means that in future censuses the Jehovah's Witnesses may prove to be somewhat less underrepresented than they were in the past, as indeed the 1981 census shows (compared with other provinces Quebec had only one-third of Jehovah's Witnesses in 1971; in 1981 the figure had risen to one-half).

Originally the Jehovah's Witnesses (then called Bible Students or Rus-

sellites) were a rather democratic organization of people engaged in searching together the Scriptures for clues about the end of the world and the
Second Coming of Christ. Yet this very search for a concrete fulfilment of
time and for an outline of the future was, by implication, a search for an
authoritative blueprint for existence. Inevitably therefore, the sect moved
towards greater autocracy of the ruling body (the Watch Tower Society in
Brooklyn, New York), although the Witnesses themselves rather think in
terms of theocracy (the rule by God). In actual fact, the undisputed rule by
the Society and the unquestioned rule by God become one and the same in
the mind of the membership.

The authoritative aura of Bible interpretation fits in with the personality
requirements of the prospective Jehovah's Witness. If self-confidence is
precarious and easily torn into shreds, a pervasive, charismatic authority is
all the more eagerly endorsed. The advantage of divine and scriptural
authority is that it stands far enough above the immediate existential
turmoil to be the hallmark of stability and the antidote to disorder.
Jehovah's Witness doctrine was strongly influenced by the orthodox Presbyterianism of its founder. As a teenager Russell "felt so strongly about the
prevailing doctrine of predestination and the harsh Calvinism of nineteenth-
century Appalachia and God's consignment of the sinners to an eternal hell,
that he went around town writing scriptural passages on walks, walls and
the sides of buildings, that all who passed might heed the possible loss of
their own souls" (Sterling 1975, 8). The appeal of an incorruptible order
unaffected by human corruptibility is as strong for the average Jehovah's
Witness as it was for Russell a century ago. Mann's observation (1955, 36)
that in Alberta the Witnesses particularly appealed to the more depressed,
backwood farmers who resented city ways and middle-class values therefore
makes eminently good sense. Beckford (1975, 164ff.) speaks about his
English respondents as experiencing "so much doubt and confusion about
the apparent aimless and chaotic condition of either their own lives or the
world in general that the question of overall purposes in life was coming to
occupy ever greater prominence in their thinking." They therefore responded to Watch Tower evangelism as a "chance to create for themselves a
new sense of personal integrity and a meaningful view of the world."

The need for authority in general rather than for its specific forms
accounts for the continuing strength of the movement, in spite of its
persistent failures to predict the Armageddon. Russell predicted it for 1878,
1881 and 1914, and latter predictions included 1918, 1925, 1941, and, most
recently, 1975. It was not easy to steer the feverish anticipation of each of
these predictions into calmer waters when they proved to be wrong, and, as
a consequence, many defected. Yet its continuing appeal suggests that the
concreteness of the prediction and the authoritativeness of God's intervention are more important than the actual time and place of the Second
Coming.

Presently the sect continues to expect the end of the world (as it is now)
at any time. A visit by a Witness to one's door usually begins with a

reminder of the latest plane crash, earthquake, war or other catastrophe. These events are then woven into an account of God's plan for the world. For the Jehovah's Witness, event and account fit like hand and glove. They compensate for one another as a plus compensates for a minus. To them there is an equal amount of order (summed up in God's decree) for the actual disorder one experiences. Yet subtle differences have slowly crept into the Jehovah's Witness view of the past and the future. In contrast with the earlier predictions, it is now believed that Christ has appeared invisibly in 1914 and that He is now preparing for the final battle with Satan. The task of the Witnesses is to warn all and sundry about the coming end so that individuals can side with those who alone will survive the holocaust.

Door-to-door canvassing is probably the major reason for the numerical success of the Witnesses. They catch the troubled and unhappy where they are. Therapy is offered for nothing on the spot in comparson with that available in a downtown office for a price. Also, the publishers present themselves well and have been trained to use the concern most people have about threats to order, be it delinquency, crime, earthquake, vulcanic eruption, insurrection, war, corruption or injustice. They use current events as ever so many manifestations of Satan and make them meaningful through linking them with biblical predictions and the wider context of God's inscrutable plan and certain victory over Satan. Confused individuals who answer the doorbell are attracted by the commitment of the publishers. Their message about the inerrancy of the Bible and the trustworthiness of God's blueprint for the future appeals. This concrete clarity contrasts sharply with one's marginality and overshadows the rational concern with the content of the message (for instance, specifying that only 144,000 specially selected Christians (Revelation 7:4) will assist Jesus in ruling heaven and that the rest of the committed Christians will have the job of burying the bones and clearing the débris of the Armegeddon). Being caught up in the perpetual dialectic between good and evil, wholeness (which one desires) and fragmentation (which one experiences), salvation and sin, God and Satan often proves to be attractive to ordinary citizens who have become estranged from institutional Christianity. And so participation in the ancient drama of binary oppositions proves to be as compelling for some individuals listening to an articulate Jehovah's Witness at his door as for tribesmen listening to a myth around the campfire.

Door-to-door witnessing has also an advantage for Jehovah's Witness group identity. The publishers become experts in their faith through defending it against a skeptical public, and their commitment grows with their witnessing. Even when the door is slammed in their faces, or when they get verbally abused, their resolve is only strengthened. After all, the behaviour of the abuser confirms the reality of Satan and produces the comfortable feeling of being martyred (a word which actually meant "witness" in the original Greek New Testament) for God's cause.

Sectarian identity is further strengthened by the flurry of weekly Bible studies, training programmes in proselytization, coaching techniques, communications with headquarters in Brooklyn (New York), religious services, and discussion of a perpetual stream of literature from the Watch Tower Bible and Tract Society. Both family life and occupation often suffer from this "totalizing" dedication to Witness activities. There is never any regret expressed over the monopolization of time and money of the membership. The sect insists on having top priority in the lives of all its members. Why should one put so much effort in being a model housewife and employee if the cosmic drama of Christ versus Satan is being played right under one's eyes? If the end of time is close, mundane affairs of necessity lose their urgency. "Witnesses prefer an average, regular income and do not seek to excel in their occupations or careers, nor do they seek to work over-time as this would necessitate a loss of time that could be spent for religious purposes" (Lottes 1972, 177).

Total dedication to the activities of the sect is synonymous with strengthening Jehovah's Witness identity at the expense of other group allegiances (family, community, occupational) and particularly at the expense of national identity. Witnesses insist on the state being Satan's preferred instrument, and therefore adamantly refuse to salute the flag, sing the national anthem and observe national holidays. To them such practices symbolize evil. A Jehovah's Witness who directly participates in political activities can be excommunicated (Penton 1976, 28). And as for any international system (the League of Nations, the United Nations), they are the wild beast of Revelation 17,3, "full of names of blasphemy, having seven heads and ten horns." The scarlet woman, the mother of harlots sitting on the beast, is to Jehovah's Witnesses the symbol of organized religion - the Catholic Church, the National Council of Churches in the U.S.A. (Sterling 1975, 174). They therefore also reject religious holidays and scrupulously use different terminology to distinguish themselves from all other religious organizations. Instead of minister or priest they use overseer, instead of bishop, servant, instead of churchmember, publisher.

Yet, in spite of the forceful demarcation from competing systems of allegiance, Jehovah's Witnesses' values are conservative and fit well with the norms of decency and responsibility prevailing in Canadian social institutions. They abhor adultery, masturbation, homosexuality and pre-marital sex, and it is an embarrassment to them that their first president Russell was rumored to be an adulterer who divorced his strong-willed wife. "(A) member of the congregation may also be excommunicated for drunkenness, the non-medical use of drugs, lying, stealing, physical violence, the willing acceptance of blood transfusions and apostasy" (Penton 1976, 28). Nowadays one can also be "disfellowshipped" for smoking tobacco or marijuana. They insist on love and discipline in the home and the authority of the father and husband. They visit the sick and have great respect for the old. They do not object to television, films or alcoholic beverages, but stress quality of programmes and moderation in eating and drinking. They are against mini-skirts and long hair and insist on modesty in clothing and appearance.

As we have seen, the Watch Tower Society began as a small group of people interested in eschatology (the doctrine about the "last things," the end of the world, Armageddon, the return of Jesus, death). It developed into a large-scale organization, with extensive publication facilities spread over a number of city blocks in Brooklyn, claiming to possess the only valid interpretation of the Bible and to be God's only vanguard in a world ruled by Satan. Marxists would explain this development as the inevitable outcome of leadership consolidating their lust for power and maximizing the exploitation of the ignorant masses. Yet this picture distorts the situation. Jehovah's Witnesses have always been attractive to those people for whom God's word and God's plan was the fitting antidote to what they considered to be a dangerous, out-of-kilter existence. The need for authority was naturally projected on, and identified with the organization which articulated the theology of predestination and election.

Leeway of interpretation could (and did again and again) threaten both membership appeal and organizational cohesion. How can one witness so single-mindedly and whole-heartedly to a truth which is not secure? Yet in democracies individual integrity and independent thinking are at a premium, and one can therefore expect the Watch Tower Society to be often in conflict with both Canadian culture and individuals within the organization.

The conflict with Canadian culture has indeed been more than just occasional. As we have seen, the Jehovah's Witnesses were driven underground in World War II because to them nationalism and war were abominations. There were other pacifist sects in Canada, such as the Doukhobors, Hutterites and Mennonites. The Jehovah's Witnesses, however, deepened the moat between themselves and the culture even more through their stress on the evil of blood transfusion. They insist on the basis of Genesis 9:4, Leviticus 3:17, and Acts 15:20 (prohibiting the 'eating' of blood), that transfusions violate God's law. Numerous are the clashes with doctors who insist that the Jehovah's Witness patient will die unless blood is administered and with judges who take custody of a child away from Jehovah's Witness parents when they refuse to allow transfusions. The Witnesses insist that to die is better than to go against God's law, and some judges agree that compelling Jehovah's Witnesses or their children to accept blood therapy is an infringement on legal rights. Penton (1976, 224- 254) provides details about the many blood transfusion wrangles in Canada.

When James Penton wrote his 1976 book on the Jehovah's Witnesses in Canada, he was a fourth-generation member of the sect. He was also an associate professor of history at the University of Lethbridge in Alberta. The book was an apology for the Witness position. Since 1976, however, Penton has proved to be less in sympathy with the inflexibility of the Watch Tower Society. A university setting encourages skeptical thinking (the Witnesses therefore traditionally suspect the educated) and a fourth-generation Jehovah's Witness is likely to have fewer illusions about the organization than a neophyte. Accordingly, Penton began to have problems

with the Watch Tower Bible and Tract Society headquarters about proselytization and the date-setting for the Armageddon. In 1981 he was tried
for heresy and excommunicated from the Lethbridge Kingdom Hall (Testa
1981, 47). Others, who like Penton refused to toe the party line, were also
"disfellowshipped." They formed a breakaway Christian Fellowship.
Similar defections and splits have occurred in other areas and the dissension
may be at the back of the 1981 drop in numbers.

Yet the Jehovah's Witnesses are used to internal controversy and disillusionment, particularly at times when the predicted cosmic catastrophes fail
to take place. They continue to make an impact, however, if only because
their firm stand on ancient biblical traditions and their concrete structuring
of future time balance the threat of alienation, anomie and meaninglessness
of industrial and other societies in the throes of rapid change. In other
words, they provide the counterfoil of faith and indelible structure when
much of existence proves to be frail, fragile and transient.

PENTECOSTALISM

On November 17, 1906, Mr. and Mrs. A. Hebden, recent immigrants
from England, were conducting a mission in a small store at 651 Queen
Street East, Toronto. Suddenly Mrs. Hebden, against her own will, began
to speak in tongues. She had been praying for healing power and the ouster
of demons but instead found herself speaking an unknown language. This
had an electrifying effect on her audience. Very soon the store became too
small for their meetings and had to be extended to three times its length.
Still it was not large enough for people who came from all over the city every
night to witness the outpouring of the Holy Spirit and very soon new
missions were established in Toronto (Frodsham 1946, 53-4).

The tidal wave of Pentecostalism (named after the events in Acts 2 on the
day of Pentecost when the apostles saw tongues of flames on the heads of one
another, were all filled with the Holy Spirit, began to speak in foreign
languages, and converted 3000 people) had now also begun in Canada.
Although Mrs. Hebden was the first in Canada to be baptized by the Holy
Ghost, a Canadian, Robert Edward McAlister from Cobden, Ontario,
underwent the same experience in Los Angeles around the same time. He
eventually carried the flame of revival all over the Ottawa valley and became
one of the most prominent Pentecostal ministers in Canada. J. Roswell
Flower, born in Belleville, Ontario, also received the fire of the Holy Spirit
around that period in Indianapolis, Indiana, and became the staunchest
pillar of the Assembly of God in the United States, the largest of the
Pentecostal family of sects in that country (Gaver 1971, 135).

Pentecostalism had its origins in early Christianity and was fed by the
revivals of Finney and Moody in nineteenth century America, which had
laid the foundations for the Holiness Movement. In this movement the

sanctifying, whole-making power of the Holy Spirit received the dominant attention. Ecstasy, barking, jerking, falling, rolling, dancing and glossolalia (speaking in tongues) were all regarded as evidence of the dwelling within of the Holy Spirit. Pentecostalism which particularly stressed speaking in tongues and healing, developed strongly in the expanding urban and industrial centres at the beginning of the twentieth century. Its birth as a separate movement is generally associated with Bethel College in Topeka, Kansas, where its leader Charles F. Parham, received the Holy Spirit in 1901 (Bloch-Hoell 1964, 21). It became strong in Texas and particularly flourished in expanding areas such as Los Angeles and Chicago. In the latter city Mr. A.H. Argue, a real estate agent from Winnipeg, received the baptism of the Holy Spirit and brought what he later called "a prairie fire" back to a Manitoba where, in 1907, an increasing number of whites and Indians were also awakened (Kulbeck 1958, 139ff).

Although the terms "tidal wave," "prairie fire," "Pentecostal explosion" (which Lalive d'Epinay, 1969, 15, uses for the experience in Chile) seem rather strong, the growth of world-wide Pentecostalism since the early beginnings has been remarkable and consistent. A conservative estimate is that, presently, at least 10 million people in the world regard themselves as Pentecostal. According to the 1981 census at least 338,000 (1.4%) of the Canadian population thinks of itself as Pentecostal. McDonnell (1976, 146) writes about "possibly thirty-five million participants in the Pentecostal-Charismatic renewal at the world level," but this includes a large number of charismatic Catholics, Anglicans, Lutherans, Presbyterians, Methodists and Baptists.

More importantly, from one census to the next Pentecostalism in Canada has grown consistently faster than the population. In the 1911 census 515 persons claimed to be Pentecostal; in 1921, 7,012; in 1931, 26,349; in 1941, 57,742; in 1951, 95,131; in 1961, 143,877; in 1971, 220,390; in 1981, 338,790. This means that in 1911 about 0.1% of the Canadian population regarded itself as Pentecostal, but that in 1971 as much as 1% did so and 1981, 1.4%. From 1921 to 1931 Pentecostalism grew 276%; from 1931-1941, 119%; from 1941-1951, 65%; from 1951-1961, 51%; from 1961-1971, 53%; and from 1971-1981 54%. At least two-thirds of these people belong to the Pentecostal Assemblies of Canada (Gaver 1971, 132), but Pentecostals think of themselves primarily as a movement rather than an organization. Denominational cohesion is (or certainly was) rather unimportant to them and there are many independent splintergroups such as the Apostolic Faith Assembly, the Apostolic Church of Pentecost, the Holy Rollers, and the Free Gospel Assembly which are regarded as Pentecostal.

One of these small groups (the International Church of the Foursquare Gospel) has strong links with Canada through its founder but grew much faster in the United States. Here it has two dozen churches at the most, but south of the border it had 614 churches and 87,582 members, according to the 1980 Yearbook of American Churches. The founder and undisputed leader of this church until her death was Aimee Semple McPherson (1890-

1944). She was born Aimee Kennedy on a farm in Ingersoll, Ontario. Both her parents were very religious (her mother was an officer in the Salvation Army). At the age of seventeen she was converted by Robert Semple, a boilermaker, who had shortly before been baptized by the Holy Spirit at the Hebden's mission in Toronto. A few months later Aimee also received the Holy Spirit. She wrote (McPherson 1923, 45): "I shouted and sang and laughed and talked in tongues, until it seemed that I was too full to hold another bit of blessing lest I should burst with the glory." In the same year (1908) she married Semple, and they both left for China as missionaries. Soon they both contracted malaria. Robert died, but Aimee survived, gave birth to a daughter and returned to the United States. Here she married Harold McPherson, a wholesale grocery salesman with whom she had a son, Rolf, who succeeded Aimee as president of the International Church of the Foursquare Gospel after her death.

Aimee was very beautiful. She was also a compelling speaker who made dramatic use of her white robes. Her charisma drew thousands, and soon she was much in demand as a revivalist from Washington, D.C., and Key West, Florida, to San Jose, California. In St. Louis, Missouri, her revival was sponsored by one, small, sixty-seven member church, but after three weeks the 12,000 seat Coliseum had to be hired. At this occasion (McPherson 1923, 318ff.) many of the sick were healed, crutches, braces and wheelchairs cast aside. Goiters melted instantly while thousands were looking on. At an evangelistic crusade conducted by "Sister" Aimee in Montreal, the invalid wife of a Baptist minister, Mrs. L.R. Dutaud, was cured of tuberculosis of the throat and of limb infections (Kulbeck 1958, 93). In Los Angeles in 1923 she built the enormous Angelus Temple, which cost $1,500,000. During the Depression more than a million people were fed and clothed by the Angelus Temple (Durasoff 1972, 73). She established a Bible college, a publishing house, and a radio station as well as many books.

Both her private and public life were rather controversial. In Los Angeles she became heavily involved in cleaning the city of the vice lords. She often served as the conscience of her hearers, exhorting them to pay their debts and straighten out their relationships. She was allegedly kidnapped in Mexico in 1926 but escaped after a month of captivity, astounding her congregation which had just held a memorial service in her honour. She died two weeks before her fifty-fourth birthday of an overdose of Seconal (sleeping tablets). She also had an affair with her radio operator, a married man, and was twice divorced (Hollenweger 1972, 487).

Pentecostals expect their leaders to be charismatic, transmitters of the fire of the Holy Spirit. Search for sensation is less important (although a spectacle is never unwelcome) than search for fulfilment. A good charismatic leader evokes in his charges an exuberant sense of fit. The awkward teenager, the shy high school wall-flower, the lonely housewife, the friendless introvert, the childless widow, the unemployed drug addict, the depressed hypochondriac, the mousy office clerk, the uprooted immigrant - all struggle with their marginality. Pentecostal leaders exude an infectious warmth which permeates the membership so that those who are at odds with themselves or on the periphery of their family or society get the overwhelming comfort of genuine belonging. Jesus loves them and heals all hurts, the leader asserts. And so he guides the individual from fragmentation to wholeness, from sin to salvation, from marginality to integrity, from the painful past to the fulfilled present. Again and again the process of transformation is dramatized to prevent mere words from drowning the life-giving experience.

The dominant role of Pentecostal leaders has been noted by many scholars of glossolalia (speaking in tongues). Kildahl (1972, 50) contends that tongues only originate after complete submission to the leader. However, Hine (1969, 218) and others (for instance, McDonnell 1976, 135) have interviewed loners who spontaneously and on their own began to speak in tongues. As there seems to be a considerable bulk of opinion that glossolalia has strong links with regression (Ibid., 132), charismatic leadership is likely to aid the process of stripping an old identity (through facilitation of the return to more elemental patterns of behaviour, such as unstructured language or memories of mother love), and the welding of a new one (being made new in Christ) without glossolalia being necessarily a prerequisite for identity renewal.

The more forcefully the charismatic leader can contrast the bleak rut many of his audience find themselves in with the infectious flame of the Holy Spirit, the greater his success. In Canada, large Pentecostal congregations are always the product of charismatic forcefulness and organizational bustle, nowadays aided by a variety of radio and television programmes from the United States. Oral Roberts is a household word to Pentecostals and so is David Wilkerson who, inspired by the Holy Spirit, transformed a gang of hoodlums and dope addicts. Because tithing is stressed in Pentecostal congregations, many have become prosperous and well equipped. And this means that organizational embeddedness has tended to modify the exuberance of an unshackled (in the early beginnings, sometimes disorderly) movement.

In the meantime, the spirit of Pentecost has also penetrated the established denominations and churches. Leaders of major Protestant seminaries, such as Union Theological in New York and Princeton in New Jersey, have paid serious and sympathetic attention to the revolutionary effect of the Pentecostal movement. This means that nowadays one can find in Canada, too, clergy and individuals in the major denominations (Catholic, Anglican, United, Presbyterian, Lutheran) speaking in tongues. Some of them practise healing by anointing or laying on of hands, and many stress the perceptible indwelling of the Holy Spirit. In 1975 the Catholic bishops of Canada issued a *Message to All Canadian Catholics* in which they affirmed the importance of charismatic renewal for the Church. While warning against excessive sensationalism and exclusivity, they did favour religious spontaneity over stereotyped forms of communication (p.5).

For the first fifty years of its existence (until approximately 1960) Pentecostalism was regarded as unconventional, if not downright weird. Scholars, even more than average churchgoers, felt that the lack of emotional restraint, the irrational babbling, the faith healing and the strong belief in the return of Jesus were both absurd and abnormal. Those who joined the various Pentecostal movements were therefore, by definition, people who were on the periphery of established opinion, often sustained in their beliefs by their undisputable, scriptural legitimacy. The early Pentecostals were generally not well educated and came from the poorer classes. The Hebdens, for example, were English immigrants with little education. The original meeting places were very humble indeed and the membership "under great reproach" (Ward in Kulbeck 1958, iv).

Change was the order of the day. Millions of immigrants streamed into North America in the first decade of the twentieth century. Industrialization and urbanization increased by leaps and bounds, and some of the rootless immigrants who flocked to the cities found in the Pentecostal movement the forge for identity crystallization. Both the theology of the movement and the fellowship of caring brothers and sisters were antidotes to the harshness and meaninglessness of the times. To many that antidote was more urgent than the reproach of established opinion. This was true both for rural migrants and for immigrants from Britain and Europe. Kulbeck (1958, 136,166) mentions the various Slavic, Ukrainian, German, Finnish and Italian congregations in various parts of Canada.

With the increasing pluralism of Canadian society since World War II grew tolerance of unconventional speech and behaviour. Instead of reproaching the unusual, a television-saturated people actually seek the titillation of the uncommon. There is now nothing disrespectful about Pentecostalism and there is little need of Pentecostal congregations to zealously build a bulwark against a hostile world. There are also internal reasons for this development. More and more members of Pentecostal churches are children of Pentecostals, and the congregations therefore tend to become reinforcers of existing, rather than crystallizers of new, identites.

Yet the roots of Pentecostalism in the poorer and disprivileged strata of the Canadian population are still visible in the census data today. As in the United States where Pope (1942, 124) observed that the Pentecostals belonged to the poorest groups in Gaston County in North Carolina, so in Canada too, Pentecostals had an average income in 1971 of $4,014 as compared with $5,270 for Anglicans and $5,033 for the population at large. The same census shows that only 4.6% of Pentecostals as compared with 10.3% of Anglicans and 8.5% of the total Canadian population earn more than $10,000 per year. Pentecostals are also underrepresented in the top professional strata. Of all Anglicans, 8.5% are managers, teachers, or work in the field of natural and social sciences. The corresponding figure for Pentecostals is only 3.8%. One can safely predict that in future censuses, these figures are likely to converge. In Canada, Pentecostalism is overrepresented in the less affluent Atlantic provinces. Eleven percent of all Canadian Pentecostals are in Newfoundland, although only 2.3% of the population lives there (1981 census). Similarly, 6.3% of Canadian Pentecostals can be found in New Brunswick, yet only 2.9% of the population lives there. One reason for the high Newfoundland figures is the educational system in that province which is based on religious denomination and thereby favours those smaller churches which evangelized the smaller outposts. Parents would tend to write "Pentecostal" on the census form if their children attended the Pentecostal school.

Pentecostal theology combines both an age-old tradition (going back to the very beginnings of Christianity) with strong personal experience and witness. Without the latter both denominational growth and bubbling exuberance would be very subdued. It is the commitment of the individual Pentecostal and, by extension, the vitality of Pentecostal congregations which is closely intertwined with those elements of the tradition that stress charisma and movement of the Spirit. Theology expresses the heart-felt commitment and the latter is again and again reflected in the kind of sermons one can hear in Pentecostal churches. There are four elements in this theology.

The first is salvation, and it sums up the other three. For Pentecostals it is not an abstract, faraway notion but an experiential reality. Indeed, the drama of God saving mankind through Christ's death on the cross·is in no way neglected. Yet for the average churchgoer the way the Holy Spirit produces a sense of salvation in one's heart is more central than the sacred story of days gone by. The story speaks of origins to them, but the Holy Spirit seals it in one's heart so that it infuses the entire personality, providing the individual (or rather the convert) with an exhilarating feeling of wholeness and well-being. The sense of well-being and wholeness is unfortunately elusive, and therefore the church services re-enact again and again the contagious inspiration, even though the average Pentecostal will admit that the Holy Spirit cannot be produced but has to be allowed to find its own unfathomable way. Yet, anything is done in Pentecostal ritual to facilitate the entrance of the Holy Spirit into the individual or collective heart.

The second element in Pentecostal theology is speaking in tongues, or glossolalia. Those who do, appear to be in a trance and speak in a foreign language. Acts (2:9-11) mentions that at the original Pentecost Parthians, Medes, Egyptians, Libyans and Romans all heard themselves addressed by the Holy Spirit in their own languages. Modern-day Pentecostals have numerous examples of the same. Kulbeck (1958, 176) mentions how in the 1920s in Vancouver, a city girl began to speak fluently in Japanese. Frodsham (1946, 230) relates the story of a Jew in Oakland (California) who, in a Pentecostal meeting, heard the Holy Spirit telling him through a Scandinavian woman that he was lost and should turn to God, all this in Hebrew, which the woman had never learned.

Yet scholars (such as Samarin 1972, 227) who have extensively recorded and studied glossolalia have never been able to actually locate the foreign language, even though the majority of Pentecostals are convinced that such a language is spoken. Samarin was a participant observer in many Pentecostal services for five years and concluded that glossolalia is an extemporaneous pseudolanguage, "a meaningless but phonologically structured human utterance" (Ibid., 2). The sounds (or phonemes) produced by those who speak in tongues are structured; they have the pitch and the pattern of the language of the speaker. In other words, speaking in tongues seems to represent a return to the basic form or deep structure of language. This is what Samarin surmises in a later article (1980, 95) when he says that glossolalia is "the reduction of one's native language .... simplified to its basic and frequently used sound and syllable units." Hutch (1980, 256,262) argues that speaking in tongues is a non-linguistic expression of basic modes of human feeling, a rehearsal of experimental parameters such as joy and pain, birth and death, a bridge between subcortical arousal and cortical (cognitive) interpretation. The benefits of speaking in tongues are beyond doubt, tongue-speakers report a general sense of well-being and euphoria after the event.

Scholars (Samarin 1972, 277; McDonnell 1976, 116) and Pentecostals differ as to whether glossolalia is natural or supernatural. Essentially the conflict hinges on one's view of reality. The secular, scientific view assumes that order is self-explanatory and generally underestimates its own emotional commitment to such a view. The Pentecostal view assumes that God sums up order and that one's deep personal commitment to this order enhances one's wholeness or salvation. In this view, glossolalia is an important element for fulfillment or for being filled with the Holy Spirit. Generally those scholars who deny the supernatural quality of glossolalia fail to understand that objectification and transcendentalization (the gift of speaking in tongues being attributed to an extraneous source) have important ancillary, efficacious consequences for personality integration. What is worse, they ignore the objectified quality of their own view of order.

The third major element in Pentecostal theology is healing. Again there is ample scriptural precedence: Jesus restoring sight to the blind, Peter curing the lame, Paul healing the sick on Malta. Pentecostals see direct proof of the working of the Holy Spirit when, through prayer or laying on of hands or anointing, an individual is cured. Healing services are therefore regularly held. Pentecostals believe that redemption is both spiritual and physical. Numerous are the stories in Pentecostal literature about divine healing.

The fourth element in Pentecostal theology is the belief in the Second Coming of Christ. Particularly in the early beginnings of Pentecostalism, the imminent return of Jesus was strongly emphasized in the services, and the many New Testament verses dealing with His return were popular topics for preaching. The Second Coming is not spiritual, but visual and physical. When Jesus arrives, many Pentecostals believe, Christians will be taken away to heaven ("the Rapture"), leaving all others behind to face the Great Tribulation when the vials of wrath will be unleashed upon the world. As the Lord is expected to return soon, it is important to be found blameless. This means practical holiness and purity (one would not want to be found by Jesus doing something un-Christlike) and liberal giving (one must not be shackled to the material things of this world).

PENTECOSTALISM AND IDENTITY

There is a close connection between identity and salvation in that both have to do with integration and wholeness. Both are bounded off against fragmentation or destruction of integrity. The fragmentation, erosion, or breakdown of various concrete forms of identity find their equivalent on a more abstract, spiritual level in sin, evil, suffering, disobedience to God, breaking the covenant. All major theological elements of Pentecostalism are aspects of salvation and, as such, cannot help but be linked to the various levels of identity, whether personal, family, group, social or denominational.

On the personal level, doctrines of the Second Coming sharply edge the future, thereby eliminating its meaninglessness, its ambiguity, its vagueness, and its precariousness. The barriers of death and destruction are relativized. Being ready for the Second Coming involves a blueprint of approved and condemned actions. Through the doctrine of the Second Coming, ethics gain both urgency and concreteness. Through the belief in the return of Jesus, the uncertainty of the times is changed into outline and structure. The believer regains his composure and focuses his purposes, in this way reinforcing his integrity.

This is also obvious in divine healing. In its physical variant, sin is thrown out and faith and confidence take its place. The Holy Spirit infuses the individual with healing power. A healthy body preserves identity, a sick one puts it in jeopardy. In its spiritual variant, sin has thwarted mental integrity. Depression, frustration, and alienation take away from spiritual well-being and Pentecostals again and again witness to the Lord taking away their burden and making them whole.

Speaking in tongues is God making use of a human organ (the tongue) for the purpose of edifying the individual's soul, so Pentecostals think. Many scholars similarly say, but in psychological language, that glossolalia can have therapeutic effects (McDonnell, 1976, 107). Wood (1965 103-7), on the basis of Rorschach tests, speaks about the re-orienting and integrating effects of speaking in tongues on the personality. Kildahl (1972, 59) compares tonguespeakers with people obsessed with handwashing. In other words, it is a personal ritual alleviating a neurosis. Most psychologists relate it to regressive behaviour, which can be interpreted to mean behaviour reviving patterns of the past which the memory has selectively stored away as emotionally unifying and satisfying. Certainly the comfort of memories and the re-enacting of basic forms and structures (and glossolalia relates to common speech as the archaic relates to the differentiated present) compensates for the pains and discomforts of actual existence. This is also what

Schwartz (1970, 156) has in mind when he observes that Pentecostalism "provides the believer with a valued personal identity" through presenting worldly difficulties in a new, less confining perspective, thereby improving self-esteem.

Yet, however beneficial tongue-speaking may be for the individual, it can disrupt social or group identity. It is for this reason that already in the New Testament Paul exhorted the Corinthians (1 Cor. 14) to use glossolalia not just for personal benefit but also for the community of believers. And this means, he said, that tonguespeaking should be done in an orderly manner, by two or three people at most, and always with an interpreter present. In modern Pentecostal or charismatic services the danger of disruption has been real. Schwartz (1970, 146-7) mentions how, in a large American Pentecostal church he studied, the individuals were so concerned with getting the benefits of oneness with Jesus for themselves that bringing the in-filling of the Spirit to others suffered. He observed in a smaller group how jealousies about spiritual distinctions tended to disrupt, making it necessary for the minister to be always ready to repair cohesion. Kildahl (1972, 85) found the same disruptive tendencies in charismatic churches within the major denominations. McDonnell (1976, 75) reported that the charismatic movement had been divisive in the American Lutheran churches. In the Presbyterian Church of Canada, the Rev. Calvin Chambers of New Westminster, B.C., was asked to relinquish his charge in the early 1980s because the tongue-speakers who had gathered around him made the rest of the congregation feel that they were second-rate Christians. Yet in the Anglican, Catholic and Lutheran churches of Canada, the charismatic movement is regarded as having a positive effect on the life of the various parishes.

Denominational identity and loyalty to the congregation are increasingly stressed as a counterfoil to too much spiritual individualism. Yet the rationing of tongue-speaking for the sake of organizational order crimps the very spontaneity which is so characteristic for Pentecostalism as a movement. The insistence on the interpretation of tongues is a successful attempt to make the utterances socially meaningful and to break the isolation of merely personal benefits. The interpretations usually include messages from the Lord about social behaviour. Tithing (giving ten percent of one's income to the church - in Canada a substantial majority of Pentecostal engage in this form of giving) also strongly contributes to denominational cohesion. Much of the money goes to the mission field or building programmes of the local church. As congregational consensus about the forms of expenditure has high priority, present-day affluence has its own separate effect on denominational solidarity. Pentecostal congregations in Canada have pride in their progress from little storefronts to well-appointed plants. They increasingly expect their ministers to be well-educated, although they hope that education does not diminish their charismatic efficacy. Although, again with pride, Pentecostals will point to professionals in their midst (thereby showing an acceptance of secular status divisions) they still tend to rate career and income as less worthy of commitment than being united with Jesus. Yet Pentecostal success is inextricably linked with corporate acceptance of the prevailing status hierarchies in their environment.

Although to the Pentecostals the mundane world is full of demons and devils, their separation from that world is more overt than covert. Much of Pentecostal belief and morality is deeply congruent with prevailing views of what constitutes a good citizen or a good familyman. Being a vessel of the Holy Spirit is thought to be visible in conduct. One cannot be a good Pentecostal and be a drunken wife-beater. On the contrary, the mark of a good Pentecostal is to have, or belong to, a decent and respectable family.

Social identity is also reinforced (directly as well as indirectly) by Pentecostal beliefs and morals. In the early days sermons clarified what was expected of believers who were filled with the Holy Spirit. They should not smoke, drink alcoholic beverages, frequent the theater, engage in idle gossip, or wear lipstick. Nowadays Pentecostals are more tolerant of minor vices. They allow newcomers particularly a certain degree of latitude. They reason that ethical behaviour does not proceed, but follows the baptism by the Holy Spirit. Once the Spirit has taken hold of a person, it cannot help but bear abundant fruit. So why be rigid and force the issue? Social identity is reinforced by the focus on inner motivation. Once the proper spiritual state has been achieved, the ninefold fruits of the Spirit (love, joy, peace, long-suffering, gentleness, goodness, faith, meekness, temperance - Wilson 1961, 17) follow naturally. One might add to this list the practice of generosity, which is well developed in Pentecostal congregations and which, like the other fruits of the Spirit, bolsters those values which advance social solidarity and the smooth functioning of a community.

Over its eighty-year history in Canada, Pentecostalism has changed dramatically. The early pioneers living on the periphery of their society would stand agape at the prosperous plants and be amazed by the extensive worldwide network of foreign missions. Often, institutionalization and elaborate organization go together with lesser growth. If this does not seem the case with Pentecostalism, it is because in those years Canadian society has changed from one that took a system of well-functioning, integrated values and norms for granted to a society in which a considerable number of these values have become optional. It is in an atmosphere of optionality and fuzziness of guidelines that sectarian groups who preserve motivation and standards are at a greater premium.

CHAPTER 9

NEW RELIGIONS AND SCIENTOLOGY

For many, modern Canada, like other highly urbanized societies, resembles a poorly stitched together crazy quilt. Politically, the provincial governments, bent on maximizing their independence from the federal bureaucracy, insist on owning and trading the natural resources, on cultural and linguistic self-determination, and on separate family laws. Economically, the richer regions of the nation resent being responsible for the poorer sections with their higher unemployment and lower average income. Unions (the postal union, for instance) and professional associations fervently augment their place under the economic sun without much consideration for the nation as a whole. The greed of the subsystems is not sufficiently countered by a sense of national purpose which the older generation fondly remembers from the days of World War II.

By contrast, the younger generations (to which the new religions appeal) feel aloof from the national, provincial or local political scenes. Never having suffered together for the common good, their loyalties are latent, if they exist at all. The complex political and economic machinery of the nation operates under its own steam. Its norms are sufficient for low-key integration, guaranteeing a fairly high standard of living for everyone. Yet loyalties which go beyond the bread-and-butter issues and which could fill out the economic and political form are missing. Of course this is the problem of any highly differentiated society: meaning and commitment are not intrinsically and naturally located in the economic, political (and we may add, scientific) subsystems. If the principles of the latter (money, power, objectivity) become overlain with deep sentiments of devotion, they soon begin to wear thin. They cannot bear the burden of cosmic comprehension.

And so anomie prevails. Not anomie in the sense of narrow normlessness (the actual meaning of the term). After all, the major subsystems of Canadian society continue to operate in the familiar grooves. But anomie in the sense of the absence of a meaning system which straddles the differentiations and which commands a reasonably unanimous allegiance. Nomos means both law and order. Anomos means "without law or order." In Canada, as in most Western, highly differentiated societies, the specific injunctions of the law are kept and continue to oil the social machinery. However, consensus and commitment to a more comprehensive moral and social order which provide the matrix for the specific injunctions are held precariously, at best.

The widespread alienation of individuals from both the social system and its subsystems is symptom, cause and consequence of the prevailing anomie. It is a symptom in that the impassiveness of the great majority expresses a lack of commitment to any overarching meaning system. It is a cause in that Western devotion to individual autonomy precludes the emergence of collective dedication to a comprehensive system of meaning. It is a consequence in that the dissipation of meaning encourages withdrawal to the bastion of selfhood.

Yet the bastion of selfhood is a rather awkward and regressive solution. Our complex world could hardly have come into existence if it had not been for the progressive capacity of the individual to surrender part of his autonomy for the sake of the larger whole. However ingeniously the industrialized West has used man's basic aggressive instincts, it has also required that at crucial moments they be disciplined for the sake of the integrity of families, communities, working places, service organizations, trade unions, nations, and any other unit of social organization. The bastion of selfhood is therefore severely handicapped in that it has to constantly balance aggressive foray with meek surrender or, to abandon the metaphor, expression with repression. Withdrawal to the fortress of self is not an option in a viable society. Social viability requires that the individual fits and does so willingly. A well stitched together meaning system guarantees motivation and minimizes alienation. Yet Canadian society is not well stitched together, even though the pervasion of its culture into ethnic groups should not be underestimated.

It is in this climate that the new religions operate. They mop up pockets of alienation. They are helped by alienated individuals discovering that self-indulgence and self-gratification (doing your own thing) are counterproductive to a fuller humanity. Humans (and many other mammals as well) are programmed to exchange repression for acceptance and love. It is love which the new religions abundantly shower on the convert. Yet, in the exchange, aggression towards the group is now fully repressed and deflected onto the nasty world outside the religious haven. The convert exchanges his personal alienation for group alienation because the religious movement leaves no stone unturned to demonstrate its separation from the world.

In response to the predicament of a loosely structured society and the confusion of many well-educated young people, a variety of religious groups has emerged in Canada, as they have elsewhere. Sociologists tend to call them *new* religions rather than sects or cults, partly because they all arose since World War II, partly because they want to reserve the word *cult* for religious groups which are voluntary associations of people with a common interest in esoteric subjects. In contrast with the new religions, cults do not generally claim the exclusive allegiance of their members.

Most of these new religious had their origin in other countries, particularly the United States (California), yet some are native. The *Brotherhood of Kenneth Mills (Unfoldment)* is centered in Toronto and has about 150 persons attending Mills' lectures. To his followers Mills is a prophet who exudes heavenly peace. They have bought him houses and are spell-bound by his speeches which make little sense to outsiders. There are now approximately 5000 disciples of Mills in Canada. However, most of new religions mentioned in the Hill report (1980, 77) were branchplants.

Four of them borrow heavily from Hinduism and are usually led by Indians. At the beginning of the 1980s, *Ananda Marga* had only about fifteen members in Toronto, five of which lived in the commune at regional headquarters. (There is another centre in Ottawa.) This new religion has a history of violence and arson, particularly in the latter half of the seventies when it wanted to draw strong attention to the incarceration of their leader in India. In a number of countries officials of the Indian High Commission were kidnapped, and fires were set to a number of embassy buildings. Ananda Marga is particularly interested in its members achieving cosmic consciousness.

Somewhat larger is the *Divine Light Mission*. It counts its world membership in the millions, but has less than a thousand followers in Canada, about 200 of them in Ontario, mainly in Toronto, London and Ottawa. It is led by an Indian boy guru, Maharaj Ji, who was born in 1957 and at the age of eight succeeded his father, the originator of the movement, on the latter's death. Ji is considered the latest in God's incarnations. This movement was brought to the United States in 1971. For awhile, Ji's fast life (expensive cars, meat-eating, alcohol) estranged him from his mother and older brothers, but the family differences seem to have been patched up. The goal of the movement is mystical union with God who is in everything. After initiation members usually adhere to the unwritten expectation to remain celibate and to surrender all possessions to the Divine Light Mission.

Celibacy and communality are also practised by another Hindu group, the Hare Krishnas, or, more formally, the *International Society of Krishna Consciousness*. It was brought to the West by a Hindu monk, Swami Prabhupada, who claimed to be a direct descendant of an Indian mystic who, in turn, was a reincarnation of the God and Supreme Lord Krishna. The Swami, already in his sixties, appeared on the streets of New York in 1965 and began to attract a following of hippies. The Hare Krishnas believe that Krishna is present in everything and is therefore the center of their long, early morning devotions and their chanting and dancing in the streets. Their income is derived from begging and peddling, and they live in temples run by temple presidents, generally the most ascetic and talented of all devotees. In 1980 the Society had eighty full-time members in the

Toronto temple with several thousands of part-time associates. Ottawa apparently had eighteen full-time members at the time and about 500 adherents.

The largest of the Hindu new religions is *Transcendental Meditation (TM)*. According to Hill (1980, 78) it claims to have 33,563 practitioners of its meditation technique in Ontario alone and maybe as many as 190,000 in all Canada. TM claims not to be a religion. It professes to be only interested in helping humans to achieve their highest potential through bliss consciousness which is attained through the seven steps of transcendental meditation. The movement began as a Hindu sect, founded in 1959 by the Indian guru Maharishi Mahesh Yogi. He had been a disciple of Guru Dev who had brought a spiritual revival to northern India. Towards the end of the sixties Maharishi eliminated all religious terminology and began to use only scientific and psychological terms - and so God was now impersonal creative intelligence to be found within man. Through meditation, twice a day for twenty minutes, this divine source can be awakened and allowed to strengthen one's inner essence or the core of one's identity. Its success has been attributed to the easy simplicity of its demands and to the hunger for self-realization on the part of a very mobile generation.

Four other new religions in Canada are, like TM, primarily interested in personality improvement. Also like TM, they charge for their courses, some after the initial free lecture. The biggest of these movements is *Scientology*, and a special section will be devoted to its history and goals. Lesser known are the *Institute of Applied Metaphysics (IAM)*, which has about 2000 members in Canada and residences, retreats and campuses in Ontario, Saskatchewan and Quebec; *Mind Awareness* (it has no formal membership but has thirty New Age Centres, mainly in Ontario where courses are provided on mind improvement); *People Searching Inside (Psi,* mainly in Ontario where about 4000 people have taken its courses dealing with improving memory, perception and meditation).

A third group of new religions are grafts of Christianity. *The Children of God* belong in this category. They were much more active in Canada round the middle of the seventies than they are now, and they make up in dedication what they lack in numbers. The movement was started by David Berg in the United States in the late sixties. His parents were evangelists, but David (later calling himself Moses David) fell out with organized religion and became an itinerant prophet, establishing small colonies of followers wherever he went. The colonies, too, are rather nomadic. Its members sign away their goods and income, obey officers (or shepherds) on command, allow them to open their mail and never leave without permission. Berg keeps in contact with his colonies through Mo-letters in which he gives advice about mundane as well as spiritual matters, particularly those dealing with the end of the world. Income is derived from the sale of Mo-letters. Usually the Children of God regard the families, the churches and the communities in which they were brought up as ever so many domiciles of Satan. Berg, together with the colony, represent salvation in a very evil world.

Another new religion grafted on Christianity was established by Moon Sun Myung in Korea in 1954 and called the *Holy Spirit Association for the Unification of World Christianity*. In 1970 the USA was made the new headquarters for the Unification Church, as it is now generally called. It has approximately 1000 members in Canada, fifty of which live at the national headquarters in Toronto. It also has centers in Ottawa, Montreal and Vancouver and conducts retreats on a farm at Rice Lake in Ontario. Moon claims that Jesus Christ was not fully God, as he failed in his mission. Moon, on the other hand, is now charged with concluding the mission to unify the world. He and his present wife (there were other wives before) are the True Parents, called Father and Mother by devoted Moonies. The latter think of themselves as being adopted by the True Father and Mother of mankind. As a consequence, they sever the ties with their more earthly relatives so that they can be all the more single-minded in the service of communes and leaders. Life in a Moonie colony is very hectic, and individuals are never alone although sexes have separate sleeping quarters. Marriages are arranged by Moon, often on very short notice, and celebrated in mass ceremonies, with hundreds of couples being wedded at the same time. Moonies usually dress very conservatively, partly because the Unification Church belongs to the moral and political extreme right, partly because its income (from peddling flowers, candles, but also from running a variety of successful businesses) depends on an image of middle-class decency and propriety.

Moonie communities excel through strong cohesion. All members are kept busy with working for the common goal. Each supports the other and there is a strong taboo on hard feelings, asocial conduct and withdrawal. Communal participation in singing, dancing, working, eating, discussing is almost frenzied. Sleep is often not adequate. Individuals become very impressionable and are soon caught up in the Moonie way of thinking. Only after thorough indoctrination does the convert begin to discover how central the figure of Moon is in the movement. In the early stages Moon's name is never mentioned, and the organization usually carries a name which is not even remotely associated with the Unification Church. Conversion to the movement and total dedication to Moon are strong antidotes to previous meaninglessness and alienation. Existence now has an exhilarating goal for bright, idealistic young people. Yet parents and friends are sometimes rather upset about this fast and unexpected severance of old ties and, in some instances, spare no effort to reverse the process of "brainwashing" as they tend to call this kind of rigorous adult socialization. An example of de-programming or de-brainwashing - that of a Canadian from Montreal - is provided in the following based on articles and a book (*Moonwebs: Journey into the Mind of a Cult*) by Josh Freed.

DE-PROGRAMMING

Benji Carroll, a McGill graduate, was in his middle-twenties when in 1977 he became involved with the Creative Community Project (a front organization of the Unification Church of Sun Myung Moon) in San Francisco. After eight months his Jewish family and friends in Montreal became alarmed. News had become very scarce and relations were on the verge of total breakdown. To Carroll, all relatives and friends were now instruments of Satan, and, as as result, ties had to be cut completely. The family met and decided that he should be kidnapped and deprogrammed, a venture that proved to be both dangerous (his parents were picked up by the police) and costly (in all $15,000 was spent).

After the kidnapping Carroll was secluded in a Berkeley hotel room, guarded by Freed and his other Montreal friends. However, both the Moonies and the police discovered the hideout and were hot on their trail. At the very moment that they reached the room, Carrol was carried down the backstairs, bundled into a car, and taken to another hideout, this time a private residence. Here the friends tried to persuade him to voluntarily return with them to Montreal, but they were met with stoney silence and expressionless eyes. The next day they hired a de-programmer who was an ex-Moonie himself and who took on the job for $750. Long, arduous sessions followed, with constant attacks on Moon and his doctrines. There was no letup. The deprogrammer is described by Freed as bright, articulate, intense, loving and electric, so much so that the friends like Carroll originally agnostic, began to feel sorry for the exercise in exorcism. Finally Carroll began to react and respond, slowly at first, but gradually more articulately. Moon and his doctrines were still strongly defended until the deprogrammer began to win some arguments about the inconsistency between unconditional love and hating everyone outside the movement or between total obedience to Moon and personal ethics. The unwinding of the Moon doctrine, the unravelling of knots in Carroll's mind, and the untwisting of half-truths, says Freed (The Spectator [Hamilton, Ontario] February 16, 1978, p.44) was a painstaking process that slowly began to succeed. The breakdown finally occurred when it dawned on Carroll that his parents and friends had spent as much as $15,000 for his return, because they loved him. He broke into tears. "The next thing we knew Benji's arms were pulling us in as we hugged and cried in a mess of tears and affection, losing ourselves to the sense of relief" (Ibid.). After this he signed papers convincing the police that he was leaving California by his own free will. Thereupon he was re-united with his family. On return to Montreal Benji Carroll was involved in deprogramming others for a while.

Deprogramming is a relatively recent term used to describe the process by which individuals, previously programmed (or "brainwashed") into dedicated membership in a group are now weaned away, or deprogrammed, from total subservience. Deprogrammers are individuals who, for a considerable fee, assist parents in transferring deep loyalties of their child from the sect or new religion back to the family. As the process nearly always involves kidnapping of the individual, deprogramming is illegal, particularly when it involves a mature adult. In Canada a well-known American deprogrammer, Ted Patrick, who wrote a book about his experiences (*Let our Children go*) has been barred from entering the country, but native-born Canadians apparently have taken his place (Hill 1980, 152).

As in the case of Benji Carroll, deprogramming generally begins with a cloak-and-dagger operation. Under some pretext the convert is enticed away from the commune or compound where he lives with other members of the new religion. He is then quickly bundled into a car and taken to the home of friends of the family or the deprogrammer. Here he is kept under surveillance. Escaping is made impossible. He is then cajoled and persuaded without interruption to voluntarily return to his erstwhile friends and family. They are often there to add force to the argument with tokens of affection and tears. The persuasion can last for hours, sometimes days. The individual is not allowed to go to sleep or be on his own, as the deprogrammer knows that the "break" is more likely to come after exhaustion and weariness. Often a reconcilation or "break" is faked, and the convert returns to the commune at the first opportunity.

One reason for the failure rate of deprogrammers is that they can only offer a return to past relationships from which the convert originally tried to escape. Often poor family relationships were a major inducement for leaving and for seeking the warm affectionate environment of the new sectarian friends. The convert is rather loath to give up a new-found confidence and heightened self-esteem for the alienation and unhappiness he associates with earlier days. The Hill report to the Attorney General of Ontario (1980, 581-583) gives other reasons for the failure of the deprogrammers. The practice is illegal it says, and the police has brought charges against the deprogrammers rather than the sects because of abduction and involuntary confinement. The report mentions that the two professional deprogrammers in Ontario are now out of business.

"Programming" (becoming more deeply entangled in the doctrines and ways of a new religion) and "deprogramming" (becoming less so) are both symptomatic of loosely woven societies where havens of belonging, security, and trust are at a premium. The new religions attempt to take the place of a closely knit family, but they cannot do so unless they combine love and affection with mutual acceptance of discipline and a considerable dose of self-denial. Too much individualism and permissiveness erodes the boundary around either group, and it is this boundary which keeps the impersonal, uncaring, whimsical world at bay. Programming then is socializing the individual into the tight structures of the new religion. Its strong beliefs about the world, its programme of salvation, and its ascetic demands keep it separate from the world at large.

Yet precisely because of its exclusiveness, the new religion has to take the potential convert through its paces. The process is rather similar to the incessant ways the culture of a new country impinges and finally absorbs the foreign immigrant. Both the culture and the new religion engage in adult socialization, and both demand loyalty and increasingly stronger emotional attachment to core values and ways of acting and reacting. The major difference between a national culture and the culture of a new religion is that the former takes that culture for granted (the way normal Anglo-Canadians behave), whereas the latter has to articulate the differences. It is hostile to society and its success with recruitment depends on not being prematurely labelled. The Unification Church therefore works with extensive aliases and only begins to mention Moon and his doctrines when the potential convert is securely within the fold. The new religions also have to separate the individual from his world, and therefore the Moonies "brainwashed" Benji Carroll in an out-of-the-way farm where access could be controlled. The individual must also be separated from competing sources of attachment. Verse 26, Chapter 14, of the Gospel of Luke is therefore a much-quoted passage of the Bible because Jesus here exhorts his followers to hate "father, and mother, and wife, and brethren and sisters, yea and his own life also...." Some of the new religions insist that they are the only true disciples and therefore the only legitimate alternative to the family. "Now we are your family" is a much heard statement in many new religions.

The future of the new religions is hard to predict. Some of them may come and go as meteors, or flashes of protest. They may be temporary signals that all is not well with our society and its isolated narcissisms. Yet others, such as the Church of Scientology (which will be the topic for the next section), may very well persist and take its form as an accepted sectarian movement, eventually becoming as respectable as other churches. Yet at present all of them are catalysts or vehicles for transforming individuals and societies into better adjusted wholes. For this they use the ferment of change. They crystallize new social forms out of older decrepit ones, and revitalize society by challenging the configurations of power, wealth and tradition. In this way they may contribute to a new integration.

SCIENTOLOGY

The attraction of Scientology lies in its promise of calmness and confidence to people who feel anything but calm and confident. The movement was started by L. Ron Hubbard, born in Tilden, Nebraska, in 1911, the son of a Navy Commander. He spent his childhood in Montana with his maternal grandparents. In his teens he studied Freud, and the influence of psychoanalysis was and is still much in evidence. There is little known about his formal education, except that at one time he attended George Washington University Engineering School. His claim to fame, however, came from science-fiction writing. In 1950 he published a book on Dianetics (exploration of the human mind) which became an instant success and topped the New York Times best-sellers list. In it he analyzes man's brain as a computer, programmed to assist the innate urge to survive. He found that the brain did not always function as smoothly as it should, even though all men were fundamentally good. Therefore Dianetics set out to restore man's full self-determination by making him relive the aberrant imprints ("engrams") and by erasing impediments to self-affirmation. Nowadays, for a handsome price, "auditors" (lay psychotherapists of Scientology) assist their clients to get rid of these aberrations so that they can become "Clear" (a state of bliss achieved when the individual has control over his mind). The "auditors" do this initially by means of an E-meter, a simple skin galvanometer which, like a lie detector, records emotionally-troubling memories impeding spiritual awareness. The auditors themselves often use their meager salaries to pay for the more advanced courses in Scientology.

In the 1950s Hubbard developed Dianetics into a full-fledged philosophy of life, which he called Scientology. It centers around a scientific account of the spiritual, and the effect it has on certainty and sanity. Scientology claims many "firsts": it is the first to discover the cause of war; it is the first to discover the means for accurate measurement of a person's contribution to group viability; it is the first applied system of bettering individuals; it is the first to prove that IQ and intelligence can be improved; it is the first to make a technical breakthrough in the subject of psychosis; it is the first and only completely workable means of handling drug addiction; it is the first to discover the basic nature of man (Hubbard 1978, 5-6).

Scientology also developed its own code of honour (item 3: never desert a group to which you owe your support; item 9: your self-determinism and your honour are more important than your immediate life; item 12: never fear to hurt another in a just cause). It has a creed which strongly stresses equal rights, but also has a credo for a variety of positions in its hierarchy (item 4 for a manager: he must never falter in sacrificing individuals to the good of the group....).

Scientology has an elaborate catechism (Ibid., 197-220). It regards itself as a religion of religions because it helps other religions to attain its goals. It has no intention to quarrel with any creed and has no dogmas of its own. By encouraging greater awareness Scientology helps each individual to attain his own certainty as to who God is and exactly what God means to him. Two pages of the catechism deal with L. Ron Hubbard. He is an individual of great warmth and stature and a much-loved friend and teacher. Full of adventure, his courage and concern for his fellow man has no bounds. In addition, he is possibly today's highest paid writer. He left the United Kingdom in 1966, ostensibly for good, after being informed that his visa would not be renewed. (One question in the catechism asks: Does L. Ron Hubbard eat food and sleep? (he does). Another one: Was L. Ron Hubbard Jesus Christ? Answer: L. Ron Hubbard personally states he is a man as others are men).

The catechism does not mention that Hubbard moved his empire in 1959 from Washington, D.C. (where the tax authorities began to be unhappy about the tax-exempt status of the wealthy organization - Wallis 1979, 29), to Saint Hill Manor, East Grinstead, in England. He resigned all his directorships of Scientology in 1966 and lived for years on a fleet of nine yachts and vessels. This fleet was the headquarter of Sea Org, which provided the senior management courses for Scientology. It is an honour for a Scientologist to be able to join the uniformed elite of Sea Org. According to the catechism its members sign a billion-year contract to express their commitment to the organization (it believes in a future life). Sea Org now has its headquarters in Clearwater, Florida (Hubbard, 1978, 206).

The catechism mentions the mid-1960s as a period when Scientology was hit by a vicious media and political attack. All this happened because it called for reforms in the areas of vested interests like psychiatry and mental health, it says. It still accuses psychiatry of being authoritarian and is appalled by electro-convulsive shock treatment and lobotomy (Ibid., 220).

The Church of Scientology claims to have increased its worldwide membership from 200,000 in 1954 to 5,437,000 in 1977. Of these, almost three-quarters live in North America. In 1980 Canadian membership was estimated to be 15,000 (Hill, 1980, 77). In 1977 it had four churches (with 319 full-time staff members divided among Ottawa, Montreal, Toronto and Vancouver), and eight missions (with 116 staff divided among Vancouver, Calgary, Edmonton, Windsor, London, Kitchener, York and Quebec). It has been involved in many court cases in Canada. In 1974 it sought to restrain a Vancouver broadcasting corporation from repeating libelous remarks about the organization. In the same year it managed to get a court order in Ontario for Nancy McLean to refrain from making public statements on television or radio which might attack or defame or impugn the Church (Ibid., 174). According to Wallis (1976, 220), the McLeans had become disaffected with the movement and suffered extensive harassment when they aired their dissatisfaction on the local news media. Members of Scientology in Toronto held a mock funeral for lost souls in the McLeans' hometown, "carrying a coffin and handing out leaflets charging that the McLean family had betrayed all God-fearing Canadians and was succumbing to the mysteries of evil." They have also taken a number of booksellers and publishing firms to court for selling a variety of books which the Church of Scientology deemed to be defamatory (Hubbard 1978, 174-5).

In Canada the Church of Scientology claims to be active in reform movements dealing with psychiatric abuse, alcoholism, care for the aged, police reform, access to government files, rehabilitation of criminals, and mental retardation (Ibid., p.217).

Worldwide Scientology conducts Sunday services, but annual attendance for 1976 was only 17,468, which means that only one in 300 Scientologists attended Sunday services in that year. In 1976 the figures for marriage services were 4,854, for naming ceremonies, 1,127 and for funerals, 27. There were 5,950 ordained Scientology ministers and 13,068 pastoral counselors (Ibid., 231).

In 1977 Scientology drew a sample of 3,028 members all over the world and came up with the following, rather interesting, profile (Ibid., 238ff.): more than 60% of the membership is between twenty and thirty years old, more than 90% regards itself as either middle- or upper-class, 50% is single, 10% divorced, 37% has a university education. Before their Scientology days 62.3% took drugs, but now 98.2% take no drugs at all. Of the same group, 71.4% report that they now use less alcohol, and as much as 94.1% regard alcohol as unnecessary. Of its members, 41% is Protestant, 26% Catholic, 7% Jewish, 21% no religion and 5% other religion. There is no reason to believe that the Canadian segment of this profile differs from the total sample, and that here, too, Scientology draws its members overwhelmingly from the young middle-class and the well-educated.

At first the movement appears to be largely a successful self-help organization that makes astute use of the alienation of individuals in Western societies. It promises exactly what younger, well-educated individuals feel they need: a sense of wholeness and integrity which leads to greater competence and efficiency in a society which rewards achievement, but is disappointingly vague about other expectations. They long for an anchor to balance their lack of certainty as to who they are or what they should be. They are too young yet to withdraw and give up the world as a bad job. Nor are they particularly comfortable with a Machiavellianism which subsumes all values to personal advancement and power. First, Dianetics and, later Scientology promised solutions to these problems of fuzziness, doubt and uncertainty by providing specific mental health guidelines and scientific legitimation for a programme of personal betterment.

Yet the development from Dianetics to Scientology did not just consist of enlarging an idea or providing a cosmic couch for a less ambitious, more specific mental health programme. In the early 1950s Hubbard had become increasingly embroiled with both amateurs and professionals who took Dianetics at face value and applied it to their own individual identity problems in often idiosyncratic ways and left it at that. He began to call this "Black Dianetics" (Wallis 1976, 83) to distinguish it from his own brand. He began to restrict copyrighted treatments and procedures to a much more exclusive, tightly knit organization. In the process Scientology became much more secretive than Dianetics ever was. From a disinterested writer of a popular book, Hubbard became the central authority in a streamlined, well-oiled movement having all the characteristics of a sect.

The change in role was not difficult to make. Hubbard had never been plagued by an exaggerated sense of unworthiness, self-doubt and humility and the mantle of charismatic leadership seemed to fit him well. Even in pre-Scientology days Hubbard's personal magnetism had been a source of attraction to groups of admirers. His self-assurance was salve for the wounds of those who were not so sure of themselves and his personal charisma (even a renegade such as Vosper [1971, 44] calls him incredibly dynamic, disarming, overwhelming) changed lukewarmness and meaninglessness into purpose and a sense of mission. He has described himself as a Meteor, but his admirers and followers ascribe to him messianic attributes. To advanced students he has been presented as the Maitreya Buddha who, according to the original Buddha, would appear after a period of decadence and corruption and would usher in a new spiritual and world order (Wallis 1976, 250).

Scientology also has its gods. Thetan (from the Greek letter Theta, the first letter, for instance, of theos, god) is the spiritual, immortal essence of man, his soul and his true identity. Scientologists learn to foster this divine, metaphysical element within themselves by practising being three feet back of one's head. By detaching the spirit from the body Scientologists transcend the limit of just one lifetime and thereby expand man's potential (Hubbard 1978, 6). In other words, Thetan is an objectified point of reference that not only orders existence but also provides a leverage for it. It is the overt, professed theology reinforcing personal identity.

Just as mysterious and powerful is the covert, practised theology reinforcing the group solidarity of Scientology. It centers around the god-like qualities attributed to Hubbard. His words and writings are the final revealed truth to his followers. They are studied for edification and spiritual enlightenment, never as a source for critical argument and independent interpretation. The followers think of his books as divinely inspired and Hubbard sees no reason to disagree with them. In a world of devils and aberrations playing havoc with man's mind, Hubbard is a saintly figure who has courageously battled with the Wall of Fire which billions of years ago caused the Thetans to be locked up in the human form (Ibid., 325; Vosper, 1971, 127). Through his heroism humans can now become free Thetans determining their own destiny. Scientology, however, does not just engage in aery-fairy speculations. It has very concrete ideas as to what qualities in human beings are to be preferred. To have power and to be affluent is admirable, to depend on welfare handouts (Scientology tends to be right wing), to doubt, and to be humble is base. Humility, however, is appropriate where the supreme authority of Hubbard is concerned.

With all this emphasis on self-affirmation and individual self- development, the Scientology organization would naturally fall apart if it were not for a strong social commitment permeating the collectivity. Typical of any modern bureacracy is not commitment to fellow workers but to rules and ultimate authority at the top. Scientology is no exception. The rules, flowcharts and intricate procedures keep the organization serenely humming and instill in workers a strong sense of conviction and purpose. A messianic glow adds piety to the purpose. Hubbard's authority (he is the Founder, spelt with capital F) is the final cappingstone to which a unifying devotion is directed. On the other hand, the relationship among the workers is sometimes one of competition and mutual distrust, even if on the surface everyone is friendly and relaxed. Vosper (1971, 138) was twelve times demoted to the Condition of Liability. This meant that he became nonexistent as a team member because he was deemed to have damaged the organization. The accusation was usually a flimsy pretext to punish people who had shown too much independence and not enough respect for the rules. It meant that he could not receive any income until he had become rehabilitated, had to wear a dirty grey rag tied around his left arm, could not eat and drink more than stale cheese sandwiches and water and was not allowed to have sexual intercourse with his wife. During this period his erstwhile friends were distant, distrustful, and uncommunicative. Only by working twice as hard and by asking each member of his group permission to rejoin could the Condition of Liability be lifted.

All this has the effect of enslaving the individual to the group or organization. He or she has to be constantly on the alert to fit in with expectations in order to advance or even just to stay in place. According to Hubbard (1965, 31), self-denial is the only aberration. Yet it is precisely self-denial which is the prerequisite for being anywhere in the Scientology hierarchy. One can even sink deeper down the organization through assignment to the Condition of Doubt or, even further down the abyss, to the Conditions of Enemy and Treason.

Doubt cannot be tolerated. Hubbard himself (Ibid., 17) declared that only the Merchants of Chaos, some very disturbing elements in our civilization, could disbelieve the truth of Scientology. For these powers to exist at the very heart of the organization calls for eradication. The individual has to wear handcuffs made of paper-clips, "is thrown off the premises, or is locked up in the most dungeon-like part of it" (Vosper 1971, 140). To be an enemy or traitor in Scientology (writing a critical book about the organization can bring this judgment) means that one is now effectively shunned and declared Fair Game.

Garrison (1974, 171), who is generally sympathetic to Scientology, explains Fair Game as follows: "Any person so designated (by an Ethics Order) could be deprived of property or injured by any means, fair or foul. He could be "tricked, sued, or lied to, or destroyed." As this practice created mounting hostility, Hubbard, in 1968, cancelled it. He explained security-checking and fair game as resulting from the need to develop "a tightly disciplined organizational structure" to counter "19 years of attacks by the minions of vested interest, psychiatric front groups." But he said, now "such duress is not necessary when one has a technology which sets man free" (Ibid., 172-3). Yet in the early seventies the sociologist Roy Wallis (1979, 204), who had written a book about the movement, was severely harassed by a series of forged letters to the University of Stirling (where he taught). There have been numerous incidents of this kind in other parts of the world. Obviously Scientology cannot very well loosen its organizational structure when it is dead set on maximum witness to the truth, as Hubbard sees it.

The Church of Scientology seems to be aware that there is a rather deep chasm between its sacralization of personal identity and its sacralization of group identity. One of its officials said to Garrison (1974, 172): "You see, any perception of truth has to be organized, and with organization comes the imposition of human frailty. So we try to strike a balance, a golden mean, between truth and organization." In other words, Scientology has to stifle individual independence to keep its organization afloat. It has developed a variety of means to perpetually cleanse itself from subversive elements within. Someone who has been declared a Suppressive Person is regarded as a traitor and incurs the collective hatred of the movement. It is this collective hatred of the deviant which binds the membership closer together and invariably increases the awe for what it defends. Yet this collective hatred is also often directed to subversive elements without, such as elected officials who vote against granting local permits to Scientology, or medical associations who warn the public in no uncertain terms against what they regard as quackery and chicanery.

Another example of commitment as the means to sacralize corporate Scientology is seen in subtle recruiting methods which ease clients into becoming loyal members of the organization. At first individuals come just to hear a free lecture and to improve themselves. But the staff is under instruction to never "let anyone simply walk out. Convince him he's loony if he doesn't gain on it ...." (Anderson 1965, 103). To make further personality improvements the individual undergoes auditing. He feels encouraged by the discovery of blocks to his progress. In the meantime he is surrounded by supportive, bright, young people who shower him with the reassurance he nostalgically remembers receiving from his mother when he was a child. He therefore wants to increase the pleasurable contacts, and soon he begins to adopt the interests and enthusiasms of his new friends. This leads to signing up for yet another course and all the way up to auditorship which qualifies him to practise for a fee. By this time he has also become convinced that he must join the awe-inspiring goal of Hubbard to clear the planet and of Scientology to save the world. After all, rumors of war and the injustices of society cry out for the mobilization of Thetans, the superior forces lurking behind the evil, obstructing engrams. To join a movement with noble intentions, he is now persuaded, gives life a worthwhile goal and makes him into a better person, confident as to what he is all about. If the evil world outside Scientology is not ready for these changes, he further reasons, this is just too bad. If people don't want to hear, they must suffer the consequences. As a zealous new member of Scientology he has no qualms about going to considerable lengths toward bolstering the movement against anyone who stands in the way of pitiless progress.

Apart from theology and commitment, various rituals also cement the corporate identity of Scientology. As mentioned before, there are the church services as well as the marriage, naming, and funeral rites. Yet they do not seem to be as important as the routines of the auditing sessions, the meetings, and other forms of interaction, which are indistinguishable from what makes other modern bureaucracies into a unity. One ritual which it has in common with schools and universities is the one described by Vosper (1971, 117), who defected after fourteen years of high office within Scientology. On Friday afternoons staff and students assemble in the Chapel. Those students who have become Clear during the week are handed their ornate certificates and make short speeches, usually "exuberant eulogies to the wonder of Scientology and L. Ron Hubbard." Still glorying in their successful arrival at this milestone of self-knowledge and surrounded by congratulating staff members, a candidate then feels sufficiently encouraged to proceed to the office where he can enrol for the next, equally expensive course.

As is often the case with sects or movements which are "total" in that they tend to monopolize the attachments of the individual, Scientology brooks little interference from the family if there is a conflict of interest. The family of their members or charges are sometimes treated as an unwanted source of interference. According to Scientology, parents sometimes prevent an individual, or preclear, from making satisfactory progress towards the goal of becoming a Clear. These relatives then get rather upset by letters from the person concerned refusing any further mail or phone calls, in short, cutting all ties. Hubbard (1965, 64) calls the family "a basically impractical institution," presumably because it is a potential source of competition for a person's loyalty and a hindrance to his self- development. Certainly his own divorces seem to indicate that, for Hubbard, marriage can be serial rather than perpetual. When Vosper was shown off the premises at the Scientology headquarters in England, he was not allowed to see and say goodbye to his children, and he comments: "The word of Hubbard is senior to any minor thing like smashing up my family." Elsewhere he says, "If families are broken up, if friends are turned against friends, if suicides occur, if an entrapment of the very spirit that makes humans human should occur, then that is subsidiary to the aim to prove Hubbard right" (Vosper, 1971, 16,13,142). In 1965 Ralph Glaser was declared a Suppressive Person because he "failed to handle or disconnect from his wife as ordered ...." (Wallis 1976, 261). Certainly at that time the organization had no qualms about separating families in order to preserve its own corporate integrity.

With Hubbard getting older and Scientology becoming of age, there is evidence that both have become somewhat less sensitive about adverse public opinion. They now think (Hubbard 1978, 220) that some Scientology executives overreacted to the attacks in the 1960s. One can expect the organization to institutionalize and mellow further as time goes on. Yet it depends for its obvious success on the problems of personal alienation of the young and the anomie of society at large for its perpetuation. With its strong emphasis on improving the mind of the individual, there is a tendency to stress its finite mental health accomplishments at the expense of the never-ending dramatization of sin and salvation of the older religious organization of the West. It would be interesting to see whether it will become less exuberantly optimistic about the human condition and human progress. If it is going to develop in that direction, Scientology is likely to downplay the ultimacy of being a Clear and, beyond that, an Operating Thetan (a state of recovering one's full abilities and freedom) and to stress man's essentially tragic interplay with the forces around him instead of the celebration of the victory over these forces. Yet this is not the way that Scientology conceives of the future now. Its optimistic individualism or overt theology is as strong as ever and can only see a "broad hope of a new and better way that shines as a beacon to an ever increasing number of people" (Ibid., 286). And of course that "way" is the way of Scientology - making Thetans stronger and thereby solving all man's problems, whether they be nuclear holocaust, drug addiction, corruption in government, or just plain existential *Angst*.

In the early eighties Scientology suffered some major setbacks. On January 7, 1983, Mrs. Hubbard (Ronald's third wife and the church's second most powerful official) was sentenced to four years in prison by a federal judge in Washington, D.C. She and ten other Scientologists were convicted of bugging and burglarizing the offices of the Internal Revenue Service and of the Justice, Treasury and Labor Departments, among others. During this period a palace revolution shook the organization, leaving a group of young zealots in charge. As though this was not enough, highly placed defectors from the church claimed to have solid evidence of Hubbard's academic failures and mediocre war record (he pretended to be a war hero). They also claimed that the active membership had dropped from a high of 2,000,000 in the early and mid-1970s to 100,000 in the USA with an equal number abroad. While all this was going on Hubbard himself went into hiding (*Time* magazine, January 31, 1983, 54-57).

In December 1984 the Church of Scientology in Toronto was charged with possession of stolen documents from the police, the Canadian Mental Health Association and the College of Physicians and Surgeons of Ontario.

PART IV

THE MAJOR DENOMINATIONS

The identity approach to religion looks at denominations as reconciling rather than provoking conflict within and between social systems. Denominations attempt to both mute *and* motivate individuals, to both constrain *and* co-opt recalcitrant groups, to both reform *and* reinforce the society. They channel personal motivation and group cooperation into directions advantageous for society at large. By contrast, sects tend to give up society as a bad job; its members must either withdraw from such a society or, at best, feel that society must be thoroughly reconstructed.

In Canada the denominations, or "mainline churches" as the 1981 census calls them, have moved away from the preservation of specific old-country mores towards the defense of "charter race" Canadian culture. Yet that culture is anything but cohesive. Not only is it divided into Anglophone and Francophone parts, it also has to contend with an increasingly greater independence of individuals and groups. This, of course, is the affliction of all modern industrial societies: the advantages of complexity and differentiation can be reaped only at the price of a weakened social conscience, anomie, and meaninglessness.

The statistics of chapter 10 illustrate this theme of the weaker hold of the major denominations on the population: the number of those with "No Religion" rises from census to census, and the percentage belonging to the mainline churches drops accordingly. Within each of these religious organizations the proportion of purely nominal members is also on the rise. Most dramatic is the fall in church attendance from 1946, when two-thirds of the population had been to church on the preceding Sunday, to 1980, when only one-third had done so. The Protestant denominations have always had a much lesser hold on their members than the Catholic one. Yet, particularly since Vatican II and the Quiet Revolution, Catholic church attendance has dropped even more than the Protestant one.

Chapter 11 traces the close alliance between Catholicism and Francophone culture. The French bishops and clergy fiercely protected the integrity of family, community and nation from the earliest seventeenth century beginnings to the post-conquest period when, almost single-handedly, they kept French culture intact. Only in the last twenty-five years

has this close alliance come to an end, so that at present (1985) the secularization (or waning power of Catholicism over the systems of which Quebec
society exists) has become a fact of life.

Chapter 12, English Catholicism, concentrates less on history than on
how a denominational identity was forged, first out of pockets of Irish,
Scottish and American settlers, later out of the German, Polish, and other
settlers. It stresses the importance of Catholic schools for this process of
consolidation, yet it in no way ignores the divisiveness of ethnic loyalties and
the struggle for power within the Catholic fold. Thanks to the international
vision of the various popes, the Catholic Church also helped to make
Canadian society more just through its concern for the disprivileged and the
powerless. Its internal solidarity suffered particularly since the early 1970s,
when Vatican II deliberately weakened organizational boundaries in order
to be more relevant for a secular society. Yet its deeper understanding of the
modern world could not avert the increasing breakdown of families, the
main carriers of its beliefs and values.

The next two chapters take the main Protestant denominations, in
alphabetical order. Over its long history, Anglicanism in Canada has moved
from uncritical preservation of English culture and class structure to critical
independence. Its denominational boundaries are now drawn more strictly,
and it can therefore afford to speak out freely against the ills of a society with
which it once was allied politically. The Baptists in Canada became the heirs
and consolidators of the exuberant Alline revivals in the Maritimes. In more
recent times, those Baptist groups which favoured openness towards secular
culture have not increased as much as the ones who shut themselves off
through fundamentalist beliefs.

Methodism and Presbyterianism in Canada have a long history of opening and closing denominational boundaries. In the nineteenth century the
intradenominational divisions were resolved. In the twentieth, both denominations, together with the Congregational Churches, took the initiative for amalgamation in the United Church of Canada, now the largest
Protestant denomination in Canada. The strength of a common national
vision (Christianizing Canada), the practical necessity for cooperation in
matters of temperance, Sunday observance, Sunday School materials, and
ministerial training, all contributed to the weakening of the existing denominational boundaries and to the formation of a new interdenominational
one.

CHAPTER 10

RELIGIOUS COMPOSITION AND RELIGIOUS PRACTICES

Denominational composition in Canada reflects the ethnic origins of the population. The immigrants maintained their culture, language, beliefs and rituals, however much economic opportunities and social structures changed. And so the earliest French inhabitants established Catholicism deeply in Canadian soil, so much so that in 1981 88% of the Quebec population put "Catholic" on the census form as its

Table 10.1

Percentage Distribution of the Major Denominations in
Canada for selected years from 1871 - 1971

Denomination	Percentage of the Population						
	1871	1891	1911	1931	1951	1971	1981
Anglican	14.1	13.7	14.5	15.8	14.7	11.8	10.1
Baptist (2)	6.8	6.4	5.3	4.3	3.7	3.1	2.9
Congregationalist	0.6	0.6	0.5	—	—	—	—
Greek Orthodox (3)	—	—	1.2	1.0	1.2	1.5	1.5
Jewish	—	0.1	1.0	1.5	1.5	1.3	1.2
Lutheran	1.1	1.4	3.2	3.8	3.2	3.3	2.9
Methodist	16.3	17.8	15.1	—	—	—	—
Pentecostal	—	—	—	0.3	0.7	1.0	1.4
Presbyterian	16.2	15.9	15.6	8.4	5.6	4.0	3.4
Catholic	42.9	41.6	39.4	41.3	44.7	47.3	47.3
United Church	—	—	—	19.5	20.5	17.5	15.6
Other	1.9	2.5	3.7	3.9	3.9	4.9	6.4
No Religion	0.1	—	0.4	0.2	0.4	4.3	7.3

Total (1)							
Percentage	100.0	100.0	99.9	100.0	100.1	100.0	100.0
Absolute	3,579,782		7,206,643		14,009,429		24,083,495
		4,833,239		10,376,786		21,568,315	

(1) Exclusive of Newfoundland prior to 1951. (2) Includes Mennonites in 1871. (3) Includes Russian, Ukrainian and Syrian Orthodox.
Source: Census of Canada.

denomination. In the same census 94.6% of Canadians of French origin also claimed to be Catholic. Similarly, Protestant immigrants from Britain and the United States established the Church of England (Anglicanism), the Church of Scotland (Presbyterianism), Methodism, and Baptism, first in Nova Scotia (where in 1827, 77% belonged to these four denominations) and later in Upper Canada (with a corresponding 62% in 1842). Yet ethnic origin is not the only factor responsible for the denominational composition of Canada as described by Table 10.1.

A second factor is the birthrate varying from one denomination to another and therefore increasing or decreasing the percentage of the population belonging to that denomination. One reason why the Anglican, Baptist, Presbyterian and United proportion of the Canadian population declined (see Table 10.1) and why the Catholic proportion increased or remained the same is that the Protestant birthrate (as measured by the number of 0-4-year-old children per 1,000 women, aged 15-44) has traditionally been below the Catholic one. For instance, in 1961 the average birthrate for Canada was 606, but for Catholics it was 666, Anglicans 533, Baptists 565, Presbyterians 487 and United Church adherents 574. For some of the smaller denominations the birthrate differences were even greater: in 1971 the Hutterite rate was 745 but the Jewish only 292, leading to the confident prediction that, relative to the Jewish one, the Hutterite share in the Canadian population will increase if the trend persists (Kalbach and McVey 1976, 238).

A third factor affecting denominational composition is continuing immigration. Before and after World War I, large numbers of British immigrants doubled the number of Anglicans and increased the Anglican proportion of the population from 12.8% in 1901 to 16.1% in 1921. After World War II, large-scale immigration of Eastern European refugees and Greek immigrants increased the proportion of Orthodox from 1.0% in 1931 to 1.5% in 1971. Post-World War II immigration from such traditionally Catholic countries as Poland and Italy has further contributed (apart from the higher birthrate) to the Catholic proportion tion increasing from 44.7% in 1951 to 47.3% in 1981. Immigration is also responsible for the overrepresentation of some denominations in specific areas. The large-scale immigration of Germans and Scandinavians to the Prairie provinces at the beginning of this century accounts for 42% of all Lutherans in Canada living there, although only 17% of the 1981 population resided in Alberta, Saskatchewan and Manitoba.

A fourth factor shaping the pattern of Canadian denominations is the gradual fading of some denominational boundaries which had originated in European history (there were nine separate Presbyterian and eight Methodist denominations in the nineteenth century) and the emergence of several thousand local union congregations, particularly on the frontier where economic necessity and communal spirit spawned many ecumenical ventures (Mann 1976, 388-92). Table 10.1 (1931 column) shows the disappearance of the Congregational, Methodist and a substantial portion of the

Presbyterian denominations. These churches consolidated in 1925 to form the United Church which is now the second largest denomination in Canada.

A fifth factor has to do with proselytism, which was more successful in some denominations than in others. Although only 10% of the Canadian population is Anglican, as much as 20% in the Yukon and 34% in the Northwest Territories belonged to this denomination by 1981, because in a previous era the Church Missionary Society of England made much effort to convert the natives in the Canadian North. This is also true for some of the smaller denominations: the robust growth of the Jehovah's Witnesses in the Canadian population, from 68,000 in 1961 to 175,000 in 1971, is mainly due to their active door-to-door witnessing. The same applies to the Pentecostals, whose denominational share rose from 0.3% in 1931 to 1.4% in 1981 (see Table 10.1) primarily because of a vigorous programme of evangelism.

A sixth factor influencing the percentage distribution of Table 10.1 is the increasing secularization of the Canadian population. "Secularization" is used here to mean the weakening hold of religious denominations on the people, culminating in an increasing percentage writing "No Religion" on the census form. As recently as 1961, the percentage doing so was only 0.5, but in 1981 the figure rose to 7.4%. One reason for this large increase is an administrative one, as in 1971 "No Religion" was for the first time mentioned as one of thirteen specific entries an individual could make. Yet even the 7.4% covers only a small proportion of the Canadian population whose membership in a denomination is rather nominal. In 1971 the actual membership of the United Church of Canada, according to its yearbook, was 1,016,706 which is only 27.0% of those who were entered on the census form as such (3,768,805). The comparable figure for 1981 is 24.0%. The corresponding percentages for Anglicans are 27.3% for 1971, 23.5% in 1981. This does not mean, however, that 76% of United and 76.5% of Anglicans are now nominal: unconfirmed children and churchgoing adherents are also hidden in these percentages. Yet it means that a majority of Canadians who think of themselves as United or Anglican at census time in actual fact have little or no contact with the churches to which they belong. They are hardly distinguishable from those who put "No Religion" on the census form. What is more, in the United Church for instance, their percentage has slowly risen from 66.3% in 1931 to 67.5% in 1941, 70.8% in 1951, 71.7% in 1961, 73.0% in 1971 and 76.0% in 1981.

RELIGIOUS PRACTICES

The boundaries around the various denominations in Canada can be drawn using a variety of criteria. The census draws them according to the criterion of individual self-definition. This means that individuals may define themselves as belonging to a particular denomination because they were baptized by a clergyman of that denomination or because their parents were married in such and such a church. Yet the denominations themselves define membership much more narrowly. Usually, only those who have made a confession of faith or have been confirmed in a special ceremony are regarded as within the fold. Even this may have little to do with sustained activity, and so the Anglicans, for instance, publish figures for those who took communion "during the Easter Octave." In 1971 there were 399,221 of the latter. This category of active members was only 63.6% of the confirmed members on the parish rolls, or 15.7% of Anglicans who appear as such in the census records. In 1981 the comparable percentages were 69.2% and 16.3%.

Individual congregations usually measure their viability by church attendance. The advantage of this criterion is its concreteness. It is easier to count people than to investigate whether they adhere to beliefs or whether they practise their Christianity. Most religious organizations are more likely to state their goals in terms of beliefs in salvation or of outreach to others. Yet church attendance at the least expresses a degree of organizational loyalty and is therefore a useful measure of organizational performance.

In Canada, church attendance can be fairly accurately described and compared. The major part of this chapter will therefore be devoted to this task. However, other practices and beliefs have also been investigated and should be summarized. First beliefs.

The Canadian Institute of Public Opinion (Gallup Poll) has at various times asked a question about belief in God. It found that Canadians, compared with other major Western countries, rank close to the top as far as affirmation of a belief in God is concerned. In 1950, 95%; in 1969, 92%; in 1971, 89%; and in 1975, 88% of adults said that they held such belief. The Gallup Poll also found (for instance, in 1969) that Catholics, women, and older people were more likely to hold these beliefs than Protestants, men, and younger individuals. Reginald Bibby provided more detail about Canadian beliefs in God in a 1975 study. This survey had the advantage of being specifically designed for the investigation of religious patterns, even though its sample was drawn from telephone directories and had only a 52% return rate. In spite of these disadvantages, it is likely to fairly reflect the Canadian situation. Bibby (1979, Table 1, p.6) found that 90% of his respondents fell into four categories: 48% who had no doubt about God's existence, 22% who believed in spite of occasional doubts, 4% who believed in God some of the time and 16% who did not believe in a personal God, but in a higher power of some kind. Only 5% were agnostic (did not know whether there was a God), and 2% were atheist (did not believe in God). These findings are remarkably close to a similar survey done in Australia in 1966 (Mol, 1971, 43-4) where the corresponding percentages were 88%, 49%, 20%, 7%, 12%, 6% and 2%.

Twenty-six percent of the Canadian population prays daily and privately, but the percentage rises to sixty-five percent for the members of conservative religious organizations such as Baptists, Brethren, Church of God, Pentecostal, Mennonite, Nazarene, Salvation Army, Christian Reformed. Most Canadians (56%) pray weekly, sometimes, or at special occasions, and only 18% never prays (Ibid. Table 5, p.8). Twenty-two percent of the Canadian population has had a definite feeling that they were somehow in the presence of God. Again the percentage rises to 61% for the members of, what Bibby calls, the conservative churches (Ibid. table 7). The latter group are also the best Bible readers; 26% read the Bible daily, although only 2% of the population at large does so (Ibid. table 6).

As has been said above: however inadequate as a measure of religiosity, church attendance is a fairly useful indicator of organizational loyalty. In Canada, church attendance has dropped severely over the last thirty-five years, but it has dropped much more for some denominations (e.g., French Catholicism) than for others. The National Institute of Public Opinion (Gallup Poll) has at regular intervals asked its Canadian panel whether or not they had attended a church or a synagogue within the last seven days. In 1946 67% had done so, in 1956 61%, in 1965 55%, in 1970 44%, in 1975 41%, in 1980 35% and in 1984 36%. The Gallup Polls are not very discriminating in that they do not distinguish between French and English-speaking Catholics or between the various Protestant denominations. However, in most surveys it distinguished between Catholics and Protestants. These polls show that attendance dropped among both: in 1946 83% of Catholics had been to church in the previous 7 days, in 1956 87%, in 1965 83%, in 1970 65%, in 1975 61%, in 1980 50%, in 1984 also 50%. For Protestants the corresponding percentages were 60%, 43%, 32%, 28%, 25%, 26%, and 29%. The figures show that from 1965-1980 Catholic attendance dropped severely and Protestant slightly, but that from 1980 onwards it has remained steady.

It is possible to get more discriminating data by doing a secondary analysis of the 1965 and 1974 Canadian National Election Studies. The time between these two studies was the period of the sharpest drop. The first study was carried out by Philip Converse, John Meisel, Maurice Pinard, Peter Regenstreiff and Mildred Schwartz; the second one by Harold Clarke, Jane Jenson, Lawrence LeDuc and Jon Pammett. Both samples are stratified probability samples of Canadians eligible to vote. It is also possible to divide both samples into regular churchgoers (at least twice a month - usually weekly) and irregular ones (those who go at best once a month, but usually only a few times a year or never). In the 1965 study 50% (n = 2055) were regular; in the 1974 study the corresponding percentage was 43 (n - 2250). As church attendance varies from denomination to denomination, we must examine the percentage of regulars separately for each major church organization.

Denomination

The samples of the two studies only approximate the denominational distribution of the population. For instance, English Catholics were underrepresented and French Catholics overrepresented in the 1965 study. Be this as it may, the trends of Table 10.2 are not likely to be strongly affected by the sample distribution. There is evidence also from other sources (see the chapter on Catholicism in Quebec) that the Quiet Revolution of the 1960s in Quebec has had a severe effect on regular attendance in that province, for, although there was a 10% decrease in the percentage of English Catholic attenders over the period, the drop amongst French Catholics was 32%. Protestant attendance went up, if anything, over the 1965 to 1974 period. However, the increase could very well be due to sampling error.

Table 10.2

Percentage of regular churchgoers (at least twice a month, usually weekly) for the major denominations in 1965 and 1974

YEAR	ANGLICAN	CATHOLIC (ENGLISH)	CATHOLIC (FRENCH)	UNITED CHURCH	OTHER
1965	19 (n = 245)	69 (n = 283)	88 (n = 619)	23 (n = 474)	29 (n = 434)
1974	23 (n = 283)	59 (n = 504)	56 (n = 577)	28 (n = 456)	39 (n = 430)

How do these figures compare with church attendance records in other countries? There are very few Catholic nations in the world with the same high church attendance figures we found in French Canada in 1965. It is interesting that the only nation with even higher church attendance, Ireland (Ward, 1972, 297-298), has, like French Canada, a history of close alliance between the Catholic Church and a national identity actually threatened or felt to be threatened by a Protestant English overlord. The drop in the attendance level of English Catholics suggests that now the secular culture or a political party such as the Parti Québecois may have taken over the function of identity sacralization from the Catholic Church.

The figures for the English-speaking Catholics in Canada are very comparable to the figures we have for those countries where Catholics are, or at least were, in the minority and where Catholic identity could not be taken for granted and had to be defended. Catholic attendance in such countries as Australia (Mol 1971, 14), England (Martin 1972, 232), Netherlands (Laeyendecker 1972, 335), New Zealand (Mol 1972, 371), South Africa (Higgins 1972, 449), United States (Lazerwitz 1964, 430; Alston 1971, 234) is or was, in the second half of the sixties, generally in the neighbourhood of 60 to 70%. By contrast, Catholic Church attendance in such traditionally Catholic countries as France (Isambert 1972, 180), Italy (Acquaviva 1972, 308), Portugal (Querido 1972, 428), Spain (Almerich 1972, 469ff.) is much lower and appears to be much more strongly determined by internal divisions, such as class boundaries.

The Protestant attendance figures in Canada also fit an international pattern. Everything else remaining the same they are usually much lower than Catholic figures. Protestant individualism everywhere seems to have an inevitable weakening effect on institutional hold as compared with collective Catholic identity. Yet there is similar variation, as with Catholicism. In Lutheran countries such as Denmark (Thorgaard 1972, 487), Finland (Seppanen 1972, 155), Norway (Vogt 1972, 393) and Sweden (Gustafsson 1972, 487), average church attendance stays below 5% of the population. Anglicanism in England is also in this category. On the other hand, Protestant sects in any part of the world provide a picture of well-buttressed identity in what is regarded as an essentially hostile camp, and church attendance here is uniformly high. The Canadian figures for the middle-and-upper class denominations such as Presbyterian, United, and Anglican fit neither of these two patterns. The middle classes (and the term has much less meaning here than in most European countries) uphold the status quo rather than defend a radical position, as the sects do. Yet their churches have to compete with other religious organizations, in contrast with the state churches of Scandinavia. Church attendance figures of Protestants in Canada are much more comparable to the figures we have for the United States, Australia, and New Zealand where the denominations also have to compete and therefore develop separate identities, and yet, on the other hand occupy an established undisputed position in the communal network.

Age

In the 1965 study the age difference proved to be relatively small. In the group aged 21 to 30 years, the percentage of regular attenders was 46%. It rose to 51% in the 31 to 40 years category and remained virtually the same (50% and 49%) in the groups aged 41 to 50 and 51 to 60. The percentage increased again (56%) for the respondents who were 61 years and over. In the 1974 survey the picture had changed. In the group aged 21 to 30, the percentage of regular attenders dropped from 46 to 31. In the 31 to 60 category the percentage had not changed much (47) and in the 61+ age group it had decreased from 62 to 52.

Table 10.3 shows that the changes in the youngest age group were almost entirely due to a decrease from 84 to 32% for the 21 to 30-year-old French Catholics. There had also been a much slighter decrease for English Catholics in all age groups, but Protestants increased attendance in most categories.

Table 10.3

Percentages of Regular Church Attenders
by Denomination and Age in 1965 and 1974

AGE	YEAR	ANGLICAN	CATHOLIC (ENGLISH)	CATHOLIC (FRENCH)	UNITED CHURCH	OTHER
21 - 30	1965	10	54	84	14	21
	1974	16	48	32	12	32
31 - 60	1965	20	72	90	20	30
	1974	24	61	64	30	42
61+	1965	28	78	87	40	46
	1974	36	68	82	37	37

The conclusion can be drawn that when denominational identity is weakening (as is the case in Quebec) and is less able to straddle competing identity structures such as age groups, the young adults tend to loosen their allegiance to the institutions identified with previous generations or to a meaning system identified with an earlier personal identity phase. In the 1984 Gallup Poll the age differences continue to be substantial. Of those 18 to 29 years of age, 25%, of those 30 to 49 years of age, 36%, and of those 50 years and over, 45% had attended church in the previous seven days.

Education

Important changes took place also in the areas of education and church attendance between 1965 and 1974. In 1965, 59% of those with only primary schooling (eight years or less - n = 750) were regular attenders; in 1974 this percentage had dropped to 53 (n = 647). In 1965, 45% of those who had either finished or had had at least some secondary schooling (n = 939) were regular; in 1974 this percentage had dropped to 40 (n = 1388). Most severe was the drop among those who had a university degree or had at least finished some tertiary education. In 1965, the percentage of regular attenders was 50 (n = 366); in 1974 it was 37 (n = 364).

Yet, as Table 10.4 shows, the decrease was much larger in some denominations (such as French Catholics) than in others (such as the United Church).

Table 10.4

Percentage of Regular Church Attenders by Denomination and Education

EDUCATION	YEAR	ANGLICAN	CATHOLIC (ENGLISH)	CATHOLIC (FRENCH)	UNITED CHURCH	OTHER
Primary Only	1965	15	66	87	24	33
	1974	29	60	70	26	43
Secondary Only	1965	13	69	90	19	29
	1974	21	57	50	29	39
Post-Secondary	1965	35	75	88	32	34
	1974	22	63	39	28	31

In the Catholic Church in Quebec, a massive exodus of the young and the educated seems to have taken place, bringing attendance down from close to the world's highest to the average for pluralistic societies. The severest drop in church attendance was from 84% to 32% in the 21 to 30 age group of French Catholics (Table 10.3) and from 88% to 39% among those French Catholics who had at least some post-secondary education. The differences among the other denominations pales by comparison and often can be attributed to sampling error, particularly when the sample is small (for instance, the n for Anglicans with primary education was 47 in 1965 and 66 in 1974) and the percentage difference is less than 10%.

In 1974 there was certainly very little evidence that in Canada the better educated tend to be more regular in their church attendance, even if one does not consider the French Catholics among whom the opposite is clearly the case. In other countries there is a correlation between higher education and better church attendance, for instance Austria (Bogensberger and Zulehner 1972, 57), Belgium (Houtart 1972, 76), West Germany (Kehrer 1972, 197), Switzerland (Campiche 1972, 520) and the United States (Alston 1971, 235). The fact that in Canada the denomination to which one belongs is much more significant for church attendance patterns than the amount of education one has received seems to point to the educational and religious subsystems functioning largely independently of one another. Yet the strength of the Catholic subsystem and its hold on the membership is also in Canada likely to be related to the capacity of Catholicism to socialize the young in its own school system (see, for United States, Greeley and Rossi 1966, and for Australia, Mol 1971, 183-196).

There is also the possibility that the young and the educated spearhead the secularization of a denomination. If that is the case, one can expect the older and the less educated segments of the French population to follow the increasingly lower level of church attendance in Quebec, until, as seems to have become the case with Protestants since 1970, all attendance levels out at a lower point. Yet the 1984 Gallup Poll showed that the differences remain substantial: of those with a university education, 29%, of those with high school, 35%, and of those with primary school only, 43% had been to church in the last seven days.

Income

In both the 1965 and the 1974 survey, those who belonged to families in the highest income brackets tended to attend somewhat less. Those in the lowest brackets attended most regularly. As in the intervening period income levels in Canada had risen rapidly, these levels were defined differently so that roughly one-third of the sample would fit in each category. In 1965 those families with a total income of less than $4000, were put in the lowest group (n = 663); in 1974 the ceiling on the lower-income category was raised to $7500 (n = 751). The middle income bracket in 1965 was defined as the income of those families where the combined income was between $4000, and $7000, (n = 851); in 1974 the limits of this category were $7500 and $15000, (n = 898). The high-income bracket included individuals who belonged to families in which total income was more than $7000, in 1965 (n = 471) and $15,000 in 1974 (n = 705).

The percentage of regular attenders in the low-income group was 55 in 1965, 51 in 1974. In the middle income group the percentages were 50 and 42. In the top category the percentages were 44 and 36. This appears to show a decrease in all income categories over the period, but when the denominational variable is introduced (Table 10.5) it becomes clear that the decrease is confined to Catholicism.

Table 10.5

Percentage of Regular Church Attenders by Denomination
and Income in 1965 and 1974

INCOME	YEAR	ANGLICAN	CATHOLIC (ENGLISH)	CATHOLIC (FRENCH)	UNITED CHURCH	OTHER
Lower	1965	22	65	85	25	36
	1974	37	60	66	33	42
Middle	1965	12	67	91	23	31
	1974	17	58	53	26	39
Higher	1965	27	74	88	21	29
	1974	11	57	45	24	32

Again French Catholicism shows a much sharper decrease than English Catholicism, the sharpest drop being in highest income families (43% for the French and 17% for the English category). Among Protestants all categories increased the percentage with the exception of the top Anglican category, and here the cells (82 in 1965 and 87 in 1974) were so small that the odds are one in twenty that the difference is chance.

Residence

In Canada city-dwellers attend church less regularly than those living in towns and rural areas. In 1965 the percentage of regulars rose from 39% in the cities (with more than 100,000 inhabitants) to 62% in towns (with less than 100,000, but more than 2,500 inhabitants) and 53% in rural areas. The comparable percentages for 1974 were 35%, 47%, and 53%. Table 10.6 shows that the drop in attendance from 1965 to 1974, according to residence, is again primarily due to the changes in French Catholicism. If anything, Protestant attendance tended to be slightly better in most types of residence. The drop in church attendance, however, was not equal for all categories of residence in French Catholicism. It was much more severe in the large cities where the decrease amounted to as much as 39%.

Table 10.6

Percentage of Regular Church Attenders by
Denomination and Residence

RESIDENCE	YEAR	ANGLICAN	CATHOLIC (ENGLISH)	CATHOLIC (FRENCH)	UNITED CHURCH	OTHER
City	1965	19	59	83	17	25
	1974	17	49	44	23	33
Town	1965	22	74	91	29	37
	1974	22	62	60	31	39
Rural	1965	17	74	88	25	37
	1974	39	68	74	31	48

In spite of this, the rural-urban differences are usually much more pronounced in Europe than in the newer countries. The European literature on church-going hardly ever fails to note the better church attendance in rural areas (see for Austria, Bogensberger and Zulehner 1972, 56; for Belgium, Houtart 1972, 73; for Denmark, Thorgaard 1972, 138; for West

Germany, Kehrer 1972, 197; for England, Martin 1972, 233; for Ireland, Ward 1972, 297; for Italy, Acquaviva 1972, 317; for the Netherlands, Laeyendecker 1972, 335; for Spain, Almerich 1972, 466; for Sweden, Gustafsson 1972, 497; for Switzerland, Campiche 1972, 516). One of the reasons why the rural-urban differences tend to be more pronounced in the older countries may be the convergence of the one local church with local identity in European villages (e.g., for Spain, William Christian 1972). In the newer countries denominational competition and, consequently, denominational identity tend to offset, rather than converge with, local community feeling. Yet in the cities, denominational competition and denominational identity would be an advantage by providing organizational strength and boundary defense against the many other foci of identity existing in modern, industrialized, urban societies. This advantage would be less available to the religious monopolies in European cities steeped in the past, *Gemeinschaft*-type, traditions.

Party Identification

In both the 1965 and the 1974 studies the question was asked: "Generally speaking, do you think of yourself as Conservative, Nationale or what?" Concentrating on those respondents who identified with the three major parties, the percentage of regular attenders who attenders who thought of themselves as Liberal in 1965 (61%, n = 757) was considerably higher than among those who thought of themselves as Conservative (39%, n = 535) or NDP (34%, n = 197). In 1974 the rank order was maintained (Liberals most regular and NDP-ers least), but the distance between percentages of regular Liberal (47%, n = 1134) and Conservative (42%, n = 544) attenders had narrowed considerably. On the other hand the distance between the percentages of Conservative and NDP regular attenders had widened to 23% (n = 194).

The percentage changes come as no surprise to those familiar with Canadian voting patterns. The association of Catholicism and the Liberal Party has been pointed out by many scholars (see Meisel 1956, 486; Laponce 1958, 256; Alford 1964, 213; Engelmann and Schwartz 1971, 48; McDonald 1971, 169; Jacek and others 1972, 196). One can therefore expect an overrepresentation of Catholics among those identifying with the Liberal party and a corresponding underrepresentation of Catholics among those identifying with the Conservative party. Catholic attendance being higher than Protestant attendance is therefore reflected in the higher attendance of Liberals, much more so in 1965 than in 1974 when, as has been noted, Catholic regular attendance had decreased considerably while Protestant remained the same. The breakdown by denomination is shown in Table 10.7.

Table 10.7

Percentage of Regular Church Attenders by denomination
and party identification in 1965 and 1974

PARTY IDENTIFICATION	YEAR	ANGLICAN	CATHOLIC (ENGLISH)	CATHOLIC (FRENCH)	UNITED CHURCH	OTHER
Conservative	1965	23	65	83	25	42
	1974	26	63	68	26	51
Liberal	1965	24	72	90	30	25
	1974	23	63	57	33	34
N.D.P.	1965	10	57	74	20	24
	1974	15	31	29	19	17

The table shows that there is little difference between the percentages of regular churchgoers who identify with the Conservative or the Liberal parties once denomination is controlled. It is interesting that the percentage of regular churchgoers is lowest amongst those in any denomination who identify with the New Democratic party. This has also been observed by McDonald (1969, 134) and Anderson (1966, 33). As in most Western countries, left-wing parties tend to be perceived as demanding the kind of commitment usually reserved for religious organizations. Individuals belonging to the major denominations do not think of salvation in terms of the political and social change at which the political left aims.

SUMMARY

The denominational composition of Canada is typical for a country settled by immigrants from a large variety of European countries. The two founding nations brought their own French Catholic and British Protestant ecclesiastical organizations, and those that came later from northern, eastern and southern Europe made their separate contribution to the religious mosaic. Yet the pattern was not static. Differential birthrates, ethnic migrations, ecumenical undertakings, sporadic proselytisms, pervasive secularization - all had their diverse effect on the dynamic configuration of denominational membership.

Yet membership can be defined in a variety of ways. The census figures used for the description of denominational composition rely on self-definition of the population. The religious organizations themselves, however, tend to be somewhat more restrictive. To be a member in good standing one usually has to be baptized, confirmed and, in many instances, be a participant in ceremonies and services. Church attendance therefore becomes an important criterion for organizational loyalty. In Canada church attendance used to be among the highest in the world: after World War II, for instance, two-thirds of the population could be found in a church or synagogue on an average Sunday (on Sabbath). In thirty-five years attendance has dropped to levels corresponding more to the practices of other nations composed of many immigrant groups. At present a little more than one-third of the population attends a religious service on an average Sunday. The Catholic half of the population has a better record for attendance than the Protestant one: in 1984, 50% had gone to church within the seven days previous to the Gallup Poll, whereas the percentage for Protestants was 29%. Since the 1960s, attendance at mass has particularly dropped in the French Catholic part of the population. In 1965, 88% of French Catholics would attend church at least twice a month, usually weekly, but in 1974 the corresponding percentage was only 56. The mass exodus from the churches in Quebec was spearheaded by the young, the educated, those living in the cities, and those belonging to the higher income groups.

CHAPTER 11

FRENCH CATHOLICISM

NEW FRANCE

As much as 150 years before the first English-speaking migrants settled in Nova Scotia, French explorers, traders, and priests roamed over what is now Canada. Explorers, such as Cartier in 1534, were interested in finding a way to the exotic East. At the beginning of the seventeenth century Champlain inspired royal visions of a French empire in North America with loyal settlements, a profitable fur trade, and a converted native population. French settlements of any significance did not appear until the second half of that century, but the fur trade and the mission to the natives soon began to flourish. First, the Récollects (originally a popular branch of strict Franciscans) and after 1625, the wealthier and well-organized Jesuits carried out energetic missions to the Indians. They were buoyed by the infectuous evangelical zeal of seventeenth century counter-Reformation France, by impressive financial contributions of patrons and by the formidable power of Cardinal Richelieu. Under the Jesuits New France became "a virtual preserve of their Society," so much so that the Jesuit missionary Paul Le Jeune could write in 1636 that the Church in Quebec imposed and carried out penalties for "blasphemy, drunkenness, failing to attend the Mass and divine services on Holydays" (Moir 1967, XIV, 3). The punishment consisted of both fines and being placed on a wooden horse for a set time near the church.

French settlements began to grow later in the seventeenth century. New France counted only 240 souls in 1641, but in 1653 this number had increased to 2000, in 1673 to 6,705, in 1683 to 10,274, and in 1700 to 15,000. By that time there were also approximately 1000 inhabitants each in Acadia and the Gaspé Peninsula. Many of the settlers were engaged in the fur trade. According to the 1681 census, as many as 800 heads of families were absent, presumably trading as *coureurs de bois* in the vast wilderness to the west of the settlements (Dominic 1956, 2-5). Those men who stayed in one place, cleared their allotted piece of land along the banks of the St. Lawrence. After the peace treaty with the Iroquois in 1666, some officers of the disbanded Carignan-Salières regiment became seigneurs, and many soldiers, became tenants. At that time close to a thousand settlers arrived from France, among them "the King's daughters," prospective brides for the preponderantly male population. Early marriages and large families were encouraged by the authorities (Walsh 1966, 140), and obstinate bachelors were fined (Jaenen 1976, 117).

The domination of the Church over the civil affairs of the settlers did not go unchallenged for long. In 1659 François de Laval de Montigny (1623-1708) had been appointed as vicar apostolic for New France. He was chosen because of his sympathies for the Jesuit Ultramontane (Rome-oriented) rather than Gallican (France-oriented) position. Yet he soon ran into trouble with Governor d'Argenson who objected to Laval's excommunication of anyone selling alcohol to the natives. King Louis XIV allowed Laval to nominate a new governor, and Laval chose a friend, Saffroy de Mésy. The latter also got into difficulties when he insisted on a more democratic election of members of the Quebec council supposed to deal with the control of the liquor traffic (Laval had filled that body with people sympathetic to his strict views). Laval had been unbending about liquor because of the havoc it created among the Indians. Yet the civil authorities, such as intendant Talon, pursued an energetic policy of trade and settlement at the end of the 1660s, soon discovering that they could only compete with the free trading, adventurous *coureurs de bois* in the wilderness by also exchanging brandy for furs. And even so, the English who bartered with rum sometimes got away with the best furs. The issue remained unresolved and became part of the general jostling for power between the ecclesiastical (primarily Jesuit) and civil authorities. In the 1670s Governor Frontenac became dissatisfied with the low position of civil authorities in church processions, but the king wrote in 1676 that only at the high and solemn feasts of the year could the Sovereign Council precede the church wardens, and that on ordinary days the order should be reversed (Moir 1967, 17). Laval had also centralized ecclesiastical power by making all clergy members of the Grand Seminarie in Quebec so that they could be moved at will rather than be given a permanent appointment to a parish, as was the case in France. In 1679 Frontenac managed to have this policy modified (Provost, 1955, 90).

In the meantime the parish rather than the seigneurie had become the pivot of civil administration in New France. The seigneur was often absent, and the parish priest, being the most literate member of the community, usually ran its temporal affairs. He registered births, marriages, and deaths, prepared legal documents and wills for his parishioners, and settled disputes. He was assisted by the *fabrique* (board of churchwardens), elected for three years by the parishioners. It looked after the upkeep of the church property and the primary schools attached to the parish. At the end of the seventeenth century there were as many as twenty-four of these schools.

The parish church both reflected and stabilized communal relations. The seigneur had a special pew and if he had financed the building of a stone church and if there was a vacancy could even nominate the priest. (However, only few of the seigneurs could afford the expense.) The pew of the seigneur was in the most honorific place - to the right, when coming in, and close to the communion rail. Behind the seigneur was the pew of the captain of the militia. The church wardens also sat in a special seat, and like the other dignitaries, had their fixed position in the religious processions (Fallardeau 1976, 109-10). It was the parish church which proved the prime preserver of New France culture after the English conquest of 1759.

Laval retired to France in 1684 but returned after a number of years, even holding office from 1700-1708 when his successor was captured at sea by the English and held hostage. Laval died in office in 1708 at the ripe old age of 86. The successor was Jean Baptiste de Saint-Vallier, a nobleman who had been a royal chaplain. Like Laval, he was austere, devout, and dedicated. He spent his considerable fortune on his diocese. His formidable energies were directed at the building of sound family life and strong parishes, and as a result he passionately (but often vainly) opposed the license of the *coureurs de bois* who were in the habit of celebrating their return from the wilderness with drinking, gambling and wenching (Wade 1968, Vol. I, 38) and of the soldiery who were equally inclined to wile away their spare time in places of ill repute, as they were not permitted to marry (Jaenen 1976, 139). He managed to prevent Molière's *Tartuffe* from being put on but had his windows smashed when he proceeded to bring charges against the would-be leading actor (Walsh 1966, 164-5). In Montreal he insisted that the prayer stool of the governor be removed to a less prominent position in church. Behind this fierce determination to quench the exuberant spirit of the young adventurers and to put the authorities in their places was much more than a spoilsport spirit. Saint-Vallier wanted the Church to be as strong as he could make it in order to better safeguard the vulnerable institutions of the new society. Much effort was made to shelter and protect the poor, the indigent, the bastards, the orphans, the sick, the dying and the crippled. Existence was harsh enough. Irresponsible parenthood, illicit sex, drunken brawls and shiftlessness did not have to make it worse than it already was. And so that bishop insisted on deviance being nipped in the bud. His clergy were encouraged to make denouncements from their pulpits about someone's misconduct, card-playing, or dancing. Excommunication was freely used to keep a freedom and pleasure-loving people in line. Yet when the community was endangered, as when a New England fleet besieged Quebec in 1690, church and people would be as one. Bishop Saint-Vallier and his priests inspired courage and confidence, and when the English left, defeated, "church and state joined in a procession with the captured flag of the enemy; then followed a service of thanksgiving conducted in the Lower Town Church which was renamed Notre-Dame-de-la-Victoire" (Walsh 1966, 158).

When Saint-Vallier died in 1727, the church fell on bad times. The mother country had lost its religious zeal, the enlightenment was becoming fashionable, and financial support for various ecclesiastical enterprises in New France began to dry up. The hierarchy began to run its own seigneurie to defray expenses, and this started a veritable epidemic of commercial and industrial enterprises among the Canadian clergy (Gosselin Vol. II, 199-201). More and more Canadian-born clergy began to take the place of the incompetents which the mother country sometimes dispatched to the colony. Yet the tendency remained to fill the top positions with noblemen from France. Bishop Henri Dubreuil de Pontbriand was one of these. He came in 1741 and died in 1760 in Montreal, where he had fled from the British forces. As his predecessors, he was unable to prohibit the traffic in brandy. Nor did his denouncements of cabarets, sexual laxity, crime, boldness, brashness, materialism, independence of mind and the "perpetual murmurings against authority" (Jaenen 1976, 129, 156) meet with much success. And so at the eve of the conquest, the people of New France tended to be dissolute, whereas the troops who under Montcalm had come to protect the colony introduced the democratic ideals and anti-clericalism of the mother country.

AFTER THE CONQUEST

The destruction of Quebec in 1759 and the conquest of Montreal in the following year left the population desolate. At the Peace of Paris in 1763 the elite was allowed to return to France, but only the officials, the soldiery and the fur traders made extensive use of the opportunity. "The clergy remained at their posts, and since their position alone among the elite was not affected by the conquest, their prestige as leaders of the people was strongly reinforced" (Wade 1968, Vol. I, 50). This is not altogether true, as during the period 1759-1765 the number of priests dropped from 181 to 138; also, the high clergy returned in large numbers (Fallardeau 1971, 346) even though the lower clergy remained. By contrast, the population increased from 65,000 to 69,810 (Dominic 1956, 99). It was as though the people felt that its power lay in multiplication: from 1760-1770 the birthrate was an incredibly high 65.3 per 1000 (Wade 1968, I, 47). The "revenge of the cradle" had begun.

As the numbers of English settlers were negligible at that time, it made only good sense for the military governor, James Murray, to minimize friction with the population. He therefore ordered his officers to show respect for Catholic processions and to deal fairly with the people. He correctly assumed that the latter would prove to be staunchly loyal, provided that religion remained untouched. In return, the hierarchy in Montreal decreed in 1762 that a Te Deum be sung on the occasion of the coronation and marriage of George III (Moir 1967, 74). Murray also arranged for Jean-Olivier Briand (a protégé of de Pointbriand) to be consecrated as bishop.

It was Bishop Briand who in the following decades proved to be both an excellent power broker and diplomat. He strengthened the only institution to survive the conquest intact and made the Church into an embodiment of French-Canadian culture, all the while remaining on the best possible footing with the English authorities. He had a strong hand in the preparation and passing of the Quebec Act of 1774 which virtually established the Catholic religion and allowed the Church to continue to tithe its people. By implication, the Act was a defeat for those Protestants, who, in the preceding years, had vainly attempted to attract sufficient British settlers to make Quebec into an English colony with English institutions and Church of England parishes.

The policy of accommodation paid off during the War of Independence (1776-1783). The Catholic hierarchy and clergy remained loyal to the British crown, even though that loyalty was not translated into joining the forces of Carleton (the governor at the time) in his effort to oust the American rebels when they invaded the Montreal region. The French were suspicious of both the British conquerors and the anti-papist Americans. With the arrival of 30,000 British Empire Loyalists from the south there were renewed pressures to make the English language, law, and religion supreme. They were reduced for a while due to the 1791 separation between Upper (the western region where most of the Loyalists had settled) and Lower Canada (the eastern, predominantly French areas) and the granting of representative government. They became strong again when Jacob Mountain, who was appointed Anglican bishop of Quebec in 1793, resented the sharing of power with a Catholic colleague. Yet the number of Catholics had risen to over 160,000 (which was eight times the number of Protestants in Canada at that time - Walsh 1956, 81) and the Church, helped by an influx of priests exiled from the French Revolution, had a clear superiority over the poorly staffed Church of England. The War of 1812 between Great Britain and the United States was another occasion at which the British government handsomely rewarded the loyalty of the French hierarchy: it gave Joseph-Octave Plessis (the very able French bishop at the time) an annual stipend together with the official title "Catholic Bishop of Quebec" and a seat in the legislative council.

While Catholicism and the civil authorities of Lower Canada developed a cordial relation, a number of problems arose which tested the cohesion of the Church. First, there was the immigration of the Irish. Edmund Burke, an Irish priest, had become dissatisfied with French supremacy and had managed to have Nova Scotia made into an apostolic vicariate, outside the jurisdiction of the see of Quebec. A second problem arose when the French members of the popular assembly in Lower Canada began to use their majority as a bulwark of French language and culture. This was partly in defense against the anti-papist and anti-French position of the Empire Loyalists, partly against the curtailment of the power of the assembly by the English- dominated legislative council. At first the Catholic hierarchy was sympathetic to the views and policies of the French majority and their leader

Louis-Joseph Papineau, but when in 1837 he and other radicals came to blows with the British troops, it sternly denounced the rebellion. It thereby lost considerable support from the population but again gained the gratitude of the British authorities (Walsh 1956, 82-4). The Catholic Church defended its policies through the doctrine that Christians owe obedience to the lawful sovereign. And so *Te Deums* were sung when Queen Victoria succeeded to the throne in 1837, but many churches ran empty as soon as the singing started (Dominic, 1956, 113).

The problem of conflict between the various Catholic ethnic groups remained. In 1860 Bishop de Charbonnel resigned, to resolve the tension in his Toronto diocese. He was succeeded by his anglophone coadjutor, Bishop Lynch. On the other hand, tension between hierarchy and laity about the relation to the state had weakened considerably by the time of Confederation in 1867 when the provinces became autonomous in the areas of education, property, laws, justice, welfare and municipal administration. These were the areas which were considered to "make up the intimate and real life of a nation" (Silver 1975, vii), and therefore satisfied many of the French patriots.

In the final quarter of the nineteenth century the theme of Catholicism and French Nationalism being one and the same could also be detected in the secular press. The journalist Jules-Paul Tardivel brought it out rather well in his widely read book *Pour la Patrie*, published in 1895. In it, the Church and those loyal to it save the nation from a takeover by the Orange Order and prevent the extermination of French Canada. To Tradivel and many of his contemporaries French Canada was the harbinger of Christian civilization haveing taken over the torch from the corrupted motherland. Not that French Canada had now become heaven on earth. Yet it, more than any other nation, had protected the divine seed, particularly in the rural areas where it was easier to defend its purity than in the cities.

The local parish was indeed a formidable ingredient for the cementing of French-Canadian identity just as much if not more so than an astute episcopal diplomacy. In actual fact, the bishops could not have carried out their strategies without populist links at the communal level. By 1851 the French-Canadian population of Quebec had risen to 670,000 through a vigorous birthrate (immigration had added another 220,000 to the Quebec population, of which 77,000 were Catholic. What is now Ontario had just surpassed Quebec: its population in 1851 was 952,000, of which 168,000 were Catholic and 26,000 French - Dominic 1956, 124). It was on the local, parish level that the Catholic Church in Quebec continued to dominate and reinforce communal identity. The clergy was primarily recruited from the lower classes. Families regarded it as an honour to produce a priest or a nun, and most of them did. Therefore the cleric innately understood the people of his parish. If there were differences, it was because the priest stood for the moral rectitude of which the laity fell short. Hence the need for confession and constant bridging between the actual and the ideal. It was particularly in the rural areas that religion and community were strongly intertwined. In the eyes of the clergy the towns were often dens of iniquity. The 400 prostitutes in Quebec City in 1810 (the population being 13,000) seemed to prove their point (Wallot 1971).

The pivotal position of the Catholic priest in the French-Canadian villages is clearly brought out in a number of novels about Quebec in the first half of the twentieth century. Ringuet's *Thirty Acres* describes the life of Euchariste Moisan, a typical French-Canadian farmer with twelve children. The land is sacred to Moisan. (In the introduction to the novel Albert le Grand traces the history of the French-Canadian rural novel back to the middle of the nineteenth century and points to the recurrent theme that the national virtues responsible for French Canada's survival flourish most naturally and vigorously on the land.) With frugality and practical shrewdness Moisan builds up his farm, meanwhile adding to the family prestige by allowing his oldest son, Oguinase, to become a priest. Another daughter goes into a convent and Euchariste himself becomes a church warden. The priest in Moisan's village counsels about marriage, reinforcing mutual understanding, kindness and altruism as values which guide the interaction between the people. He also arbitrates disputes and is described (p.79) as "knowing everything." At the end of the story we find Moisan in a Massachusetts town where his wild, third son Ephrem now lives with his Irish wife and where the only remaining link with the past is the weekly Mass and the socializing afterwards with compatriots.

In Hugh MacLennan's *Two Solitudes*, Athanase Tallard, seigneur and a federal member of Parliament, is pitched against Father Beaubien, priest of Saint-Marc-des-Erables. Tallard represents cosmopolitan anti-clerical progress. He wants a mill to be established in the village to provide employment but is thwarted by the priest and the people who fear the destruction of their rural values through urbanization. The priest blames the English Protestant entrepreneurs for ruining the simple morality in his previous church and is determined not to let Tallard "spoil his parish" (p.167) this time. Father Beaubien wins the battle. From his pulpit he warns the people against the seigneur and they cold-shoulder him to the point where even his servants leave his employ.

Although both novels are placed primarily in the first quarter of the twentieth century, their values, beliefs and myths find roots in earlier periods of French-Canadian history: true Christianity has been preserved in Quebec. The people were abandoned by the mother country after 1760, but this was a blessing in disguise, as now the Enlightenment with all its anti-clerical revelry can have little effect. Since the conquest, the materialism of the English financiers has been a continual threat, and although this materialism has found a foothold in the urban and industrial areas, the noble, simple virtues of Christianity are still preserved in the rural parishes.

The Catholic Church sees a close connection between its tasks as a protector of communal and of family life. The pulpit, the confessional, and the pastoral visits have been the means of the church throughout its history in Quebec to bolster marriage and to channel man's unruly instincts into the safety of monogamy and fidelity. The Church has always felt that deviance could be best controlled through the authority of parents acting in concert throughout the entire process of socialization, therefore divorce and adultery have been decried as unmitigated evils for they would destabilize the very matrix for upbringing and would jeopardize an always precarious communal system of norms and values. Too much thinking for oneself, not enough obedience, and exaggerated individualism were similarly seen as threats to both family and community cohesion. The Catholic Church in Quebec therefore became the guardian of the entire educational process, as it was in full agreement with the Syllabus of Errors attached to the encyclical *Quanta Cura* of Pope Pius IX in 1864. In this document the pope strongly condemned liberalism and the idea that education should be subject to civil and political power. It therefore also unleashed its fury on the few institutions of Quebec society in the second half of the nineteenth century which represented the spirit of free thought and speech. The major one of these was the Institut Canadien, a centre of French-Canadian intellectuals, whose yearbook was placed on the Index in 1868 at the instigation of Bishop Bourget. The Church felt that its beliefs about life and morals could only be safeguarded when it exercised undisputed authority in all areas enveloping the growing child: family, community and school.

The problem was that, in the last quarter of the nineteenth century, the high birthrate, poverty, and overcrowding of the rural population created strong pressures to leave the protective shield of the rural community and family. There was extensive emigration to the United States. Urbanization and industrialization of Montreal, Quebec City and other centres began to siphon off the more ambitious from the country. In 1875, 88% of the Quebec population was still rural, but in 1911 the percentage had already dropped to 50% and would continue to drop throughout the entire twentieth century. In 1971 as much as 80% of the population was urban (Rioux 1971, 34). The Church vainly attempted to halt the exodus from the countryside, yet around the turn of the century, many clergymen who saw the writing on the wall tried to promote industry (Ryan 1968, 86ff.). The Church continued to feel responsible also for those who had migrated to the cities. Extensive welfare provisions, hospital care, and orphanages were examples of that care. In 1950 the archbishops and bishops of Quebec published a pastoral letter in which they expressed their concern for the disrupting of industry and city life on the family. They attacked not only materialism and the frivolous use of leisure time, but also the conditions which made for family breakdown, such as inadequate housing and the lack of opportunity to develop satisfaction in one's job (Barnes 1961, 68).

The Church's involvement in the trade unions was closely related to its concern for good family life. However much *La Confederation des Travailleurs Catholiques du Canada* (C.T.C.C.) "was a negative response: it was anti-socialist, anti-communist, anti-international, anti-American, anti-Protestant and anti-neutral" (Milner and Milner 1976, 165) it was also positively the champion of decent wages for good Catholics with large families. In Quebec the relation between the working classes and the Church had always been a close one. The reason was not only that the clergy were mostly from these classes but also that the Church was suspicious of the rich and powerful with their penchant for hedonism. Secularism, liberalism and anticlericalism also prevailed more among the educated middle-classes. By contrast, the Church found the poor manifesting some of its own most cherished values: a Christ-like powerlessness, the austere life (albeit not by choice), and a developed sense of sin. It was because of this close relation that neither socialism (as protest against capitalist exploitation in Europe) nor sectarianism (as protest against establishment religion in the United States) got any foothold in Quebec. Some of the Catholic lay organizations, such as Catholic Action, was usually most militant in the lower class parishes and least so in the richer suburbs (Hughes 1976, 182-3).

Until the Quiet Revolution in 1960 (when the Liberal, socially sensitive, Lesage regime took over from the Conservative, big business oriented, Duplessis government), there had been extensive consultation between the ecclesiastical and political spheres, so much so that "no government would consider submitting a bill of any importance without first being assured that it would receive the favour, or at least the tacit approval of the episcopate" (Fallardeau 1971, 356-7). This cosy arrangement had already begun to crumble in 1949 when the Duplessis government used every legal, and less than legal, means at its disposal to quell an asbestos strike. At that time both Bishop Roy of Quebec and Bishop Charbonneau of Montreal backed the workers in no uncertain terms. Charbonneau justified his intervention by calling the workers victims of a conspiracy and by forcefully pointing to the Church's duty to give priority to the human factor over financial interests (Wade 1968, II, 1109). Since the 1960s, the political and religious sphere have become much more widely separated, so much so that French-Canadian consciousness seems now more closely associated with politics than religion.

It was also in the 1960s that the 24th of June celebrations of French-Canadian nationhood changed from being very Catholic (St. Jean Baptiste Day) to being rather secular (La Fête Nationale). The St. Jean Baptiste Society was founded in 1834 by Patriotes (who a few years later were to instigate the 1837 uprising) to defend and promote French institutions and language in North America. The parades had been purely political (the Church had come out against the Patriote party), but after 1840 they began to include a carriage on which John the Baptist was represented by a young boy with a sheep slung over his shoulder and a cross in his hand, symbolizing Christian leadership of the flock (Quebec). The parades led to the local church which all the people were required to attend on that day. After the service, the parade was reformed and proceeded to the city square where public addresses were held. It was the most important and largest annual parade in Quebec, but in 1968 it was used by separatists as a protest against Prime Minister Pierre Trudeau, who had opposed any special status for

Quebec and who was on the reviewing stand. After this the holiday reverted back to its original political purposes and became La Fête Nationale. During their heyday the parades expressed the unity of the French Canadians supremely guided by a Catholic saint (Chapin 1955, 145).

The close alliance between Catholicism and French-Canadian nationalism during that period, says Fernand Dumont (1966, 36), was the only means for survival of the latter, as apart from the Church there were no other institutions powerful enough to support the patriotic sentiment. It was the Church which provided the skeleton and the consciousness for an otherwise powerless society. However, the present secularization means that the Church has to give up control over secular institutions. Therefore, the question arises as to whether each of these separate entities can produce sufficient effervescence to bolster its internal unity (Ibid., 37). This is the situation of the 1980s. The profound changes registered in the severe drop in French Catholic church attendance in the last twenty years suggest that the erosion of its national sacralizing function has not been altogether painless for the Church. Yet it continues to have a firm hold on the way most French Canadians shape their personal and family identity, even when there are now non-Catholic and non-Christian alternatives for self-definition.

SUMMARY

Throughout its long history the Catholic Church has been the prime defender of national solidarity, communal integrity, family cohesion, and personality integration in French Canada. Before the Peace of Paris in 1763 when New France permanently lost its autonomy, the Church often successfully, yet never incontestably, guarded the morals of the nation. After the English conquest there was no letup in the see-saw battle with civil authorities, other denominations, the spirit of liberalism, secular individualism, and the forces which tended to shatter the precarious wholeness of community, family and individual. Since the Quiet Revolution and the Second Vatican Council of the early 1960s the Church appears to have lost much of its former hold on the young, educated city-dwellers. It certainly has lost its grip on the political machinery of the province. Yet it continues to inform the major part of the population about its expectations of behaviour, its specific blueprint for existence and its solutions to the ambiguities and dilemmas of living.

CHAPTER 12

ENGLISH CATHOLICISM

In 1981, 46% percent of Catholics in Canada (11,212,000 Catholics minus 6,088,000 individuals of French origin), were of non-French origin in spite of the fact that almost all of the 70,000 Catholics inhabiting Canada in 1766 were French. After the English conquest, the immigration of the French came to a standstill. By contrast, Catholics from the British Isles came to Canada in increasing numbers. There were about 1000 Irish in Halifax, N.S., in the 1750s, and later in that century many Catholics from the Scottish Highlands began to arrive. At first Catholicism was hardly tolerated in Nova Scotia, but in the 1780s the laws against popery were repealed, if only to accommodate those Catholics who had come with the Empire Loyalists from the United States. In the absence of priests, and quickened by the spirit of religious initiative in their Protestant fellow citizens, a number of Catholic laymen in Halifax bought land, built a church, and in 1785 persuaded a Capuchin priest from Ireland, James Jones, to become their pastor and, thereby, the first English-speaking Catholic priest in Nova Scotia. However, the lay people were in no mood to relinquish the power they had acquired in organizing the parish and kept control over church property and burials in the churchyard. Neither were they very pleased when Jones appointed a successor without consulting them, and in 1792 they threatened legal action over the use of mission funds. The issues were resolved and Jones managed to attract eight more missionaries to Nova Scotia before he returned to the British Isles in 1800 (Murphy 1981, 26, 33-4).

After the American Revolution, several hundred Catholic Highlanders crossed the borders into Upper Canada to escape an anti-Catholic crusade in New York State. They settled in Glengarry and were joined in the first decade of the nineteenth century by many other Catholic Highlanders who had been evicted from their farms and demobilized from their regiment, the Glengarry Fencibles (Scott 1914, 41). They formed the bulk of Catholics in what is now Ontario. Father Alexander Macdonell was appointed pastor of their church and eventually (in 1820) became the first bishop of Upper Canada. His flock was relatively small (about 15,000 in the year of his consecration), but it grew dramatically from that time onwards. In the short span of five years, more than 65,000 Catholics arrived from the overpopulated estates of Irish landlords, and the flow did not diminish until 1848 when approximately 700,000 Irish died as a result of the potato famine. Those who escaped the ordeal in their home country in 1847 often caught typhus on the way over and carried it with them into the new country. In that year, the typhus fever spread from Montreal to Toronto, claiming thousands of victims including eight Anglican and Catholic clergymen in the quarantine station on Grosse Isle (Moir 1972, 174).

Meanwhile, some immigration had taken place beyond the boundaries of what is now Ontario. Lord Selkirk had bought 110,000 square miles of territory along the Assiniboine, Red and Winnipeg Rivers, land he planned to settle with depressed and landless crofters. In 1812 the first contingent of Scottish Presbyterians and Irish Catholics arrived. The settlement grew rather slowly: thirty years later there were still only about 2,600 Presbyterians, and 2,800 Catholics in the entire area. Yet the Catholic Church in Quebec had provided the field with a very active bishop (Provencher) and four secular priests, assisted from 1845 onwards by the French order of Oblates of Mary Immaculate (Moir 1972, 200). Although its leaders scrapped with both the employees of the Hudson's Bay Company and the natives, on account of drunkenness, immorality and debauchery, the Catholic Church was now ready for the large-scale immigration of German, Polish and Ruthenian Catholics towards the end of the century (Morice 1914, 122, 185).

Yet the Catholic Church, like the various Protestant denominations, did not find it easy to provide religious services for the widely-separated settlers after the flood of immigration began. The immigrants usually came from countries where the state supported religion, and they were often both incapable and unwilling to contribute financially. This meant that the successful outreach to the newcomers depended on the established churches further east having both funds and personnel to spare. Those churches who could rely on a steady stream of finances and missionaries had an advantage over others not so well equipped.

DENOMINATIONAL IDENTITY AND CATHOLIC SCHOOLS

A good example of the efforts to strengthen denominational identity in order to meet the demands of the frontier is George Thomas Daly's *Catholic Problems in Western Canada*, published in 1921. Daly used his considerable journalistic talents to convince Catholics further East that the low moral standards and the materialism of the newly settled areas ("....elevators are in our prairie landscapes what the church spires are in the Quebec villages" p.146) could only be countered by a stronger Church. Support in any form (prayers, priests, funds) would stop the great leakage of immigrants for whom the faith was no longer "wrapped up, we would say, in the folds of their national customs and celebrations" (p.34). In addition, the vacuum of Catholic tradition and surroundings was being filled with secular and Protestant ways of thinking. "God alone knows how many of our Catholic boys and girls have been lost to the faith through mixed marriages and marriages outside of the Church" (p.36).

To Daly (as to his Protestant colleagues at the time) denominational organization and strength formed the mother-cell of moral and religious standards. Although he was much aware of unity being the essence of religion (p.21), in actual fact he set himself off from his fellow competitors for the souls of the settlers. That in the process denominational identity was considerably bolstered escapes his attention, although it is precisely this competition which has made Catholicism in countries where it is a minority a much more formidable force than it is in countries where it is or was the state church. He raves against "unscrupulous and most aggressive pro-selytizers" (p. 66) shooting amongst the Ruthenian pigeons, but later (p.134) makes a stirring plea for an aggressive "apostleship among our non-Catholics."

Yet in the tradition of good sportmanship, the competition was also given homage. The Methodist Church, says Daly (p.48), pledged eight million dollars in 1918 for their missions in the next five years, whereas, for Catholics, charity began and ended at home. "When one has paid his pew-rent and his dues, bought a few tickets for a sacred concert or bazaar, thrown on the collection plate each Sunday a few coppers or a small piece of silver, he thinks he has accomplished all his duty to the Church" (p.49). And this argument of one's side being outdone seemed a more effective spur to action than general pleas for commitment and generosity.

Daly was particularly wrapped up in the evils of public schools. They are the most powerful weapons in the hands of the enemy (p.76) and bring "young minds under the spell of worldliness" (p.156). "The monopoly of State education is nothing else but the conscription of the minds, an 'intellectual militarism', which eventually leads to the absorption of the individual and the family and to greater disasters than war" (p.160). Neutral schools are irreligious, Daly claimed, or amoral (although he does not use that term) because they do not work hand in glove with the values and norms of the family (the pivotal social institution), which in turn depends on the Church for its sustenance.

In other words, the Catholic Church (and Daly represented traditional Catholic thinking) claimed to have a monopoly on moral and religious instruction; and, as religious truth and religious organization are one and the same, Catholic schools were in fact valuable forces for the strengthening of denominational identity. To the Catholic bishop of Toronto, Armand de Charbonnel, it was therefore not at all out of keeping to say in his 1856 Lenten pastoral message that "Roman Catholics who did not use their vote to promote separate schools committed mortal sin" (Moir 1972, 185). Ul-tramontanism, particularly, saw "education as the most vital issue in the struggle against infidelity" (Grant 1972, 17).

For most of Canadian history from the first half of the nineteenth century up to the second half of the twentieth, the Catholic Church fought tooth and nail for the right to shape its own educational programmes. As education was generally a provincial matter, it had to fight the battle on a large number of fronts. It won handsomely in Quebec (where schools were attached to the local parish and supported from taxes) and Newfoundland (where the schools even now are controlled by the churches and 90% of school costs are paid by the provincial government). It was also relatively successful in Ontario where the province supported the Catholic, separate, school system up to grade 10, and, since 1984, up to and including grade 12. Both Saskatchewan and Alberta support separate schools on an equal basis to public ones even though, at the beginning of the twentieth century, there had been much opposition to denominational schools by those Protestants who hoped that one public system of education would weld the various ethnic groups into one English-speaking unity (Noonan 1979, 77).

Manitoba became engulfed in bitter controversies when, in 1890, the new Liberal government abolished the dual school system. Catholics had become a decreasing minority, and they faced a militant Protestantism which thoroughly disliked denominational schools. Various federal gov-ernments became involved in the controversy (the Catholic Church claimed that the British North America Act of 1867 guaranteed educational rights to a minority - Daly 1921, 166) and made some compromises. At present, denominational schools in Manitoba receive grants for textbooks but cannot claim aid for teachers' salaries. In Prince Edward Island and New Brunswick there is now only one public school system. There are many separate Catholic schools in British Columbia, but they receive no govern-ment aid.

For the Catholic hierarchy, preservation of the separate school system in Ontario and the prospect of a greater independence for the province of Quebec weighed the balance in favour of Confederation in 1867. The bishops were not overly enthusiastic, but they decided that they could live with the new political plan. The Quebec bishops, particularly, were not happy with Anglicization, but they felt that Confederation gave them a sufficient guarantee for the survival of French-Canadian culture. They and their English-speaking colleagues felt oppressed by much anti-Catholic feeling in the country, but they did little to allay the fears of monolithic religious power. Indeed, they worked at optimization of denominational identity and were therefore less inclined to bring into the open some of the internal divisions apparent only to the insider.

ETHNIC LOYALTIES

One of these divisions had to do with conflicting ethnic loyalties. Both in the nineteenth and twentieth century Catholic immigrants came from a variety of national and linguistic sources. The 1981 census shows the many ethnic components of the Catholic population. Apart from the French (95% of which is Catholic), 95% of Canadians of Italian origin, 75% of Polish, 53% of Indian and Inuit, 25% of German, 22% of Dutch, 21% of British (Irish and Scottish), 17% of Ukranian, and 7% of Scandinavian are Catholic. As in most of these groups being Catholic is closely associated with ethnic loyalties, the Church had to face the formidable problems of coordinating the various old world allegiances with an emerging Canadian way of thinking. Much commotion and maneuvering went on behind the scenes and only occasionally does the outsider get a glimpse of the friction between the Church and its ethnic components. The Polish National Catholic Church came into being as a protest against what the Poles felt to be inadequate support for their native distinctiveness by the Mother Church. Although this Church originated in the United States some disgruntled Canadian Poles formed affiliates.

Yet this was the exception rather than the rule. Catholic bishops were often elevated to high office because of their tact and diplomacy. They generally managed to juggle personnel and building requirements so that unassimilated immigrants did not have to go elsewhere or start up an independent religious organization. When a specific ethnic group was sufficiently large, bishops often promoted an ethnic parish for the area. When numbers did not warrant such an expense, they often attached Polish, Italian, Lithuanian and other priests to local parishes, encouraged social affairs for specific native groups, and (after Vatican II) offered masses in the old world language. By combining foreign and English masses in the one parish, the hierarchy also kept a hold on the younger generation, which too often tended to become disenchanted with the un-Canadian (as they thought) parental tradition.

In the early days of settlement in Canada ethnic groups often bought land together so that they all could stay in the same place and reconstruct a home away from home. About 1800, French-speaking Acadian settlers were almost the only Catholics on Prince Edward Island. On Cape Breton and around Antigonish, Scottish Catholics predominated, as did the Irish Catholics in Halifax. Neither of these groups was well cared for by the French hierarchy in Quebec. The Irish priest Edmund Burke made this plain when he paid an unauthorized visit to Rome, whereupon, in 1817, he was made vicar apostolic for Nova Scotia. His successor was the Gaelic-speaking Scot, William Fraser, who proved to be much more acceptable to his fellow countrymen than to the Irish in Halifax, of which city he became the titular bishop in 1842. Because of the friction between the Scottish and Irish Catholics, Fraser moved to Antigonish, leaving Halifax to his coadjutor, William Walsh, with whom he was not on speaking terms. The tension was resolved in 1844 through the creation of a new diocese of Arichat which included Antigonish and Cape Breton with its Scottish Catholic population and left the Irish bishop of Halifax to an Irish consti-tuency (Grant 1972, 137, 145).

In later years, matching settlers and bishops of the same ethnic origin proved to be less easy. Immigrants from a variety of countries would come to the same area, and, as a result, the ethnic balance would shift from one nationality to another. This was particularly true for western Canada, where the changes in ethnic composition put considerable strain on denomina-tional unity. Until the end of the nineteenth century most Catholics had been French. Often they were Métis (the offspring of Indian mothers and French furtraders). But at the beginning of the twentieth century the balance began to shift. French Canadians became a decreasing minority in the Prairie provinces, yet the bishops remained French. In 1906 a delega-tion of English-speaking Catholics in Winnipeg requested from Bishop Langevin the appointment of English clergy and an English bishop. How-ever, Langevin was less in favour of the request than the Apostolic Delegate who correctly surmised that English rather than French culture would soon dominate the West. Against the advice of the French archbishop, the Vatican appointed an Irishman, John Thomas McNally, to the diocese of Calgary in 1912. McNally removed four French-speaking orders but was rebuffed by the Oblates.

Meanwhile in Winnipeg the English and French groups remained at loggerheads, and so in 1916 the Pope decided to divide the Archdiocese of St. Boniface and appointed an Irish prelate (A.A. Sinnott) to the new Archdiocese of Winnipeg. The French bishops continued to agitate, point-ing to the inequity of all three archibishops of Ontario being Irish while more than half the Catholics were French. They lost again when one Irish priest was appointed to the Archdiocese of Edmonton in 1921 and another one to Regina in 1929. Still, they won out in 1933 when Archbishop Villeneuve of Quebec was created cardinal in spite of strong representations to the pope by Prime Minister Bennett, who pointed out that all three previous Cardinals had been French and that the time had come "when the head of the Canadian Church should use his influence to promote national unity" which meant chosing an English-speaking cardinal (Huel 1976, 67). Ethnic conflicts of a similar kind existed at one time or another between the Acadians and the Irish in the Maritimes (Murphy 1981, 29) and between the French and the Germans on the Prairies (Painchaud 1975, 57).

THE CATHOLIC CHURCH AND CANADIAN SOCIETY

Although the assimilation of immigrants in Canadian society appeared to be "of less concern than their harmonious integration into church life" (Grant 1972, 97)", this did not mean that integrity of society in general and its communities in particular was unimportant to the Catholic Church in

Canada. Indeed, it has attempted to protect the powerless and restrain the powerful in order to minimize conflict and, in this regard, it has followed the leadership of the various papal encyclicals as they addressed themselves to the ills of the times. In 1891 Leo XIII published *Rerum Novarum* on the plight of the workers in industrial societies. He recognized their helplessness and the hard-heartedness of capitalism. Unions, he suggested, might help them to increase both material benefits and to solve the problems at hand with Christian principles. Employers were urged to pay fair wages and to promote morality and health in the working place. Yet he defended private property and pointed to the danger of strikes. Cooperation rather than conflict between workers and employers should be the order of the day. In Canada the clergy sometimes stressed the conservatism of *Rerum Novarum* to counter socialist ideas, but, particularly in Quebec, many initiated Catholic unions.

The hardship of the Depression led Pope Pius XI to publish *Quadragesimo anno* in 1931. Like *Rerum Novarum*, it aimed at reconciling the warring forces within society. Christian principles, social attunement, and striving for the common good were assumed to be closely allied, if not identical. Yet developments in both capitalism and socialism made for lesser rather than greater social justice. Capitalism, the pope indicated, had become monopolistic and despotic. Economic dictatorship had replaced the free market. Unbridled ambition had made the few survivors of the competitive struggle hard, cruel, and relentless, and this had enslaved the state. Yet some forms of socialism (for instance, the communist variety) were not any less materialistic, for they advocated militant atheism, class warfare and abolition of private property. These programmes also undermined the common good and the dignity of the individual. There were, of course, other more moderate forms of socialism which did not differ all that much from Christian plans for social reconstruction. Usually, however, the pope suggested, they also suffered from too much stress on economic conditions and not enough emphasis on the "greed, selfishness, resentment and vindictiveness" vitiating all societies. For that reason a sincere Catholic could not be a true socialist (Baum 1980, 87).

The impact of *Quadragesimo anno* on Catholic policy in Canada was profound. When the Cooperative Commonwealth Federation (which in 1961 allied itself with the Canadian Congress of Labour to form the New Democratic Party) was founded in Calgary, in 1933, the Canadian bishops echoed the papal statement by warning against new parties which undermined the principles of private property, provoked the class struggle, and defended a materialist philosophy. This had the effect that in Canada (like Europe, but unlike Britain, Australia and New Zealand) Catholics felt that they could not in good conscience join, or vote for, a socialist party such as the C.C.F. They felt quite certain of this when, in 1934, Archbishop Gauthier of Montreal pronounced the C.C.F. programme irreconcileable with Catholic teaching. In the same year the Catholic bishops in Saskatchewan warned against socialist solutions to the moral problems of greed and materialism represented by the Depression. On the other hand, some prominent Catholics such as Henri Bourassa in Quebec and Henry Somerville, editor of the Catholic Register in Toronto, found the C.C.F. policies much more to their liking.

During the Depression some Catholic clergy felt that more than words were necessary to improve the appalling conditions of their parishioners. Two powerful, charismatic priests, Fathers James T. Tompkins and Moses M. Coady, addressed themselves to the spreading poverty and depopulation of eastern Nova Scotia. The farmers and fishermen in this area were at the mercy of the commercial firms which bought their products at a low price and charged them high prices for equipment, feed and fertilizer. With the help of the extension department of St. Francis Xavier University in Antigonish, they inaugurated an extensive system of "study clubs" which taught the villagers how to organize producer cooperatives for marketing lobster and whatever else was produced. Farmers began to establish consumer cooperative stores, thereby forcing commercial firms to become competitive. Credit unions were founded, thereby making the population (Protestants also began to join the movement, somewhat hesitatingly at first) independent from the commercial banking system. By the end of the 1930s the Antigonish Movement, as it was now called, "affected eighty communities organized into one hundred and fifty co-operative enterprizes which contained an estimated twenty thousand people" (MacInnes 1978, 2).

The movement was a successful attempt to walk the middle road between monopoly capitalism and communism. It modified the tendency of the former to let unrestricted competition erode into exploitation by the survivors, and it avoided the stifling lack of freedom typical of the state ownership of the means of production. Its goals were unabashedly economic, and yet its leaders persuaded the co-operators that the system, because it lead to a climate of social justice in which both the individual and society could thrive, was based on sound moral principles. Coady felt that Christianity could only come into its own if law, order and decency were re-established by means of a just economic programme (MacInnes 1978, 289).

Since World War II the Catholic Church has decidedly softened on he socialism issue. In his letter *Octogesima adveniens* (1971), Pope Paul VI allowed much more leeway to Catholics who were also socialists, but, he drew the line at those forms of socialism which claimed to provide an all-encompassing world-view. The Canadian Catholic bishops travelled in the same direction. In the seventies they showed little inhibition about exposing social injustice and locating Canadian problems such as the development of the Canadian North and the liberation of native peoples (Baum 1980, 213-4).

In 1983 the Canadian Catholic bishops released a report called "Ethical Reflections on the Economic Crisis" in which they expressed concern for the unemployed and the basic moral disorder unemployment has created in Canada. First priority, the bishops said, should not go to fighting inflation but to alleviating the misery of the poor, the pensioners, the natives and those who are threatened with the loss of human dignity because there is no work in which they can meaningfully express themselves. The report was attacked by government and business alike for its "idealism," yet the bishops were also widely praised for their courageous stand against the excesses of the profitmotive. Many Canadians seemed to agree that salvation of the country was advanced more through better work opportunities than through the accumulation of profits and technology. These sentiments were unambiguously endorsed by Pope John Paul II during his visit to Canada in September 1984.

VATICAN II AND SECULARIZATION

After World War II Catholic church attendance remained uniformly high until about 1965. Gallup Polls showed that both in 1946 and in 1965 as much as 83% of the Catholic population in Canada had been to church in the previous seven days. However, after 1965 the percentages began to decline rapidly: to 65% in 1970, to 61% in 1975, and to 50% in 1980 (it has stayed at 50% until 1984). English-speaking Catholics had never been as loyal to the Church as French-speaking ones, but after 1965 the former began to attend much less. It can be roughly estimated that from 1965 to 1980 the decline among the former has been approximately 20% (from 70%-50%), among the latter 40% (from 90%-50%).

What caused these pronounced changes? Some Catholics put the blame squarely at the feet of the Second Vatican Council (1962-1965) which opened its windows to the world, but in doing so introduced secular air inside its hitherto carefully preserved Catholic identity. It abolished the Latin mass and replaced it with the language of the people. (Archbishop Levèbre of France continued to say the mass in Latin and was consequently suspended by Pope Paul VI. In Canada, Father Yves Normandin and others continue to celebrate Latin masses, but until 1984 when the Vatican relaxed the rules they did so without the consent of the local bishops, and their communicants only knew about it through word of mouth or newspaper advertisements.) Vatican II also began to stress "collegiality" (rule by the college of bishops) at the expense of papal authority. When in 1968 Pope Paul VI published the encyclical *Humanae Vitae* (which condemned artificial birth control), the Canadian bishops weakened its impact by stating that, in the final resort, individual conscience was the arbiter of moral matters.

Yet it is a mistake to blame internal, organizational decisions on the weakening of Catholic boundaries. Pressures to use the vernacular for the mass and to relax proscriptions of artificial birth control existed long before the 1960s. The secular individualism of urbanized societies had infiltrated many Catholic circles, and Vatican II recognized the change taking place. In a survey of twelve parishes in Metropolitan Toronto, taken on behalf of Archbishop Pocock in the early 1970s, 73% of practising Catholics favoured the changes bought about by Vatican II. Yet in the exuberant opening of windows, the innate Catholic hankering for the stable frame of reference was underrated. Decline in church attendance shows a continuing disillusionment with the changes.

For at least some Canadian Catholics, "Catholicism is like a city destroyed by war" (Roche 1982, 10). In former days, when Catholic education depended on rote learning rather than on developmental psychology, external authority for one's actions was taken for granted. The confessional enforced the idea that evil was to be eradicated and forgiven rather than to be discussed and personally mastered. Good was excitingly demonstrated in the lives of the Christian martyrs in the beginning of the Christian era and was rewarded in heaven rather than regarded as variable with time and circumstance. The consequences of ambiguity for church-going are described by the example Roche (Ibid., 10,16) gives of her father, who was a millwright in Newfoundland. She says:

> I was never so shocked in my life as when my father told me, several years before he died, that he was no longer going to Mass...My father, whose faith through the poor times, and through my mother's agonizing death, had remained so innocent, cheerful and trusting, who until then would have rather died than miss Mass intentionally, who took Holy Communion so seriously that he wouldn't receive it if he had so much as laughed at a blasphemous joke in the mill - now for him, the miracle had departed. They had taken away his Lord, and he didn't know where they had laid Him.

And Roche concludes (somewhat excessively) that the heart of Catholicism is broken. One cannot live the Catholic life unself-consciously anymore. One can go to church out of love, "but it is love among the ruins." Gutted Masses with antic priests, manufactured excitement, and cafeteria casualness are all she can see. Clearly her opinions are not shared by many other Catholics.

Vatican II also affected divorce, or better, annulment. To the Catholic Church, marriage is a sacrament and therefore permanent and indissoluble. Before the 1960s, a marriage could be declared null and void, although it was done only in rare cases and after expensive and long, drawn-out procedures. The Church then declared that a true marriage had never existed. During Vatican II the *Pastoral Constitution on the Church in the Modern World* insisted that marriage was not primarily ordained for the begetting and educating of children (as the Church had maintained in the past) but that its provision of a communion of life and a covenant relationship based on trust, self-giving, and sacrificial love was equally important. This new definition proved to be the mechanism for the streamlining of annulment procedures, for now the validity of a marriage could be attacked on the grounds that either partner was incapable of mutually supportive human relationships or that mental problems, selfishness, homosexuality, alcoholism, extramarital affairs, or just plain immaturity had prevented marriage from being what it should be. As a result, annulments increased fifty-fold. Of course the problem with this pastoral/psychological view was that it weakened the indissolubility of actual marriages: the sacred bonds strengthening any family could now be broken asunder on the grounds of the very factors which had made the institution of marriage increasingly precarious in the first place. The new, exalted view of marriage weakened the antidote for the breakdown of actual marriages, however realistic its insights as to what had gone wrong.

Over the last twenty years or so the stigma of mixed marriages has also become much less potent. Numerous were the stories of Catholic girls who, deeply in love with Protestant boys, remained spinsters all their life because the thought of marrying outside the Church was abhorrent. Catholicism forcefully realigned its own denominational identity with that of its families and emphatically minimized the potential for divided loyalties. It insisted on Church and family strengthening one another, and therefore adamantly avoided mutual weakening. In some instances, Catholic priests even succeeded in persuading Catholic husbands to leave their non-Catholic wives (Moir 1981, 86). But all this has now changed. In 1967, joint counselling by Catholic priests and Protestant ministers was begun for couples planning mixed marriages (Bader 1968, 172-4). Also, the excommunication penalty has been abolished and Protestant ministers are now permitted to join in prayers with the priest during a Catholic marriage ceremony. No longer is it necessary for the Protestant partner in a mixed marriage to guarantee in writing that children will be baptised in a Catholic church and educated in a Catholic school. Yet the 1981 census shows how marriage with spouses of different ethnic origin can negatively affect Catholic belonging: 95% of those of French derivation are Catholic, but only 61% of those of French and British, 66% of French and other (non-British) and as few as 44% of French, British and other origins.

SUMMARY

Forty-seven percent of the Canadian population is Catholic. Twenty-five percent is of French origin and twenty-two percent is generally English-speaking, although many in the latter category have European origins (Italian, German, Polish, etc.). Ethnic diversity has taxed denominational unity, but a combination of episcopal tact, papal authority, ethnic services and religious education has safeguarded and reinforced Catholic integrity.

Like all other major denominations in Canada, the Catholic Church has taken its service function to society, community and family very seriously. It has bolstered as much as it could greater social justice, has defended the poor and the helpless against the powerful, has established and staffed orphanages, hospitals, and homes for the aged and has opposed alcoholism, infidelity, greed, and selfishness which undermined the integrity of home, family and community.

Since the Second Vatican Council (1962-1965) it has opened many windows to the secular world, but the dialogue with that world has taken place at the expense of inner solidarity. There is now more stress on individual conscience and less on obedience to institutional authority, more chance of getting an annulment of a marriage which has broken down, so that a divorced person can remarry in a religious ceremony. Mixed Catholic/Protestant marriages do not exactly get the blessing of either church, but less impediments are put in their way.

CHAPTER 13

ANGLICANS AND BAPTISTS

The Church of England came to Canada as early as the sixteenth century when Sir Humphrey Gilbert received a charter for the settlement of Newfoundland. He arrived at St. John's harbour in 1583 and took possession of the island in the name of Queen Elizabeth. The Chaplains who were attached to expeditions of this kind said daily morning and evening prayers and were the indispensable moral policemen and divine comforters for all on board. The sovereign in whose name these charters were commissioned also charged them with the conversion of "the poor infidels captured by the devil," whenever they found them. For a time, however, nothing much came of the Newfoundland settlement. For most of the seventeenth century the island was a refuge for rejects of the mother country. It was to the advantage of the ship owners not to have the island settled, in order to keep their fishing monopolies intact. Nevertheless, against the wishes of the ship owners, thousands of individuals and families remained on the island year round, and in 1697 a chaplain on one of the ships, the Rev. John Jackson, settled among them. Although he built a church, he found the drinking and disorderly conduct of the common people, on the one hand, and the cruelty and the antagonism of the powerful, on the other, too much, and after nine years he returned to England (Langtry 1892, 732). In the eighteenth century various clergymen were sent out by the Society for the Propagation of the Gospel, but the fluctuating population of poor fishermen was generally unable to contribute much to a parson's stipend. Yet it was through the work of chaplains and because of the large proportion of the English among the fishing population that Newfoundland had more than twice as many Anglicans (27.2%) than Canada at large (10.1%) at the 1981 census.

The beginnings of Anglicanism in Canada are typical of the ways religion was expected to function. Traders, soldiers and settlers alike assumed that the Church of England was an indispensable part of English morality and culture. They might have felt oppressed by it as many of the early inhabitants of Newfoundland obviously did, but they also knew that law and order were necessary for a viable community and that the Church of England was the cosmic representative and underwriter of such an order. It came in a package with everything that was refined in literature and edifying in morality. It was therefore taken for granted that its exclusive place of honour in the colonies was as necessary for civilization as language and political institutions were. They all needed the sustenance of the others for a viable society, or so it was thought.

Yet, in subsequent years, the Church of England failed to become the bulwark for English-speaking culture as profoundly as the Catholic Church succeeded in becoming the guardian for a French-speaking culture. In the middle of the twentieth century it would be as natural for a French Canadian to be in a Catholic Church on an average Sunday as it would be uncommon for an English-speaking Canadian to occupy a pew in the Church of England. There were three important reasons for this state of affairs.

The first reason was the lack of missionary drive in the early beginnings of Anglicanism in Canada. The Counter-Reformation, Jesuit zeal, and the restless dedication of Laval in the seventeenth century had put an indelible stamp on French society as it set out on an uncertain path toward autonomy. The English had their zealous Society for the Propagation of the Gospel in Foreign Parts, but somehow it was not as effective. A system of Anglican establishment in Nova Scotia (proclaimed in 1758) did not prove to be workable, even if the original contingent of 3,760 English settlers who arrived in Halifax under Lord Cornwallis in 1749 were accompanied by two missionaries of the S.P.G. There were not enough clergy for the rapidly expanding population of Nova Scotia in the second half of the eighteenth century. The eleven missionaries which the first Anglican bishop in Canada (Charles Inglis) had at his disposal in 1788 for the work in the entire eastern half of Canada from Newfoundland to Upper Canada were a motley crowd of four diligent clergymen, three indifferent ones, and four who were a blot on the reputation of the church, according to his complaining letter to the archbishop of Canterbury (Walsh 1968, 107).

The second reason for the failure of the Church of England to become the solid preserver of English culture in Canada was its increasing diversification. By the time that Bishop Inglis complained about the inadequacy of his missionaries, only a minority of the English-speaking population of his diocese had come from England. Most of them (between thirty and forty thousand) had recently (during the American War of Independence) arrived from the United States. They were the United Empire Loyalists, who had opposed republicanism, rebellion against the motherland and the kind of egalitarianism which coarsely ignored the refined distinctions of birth and wealth. Although the Anglican Church had been closely associated with the Loyalist party in the thirteen American colonies, many of the United Empire Loyalists were neither Anglican nor of English extraction. In addition, the population of Nova Scotia included numerous immigrants from New England, who tended to be Congregationalists, and many European Protestants, who settled Lunenburg. There were also approximately

10,000 Acadians (the original French inhabitants), most of whom were expelled in 1755. In the sixties and seventies Ulster Presbyterians, Yorkshire Methodists and Highland Scots began to settle in Nova Scotia. By contrast, population expansion in French Canada, after its early beginnings, came about through a high birthrate rather than by immigration, and this guaranteed smooth absorption within the existing Catholic framework.

A third reason was that the Church of England, as represented by bishop Charles Inglis in Nova Scotia, was geared to preservation of the status quo in an environment characterized by economic upheaval, frontier hardship, large-scale immigration and rapid social change. French-speaking Canada, on the other hand, was already well-settled and remained homogeneously French and Catholic. Sectarian forms of religion, usually hostile to the status quo, hardly penetrated because the clergy had strong ties of blood with the poorer classes. Not so in Nova Scotia. Bishop Inglis insisted on replicating the hierarchical society with the class distinctions he had known. He opposed free seating in his churches as this would mingle the respectable and the disreputable. Yet the situation cried out for the creation of new communal and personal identities rather than the preservation of old ones. Or as Walsh (1956, 106) has it: "The Church of England's concern to preserve traditional loyalties and cultural values of European society prevented it from developing new loyalties appropriate to frontier conditions, thus reducing its effective work to a colonial upper class society."

The preeminent place of the Church of England at the founding of Halifax is well exemplified by the building, at the government's expense, of St. Paul's Church of England in 1750, opposite the Grand Parade so that ecclesiastical ceremonies could lend suitable dignity to military parades and other celebrations. Soon, however, the government felt obliged to also assist Congregationalists and Lutherans with the building of their churches. At the end of the eighteenth century, even the last of the bitterly contested privileges of Anglicanism (the sole right to perform marriages and to keep the register of births, deaths and marriages) became thoroughly eroded as there were just not enough clergy for the many burgeoning settlements of Nova Scotia.

The same happened in other parts of Canada. At first the English conquerors and English settlers would attempt to re-create a little England on foreign soil. But soon other ethnic groups would challenge the taken-for-granted monopoly of the Church of England, and civil authorities would wisely allow them the traditional religious expression of their national or ethnic identity. In 1801, on Prince Edward Island, the legislative council made a grant to both the established churches of England and Scotland for the building of St. Paul's in Charlottetown, to be used on alternate Sundays by each. Both in Lower Canada (Quebec) and Upper Canada the Church of England monopoly soon came to an end.

The Treaty of Paris in 1763 had deeded all French possessions in Lower Canada (with the exception of St. Pierre and Michelon) to Britain, but the first Church of England bishop of Quebec, Jacob Mountain, was only appointed in 1793; his flock was small and his clergy not particularly reputable. And so, during the War of 1812, Plessis gained equality as the Catholic bishop of Quebec with a yearly stipend and a seat in the legislative council.

In Upper Canada the struggle for equal recognition with the Church of England was much more protracted. Here the established Church of England allied itself with powerful little oligarchies known as Family Compacts, who resisted all attempts for greater democracy in government and insisted on the paternalistic hierarchies of the mother country. The undisputed leader of the Family Compact was John Strachan, archdeacon of York from 1827 onwards and bishop of Upper Canada from 1839-1867, the year he died at the age of eighty-nine (Henderson 1969, 103). He was one of the younger children of a poor quarry supervisor in Aberdeen, Scotland, and it was this lowly birth which had made the authorities somewhat hesitant about giving him the bishopric, which they felt should go to gentlemen, even if they were otherwise not as well qualified. Yet John Strachan was in all respects the dutiful, diligent and learned servant of the church who all through his long life in Upper Canada did the utmost to preserve the special position of the Anglican Church. The latter had one-seventh of the land in each township preserved for financing the establishment of a clergyman and a church. But as there were not enough Anglican priests, these so-called clergy reserves often lay vacant and were in the way of road construction, as another Scot, the reformer William Lyon MacKenzie, was eager to point out. The Rebellion of 1837 which MacKenzie led was partly the result of the populist desire for more democracy in government and less power for of the Church of England.

The populist, or reform, party won the battle in 1847, and one by one the Anglican privileges were whittled away until the clergy reserves were secularized. Strachan's plans for an Anglican university (King's College) were undone, and instead the University of Toronto became a secular university. Not altogether foreign to this development were the many other religious denominations, such as the Church of Scotland, the Methodists, and the Baptists, who naturally favoured equal status. Most of them also insisted on the voluntarist principle in religious affairs, whereby parishes and congregations were financially independent and autonomous in their selection of ministers.

Losing the battle for establishment was a blessing in disguise for the Church of England. For quite some time to come it would continue to reinforce local hierarchies in church seating, and, like the colonial upper classes attending the services, it tended to frown on the emotional outbursts of frontier religiosity. Yet it now had to stand on its own feet. Buoyed by the influx of large numbers of immigrants, it spread rapidly from east to west until, by the end of the century, it covered the dominion with a network of twenty-two dioceses. Some of the missionary zeal was supplied by the very evangelical Church Missionary Society established in Britain in 1799. This organization was set on converting non-Christians and saw a fertile field in the native races of Canada. Their chaplains usually began schools also and used them to plant the Christian tradition among the young.

John West, who had become chaplain to the Hudson's Bay Company at the Red River Settlement in 1821, successfully persuaded the Church Missionary Society to begin a vast missionary enterprise to the natives. It sent out many highly capable and zealous men from England, spreading out over western and northern Canada. The large overrepresentation of Anglicans in the Yukon (25.3% in 1971) and Northwest Territories (36.4%) is the result of this energetic, dedicated body of Anglican, evangelical (low church) missionaries. Walsh (1956, 250) attributes the strong evangelical colouring of western Anglicanism to West and the subsequent efforts of the C.M.S.

Although in the second half of the nineteenth century the Church of England in Canada had decidedly moved away from Bishop Strachan's position that "a Christian nation without a religious establishment is a contradiction" (Grant 1977, 11), it remained a staunch defender of wealth and privilege. The 1872 printers' strike in Toronto was heartily condemned by *The Church Herald*, expressing the Church of England viewpoint. The editor felt that if it had not been for foreign influences the printers would have remained satisfied with job and wages. Even in the first decade of the twentieth century, the Anglican Church showed little interest in the social reform which the Presbyterians and particularly the Methodists began to demonstrate. Yet in the second decade, the Church grew more responsive to both its grassroots (the source of its income) and the social turmoil which accompanied rapid industrialization. In 1918 the General Synod of the Church of England in Canada adopted a report by its Council for Social Services roundly condemning the social ills resulting from individualism, competition, and materialism. From here onwards the Anglican Church became less a champion of the aristocracy and more the healer of the nation (Crysdale 1976, 192, 202).

The extensive immigration which took place during the first quarter of the twentieth century galvanized the Church of England into action. Like other Protestant Churches (Clifford 1977) it felt that the Dominion of Canada should become "the Dominion of our Lord" (Kuhring 37). The Church had a special duty to strengthen the Empire through religion (Ibid., 124), but above all it had to make Canada safe through immigrants who embodied the ideals of democracy, clean living and clear thinking (Ibid., 31). And this meant, as the unanimously adopted resolution of the Council for Social Service of the Church of England put it in 1923, that "decided preference should be given to immigration from the British Isles" (Ibid., 32). Mrs. Kuhring, who about that time wrote the book *The Church and the Newcomer* for the Joint Committee on Education of the Church of England in Canada, put it in more personal terms (Ibid., 39) when she expressed the wish for greater numbers of "newcomers of our stock." She did not much object to immigrants from northern Europe such as the Scandinavians, the Dutch, and the Germans, who were sturdy, self-reliant and easily assimilated into English culture (Ibid., 41), but she implied that too many people from central and southern Europe would somewhat endanger the vision of God's kingdom in Canada.

Yet the Church of England's job was to build character anywhere, a job left to the churches by the secular education system (Ibid., 101), and this meant an extensive Sunday school system which would serve all peoples, including those who were non-British, such as the Japanese, the Chinese, and the Icelanders. These activities (but also intermarriage) account for the fact that in the 1971 census a considerable percentage of Canadians of pre-World War II foreign stock regarded themselves as Anglicans. For the Dutch this percentage was 10.8%, for Asians 9.3%, for Scandinavians 8.7%, for Germans 6.5% and for the Polish 5.0%.

Other churches were engaged in essentially the same character building endeavour, but by now the denominational spirit had begun to accompany the purely national considerations of the Church of England in Canada, and so in Alberta a missionary warned that unless the Anglican Church extended its Sunday school system the Anglican children who were now attending Presbyterian, Methodist, or Union Sunday schools would end up belonging to these churches (Ibid., 119). The Church of England also felt that it needed an extensive referral system to keep all the British immigrants within the Anglican fold. To this end it had chaplains at the main ports of entry such as Quebec and Halifax, and it also kept a fatherly eye on the many Eastern Orthodox who were often deprived of priestly services. All this would be to the good of Canadianization, of God's Kingdom in this corner of the world, and of the strength of the Church of England in Canada.

Although the Anglican Church hesitated more than the Methodist and Presbyterian Churches to go out for a national vision at the expense of the Empire and denominational boundaries (it did not participate in the union attempts of the first quarter of the twentieth century), it participated actively in such inter-denominational organizations as the Social Service Council of Canada and the National Council of Churches of Canada, not to speak of many local forms of cooperation. Yet the diminishing role of the churches in an increasingly secular environment created a variety of pressures to come to terms with rapid social change. And so the Anglican Church of Canada (since 1955 the official title of the Church of England in Canada) modernized its *Book of Common Prayer* in 1959 and set up a Unit of Research and Field Study in 1962 to take the pulse of its constituency (the first study dealt with a sociological study of the Anglican clergy - Pickering and Blanchard 1967). For the first time it also began to be seriously interested in union with the United Church. Together the denominations produced a study guide, *Growth to Understanding*, and in the mid-sixties both adopted the principles for union. Yet in 1975 the Upper House (the council of bishops) of the Anglican Church recommended a delay in proceedings, and the union issue has been dormant ever since (Grant 1976, 213). There is evidence, anyway (Kaill 1976, 403), that in Canada Anglicans are less in favour of union than members of the United Church, partly because the former have been conditioned by a long tradition of episcopal government and conformity to clerical opinion, partly because in any population denominational boundaries provide their own sense of security and their own gratifying delineation from liberal tolerance.

The Anglican Church, however, was not just the preserver of English culture, class, and hierarchy (at first) or denominational boundaries and Canadian identity (later); it also had a deep and abiding interest in the well-being of marriage and the family. Like the Catholic clergy in New France, Anglican chaplains of the Hudson's Bay Company felt called upon to defend family unity against trading interests. They protested against the evil effect of alcohol on Indian family life and often infuriated the officers and other servants of the Hudson's Bay Company through their unflinching attack on the latter's irregular marital relations and the bad example they set for the Indians (Boon 1962, 17; Walsh 1956, 252).

Like other churches, the Church of England insisted that character-building of the young would suffer unless marital fidelity was preserved, divorce prohibited, and families worshiped together. For a long time the Church forbad its clergy to remarry divorced parishioners. Divorced Anglicans would often go to the United Church where the rules were somewhat more relaxed. Change came after the 1963 worldwide Anglican Congress at Toronto where, as Grant (1976, 208) noted, Anglicans began to sense the passing of Victorian Canada. From 1968 onwards, Canon XXI (On Marriage in the Church), part IV, allowed remarriage of divorced Anglicans, provided that (1) every attempt had been made to salvage the earlier marriage, (2) adequate provisions were made for the former wife and dependent children, and (3) there were "grounds for special assurance of the probable stability of the intended marriage." At the back of the mind of clergy and officials alike was always the worry that legitimizing divorce would trivialize marital stability. Yet re-absorption of sinners into a viable community was just as much a Christian duty, and therefore relaxation of the ban on divorce became accepted practice. (Also, Canadian society at large had begun to remove the stigma of divorce.) The result was that the percentage of remarriages of divorced persons rose from 1.8% in 1968 to 3.3% in 1969-72, to 6.3% in 1973-76, and to an estimated 10% in (1977-80) of all Anglican marriages (Grayston 1981, 4-5).

In the beginning, the Church of England in Canada had looked upon itself as the guardian of English culture and religion. This view of the task prevented adjustment to the conditions of newly settled countries and led to a peculiar position of both exaltation (it represented the ruling aristocracy) and marginality (it stood aloof from the rank and file). It was particularly its position of privilege which masked and retarded the imperative of Canadianization. In contrast with other ethnic groups, it could afford the relaxed posture of those to whom others adjust rather than those who have to do the adapting. It was therefore no accident that as late as the second half of the twentieth century John Porter (1966, 515) could observe that, in contrast with Catholic leadership, the Anglican bishops were nonindigenous. Of all the Catholic bishops in office in 1952, 52 out of 57 were born in Canada, he found, whereas only 10 of the 26 Anglican bishops had that privilege, the rest primarily originating in England or Ireland.

Yet, since Porter wrote, more and more bishops have tended to be native sons. Nock (1979, 50) shows convincingly that, already in earlier days, the "parachuting" of Englishmen into episcopal office was the exception rather than the rule. He says that from 1787-1927, out of a total number of 86 Anglican bishops, indeed only 21 were Canadian-born, but that an additional 27 were priested in Canada, leaving 55.8% "indigenous," according to his definition. He says that this percentage of indigenous bishops rose to 88.0% from 1928 to 1961 (59 out of 67) and to 92.8% from 1962 to 1976 (39 out of 42). Yet it may be assumed that being of English birth and having an English accent was certainly an asset rather than a liability for those who aspired to high office in the Anglican Church of Canada.

There is a general consensus in Canada that the Anglican Church represents the elite. Berton (1965, 80), for instance, wrote as follows about one of the most famous Methodist families in Canada, the Masseys:

> When the Massey farm-implement fortune was being ac-
> cumulated, the Methodist church was traditionally the
> refuge of the small and aggressive businessman, while the
> Anglican church was the preserve of the privileged classes.
> It is perhaps germane to note that, as the Masseys rose in
> social prestige, several of them joined the higher-status
> church. These include the Rt. Hon. Vincent Massey, the
> former Governor General, now a "high" Anglican, and his
> well-known cousin, Denton, the former evangelistic
> leader of the Methodist-oriented York Bible Class, who
> has been ordained an Anglican priest.

There is also less anecdotal and more concrete evidence for the prominent place of Anglicans in the Canadian elite. Wallace Clement (1975, 239-40) shows how, in 1972, twice as many Anglicans (25.3%) as Catholics (12.7%) belonged to the corporate elite even though (n = 775) in 1971 there were almost four times as many Catholics (46.2%) in the population as Anglicans (11.8%). He adds: "When only those with multiple directorships are considered, the Anglicans increase to 32%." The same applies to the bureaucratic elite. Porter (1958) shows that the percentage of Anglicans in the higher public service (22.7%) is the same as the one for Catholics (also 22.7%). Yet in the 1951 census there were almost three times as many Catholics (43.0%) in the population at large as Anglicans (14.7%). In an ecological (county by county) analysis of Ontario, Allingham (1962) found that according to the 1951 census, Anglicans and Jews were overrepresented in the upper classes, if "upper class" was defined by occupation and education.

According to 1971 census data on income, the average income for all Anglican males over 15 in Canada was $7,136; that figure was $6,538, for all

Canadian males of the same age group. In some provinces the differences were even greater: in Quebec the average income of all males over 15 in 1971 was $6,288, but for Anglicans it was $8,174. In the same year (1971) 15.8% of Canadian males over 15 earned more than $10,000. The corresponding percentage for Anglicans was 19.9%, for Catholics 12.4%, for Jews 33.2%, and for Pentecostals 9.0%. Paradoxically, the annual per capita giving of Anglicans to their churches ($93.61, according to Jacquet, 1980, 240) is much below that of other denominations, such as Presbyterian ($162.26) and United Church ($172.04).

Anglican males are also overrepresented in the managerial, administrative, and related occupations: 5.9% are in this category as compared with 3.4% of the largest denomination, Roman Catholic. Also, of Catholics, 9.0% work in the construction trade as compared with 6.8% of Anglicans. There are similar discrepancies between the percentages of those Canadians over 15 years of age who had been to university: 10.87% of Anglicans and 7.70% of Catholics were in this category in 1971.

Yet in the 1980s the picture of Anglicans representing aristocracy and establishment should not be overdrawn. The social conscience of the Anglican Church has been well developed for several generations, and the Church has learnt to take full advantage of its independence from political and economic establishments. At the 1981 hearings about the new constitution, the Primate of the Anglican Church, Archbishop Edward W. Scott, testified against the self-interest of those in power and suggested that citizens should have more say in constitution making. In line with more leftist thinking he insisted on a greater voice for the native peoples. Commenting on the testimony, Charles Lynch (1981, 2) concluded: "If the Anglican Church is still the place where the privileged come to pray, it's not because the primate wants it that way, as he made clear with his plea that the needs of the poor override the wants of the rich, that freedom of the dominated supersede the liberty of the powerful."

Of late the percentage of Anglicans in the population has been on the decrease. In 1981 it was 10.1%, whereas in 1931 it was as much as 15.8%. Immigration (or lack of it) from the British Isles, birthrate fluctuation, and ongoing secularization are probably the main factors accounting for this situation. From 1901 to 1921 the Anglican percentage of the population rose from 12.8% to 16.0%, mainly because of large scale immigration from Britain, but from 1951 to 1971 immigration from Great Britain was comparatively slight, compared with other European countries. A decrease in the percentage of those born in the United Kingdom out of the total number of those born in a foreign country (being 45.5% in 1951 and 29.4% in 1971) provides some evidence for the weight of this factor. Anglican birthrate has also been below that for the population at large: in the 1971 census there were 2,475 children per 1000 Anglican women, ever married. The corresponding figure for the population at large was 2,775. This may also have been one of the factors in the decrease of pupils in Anglican Sunday schools from 96,397 in 1975 to 92,993 in 1977, according to the 1980 Anglican

Yearbook. The third factor (secularization) is probably visible in an increase from 0.4% to 7.3% in the 'No Religion' category from 1951 to 1981 and a decrease of 4.6% in Anglican and 4.9% in United Church adherents during that same period. At least some of these changes were likely caused by purely nominal adherents of these denominations selecting the now available "No Religion" category on the census form.

The problem of secularization surfaced into consciousness in the middle-sixties when the Department of Religious Education commissioned Pierre Berton to write a critical book about the Church. *The Comfortable Pew* became a runaway bestseller. Berton had been raised as Anglican in Dawson City (Yukon) in the 1920s. He was confirmed in Victoria, B.C., but began to slowly drift away from the church. However, the Vancouver daily newspaper for which he worked appointed him church editor, and as such he had to report on Sunday sermons and other religious activities of the city. He was married in the United Church and had all his six children baptized there as he did not agree with the Anglican order of baptism which begins with the statement: "all men are conceived and born in sin." He felt rather that children were innocent slates waiting to be written upon (Berton 1965, 24).

Berton had little time for dogma, for it clashed with science. Yet he had a profound respect for "walking sermons," men such as Isaac O. Stringer, bishop of the Yukon or David Baurer, a Basilian Father who coached the Canadian Olympic hockey team during the winter of 1963-64 and imbued it with a spirit of honesty and fairness. He railed against the religious establishment, which cowardly attempted not to rock any boats, preached deadly dull sermons, and condoned war and nuclear armament while condemning pre-marital sex and other pleasures of the flesh. By contrast, he had high respect for those clergy who dared to disturb, as Christ did, and who were not afraid to innovate. Instead of bumbling do-gooders or pious moralists, the clergy should be activists such as Gandhi or Schweitzer (Ibid., 133-4).

Berton had an image of a new age for Christanity, and he saw it being inaugurated by someone who is both

> a man of vigour, humour, passion, concern, guts and above all, action. It is fairly certain that he would not move with the elders of the Church but with its youth; it is probable that he would not mingle with the leaders of society but with the rejected; it is predictable that he would be a master of contemporary methods of communication, but that his real communication would be through his own commitment to his faith. It is axiomatic to say that he would be reviled as the most dangerous of heretics for slicing through the labyrinth of myth and dogma in which the Church is currently enmeshed; it is more than likely that, being an enemy of the establishment - religious, social, and political - he would be denounced as a traitor. And it is in the cards that society would find some modern means of crucifying him (Ibid., 144).

The Comfortable Pew had an effect far beyond the Anglican Church for which it was originally intended. It showed the thinking of well-educated, articulate Anglicans who had drifted away from the Church, but were still loyal enough to long for a new age in which real Christianity could come into its own. The problem was that Berton and many others who were on his wavelength overestimated the charismatic or prophetic function of religion at the expense of its traditional or priestly function. Dogma and Christian symbolism had much greater depth and potential relevance than *The Comfortable Pew* would allow, however much its author was correct in insisting on better communication of the churches with the mundane world. Above all, it tended to be too ironic about the stabilizing contribution which the churches tried to make to the embattled structures of family, community, nation, and personality. The very ideology or open-minded pragmatism which formed the woof and warp of Berton's argument was unsettling for the many who longed for clear delineations of time and meaning. Charismatic fervour and Christian commitment are indeed necessary for changing worn-out patterns, but charisma usually reinterprets an old tradition rather than subverts it irrecognizably. Of course, Berton's respect for Christianity was great enough to have a lingering, though inconsistent, sympathy with that view.

Yet the old religious traditions, even in reinterpreted guise, seem to have a diminishing attraction for many modern Canadians, in general, and for Anglicans, in particular. *The Book of Common Prayer* is a case in point. It has been central to the worship of the Anglican Church throughout its entire history in Canada. It contains the thirty-nine articles, agreed upon in 1562, which Anglicans have always regarded as their unique summary of what the Christian religion is all about. It formulates in detail its view of man as corrupted by sin and worthy of damnation. Yet this same man is also made whole through Christ, and therefore the Anglican community thinks of itself as part of an imperfect world of disorder and pain, but also protected under the wings of God's order and salvation. *The Book of Common Prayer* has gone through various revisions, for instance, in 1918, and more recently in 1959, yet it continues to address itself to the widest possible range of human predicaments and blessings, whether on the personal (sickness, suffering, death, birth, prosperity, health) or on the communal level (war, discord, adversity, corruption, pride, adultery, peace, altruism, goodwill, harvest, charity). It puts all these human experiences, social tensions, and concords in a framework of meaning by relating them to God's covenant. In the Anglican services (inevitably structured around the *Book of Common Prayer*), the same point is made over and over again in a variety of forms: existence may be joyful or hard, full of peaks and valleys, accomplishments and failures, yet, in final resort, it receives its balance and purpose from God in whom everything connects. He represents the unity of all that is.

Yet this universality strikes a cord only with a minority of Anglicans or, for that matter, of Canadian Protestants in general. Why? The riddle increases when we consider that the *Book of Common Prayer* does more than

putting existence into perspective. It deliberately, though latently, ad-
vances the integrity of families, communities, persons, countries, and the
religious organization itself. Honouring parents, considering neighbours,
obeying authority, disciplining appetites, paying homage to the sovereign,
exalting the Church are all part and parcel of the commandments and
prayers and are constantly reiterated. And if worshipping Christians have
not lived up to expectations (as they are unlikely to), the prayers of confession and the assurances of pardon wipe the slate clean and offer a fresh
beginning. One would therefore expect the Church's contribution to to
social and personal well-being to be highly appreciated. Generally clergymen go out of their way to put their messages in easily digestible form and
the saints of the Church concretely exemplify the values to be followed.

The answer to the problem of limited relevance has to take various
forms. For one, the need for symbols and meaning can be overstated. If
acting has the required concrete result, there is often little need for fitting
that action into a comprehensive frame of reference; therefore, people often
live by borrowed or taken for granted justifications, and the Church will be
always there, they feel, if these justifications begin to totter and need
bolstering. Another reason is that to feel at one with one's environment it is
not necessary to go to church; nor do many in our individualistic age feel a
deep responsibility for social institutions. For a third, play, entertainment,
art, music, and literature feed the integrity of culture as much as the
religious institutions, or the religious system of meaning. Fourthly, beliefs,
commitments, and rituals are often expressed and enacted outside the
bounds of religious institutions and their theological systems.

SUMMARY

The Anglican Church of Canada has evolved from an institution closely
tied to English culture, ethnicity, and privilege to one which is independently Canadian and independently denominational. Its first bishop
(Charles Inglis) tried to re-establish a replica of England on foreign soil,
complete with the hierarchical relations of the mother country and a
monopoly of the mother church. Its primate in 1984 (Edward W. Scott) has
no qualms about carving out a niche for his denomination which will make it
distinct from other religious organizations and from a political, economic
and bureaucratic establishment.

Yet because English culture and language has been the major force
determining Canadian identity, its scions and privileged representatives can
be found disproportionately in the Anglican Church of Canada. Its membership is, on average, wealthier, better educated and occupationally
positioned than the constituency of all other major Canadian denominations. It shares with the latter, however, the battle for the hearts and
loyalties of the average Canadians whose personal integrity and corporate
loyalty is informed by non-religious considerations.

THE BAPTISTS

The Baptists trace their origin to those sixteenth century reformers who stressed believer's rather than infant baptism. Based on this principle, John Smyth and Thomas Helwys established a congregation outside London in 1611, but its members were persecuted. One Non-conformist, Roger Williams, took refuge in the American colonies and was baptized by immersion in 1637. He founded Rhode Island and Providence Plantations. From New England, Baptist settlers and preachers trickled into Nova Scotia and New Brunswick during the 1760s, but the first continuing Baptist congregation was not established until 1778 at Horton (now Wolfville), Nova Scotia. It came into being during the Alline revivals, and, although Henry Alline was and remained a Congregationalist, most of his followers became leaders of Baptist churches.

There were good reasons for early evangelical fuzziness and for later Baptist structuring. In the burgeoning frontier settlements of Nova Scotia, the revivals aided the unification of communal sentiment out of the variety of cultural forms and hardship experiences. Faith proved the antidote to fragility. Yet spirit itself was not enough. To guide the crystallization of new forms out of a caldron of diffuse sentiment is the contribution the Baptists made in the first decade of the nineteenth century. To Alline (1806, 48-9), the formality of religious structures tended to squash surging religious sentiment and he therefore tended to disparage "such small non-essentials, as different opinions about water Baptism." But this stress on sentiment and experience tended to lead to a relativization of all forms, and after Alline's death in 1784, the New Dispensation (the idea that all church orders are contrary to the Spirit of God) movement began to destroy some of the New Light congregations in Nova Scotia.

To counter unruliness and antinomianism (in Harris Harding's congregation in Yarmouth members of either sex would ascend the pulpit to contradict him while he was preaching - Rawlyk 1980, 23) the New Light leaders established an annual conference which provided rules for order and discipline. In 1799 this conference was still called "The Baptist and Congregational Association" for, in spite of differences about believer's baptism, both denominations stressed congregational autonomy, individual interpretation of the Bible, and distrust of central authority. But a year later "Congregational" was dropped from the name and in 1808 adult baptism became mandatory for admission to the Lord's Supper ("closed" communion) in the churches belonging to the Association. Three of the eleven Nova Scotia Baptist churches (all with close ties to Harris Harding) withdrew as they believed in "open" communion and admitted all believers to the Lord's Supper (Rawlyk 1980, 24).

The Baptist Association of Nova Scotia also became the overseer of, or arbiter for the various congregations. It reinforced and coordinated the various rules which had been drawn up by the local churches. The latter had begun to effectively function as reservoirs of moral rectitude and social cohesion in their communities. They did this by means of covenants, solemn pledges made by the membership to uphold the worship and service of God and to conduct themselves as Christians. Converts would make similar promises in order to become full members, and the covenant would be periodically renewed, usually before a communion service. Discipline was closely linked with a covenant. If a member had behaved immorally (through, for instance, fornication), had neglected his church duties, or had voiced a heresy of one kind or another, he or she could be privately admonished, publicly rebuked, suspended, or excluded from the church's fellowship - according to the severity of the sin. Discipline was always to be administered with great tact and humility, without regard to a person's status or influence. Congregations were constantly aware of the internal tensions discipline could cause, and therefore believer's baptism and the "contriteness of heart" which went with the born-again experience were also stressed as means to make discipline unnecessary (Deweese 1980, 41).

Improving the education of ministers was another Baptist way of structuring the contagious but diffuse spirit of revival. The New Light movements had been a reaction to the formality of the Old Light Congregational Churches whose educated ministers had returned to New England when their salaries had become endangered. To a man, the New Light preachers were poorly educated and even more poorly paid, but they made up in zeal and dedication what they lacked in formal knowledge (Moody, 1980, 89). Once established, however, the local Baptist churches and their clergy found it necessary to defend their own position against other denominations and to intelligently safeguard Baptist doctrine for future generations. With the help of some prominent Halifax lawyers whose evangelical beliefs had steered them out of the Anglican and into the Baptist fold, the Nova Scotia Baptist Education Society was founded in 1828. From this emerged Horton Academy and, later, Acadia University (Clark 1948, 251).

The fight for temperance became another way to delineate the conduct of the Baptist membership from a spirit of indulgence in the wider community. Drunkenness (also card playing, dancing and swearing) was regarded unbecoming to a good Baptist, and anyone found drunk would be reprimanded by the congregation and would have to repent. Yet rules of proper conduct not only served to strengthen internal Baptist cohesion, but they also began to be valued as important means of building stronger communities. Whether a man was a farmer, a fisherman, or a shipyard worker, his efficiency would decrease drastically if he was habitually drunk, and the community would also gossip about the havoc he created for his family. Therefore, the Baptist Association of Nova Scotia was rather successful when, in the 1830s, it began to promote local temperance societies. All of the major towns in Nova Scotia soon possessed a chapter, and the public began to associate religion with good citizenship, whereas not so long ago the emotional outbursts of the revivals had raised many an eyebrow. Clark (1948, 255) saw the promotion of both education and temperance as a movement away from sectarianism towards denominationalism in that now Nova Scotia Baptists accepted "responsibility for the community at large."

The revivals at the end of the eighteenth century, the Baptist structuring of them in disciplined, cohesive congregations in the first half of the nineteenth century, and the success of these congregations in becoming value models for expanding communities are the main reasons for the overrepresentation of Baptists in the Maritime provinces from that period onwards. In Canada at large the percentage of Baptists was 6.4% in 1891, but dropped to 3% in 1981. Yet in that same year the percentage was still 12% for Nova Scotia and 13% for New Brunswick; or, to say this differently: although the population of Nova Scotia and New Brunswick was only 6.3% of the Canadian population, 27.2% of all Baptists lived there in 1981. Immigration and birthrate overwhelmingly account for denominational distribution in Canada, yet the numerical strength of Baptists in the United States and in the Atlantic provinces of Canada came by conversion rather than by immigration. Vigorous home mission activities by the various Baptist associations in Nova Scotia and New Brunswick in the second and third quarter of the nineteenth century sustained the drive for winning Baptist souls (Moir 1972, 139, 150).

In other parts of Canada Baptist immigration played a much more important role. Gaelic-speaking Baptists from the Scottish Highlands began to arrive in the Ottawa Valley in 1816 and founded a number of congregations. They and other British immigrants, such as John Gilmour, pressed for improved training and education of ministry and people and established the Canadian Baptist College in Montreal with money received from English sources (Wilson 1980, 25). Apart from their views on education, the British Baptists also differed from their colleagues on revivalism (about which they were lukewarm) and open communion (which they tended to favour). The War of 1812-14 advanced the British influence on the development of the Baptist denomination and diminished the American influence, although later in the nineteenth century the work on the Pacific Coast, for instance, was mainly supported by American organizations.

In Canada, Baptist strength lies in the relative autonomy and cohesion of the local congregation. Baptist churches tend to work hard at internal consensus, membership involvement, and missionary zeal. But this entails a corresponding weakness on regional and national levels. There is a Baptist Federation of Canada which loosely combines a number of regional conventions (such as the United Baptist Convention of the Atlantic Provinces and the Baptist Convention of Ontario and Quebec), but approximately one-third of all churches (about 600) remain outside this federation. They belong to the Fellowship of Evangelical Baptist Churches, which came into being in 1953 and united the evangelical, fundamentalist wing (Davis 1980, 237; Tarr 1968, 133). Baptists have always cared relatively little about a concerted national or regional stance, and they have therefore had few qualms about organizing factions at the expense of overarching unity.

Doctrinal controversies were carried out in a much more uninhibited way than in other denominations, and this was particularly so for Ontario. After a slow start, an effective home mission system had increased the Baptist membership twice as fast as the population (from 1851 to 1891). In Quebec, too, the Grande Ligne mission begun by Swiss missionaries in 1835 had blossomed into eight churches and twenty outstations by 1888, in spite of persecution by the Catholic Church (Thomson 1980, 52-3). In Ontario the Canadian Literary Institute had become Woodstock College in 1882 which had in turn been united with the Toronto Baptist College in 1890 to form McMaster University, around which bitter doctrinal controversies began to swirl in the twentieth century.

Senator William McMaster, a member of Jarvis Street Baptist Church in Toronto, handsomely endowed the new institution which he envisaged to be a citadel of Baptist orthodoxy (Tarr 1968, 62). But in the first decade of the century a liberal professor in Old Testament, Dr. I.G. Mathews, and in 1925 a liberal professor of Pastoral Theology, L.H. Marshall, had begun to upset the evangelical Baptists and their leader Dr. T.T. Shields, the minister of the same church (Jarvis Street Baptist in Toronto) to which Senator McMaster had belonged. They founded their own Toronto Baptist Seminary and their own Union of Regular Baptist Churches of Ontario and Quebec in 1927. Later (in 1953) this body would unite with other evangelical Baptist groups to form the already mentioned Fellowship of Evangelical Baptist Churches in Canada. Presently, ministers belonging to this group unanimously believe that the Bible is the Word of God, inerrant and infallible on all matters in the original autographs. Most ministers of churches belonging to the Federation believe this too, but there are a substantial number who think that it contains errors on matters of history, science, etc. (Beverley 1980, 271). The Fellowship of Evangelical Baptist Churches in Canada seems to have a higher growth rate in the 1980s (Mikolaski 1982, 5) than the Baptist Federation.

It was the same issue (the infallibility of the Bible) which half a century earlier divided both the American and the Canadian Baptists. Pitched against one another were the modernists, who wanted to accommodate the gospel to humanist, enlightenment culture, and the conservatives, for whom the authority of Scripture was absolute. From the sociological angle, the first group favoured openness towards secular culture, the second one closure. If, in the second half of the twentieth century, the latter appears to have the greater appeal, it is because the disparate diversity of modern societies seems to summon up its own opposite: closed islands of structured meaning and infallible absolutes. Essentially, however, both groups reinforce wholeness, be it the wholeness of national culture in the former or that of a protest group in the latter.

In Canada's west, many Baptists tended to think of mending the social fabric as their main task. This was particularly so in Manitoba and Saskatchewan where the evangelical or Regular Baptists did not get much of a hold, and where Baptist progress advanced less than in Alberta and British Columbia (Richards, as quoted by Tarr 1968, 92). The census figures bear this out. The Baptist work started late in the entire West, but in 1981 only 1.9% and 1.7% of the populations of Manitoba and Saskatchewan proved to be Baptist, whereas the corresponding percentages for Alberta and British Columbia were 3.0 and 3.0.

Baptists in the Prairie provinces tended to be merchants, white- collar workers, and professionals, the sort of people who did fit easily into the liberal optimism of the urban environment at the end of the nineteenth and the first half of the twentieth century. Brandon College in Manitoba, which was established in 1899 and graduated its first class in theology in 1904, reflected the spirit of urban secular culture.*It produced such people as Thomas C. Douglas, an ordained Baptist minister for whom democratic socialism and applied Christianity were synonymous. The suffering of the depression era caused him to get involved in politics, and in 1934 he was elected to the House of Commons in Ottawa as a member for Weyburn in Saskatchewan. In 1944 he led the Cooperative Commonwealth Federation (forerunner of the New Democratic Party) in the Saskatchewan elections and remained premier of that province until 1961. To him free enterprise was the law of the jungle applied to economics. It represented the philosophy of every man for himself "as the elephant said when he was dancing among the chickens" (Ellis 1980, 174). Through people like Douglas (Stanley Knowles was also a graduate of Brandon, but went into the United Church ministry) the Baptist Church became involved not only in politics but generally in the healing of a society in which poverty, pain and powerabuse were the order of the day. Yet this very dedication to social action also lessened loyalty to the local congregations. There is good evidence in Canada that those who prefer the New Democratic Party, originally so closely tied to the Christian social gospel, are also much more likely to be non-churchgoers than those who prefer the Liberal and Conservative parties.

SUMMARY

In Canada Baptists astutely structured the exuberant Alline revival in the Atlantic provinces towards the end of the eighteenth century. Even now they are overrepresented in the population of Nova Scotia and New Brunswick as compared with the rest of Canada. They do so because originally growth depended less on immigration and birthrate than on appeal and conversion. By contrast in some of the prairie provinces (particularly Manitoba and Saskatchewan) Baptists are underrepresented in the population, even though their involvement in public affairs (through for instance Tommy Douglas) was much greater then in Eastern Canada. The history of Baptists in Canada seems to suggest that denominational growth is positively affected by sectarian separation, 'closed' communion and evangelical dynamism and somewhat negatively influenced by social outreach and dedication to healing the social fabric.

CHAPTER 14

METHODISM, PRESBYTERIANISM, AND THE UNITED CHURCH

The Church of England was not alone in its attempt to establish a replica of the old country in the emerging colony. The Scots were just as keen to safeguard their ethnic identity by planting Presbyterian churches wherever they went. Like the Congregationalists from New England and the Methodists who came from both England and the United States, they also brought with them to the new country their internal divisions. However, in the nineteenth century these three gradually united the various family factions, so that in the twentieth century they were ready to seriously work towards a United Church. The latter came into being in 1925, effacing the original ethnic and sectarian divisions. We will trace the effacing of one boundary and the drawing of a combined one for each of the participating denominations.

METHODISM

In the case of Methodism, loyalty to sectarian and to ethnic divisions were equally important. In some countries, sects had split off from the state churches and became transplanted to Canada when their members dec competition between the two bodies made a division of labour necessary: The British Wesleyans confined themselves to Lower Canada, and the Methodist Episcopal Church was now in charge of Upper Canada.

In those early pioneer days Methodism had become an important, crystallizing force. In contrast with the established Anglican and Presbyterian churches, its missionaries (or circuitriders) travelled far and wide and often became the moral backbone of expanding frontier communities. They appointed local preachers (usually artisans, farmers or teachers with a reputation for integrity) and made up in youthful, evangelical zeal what they missed in education. Their Christianity was not of the inherited type. Some of the most famous ones, such as the Ryerson brothers (Sanderson 1908,

113) or John Carroll (1967, 39), had fathers who were either against religion or drunkards (in those days almost every fifth person was an alcoholic, according to Caroll, Ibid., 79). These young dedicated circuitriders electrified their audiences with tales of their conversion experiences. They suffered many deprivations. Their income was so small that Carroll, for example, felt obliged to give his fiancee her freedom back when his horse (worth a year's salary) died. Circuitriders usually spent the night in hovels, where sometimes the tablecloth also functioned as undersheet and towel (Ibid., 170).

It was this grassroots contact which gave Methodism an important advantage. Already in 1828 the Methodist Episcopal Church became an autonomous Canadian body, which five years later united with the British Wesleyan Conference. They split again in 1840 over "voluntarism," the principle of state aid to religious organizations. The Methodist Episcopals, under the leadership of John and Egerton Ryerson, rejected this aid, while the British Wesleyans accepted grants. Seven years later the competition of Adventism (Sanderson, 1910, 53) increased the desire for a common front, and so they were united again.

Certain distinctions, once relevant and precious, tended to be blurred or erased. After 1854 when the clergy reserves were secularized, the distinction between those who accepted and those who rejected state aid disappeared. So did the ethnic (British or American) and the sectarian (Primitive versus Episcopal Methodism) differences. Instead, pride in one's flourishing community, the status of one's family, the values of success and sobriety, and a burgeoning nationhood culminating in the 1867 federation, began to predominate. Previous distinctions were also irrelevant to the Methodist missionaries now entering the West. Instead, ministers such as James Evans (the inventor of a syllabic system for writing the Cree language) became involved in controversies with the Hudson's Bay Company over his warning the Indians against alcohol and Sunday labour, "two economic essentials of the trade in the company's opinion" (Moir 1972, 204-5).

Apart from the opening of the West, the 1867 federation, the subsequent railway link between the provinces, the extension of local horizons, and the fading of old sectarian controversies, the work of powerful individuals such as Dr. Morley Punshon, sent by the Wesleyans in Britain to initiate the reunion of Methodism, influenced the coming together in 1874 of the Wesleyan New Connexion with the Conference of the Wesleyan Methodist Church of Canada and the Wesleyan Conference of Eastern British North America. Ten years later, in 1884, almost all other remaining Methodist bodies (the Primitive Methodist Church, the Methodist Episcopal Church in Canada and the Bible Christian Church) joined the others so that, from that time onwards, Methodism in Canada could and did speak with a united voice.

PRESBYTERIANISM

The Presbyterians, too, transplanted both their ethnic identity and sectarian divisions to Canadian soil. The earliest Presbyterians in Canada were French Huguenots who arrived in Acadia in 1604. They brought their Reformed minister with them, but he soon died; and after little more than two decades the Huguenots were excluded from colonization by the policies of Cardinal Richelieu.. It was not until the middle of the eighteenth century that a Presbyterian chaplain arrived with Scottish troops capturing Louisbourg and Quebec. Amongst the earliest immigrants to Nova Scotia (Truro and Londonderry) were Ulster Presbyterians who were served by the Rev. James Lyon. By 1786, of the five Presbyterian ministers in Nova Scotia, only one belonged to the traditional established Church of Scotland and four to the various factions of the more zealous Secession Church, which had seceded from the former because it wanted greater autonomy for the local congregation.

In the Canadas, the Presbyterian situation was rather similar. Here, too, the Secessionist ministers prevailed. They organized independent churches on the frontier and in 1818 formed the majority in the then-founded Presbytery of the Canadas, later the United Synod of Upper Canada. However, in 1825 the Church of Scotland formed the Glasgow Colonial Society for the purpose of providing aid to settlers in the colonies. Its ministers in Canada pressured the government to provide similar grants to the ones received by the Church of England in the form of Clergy Reserves. The government was willing to meet the requests but suggested that all the Presbyterian clergy of the province unite so that it could deal with one body only. As a result, in 1840, sixty Church of Scotland and sixteen United Synod ministers formed the Synod of the Presbyterian Church of Canada in connection with the Church of Scotland (Farris, no date, 39).

In the meantime immigrants from the British Isles continued to stream in, and this slowed the Canadianization of the Presbyterian Church. Also, irrelevant Scottish divisions were introduced on Canadian soil. The 1843 Disruption within the Church of Scotland is a case in point. The dominant evangelical section of the Church had managed to pass an act stipulating that the minister presented by the patron was not to be instituted unless approved by a majority of the heads of families in the congregation, but the House of Lords declared the act invalid. Consequently, slightly more than a third of all clergy of the Church of Scotland walked out of the Assembly and founded the Free Church of Scotland. Although there was no system of patronage in Canada and no patrons who could impose unwanted ministers on the parish, the Canadian Presbyterians took sides in the purely Scottish dispute and also divided into Free Church and Church of Scotland congregations. The former tended to be more evangelical, middle-class, and liberal in politics; the latter consisted more of the long established citizens who were conservative both theologically and politically (Silcox 1933, 66).

Other divisions within Presbyterianism were more of a local nature.

When a new minister was installed at St. Andrew's Church of Scotland in St. John's, New Brunswick, an indiscreet elder mentioned that the church would never call a clergyman of Irish extraction, whereupon the Irish Presbyterian faction of the church organized St. John's Church so that it could call a minister of the same ethnic origin. Other divisions were caused by those who insisted on sermons in Gaelic and those who were less particular. One church in Rodney, Ontario, consisting of immigrants from the island of Lewis, split because of the kind of Gaelic a particular faction preferred (Ibid., 69).

Ethnic nostalgia, sectarian memories, and local idiosyncracies, however, proved to be inadequate boundary markers for denominational divisions. Economic necessity (competing congregations being too small for adequate pastoral supervision), a sense of common missionary responsibility for an expanding population, and, above all, the political example of the 1867 Confederation exerted pressure on all Presbyterian bodies to unite. After years of committee meetings, the four major Presbyterian assemblies and synods became one body in 1875, now called the Presbyterian Church in Canada. The new church had as many as 623 ministers on its rolls (Gregg 1892, 194).

The Presbyterian Church could now engage in a common mission to western Canada which was beginning to receive its first immigrants. Dr. James Robertson was appointed superintendent of missions in the Northwest and with great energy set himself the task of extending Presbyterianism to the Prairies. Under his leadership Presbyterian membership increased twice as fast as the population during the period from 1891 to 1901 and from 1881 to 1902 (when he died) the number of presbyteries had grown from one to eighteen (Markell, no date, 57).

Yet the success of the Presbyterians in the Prairie provinces was the result not only of vigorous missions but also of the weakness of many smaller denominations with their sprinkling of members spread over huge distances, too few in number to embark on a viable church organization. As the spirit of cooperation was rather strong in those pioneer communities, the larger denominations were often able to build churches with the help of people from other denominations. In 1911 the Home Mission Committees of the Methodist and Presbyterian Churches made a "comity" arrangement whereby each promised not to compete in new areas or to build churches within six miles of another. This meant that Methodists were expected to join Presbyterian churches, and vice versa, according to which denomination had begun the work first. Actually, the formal cooperation sealed a practice which had emerged since the beginning of the century.

CONGREGATIONALISM

Congregationalism was introduced into Canada by New Englanders who had settled in Nova Scotia in the 1760s when forfeited Acadian land had been made available on rather favorable terms. For various reasons (such as economic hardship of the newcomers, the incapacity of local congregations to pay a minister's stipend, mobility of membership and Henry Alline's evangelism), Congregationalism soon fell on hard times. However, about the time that the Society for the Propagation of the Gospel began to send Church of England clergymen to the British North American colonies (the Glasgow Colonial Society did the same for Presbyterians), the Colonial Missionary Society (founded in 1836) commenced to plant Congregational Churches in the Maritimes and Upper Canada. They remained small, if only because Congregational immigrants remained few and far between - English Congregationalists were generally well-to-do and did not have to migrate to better themselves. The absence of a membership base was also the reason that, in contrast to Methodism and Presbyterianism, the Congregational Church became poorly represented in the West. In 1906 it combined forces with the United Brethren in Christ, but this did not halt their decline in membership which was only .63% of Canadian population in 1871 and even less (.35%) in 1921.

INTERDENOMINATIONAL COOPERATION

There were a variety of reasons why the intradenominational unions of the nineteenth century turned into an interdenominational union (the United Church of Canada) in the twentieth. All these reasons have a common denominator: the weakening of denominational boundary markers and the emergence of new interchurch ones.

First there was the ecumenical influence of the mission field. Both missionaries who served native populations outside Canada and those who were working amongst Indians, Inuit, and foreigners within the country became forcefully aware of the seeming irrelevance of subtle denominational distinctions for their charges. Constantly moving in a much broader Christian, as over against denominational, context, they favoured cooperation with colleagues with whom they had much in common as compared with the natives and the foreigners whom they served. In 1911 the Congregational, Methodist and Presbyterian Home Mission committees agreed to a division of labour amongst the various immigrant groups of whom almost two million entered the country in the second decade of the twentieth century. It was therefore no accident that at the 1925 founding of the United Church as many as 314 of the 337 missionaries of the seriously divided Presbyterian Church opted for union (Ross 1973, 159).

Temperance was similarly a uniting influence. The havoc alcohol wrought in native communities was only slightly in excess of the damage it did to white families, both in the country and the industrializing cities. All churches deplored inordinate drinking and prevailing alcoholism, but the Methodists stood out as particularly zealous in the cause of temperance. Their close contact with the struggling working classes and their advocacy

of values of restraint and hard work made this zeal almost inevitable. Both in
the United States and in Canada temperance movements had begun their
energetic crusade as early as 1827 and continued as late as 1898 when a
plebiscite showed that a majority of English-speaking provinces, but only a
minority of French-speaking Canadians, favoured prohibition. The
Methodist churches were always in the forefront of organizing petitions
favouring stricter laws on the sale of alcoholic beverages and "the popular
mind identified the Methodist Church with the prohibitionists, although
Baptists, Congregationalists and most Presbyterians were no less enthusiastic in their support of the movement, and, in the common crusade
against the evils of intemperance, learned to work together" (Silcox 1933,
81).

A third reason was the common stand taken by the Anglicans,
Methodists, and Presbyterians regarding Sunday observance. In 1888 the
General Assembly of the Presbyterian Church in Canada took the initiative
for the founding of the Lord's Day Alliance, which the others joined. The
Alliance was the prime mover for the Lord's Day Act of Canada, which the
Dominion Parliament passed in 1906. The Act enforced the scrupulous
observance of the sabbath, with the result that neither alcoholic beverages
could be obtained nor theaters be open on Sunday.

A fourth reason was the populist instinct for the integrity of local
communities. The early pioneers had little time or money for indigent,
struggling, unpromising denominations dividing villages. At first their
ethnic ties were stronger than their specific theological convictions, but the
longer they resided in an area the more they abandoned both in favour of
those religious organizations which straddled the community and reinforced its moral integrity. And so a large number of union churches arose.
The 1901 census counted 267, and by by 1925 there were over 3000 of these
congregations in 1245 charges, most of them in Saskatchewan and Alberta
(Mann 1976, 391).

The grass roots impetus was complemented by the common training
received by ministers of the major Protestant denominations. The four
theological colleges affiliated with McGill University in Montreal (Anglican, Congregational, Methodist and Presbyterian) pooled some of their
resources as early as 1906 and later erected a Divinity Hall where a joint
faculty lectured to a joint student body. In Toronto, Methodists and Presbyterians coordinated theological training in 1921. In Winnipeg, cooperation between Methodists and Presbyterians went back to 1889. In Edmonton it began in 1913. In Vancouver a scheme of cooperative theological
training was worked out between Anglicans, Methodists, and Presbyterians
in 1923 (Silcox 1933, 235 ff.).

A sixth reason for increased cooperation between some of the denominations lay in the pooling of resources for Sunday schools. The 1901 census
showed that there were 554 union Sunday schools in Canada. The materials
for Sunday schools often came from the United States. In 1915 the Presbyterians arranged to use the Methodist printing facilities, and the

Methodists gained the right to use the Presbyterian departmentally graded quarterlies. From this point on the common use of one another's Sunday school materials increased, the quality improved and the content became much more oriented towards Canada.

Other organizations in which a variety of denominations worked together were the Bible societies, the Y.M.C.A., the Y.W.C.A., the Evangelical Alliance and such anti-Catholic associations as the Protestant Defense League and the Loyal Orange Order. The Bible societies were active throughout the nineteenth century in Canada. They distributed Bibles and Gospels in scores of languages and dialects to natives and immigrants, and solicited subscriptions through thousands of local branches all over the country. The Young Men's Christian Association and its counterpart the Young Women's Christian Association came to Canada in the second half of the nineteenth century. Originally (as today) they carried out their clubwork mainly in the larger towns and cities, but in the heyday of their growth (1900-1915) they also carried out limited programmes in many of the smaller towns of Ontario and Quebec. The Evangelical Alliance had come from England in the second half of the nineteenth century and wanted to unite the evangelicals of all denominations to lift the moral and spiritual tenor of the local community. They promoted weeks of prayer, they staunchly supported religious liberty, and they organized protests against the Quebec Civil Code in the beginning of the twentieth century when it ruled that marriages between Protestants and Catholics performed by a Protestant minister were invalid. "When Roman Catholicism grew aggressive, the Alliance woke up; at other times it slumbered" (Silcox 1933, 87). More directly anti-Catholic were the Protestant Defense League, formed to protest against the return of lands to the Jesuit order in 1889, and the militant Loyal Orange Order which remained on the lookout for alleged abuse of political power by the Catholic Church. The effect of the latter organizations on Protestant solidarity should not be underestimated. They strongly articulated the view that only a united Protestantism could stand up to the numerical and organizational superiority of Catholics in Canada.

A major influence on Protestant cooperation was the social gospel spirit pervading the Canadian churches at the beginning of the twentieth century. It consisted of an effort to build a better society in which the poor and the disprivileged were protected rather than exploited. It was influenced by the teaching of Walter Rauschenbusch whose book *Christianity and the Social Crisis* had an important effect on the social outreach of the Protestant churches in the United States. The social gospel movement arose as a reaction to poor working conditions, bad housing, unemployment, and health problems of workers who had flocked to the Canadian towns and cities where expanding industries had beckoned with the promise of greater earnings. The social idealism of the churches was coordinated in 1907 in the Moral and Social Reform Council of Canada. By 1914 it was known as the Social Service Council of Canada. It stressed the saving of society rather than the individual, and it advanced social legislation for the betterment of the conditions of workers in industry. It engaged in those activities which could be better accomplished on an interdenominational basis, such as legislative lobbying and research. The "council could take a large share of the credit for welfare legislation protecting the more vulnerable and bringing social support to the less fortunate" (Allen 1971, 241). And the more churchleaders became convinced of the value and effectiveness of their common actions the less denominational loyalty seemed to be such a god-send. It is for reasons such as these that Richard Allen (Ibid., 256) suggests that "the social gospel, in several of its phases was a primary force in church union," and that in some respects it "had become the orthodoxy of the uniting churches."

A ninth and final reason for the drive towards interdenominational cooperation was just as important as the previous one and was closely linked with it. Around the turn of the century there was a pervasive conviction in the major Protestant denominations that Canadianizing the large numbers of immigrants entering the country was synonymous with Christianizing them. In the same way as the health of the nation requires justice for all (the social gospel), so it also demands a common loyalty to Canadian values and ideals - so the thinking went. In order for Canada to be true to its destiny it should become God's kingdom; the nation had to be His Dominion (Clifford 1976, 24ff). As well, the disparate mixture of peoples and nations had to become a mosaic in which each contributed to a pattern provided by Christianity. And that meant that Protestants should be genuinely open to the problems and aspirations of newcomers and oldtimers alike rather than shut off by ethnic and denominational loyalties. God's kingdom transcended the national divisions which ever since Confederation in 1867 were regarded as a liability and which therefore needed the unifying vision of the Christian faith.

Both the social gospel and the national vision provided important points of leverage against entrenched commitment to more segmental systems of integrity such as exaggerated individualism (the social gospel countered that by stressing the social conscience), denominational seclusion (the Kingdom of God was proclaimed to be wider than organizational boundaries), and ethnic separation (God's blueprint both transcended and incorporated the ethnic parts). The emergence of a strong movement towards organizational unity by the Congregational, Methodist, and Presbyterian Churches in the first quarter of the twentieth century would have been impossible without the combination of all these factors. They were all important, although the stirring vision and leverage were provided primarily by the social and national conscience.

THE UNITED CHURCH OF CANADA

Originally other denominations were involved in the union discussions with Congregationalists, Methodists and Presbyterians. (These three denomination formally founded the United Church in June 1925.) The Church of England in Canada made a number of proposals for Christian unity in 1881 and 1889 which led to many interdenominational meetings and discussions, but these and other plans "failed because of excess denominationalism, just as internationalism fails because of excess nationalism" (Silcox 1933, 116). When from 1904 to 1908 a joint committee of the Congregational, Methodist and Presbyterian Churches drew up the Basis of Union, the Anglicans proved to be sympathetic to the plans, but further transactions foundered on the incapacity of the joint committee to accept the historic episcopate as a prior condition for negotiations. The Baptists also appointed negotiating committees, but they took the wind out of the union sails by denying the close link between organic union and Christian unity; and there the matter came to rest.

The Basis of Union provided the doctrinal underpinnings for the uniting denominations. It had an important preamble in which the hope was expressed that in due time the United Church "may be fittingly described as national" (Faulds, 3). The doctrinal statements avoided the stern language of the Westminster Confession or the Thirty-nine Articles, instead expressing the belief "that the eternal, wise, holy and loving purpose of God so embraces all events that while the freedom of man is not taken away, nor is God the author of sin, yet in His Providence He makes all things work together in the fulfilment of his sovereign design and the manifestation of His glory" (Article III). The right of Presbyterian and Congregational congregations to call a minister was retained, but the settlement committee of the conference (a Methodist institution) had the right to appoint a clergyman to a parish with the understanding that it was to comply as far as possible with the wishes of ministers and charges. In actual practice, this led to various complications after 1925.

It took almost a generation for the union to become consummated. The Congregationalists and the Methodists were soon ready, but the Presbyterians encountered considerable opposition in their own midst. In 1912, 26% of the Presbyterian membership voted against the Basis of Union, and the General Assembly therefore decided that it would be unwise to proceed and that further efforts should be made to gain greater unanimity. But in 1915 the percentage had increased to 38. Also, because of World War I, a truce was called, and for several years church union remained unmentioned in the minutes of the Presbyterian Assembly. After the war, however, the Congregationalists and Methodists began to show some impatience, and so the matter of union was brought up again at the 1921 Assembly. As before, the minority sprang into action, this time with the well-organized Presbyterian Church Association. The result was considerable upheaval and bitterness within the Presbyterian fold. At the final ballot in 1924, 43% of its membership voted against Union. The following year, on June 10th, a procession of delegates from each of the three denominations entered the Arena in Toronto through separate entrances to be united in a solemn and stirring communion service. A large minority of "non- concurring" Presbyterians were absent and reorganized themselves as well as they could (only two professors and an insufficient number of ministers were left), but the United Church was now born and went full speed ahead with its mission to Canada.

Its demographic base of operation had become much smaller than originally envisaged. When negotiations began at the beginning of the twentieth century, the four major Protestant denominations (Anglican, Baptist, Methodist and Presbyterian) together comprised more than half the Canadian population. Even the Methodists and Presbyterians alone formed 33% of the 1901 census. But the 1931 census showed that one- fifth (19.5%) of the population professed to belong to the United Church. However, there was now no turning back. The United Church continued to be inclusive and in 1966 added the Evangelical United Brethren to its fold. It also continued to stress social conscience rather than doctrinal precision, so that as recently as 1982 a prominent ex-moderator of the United Church (MacQueen, 1982, 10) would finish his article in *MacLean's* Magazine with the comment: "....the church that talks about salvation but does not battle for human welfare and social justice will be - and should be - dismissed as" "phoney".

Yet a picture of the United Church perpetuating the social gospel tradition of the first quarter of the twentieth century is an oversimplification. The fifty years since its foundation have seen considerable changes in Canadian society, changes which have not left the churches untouched. The legislative battles for greater social justice, welfare protection, unemployment insurance, old age pension, lesser discrimination in the workplace, cradle-to-the-grave medical insurance, compensation for industrial accidents have generally been won. Therefore much wind was taken out of the social action sails typical of an earlier era. Post-World War II immigration somewhat shifted the population balance from a British, Protestant to a European, Catholic pattern. In 1941 the combined percentage of the major Protestant denominations in Canada (United, Presbyterian and Anglican) was still 41.6 of the population as compared with 41.8 for Catholicism. In 1981 these percentages had changed to 29.1% and 47.3% respectively. Crysdale (1965, 1, 2, 13) describes how this change bewildered a minority of United Church members and quotes an active older member of a village church in southwestern Ontario as upset by the closure of United Churches while "new Roman Catholic and Hungarian churches are going up all through the district".

Another pervasive change over the last fifty years has to do with rapid urbanization. Farms became increasingly more mechanized, thereby allowing a decreasing number of farmworkers to provide an increasing supply of farm products. This meant smaller rural congregations. By contrast, industry and government services expanded rapidly during the same period. Small family businesses and bureaucracies became large conglomerates and civil-service empires. And this meant many new suburbs to house employees were built, resulting in an urgent need for schools and churches. In those dormitory suburbs the sense of community became rather frail;

instead, the cohesion of such corporate bodies as militant trade unions, business associations, public interest groups grew. The religious organizations in the urban areas now had to compete with more secular sources of commitment of their members.

It was with these changes in mind that in 1963 Stewart Crysdale (1965, 10) embarked on a national survey for the United Church in which he investigated the effect of "urbanism," an urban style of life with "openness to new ideas and readiness to question old norms" and with much emphasis on rational routines, plurality of customs and a vast array of media choices. The survey consisted of a mail sample of 1,708 individuals on United Church lists of communicants and adherents and found that an increasingly urban style of life went roughly together with an increasingly liberal theology or, "that beliefs and social situations are closely interrelated" (p.78). By liberal theology Crysdale meant freedom of interpretation concerning the nature of God, Jesus and the Bible. The implication was that rationality had been a pervasive influence on both urbanism and theology. Yet towards the end of the 1960s, and in the 1970s, it became increasingly more obvious (see Mol 1969, 1970 and 1977) that the less secularized (or "rationalized") religious institutions were also the more viable ones because they formed little islands of belonging, commitment, and meaning in the modern wasteland of anomie and meaninglessness. It also seemed that a traditional rather than an accommodative theology advanced cohesion. Crysdale's own data seemed to show this trend in that the percentage of liberals in theology (46% in the total sample) drops to 40% for those who attend regularly, to 35% for core members, and to as little as 14% for those with a high religious commitment (measured by regular prayer, biblical knowledge, experiencing God's presence, etc.). All this pointed to the side-by- side existence of both a social action trait in the United Church (healing a broken community, nation, and world and empathizing with their ethos) and a tendency towards evangelical, traditional theology (stressing the religious experience and conversion of the individual), although those with a high religious commitment formed only 17% of Crysdale's sample (Ibid., 104). The survey (Ibid., 2, 99, 104) recognized some of this by observing: "Nostalgia is widespread among faithful, older members for the good old days and something like the old-time religion," but, also showed that the young were in no way more liberal and that the highly committed were in no way less urbanized.

The openness of the United Church towards its environment (rather than withdrawal from) has led to a continued interest in social research. It backed another large national project in 1975 conducted by Dr. Reginald Bibby, now a sociologist at the University of Lethbridge in Alberta. This survey too relied on mailed questionnaires (1,917 were returned), but the sample was drawn from telephone directories in thirty communities across the nation and therefore allowed for interdenominational comparisons and for analysis of the unchurched section of the population.

Like Crysdale, Bibby was interested in the phenomenon of secularization. In writing his report on *Canadian Commitment*, prepared for the United Church of Canada (1979, 4), he anticipated finding that the high level of industrialization in Canada would lead to an ever-decreasing minority of religious people and that even this minority would rationalize belief and delimit religious authority. And this is what he found. Religion is becoming more and more peripheral in Canadian society and maintains itself mainly through religious socialization in the home. Religion has little input in well-being and interpersonal relations. "Only in the sphere of personal morality and in one's response to death does religious commitment in Canada give evidence of making a significant 'difference'" (Ibid., 72-73). Twenty percent of Bibby's sample was traditionally Christian in that they believed in God, the divinity of Jesus, life after death, prayed regularly, did experience God's presence and knew the Bible. For the United Church this percentage was as low as 14%, but for the conservatives (a category in which Bibby grouped together most of the smaller denominations and sects, such as Baptists, Brethren, Mennonite, Nazarene, Pentecostal, Salvation Army) it rose to 50%. The author blames this state of affairs on a pervasive industrial world view which is propagated quite unconsciously in all institutions of Canadian society. It expresses itself, he says, in people's basic commitment to the senses and the observable world rather than to anything spiritual. And the United Church has adjusted itself so much to this outlook "that the commitment differences of United members and nonmembers - while existent - are consistently smaller than those found for other Canadian religious groups, suggesting that participation in local United congregations does not as readily foster a traditional Christian outlook" (Ibid., 15).

All this suggests that the United Church, through its deep, traditional empathy with the well-being of Canadian society, has more than any other denomination become identified with its social environment to the extent that it has allowed the leverage of traditional and sectarian Christianity to become somewhat eroded. And yet within the United Church there is also a small vocal minority, the United Church Renewal Fellowship, which is anything but inclusivist. Its membership consists of born-again and charismatic Christians for whom the Bible is literally inspired. They think of themselves as a leaven in a secular society. There is evidence that of late this movement has gathered rather than diminished in strength.

The United Church of Canada is still the largest Protestant church in Canada. At the 1981 census it had 15.6% of the population. Like the second largest denomination (the Anglican Church, 10.1%), it has acquired the internal heterogeneity of the nation it mothers and in the process has rejected the sectarian option of a united fundamental and vocal opposition to the inexorable secularity of that nation. This has the advantage of broad appeal and easy access to the secularized masses, but it has the disadvantage of blurry boundaries around its own identity. And this disadvantage will be felt all the more during times when corporate identities tend to become a refuge for unfocussed individuals.

PRESBYTERIANISM AFTER 1925

Representatives for the large minority of Presbyterians which had voted against union met on the same day that the United Church was solemnly inaugurated. It was the 10th of June, 1925, and the place was St. Andrew's Presbyterian Church in Toronto. They called themselves non-concurrents, or continuing, Presbyterians. They were well-organized, for the Presbyterian Church Association had its own publications and had left no stone unturned to bring out the anti-union vote. They harboured strong and bitter feelings, as the voting had split many congregations. They were now faced with the task of rebuilding the denomination out of the remains of the old one. The first moderator of the continuing Presbyterian Church was Dr. Ephraim Scott, the anti-unionist editor of the *Presbyterian Record*, the official house organ of the church. The anti-union movement had been largely a lay movement, and therefore many non-concurrent congregations were without a minister. A campaign for recruiting Presbyterian clergy in other countries was begun. The entire staff of Knox College in Toronto and all but two of the faculty of the Presbyterian College in Montreal had gone over to the United Church, but vigorous recruitment gradually rectified a desperate situation.

The continuing Presbyterians differed in many respects from the unionist ones. The older well-established congregations tended to be less enamoured with union than the younger, struggling parishes. Non-concurrents often had higher social status. By contrast sentiment for union was very strong in the more recently settled areas of Canada where many congregations were still aid-receiving and where social distinctions had not yet become well entrenched. Out of 1,961 Presbyterian congregations in the Prairie provinces, only 76 (4%) did not join the United Church. However, in Ontario (28%), Prince Edward Island (25%), Quebec (20%), and Nova Scotia (19%), the comparable percentages were much higher (figures based on statistics in Silcox, 1933, 282).

The non-concurrents also tended to have more pride than the unionists in things Scottish. They were more likely to bring up the contributions the Scots in Canada had made to government, business and the professions. They felt strongly about the links with the empire, even though their families might have been in Canada for many generations. To them, Scottishness and Presbyterianism went together. By contrast, the unionists tended to be more critical of the mother country and to be committed to the building of the nation. Or, as Ross (1973, 232) has it: "They were acutely conscious of the political, economic, ethnic and geographic differences that divided the nation; they believed that commitment to a national united church would overcome the divisive loyalties to secular association." This differed sharply from what Silcox (1933, 198) calls the superiority complex of the non-concurrents.

Thirdly, the continuing Presbyterians were keen to perpetuate the denominational ethos of solemnity in worship and the stately language of the Westminister Confession about God's inscrutable power. The unionists, on the other hand, had less qualms about being associated with the more emotional, bubbly, Methodist emphasis on the love of the Redeemer which had predominated in the early sectarian origins and which had been inobtrusively preserved in the amiable activism of the denomination. Although the actual theological difference between non-concurrents and the unionists should not be overestimated, it is true that the former were more imbued with an ethos of staidness and reserve for which they found as much scriptural justification as the latter did for Christian love and social action. It is therefore not accidental that the reformed, Barthian theology of the influential Dr. W.W. Bryden, who taught at Knox College in Toronto from 1927 to 1952 (McClelland 1980, 120), could stamp an entire generation of ministers of the continuing church.

Closely linked with the previous point is the lack of enthusiasm of the continuing Presbyterians for the spirit of social action so important to the unionists. They rather favoured the salvation of the individual over that of the society. To them, the reformation of society by means of political pressure meshed the sacred too closely with the secular and thereby downgraded sin and God's grace. They left themselves open to the unionists' charge that, in actual practice, separation and individualism legitimated the status quo and that their comfort had led to an unchristian lack of consideration for those who were less well off. The unionists did not hesitate to attack (if that were necessary) the business community and the liquor interests, and the result was that the latter tended to feel more comfortable with the hand-off policy of the continuing Presbyterians.

A fifth point of difference relates to the lower fertility (rate) and the relative preponderance of older people in the continuing Presbyterian Church. In the 1931 census the number of children 0-4 per 1000 women in the 15-44 age bracket was 363 for Presbyterians, 385 for those claiming to belong to the United Church, and 466 for the nation at large. This low fertility rate and the resulting decrease of membership relative to the nation has continued to affect Presbyterianism ever since. In 1941 the corresponding ratios were: 292 (Presbyterian), 344 (United), 397 (Canada); in 1951: 441, 529, 555; in 1961: 487, 574, 606; in 1971: 322, 358, 390. In addition, the continuing Presbyterian Church has had a relatively larger percentage of individuals in the upper, non-reproducing, age brackets ever since 1931. In that year the census showed that 11.0% of Presbyterians were in the over 60 age bracket, as compared with 10.4% for the United Church and 8.4% for the nation at large. In 1961 and 1971 the census grouped the age categories differently, but the same pattern showed for those over 65 years of age: in 1961, 14.2% of Presbyterians were in this category, compared with 8.5% for the United Church and 7.6% for Canada as a whole; in 1971 the corresponding percentages were 14.2%, 9.4% and 8.1%. The combined factors of low fertility rates and relatively large percentage of older Presbyterians are among the main reasons that the denomination has decreased its percentage of the population since 1931 when it still was 8.4%.

It dropped to 7.2% in 1941, 5.6% in 1951, 4.5% in 1961, 4.0% in 1971 and 3.4% in 1981.

In the early 1980s the Presbyterian Church began a campaign to double its membership in the decade ahead. On the basis of the age and fertility profile, the prospects for the campaign were dismal indeed. Of course, the Church hoped to increase its membership not through birthrate but through evangelism, and for this it had a wide open field at its doorstep. Even more so than in the United and the Anglican Churches (where in 1981 the communicant membership was respectively 24.0% and 23.5% of the denominational census figures), the Presbyterian Church in that same year had on its membership rolls only 20.6% of those who regarded themselves as Presbyterians. In other words, by activating only one-fifth of its nominal membership, the church could double its membership. Yet the reserved, solid Presbyterian style, compared with the more exuberant, lively components of the Canadian Protestant mosaic, does not appeal to this inactive, presumably secularized, section of its flock.

PART V

NATIONAL IDENTITY AND CULTURE

The advantage of the identity (or dialectical) theory of religion is its applicability over a wide range of phenomena. It draws the attention to transcendental ordering, emotional anchoring, sameness enacting and dialectic dramatization as ways of strengthening or reconciling any unit of social organization, be it primitive or modern. It looks for sacralization patterns also in the secular domain, because it expects sacralization to be both counterfoil and counterpart of secularization. It fits with the usage of religious terms (such a worship, divine, sacred trust, religious commitment, holy reverence) in situations which have little if anything to do with religious organizations. It expects the sacred to reassert itself under new guises, bypassing, if necessary, the traditional religious forms.

Chapter 15 is a good example of the application of the theory to the secular domain. It first dwells on the meaning of Canadian identity and the forces which have shaped, strengthened, or weakened it. It then zeroes in on sacralization, discussing the monarchy and the crown as lofty moderators of the ruffles of political life, the national anthem as the engraver of loyalty on the minds of the people, the flag as the constant reminder and symbol of national unity, and the various myths as ever so many pointers to Canadian distinctiveness. Yet it also has an equally large section on the priestly (legitimating) and prophetic (critical) concern of the major denominations for the nation.

Chapter 16 deals with education as a separate subsystem of Canadian society which began originally as another arm of religious organizations. Catholics still look upon education in this way as they are rightly convinced that socialization of any kind has implications for beliefs and values. Yet for most Protestants the school system has become emancipated from religious control and the tertiary level is almost entirely public and neutral. The chapter does not explore the self-sacralizing assumptions in science and technology (this can be found in Mol 1976, 120ff.) and instead discusses the phenomenon that, among individuals with a university degree, there is an underrepresentation of the sects and an overrepresentation of Jews, those without a religion, and membership in some of the major denominations nations. It confirms that in Canada as well as in other nations sects tend to

247

appeal to those at the bottom and the denominations to those closer to the top of the educational status hierarchy. The chapter finishes with a discussion of the treatment of religious organizations and religious themes in eight of Canada's best-known novels. The criticism they mete out to the churches is often matched by the use they make, and the deep understanding they show, of the major theological themes of Christianity.

The final chapter takes the emancipation of the political subsystem from the religious one for granted and deals primarily with the link between voting patterns and denominational belonging. It points to the boundaries of religious organizations being strengthened by common political orientations as well as by common beliefs and practices. It then moves to arts, play, and sport as kindred arenas for the acting out of order/chaos, altruism/selfishness, cooperation/aggression, and expression/repression themes. Some of the mechanisms of sacralization are in evidence here as well, although each makes a separate contribution to personal and social integrity: religion through sacralization, art through artistic interpretation, sport through acting out the interplay between instinct and social order. Yet all three operate in the expressive as over against the instrumental spheres so typical of the economic, industrial, technical, and administrative segments of Canadian society.

CHAPTER 15

NATIONAL IDENTITY

Time and time again Canada's identity has been tottery and precarious. Mordecai Richler's description of Canada as a fragile, loosely knit confederation of "ten squabbling provinces" was used as the title of Marsden and Harvey's book (*Fragile Federation*, xiii). Even the name Canada was for quite some time a source of irritation: the Maritimers loathed it, and the French, who thought of it first, refused to call the Anglophones "Canadiens." "Les Anglais," they felt, were more interested in "home" (that is to say England, Ireland and Scotland [Lower 1946, 327] than in the new settlements. How did this "loosely knit confederation" come into being, how did it become more closely knit or loosely woven (whatever the case), and, above all, how was and is religion involved in the fusing and diffusing? First the factors which led to its formation and strengthening should be dealt with.

STRENGTHENING FACTORS

Calling Canada an accidental creation is true to a point. The War of Independence of the American colonies separated loyal from disloyal colonies, and so British North America was born. The recently conquered French colonies were charmed even less by the anti-papist sentiment in the United States than by the haughty mien of the British occupants. And so a separate, British-dominated assemblage of colonies in the north continued to include what used to be New France. For the next generation or so (until the War of 1812), more immigrants from the south joined the British Empire Loyalists to take possession of the empty northern lands, making English Canada "largely American in population and in the functioning of its institutions" (Morton 1975, 102).

The War of 1812 changed all that. It bolstered anti-American sentiments. The "warhawks" controlling Congress wanted to expel England from the American continent, and England resented the Americans taking Napoleon's side in the war with France. Polarization of sentiments and the various battles with the United States forces built a strong sense of belonging together. If a national identity was not born at the time, its maturation was certainly quickened by a war in which neither party proved to be loser or winner.

After the War of 1812, immigration from Britain rapidly changed the population balance, but this immigration strengthened imperial ties rather than Canadian nationhood. The Rebellion of 1837 by William Lyon Mackenzie's band against the monopoly of power of the Family Compact in Upper Canada (Ontario), and the rebellion by Joseph Papineau's reformers against the Chateau Clique in Lower Canada (Quebec) pitched a considerable part of the people against its rulers. These rebellions were crushed by the imperial authorities, but in 1848 the power of the public at large was recognized through the provision that the governor (appointed by these authorities) had to execute his duties "through ministers who had the continual support of majorities in the colonial legislature" (Smiley 1980, 215).

If enhanced responsibility for government fed a sense of national identity, the latter was braced even more by persistent fear (all through the nineteenth century) of invasions from the south, and the 1867 Confederation was at least partly a response to this apprehension (Brady 1958, 42). Yet this common fear could not disguise the essential cultural duality (French and English) of the new Dominion of Canada: Confederation gave each of the founding sections greater provincial autonomy (linguistic, educational, religious) than they had before. Confederation was essentially a correction of, (and retreat from), the British attempt in 1840 to swamp French ethnic identity by uniting Lower and Upper Canada into one legislative union in which English alone would be the language of intercourse.

Yet fear and expediency were not the only factors creating a sense of national unity. The spirit of confederation had its own self-propelling effect. For instance, it promoted the union of various Methodist and Presbyterian denominations hitherto happily ensconced in cloistered smugness. Authors such as H.J. Morgan and E.H. Dewart felt that literature should serve the new spirit of patriotism and break the habit of imitating the English (Watt 1966, 238-9). The Canada First movement began to kindle national pride and devotion in the new Dominion, a feeling distinct from subservience to anything British or American (Foster 1890, 25).

Yet the covertly British (as over against French) character of much patriotic pride of the last quarter of the nineteenth century became obvious at the time of the Boer War in 1899. On the whole, English-speaking Canadians felt that Canada should send troops to fight the Boers for Queen, Empire and Motherland. Prime Minister Laurier fell in with the patriotic fervour aroused by the war and decided to send soldiers (volunteers) to South Africa. Yet French Canada was less enthused. Henri Bourassa resigned his seat in Parliament in protest against the decision, and he "became something of a hero to the young elite of French Canada" for whom nationalism and imperialism were altogether separate categories (Levitt 1975, 317).

The English version of patriotism received another shot in the arm during the large-scale immigration from non-British countries during the first decade of the twentieth century. The fear of being swamped by "inassimilable lumps" of settlers from southern and eastern Europe galvanized the Canadianizers into action (Reid 1973, 41ff.). It was as though the assimilated, English-speaking Canadians felt that the virility of their culture was at stake and that only missionary zeal could counter the threat to its survival. Yet it was also true "that the years of the Laurier regime saw the rise of a Canadian national spirit, neither French nor British but wholly Canadian in sentiment" (Morton 1975, 51).

> The First World War, if anything, heightened that national spirit.

> "I've always thought that the Canadian nation was in fact, born on the battlefields of Europe. I'm sure that that's true, that the fierce pride developed in the Canadians in their own identity, in their own nationhood, was a very real thing and it survived over into the peace" (old soldier quoted in Masters 1967, 11).

The 250 acres of Canadian soil at Vimy Ridge (twenty-four miles from Lille in France) dedicated to the dead from the four Canadian divisions which overran the Germans in 1917 are an impressive reminder of that fact. In the same way as England and France fought together in the war, so English- and French-speaking Canadians were united in the common effort. Yet the Conscription Act of 1917 was bitterly opposed in Quebec and led to a split in the Liberal party.

After World War I, provincial and regional interests began to reassert themselves at the expense of a unifying nationalism. Certainly the common suffering of the Great Depression did not bind the nation together in the same way as World War II subsequently did (Smiley 1966, 100ff.). Yet even the heightened patriotism of the early forties was marred by another conscription crisis (1944) in which, as before, French Canada was pitched against the Anglophones. After the war, federal plans for post-war reconstruction (health, welfare, employment urban expansion, natural sources development) took the initiative away from the provinces and provided an exciting image of a nation on the march.

A more important factor were the millions of non-English-speaking immigrants from Europe who flooded Canada in the post-war years. In a unobtrusive way they (and their children more so) were absorbed into an Anglophone Canadianism which proved to be all the more effective for its relative lack of articulation. English-speaking Canadians have always taken for granted that schools, governments, communal institutions and the all-pervasive mass media would unselfconsciously be missionaries for a culture which was neither American nor British, but somewhere in between. And this unself-conscious Canadianism has proved, in the long run, to be much more powerful than the learned treatises of pundits.

Although multiculturalism and its twin, ethnic "mosaic" (as over against the "meltingpot" south of the border), form the official rhetoric, in actual fact, a Canadian national spirit is considered non-negotiable. The mosaic moves inexorably in the direction of the meltingpot. The major French-Canadian prime ministers were and are primarily remembered for their contribution to the unification of the country. Sir Wilfrid Laurier illustrated this national task of his office well when he said:

> I am branded in Quebec as a traitor to the French, and in
> Ontario as a traitor to the English. In Quebec I am
> branded as a Jingo, and in Ontario as a Separatist. In
> Quebec I am attacked as an Imperialist, and in Ontario as a
> anti- Imperialist. I am neither, I am a Canadian (Skelton
> 1919, 380).

Pierre Elliott Trudeau's charisma bound Anglophone and Francophone Canada together towards the end of the 1960s. His firm stand against both the militant Front de liberation du Québec (FLQ) in 1970 and the separatist Parti Québecois at the end of that decade provided the nation with a sense of unity straddling deep ethnic rifts.

Patriotic sentiments are often bolstered, as we have seen, by actual or perceived threats, by participation in the political machinery, by the necessity to defend one's culture against newcomers, by social and economic initiatives on the federal level, by the pervasiveness of the national mass media, and by strong, or even charismatic, leadership in Ottawa. There is more. A nation may develop distinct values and beliefs even within the bounds of an English- speaking commonwealth. Canadians are decidedly more egalitarian than the English and less inclined to value birth and bearing over ambition and achievement. Yet, compared with Americans, who have similar preferences, André Siegfried (1937, 97) felt that Canada could counter the vulgarity of the latter with the moral, aesthetic, and social bulwark of Anglicanism. And Lipset (Porter 1971, 6) calls Canadians "conservative, authoritarian, oriented to tradition, hierarchy, and elitism, in the sense of showing deference to those in high status" in comparison with "the strong egalitarianism of the United States." In other words, Canadians may possess some of the restraint and the reserve of the English, practice the frugality of the Scotch (they are the world's best savers), and frown on American hustle and bustle, but they are like Americans in their accents, in the materialism of their culture, and in their respect for competence, efficiency and vigour.

Most of these national characteristics are nothing more than astute hunches. Yet there is concrete evidence for at least some of them. In the various public opinion polls, dependency on the United States is regarded as not a good thing by large sections of the population, but so is dependency on the Commonwealth (Schwartz 1967, 69, 73). Archibald (1978, 237) concludes that "there has been something of a distinct English Canadian national character which can be documented in comparative-quantitive terms." Canadians seem to be more other- and less self-oriented than Americans. They are less achievement-oriented, but more self-reflective. "Whereas they have been more deferential toward elites, they have not necessarily been more conservative or conformist in general." Yet, once all is said and done, there is substantial agreement with an observation made by MacCormac (1940, 153-4) that "English Canadians are far more like Americans than they are like French Canadians or Englishmen." He admits that there are subtle differences: "Canadians take their work more calmly" and high-pressure salesmanship "never threatened to blow off the cylinder heads in Canada." Yet his conclusion that political conventions in the United States are like bedlam compared to those in Canada (they remind him of a cemetery) is much less true now than half a century ago.

WEAKENING FACTORS

There is unwitting imperialism in any culture worthy of the name. People who work and live together develop common wavelengths so that actions and reactions can fall in predictable patterns. Whichever nation is first on the scene and has the numbers usually determines the linguistic and cultural outline to which subsequent settlers have to adjust. The problem for the spread of English Canadianism is and was that the French were first on the scene and were also numerically superior for quite some time after the English conquest of 1760. Canadian identity has therefore suffered from the existence of two distinct cultures (French and English) neither of which is prepared to yield to the other. A straddling patriotism is obviously handicapped when sections within the nation can command greater loyalty than the whole. Outside Québec, where the vast bulk of the six million French-speaking inhabitants are located, English Canadian culture reigns supreme, so much so that French enclaves in Ontario are in the process of gradually becoming Anglicized. However, within Québec the Francophones hold their own, even though they do not seem to be equally capable of Frenchifying newcomers.

Loyalty to French Canadianism is reinforced by a variety of means. Language is the most obvious one, and the squabbles over language laws in Canada but represent the determination of the French culture to survive. Also, important are the ways by which each culture remembers its roots and its heroes. Quebec children identify with Francophone heroes from the pre-1760 period. By contrast, Anglophone children remember post-1760 personages of their own culture much better. Richert (1974), who carried out the research detecting this pattern, concluded that the education system of each culture widened the gulf in Canada (also Hiller 1976, 168).

There are similar differences in values and beliefs. A tendency toward individualism and pragmatic improvisation on the part of Anglophones compares with a tendency towards reverence for authority, logical consistency, systematization for its own sake, on the part of Francophones.

> In Quebec the battle of ideas and refinement of logic are more highly valued than is generally the case elsewhere .... civil liberties in English-speaking Canada have been more carefully cherished than in Quebec .... French Canadians prefer to systematize and codify the law, the constitution and, indeed a broad range of social relationships .... and (have) a natural proclivity for verbalization (McNaught 1966, 62, 69, 70).

For long periods of its history French Canada preserved its cultural heritage with the astute and competent aid of the Catholic Church. It reinforced the belief that only in Québec were the rural virtues of simplicity and integrity safeguarded and that French culture had a messianic task on the North American continent. It played a decisive part in the opposition of "the French language, authoritarianism, idealism, rural life and later return to the soil" to "the English, Protestant, democratic, materialistic, commercial and later industrial world" (Trudeau 1954, 12; Smiley 1980, 220).

There are other factors weakening the Canadian national fabric. When the 1867 Confederation became a reality, upside-down, half-mast and black flags in Nova Scotia vented the anger of many for the loss of independence. Newfoundlanders going to the mainland feel exiled, even when mainlanders refrain from telling Newfie jokes in their presence. On the other side of the continent, the sense of being first shared by many British Columbians weakens loyalty to the nation. The Prairie provinces have, for many generations, felt exploited by the wealthier East, and when the Edmonton football team (the Eskimos) came to Toronto for the Grey cup in 1952, they not only brought their own steaks, bread and other food, but even their own water (Reid 1973, 79ff.).

Class and other ethnic loyalties also prove to be sometimes stronger than the national sentiment. Marsden and Harvey (1979, 127f.) regard these and regional allegiances not only as a "direct challenge to twentieth century national identity and power," but even as more important than "all other forces for change" in Canada. Following Porter (1966) and Clement (1975), they maintain that diverging economic interests of sectors of the Canadian population (classes) clash with the national interest. Without necessarily agreeing that one's material position issues into a major identity determinant (in North America, class in this sense is much more amorphous than other groups, such as family, sect, ethnic association, gang, community, etc.), it is true that ruthless pressure of chambers of commerce, unions,

professional associations, powerful conglomerates and profit-oriented corporations flout whatever sentiments for the common and good remain
among their constituents.

Mass immigration of eastern and southern settlers did put a strain on
patriotic sentiments. Especially among those who settled in separate rural
colonies these groups could perpetuate old world loyalties for several generations to come. In the early days of their residency, the Ukrainians on the
Prairie provinces, the Hutterites in Alberta, the Doukhobors in British
Columbia, and even the urban enclaves of Italians, Greeks, or Portuguese
put more store on their ethnic than on their Canadian ties - and some of them
still do, particularly when (as is the case with the Hutterites) religion
consolidates the old-world tongues and ties. Isolation becomes less of an
option, however, when the immigrant group has to maintain extensive
occupational and economic links with the dominant culture and when
modern mass media, with comparative ease, infiltrate even the most determined ethnic bulwark.

It is this technological advance which some scholars see as loosening
national integrity. Marshall McLuhan, impressed with the lightening speed
of the electronic mass media, sees national boundaries withering away. Mel
Watkins (1966, 292, 301) thinks that military technology has rendered
national sovereignty obsolete, and that Canadians should lift their vision
beyond nationalism to world society. George Grant (1970) feels that Canadian nationalism has been defeated by American culture and economic
dependence on the United States. George Woodcock (Nelles and Rotstein
1973, 4,6) adopts Northrop Frye's idea of the post-nationalist age and
suggests that "the nation- state, as an effective unit is already obsolete," not
because of technology (if anything the mass media have strengthened
nationalism by deep and passionate involvement of the people), but because
only internationalism can secure peace, control populations, and safeguard
resources. Yet the assumption that information-processes, military
technology, economic dominance, yearning for peace, and equitable distribution of resources can determine human commitment to the various
forms of identity (national or otherwise) is to overestimate the former.
Neither knowledge, nor oppression, nor persuasive arguments for international order have weakened national identity. Ireland, Greece and Poland
are historical examples of nations in which conquest increased patriotism.
And both the League of Nations and the United Nations have lacked, and
still lack, grassroots commitment, rather than rational arguments for their
existence.

SACRALIZATION FROM WITHIN

By sacralization from within I mean those beliefs, commitments, and
rituals which are part and parcel of the national identity itself and
strengthen it, independent from religious organizations. The contribution
of the latter will be discussed under a separate heading, "sacralization from

without." Here I would like to consider the unifying role of Queen and Crown, the national anthem, the Canadian flag and civil myths.

a)   Queen and Crown

In the 1982 Constitution of Canada, the preamble to the Charter of Rights and Freedom begins: "Whereas Canada is founded upon principles that recognize the supremacy of God and the rule of law....". God was absent in the first draft, but the conservative members wanted God acknowledged and Prime Minister Trudeau was personally in favour of this, although he was not altogether sure that reference to God belonged in a secular document (McWhinney 1982, 57). Yet God is not the only unifying symbol of legitimacy for Canada's governmental structures, although he is certainly the most transcendental source. After Him, in descending order of spirituality or expanding forms of embodiment, come the Crown (a still somewhat abstract principle signifying supreme executive power) and the Queen (personifying or humanizing that power).

The Crown (monarchy) was originally absolute, but as MacKinnon (1977, 15) points out, in Canada and other constitutional monarchies, the possession of power (safeguarding laws and holding power on behalf of the people) is now separated from the wielding of power (a trusteeship temporarily invested in members of parliament to make laws, in the judiciary to interpret them and in the administration to carry them out). The Crown is like a trustee holding an estate in trust: the trustee controls it but does not possess it, whereas the children possess it but do not hold it (Ibid., 17). The analogy, however, should not be carried too far. The Crown controls permanently, a trustee does not. Unlike children inheriting an estate, those in power can wield it only within limits of time and, directly or indirectly, only at the discretion of the people. As a balance to the inevitable discontinuity of this kind of governing, the Crown provides a compensating continuity, by furnishing a transcendental, ordering frame of reference, a canopy which relativizes the power of those who wield it. It also minimizes the potential for abuse (dictatorship) by both itself and those who do the actual governing. The Crown allows itself to be exalted innocuously as a symbol of unity and continuity, thereby allowing the free flow of criticism of the power-wielders.

MacKinnon (1977, 17) compares the Crown with the soul, presumably meaning that both unify what is inherently fragile (whether government or man). He brings out the transcendent, ordering function through the analogy with

> a benchmark, or fixed location *separate* (his underlining) from a structure for surveys and observations so that distances, directions, and levels may be ascertained, in order that the structure may be accurately built and precisely related to other structures.

All this means that the Crown preserves and enshrines some of the most important values of Canada. It safeguards egalitarianism and individual rights by restricting the power of any single individual. It instills, as suggested by one of the fathers of Confederation in Canada (Thomas d'Arcy McGee 1865, 131) humility, self-denial, obedience and holy fear - virtues he strongly recommends for a burgeoning frontier society where lack of discipline and self-assertion tend to come out on top. The Crown also acts as the conscience of the nation, and, as the nation's parent, it defends the law, pardons prisoners, and rewards outstanding performances and achievements with prizes, medals, citations, and honours, in often impressive ceremonies.

The analogy with the family is not accidental. The Queen as the personal expression of the Crown is, for Canadians, the head of State to whom one owes allegiance, and this is rather similiar to the feelings of loyalty one has for parents. Yet precisely because the Crown is concretized in a person, that person is also continually matched against the lofty standards she represents. A divorce in the royal family is therefore regarded as more serious than a divorce of ordinary citizens, and the popularity of members of the Queen's household hinges, more than elsewhere, on expectations of a model family. Polls taken in Canada in 1956 and 1958 show that only a minority of the population would approve if the Duke of Windsor or Princess Margaret were appointed as Governor-General, but reasons for this may have more to do with preferences for a Canadian in that post than with concern about royal links with divorce (Schwartz 1967, 114). Commitment to the royal family is often articulated in terms of the match between symbol and actuality. Allegiance and commitment have their own intrinsic capacity for unification, yet this capacity diminishes if the focus of that commitment ruptures symbol and reality.

In Canada the Queen is represented by the Governor General on the federal and by Lieutenant Governors on the provincial level. They legitimate on her behalf the hierarchical relations between the provincial and federal forms of government and provide continuity when governments change. They put a decorative seal on the major events and accomplishments within their jurisdiction. Since 1952, each Governor-General has always been Canadian.

Yet the Crown, the Queen, and her representatives are also vulnerable when the unity they symbolize hides papered-over rifts. In Quebec British royalty has been less popular than in other provinces, and in her 1964 visit to that province the Queen was actually booed by separatist demonstrators (Reid 1973, 231). To French Quebeckers, the Crown is too much associated with the British version of Canadian nationalism. "Those in favour of the Queen's picture on money and stamps were most often found on the prairies, less often in British Columbia and least often in Quebec" (Schwartz 1967, 157).

b)   The National Anthem

Whenever the national anthem is sung, participants are solemnly reminded
of their belonging to Canada. Not that the ritual invariably warms the heart.
School children, theatre-goers and hockey game spectators may fidget alike
when the school day or the event is opened with the rhythmic strains. Yet
these same individuals may have their heartstrings tugged when the national
anthem is played at a memorial service for soldiers of both world wars, or at
the presentation of international awards. National anthems link the hearts
and minds of the people with the nation of which they are part. Periodically
keeping the bond alive and well, they symbolically retrace the grooves of the
national order. Although they cannot create patriotism from scratch, once it
exists they can provide it with "pomp and circumstance."

"O Canada" is now generally accepted as a truly national anthem. It was
written by Calixa Lavallee in 1880, and at the time its popularity in French
Canada vastly exceeded that in other parts of the country. It is highly
patriotic (the second line runs "true patriot love in all thy sons command"),
speaks about the glory and freedom of Canada, and mentions as much as five
times the "standing on guard for Canada." It also grew in favour within
English Canada after World War II, until, in 1963, close to three-quarters of
the population regarded it as the most suitable of the four patriotic songs
(Schwartz 167,42,110).

The victory of "O Canada" corresponds with a growing national, as over
against imperial, consciousness. The competing patriotic songs were
strongly British in their sentiments. "God Save our Gracious Queen" lost
out because in Quebec, particularly, the English monarchy was never
strongly acclaimed. There had always been pockets of resistance to the
"foreign" queen. The other song, "The Maple Leaf Forever" was written
by Alexander Muir in the year of Confederation (1867) and was very
Canadian indeed. It began

> In days of yore, from Britain's shore
> Wolfe the dauntless hero came,
> And planted firm Brittania's flag
> On Canada's fair domain.

It had the obvious disadvantage of making a hero of the conqueror of French
Canada in 1759 and rather insensitively assumed that Canadian history
began when the British arrived.

c)   The Canadian Flag

Like the national anthem, the flag symbolizes Canada's unity for it
represents an exclusive bond between people spread over many regions,
provinces, and communities. At times of crisis such as war, the flag becomes

a rallying point for the nation and refusal to salute the flag then (as the Jehovah's Witnesses do) is regarded as grave sacrilege. Lowering the flag at the death of a distinguished citizen shows the grief and the respect of the entire nation. Nowadays, on a more local level, municipal, educational, and commercial organizations use the lowering of the Canadian flag on their buildings and grounds to symbolize the loss of the individual for the community in question.

It is not accidental that the Canadian flag consists of a red maple leaf on a white background. The maple leaf is a way to pronounce our separateness and uniqueness to other nations: what is typical for nature in Canada is, by implication, atypical for the rest of the world. Yet this is not where the symbol comes to rest. Red and white predominate over all other colours in national flags. They send complementary messages to other nations: white (the colour of purity) for peaceful coexistence and red (the colour of aggression) for defense readiness. Although seeming to contradict each other, they belong together in that both peaceful coexistence and defense existence provide the optimal guarantee for continuity of the nation's boundary.

The Maple Leaf became the official Canadian flag on the 15th of February, 1965. Prime Minister Lester Pearson's plans had encountered heavy opposition from those for whom the Union Jack (combining the English, Irish and Scottish crosses of St. George, St. Patrick and St. Andrew) was sacred. The opponents (many of whom belonged to the Conservative party) felt that the ties with Britain should be maintained, if not through the Union Jack, at least through the Red Ensign (which has the union Jack in the top left hand corner and the Canadian emblem in the middle on a red background). Like the Canadian anthem, the flag omits all reference to Britain, thereby paving the way for sentiments of national unity comprehensive enough to also please the French Canadians.

d) Civil Myths

The sense of national distinctiveness has been strengthened by various other means. The Group of Seven artists expressed its love for the Canadian landscape in its numerous paintings. Team Canada welded the nation together in 1972 when it defeated the Soviet Union in the national game of ice hockey (Reid 1973, 180) and again in 1984. The blend of aggression and grace so typical of hockey is not only dramatized on the ice. It is also at the heart of the peculiar love relationship Canadians have with the land. The national myth has it that the harshness of climate and landscape must be tamed and yet must also be deeply respected. Bruce Hutchison (1957, 59) suggests that the basis of Canadian identity rests not on history but on the way the landscape has entered the subconscious. It made Canadians hardy and vital and capable of sublimating the loneliness inherent in the grim nature surrounding them. They return to their cottages in the wilderness to be revived by the raw essence of the land. The "land" myth interprets the basic Canadian character (whether English or French, rural or urban) as fluctuating between masculine "questing," and feminine "nesting" (Morton 1975, 5; James 1981, 161). The mosaic myth (Reid, 1973, 56) affirms that Canadian unity consists not in homogeneity, but in accepting and even extolling diversity. It is an official rather than a popular myth, because individuals (and Canadians are no exception) prefer the security of common ways of acting and reacting to the exhilaration of the uncommon. The myth attempts to discover virtue in the failure to amalgamate the various ethnic components of the nation. This can be as seriously argued as it is because the increasing amount of education, urbanization, and industrialization of Canadians facilitates the acceptance of diversity and novelty, and because the economic and financial security of these Canadians usually balance cultural and other insecurities. Yet the mosaic tolerance comes apart on the school playgrounds and in the workaday world of factories and road-building crews. Here the pressure for the mosaic to turn into a melting pot is unrelenting.

SACRALIZATION FROM WITHOUT

How have the religious organizations and their personnel contributed to the strengthening of Canadian identity? I do not want to repeat the argument that Catholicism was essential for the preservation of French nationalism, or that after the British conquest Anglicanism was at first taken as the religious arm of government, or that the Methodist, Presbyterian, and later United Churches vigorously defended the ramparts of embattled English-speaking culture when millions of immigrants from the European continent flooded Canada. Here I want to discuss how, after a period of close collaboration, the Canadian churches adopted a more autonomous and critical stance while maintaining their sense of responsibility for society at large. First, the responsibility, or legitimation, angle.

a)   Legitimation

In contrast with some sects, the mainline churches in Canada have never abandoned their priestly concern for the nation. By "priestly concern" I mean that, in spite of the widening gap between churches and culture, the mainline churches continued and still continue to provide the nation with its transcendental assurance (the love of God for the nation), its loyalties (the flag in their sanctuaries), its rites (prayers for the monarch and the government), its theology (the interpretation of national events through scriptural traditions). However secular Canadian culture may be and however much the religious institutions appear to be on the fringes of society, mainline Christianity perseveres in the firm conviction that God is a God of history, and that, therefore, the nation is part of His plan.

The transcendental purpose behind the nation's affairs was strongly and widely stressed in much of Protestantism, both in the latter part of the nineteenth and in the first half of the twentieth century. Again and again, from pulpits and in denominational literature, the dominion of Canada was interpreted to be God's dominion. God was working out His purpose in the nation. Clifford (1977, 24) called this vision "the inner dynamic of Protestantism during that period." It had, he says, "sufficient symbolic power to provide the basis for the formation of a broad Protestant consensus and coalition." Although the earlier idealism is now much more subdued, leaders of the United Church in the last quarter of the twentieth century continue to maintain (following the Old Testament model) that the nation's welfare and actions are certainly of supreme concern to God. And so do the other denominations.

If God orders history, the values of the nation are also His affair. Ultramontane Catholics as well as voluntarist Protestants, says John W. Grant (1977, 14), speaking about the effect of the missionary drive in Canada, were convinced that society needed sanctification, and they did this in "highly moralistic terms, habitually stylizing its demands into readily identifiable taboos." They felt it to be their task to strengthen "known values rather than .... discovering new values" (Ibid., 15). Anglo-Saxons and French-speaking Catholics alike were convinced that they had to make their own uniquely Canadian contribution, "either abroad in promoting peace and mutual aid or at home in developing an alternative to the materialistic society of the United States" (Ibid., 16). Although this confident missionary drive was much more in evidence in the first half of the twentieth century, the Canadian mainline churches assume that the nation's values belong within their domain.

But if God is the God of history, the relations between man's various units of social organization (systems) are, of necessity, also His affair. Canada is therefore no exception to the rule that the Christian churches constantly engage in modifying the tensions and conflicts between the subunits (individuals, classes, communities, ethnic groups) of the nation. They do so through sanctifying some values and norms over others. Crimes and offenses are obviously conflicts between what is good for a society and what some individuals think is good for themselves, and therefore rules of not stealing, killing, coveting, and those of loving one's parents are reinforced by Christianity. Hutchinson (1977, 199, 211) rightfully asserts that corporations, too, can subvert the common good, and that Christians must transform the various subunits of society in order to create a more just and humane society. Kerans (1977, 227, 263) points to a similar "dialectic relationship between individual freedom and dignity on the one hand, and community order on the other" and thinks that over against a prevailing possessive individualism, the Judaeo-Christian ideal of reconciliation must be institutionalized in Canadian society. Hall (1980, 103) suggests that the Canadian church "functions as a forum of caring in the midst of a society in crisis" but that it can only do so if it frees itself "from ethnic, economic, class and other interests and identities."

Yet God acting in history does not confine Himself to one nation and its internal reconciliation. Gualtieri (1977, 523) detects the emergence of a global society and of a world growing ever closer, and feels that a sanctified Canadian nationalism misses the point unless it allows its historic uniqueness to be in dialogue with other nationalisms in an organic international context.

National loyalties are reinforced by the presence of the Canadian flag (usually "flags") in many churches. The hymnbooks contain the national anthems and they are sung at special occasions, such as Remembrance Day in November. Allegiance to Canada's form of government (democracy) is openly assumed and encouraged. Democracy and Christianity are linked in the minds of clergy and laymen alike, and during election time religious leaders lend their voices to the civic organizations intent on bringing out the vote. They scrupulously avoid, however, to show their own party preference, particularly when they officiate. Despland (1977, 541) is aware of "the naive and immediate flow between the emotions of religion and those of nationhood," but feels that Christians should keep their priorities straight and should not allow their commitment to the city of God, to justice, and to democracy to take second seat to national allegiance. We will come back to the issue of the churches being the watchdogs of the nation in the next section.

The rites and worship of the churches converge at various points with those of the nation. The mainline churches offer prayers "for the Queen and her household," and "for those who reign over us." Often in the same breath these prayers repeat the expectation that the leadership will remain incorruptible, honest, fair and virtuous, thereby strengthening the moral foundations of Canadian government. Power as an end in itself is invariably condemned in these prayers, and power as means to advance the good of the nation is correspondingly endorsed. At times of war the churches intercede with God for victory of its armed forces. Yet they also agonize publicly over the fact that all this warfare must be an abomination in His sight. Other calamities which have befallen the community or the nation are brought before God in prayer, thereby putting the apprehension and upset in a context of love and order.

The orderly context is similarly provided in sermons which deal with interpretation rather than supplication. Only rarely do they deal with topics of national interest, and yet the values which are implicitly or explicitly espoused fit with those of the nation, if only because the religious leaders feel obliged to be relevant to the situation of their audiences. Dialectic themes are often at the heart of these interpretations. The literature on religion and nationalism mentions a few of them. Hutchinson (1977, 200) suggests that through the symbols of sin and redemption, Christians rather than Humanists attempt to do justice to the various dimensions of social reality. Gualtieri (1977, 508), in his paper about a theological perspective on nationalism, similarly interprets religious traditions to make alienation yield "to reconciliation, chaos to meaning, guilt to forgiveness, insecurity to acceptance, death to life, bondage to freedom." Hall (1980, 66, 72, 77) writes that the harsh reality of the Canadian winter climate makes the people more prone to despondency, less amenable to faith in progress, and that religion in Canada realistically accepts this spirit, while continuing to celebrate the triumph of light over darkness and hope over despair.

b)   Critique

The increasing autonomy of religious and political organizations in Canada has given opportunity to the former (the churches) to balance legitimation with critique. Ecclesiastical autonomy gives a much freer rein to the prophetic function of religion. By "prophetic function" I mean the application of standards of social justice and personal morality which tend to be trampled underfoot in the actual world of give-and-take. In the Judaeo-Christian-Islamic tradition, God's order is one of both love (the priestly facet) and judgment (the prophetic facet). Yet the first, or accepting, mode is likely to prevail if political and religious power are linked too closely.

This means that a transcendental order which started out as an agent of synthesis and integration could also become one of leverage and change when it became separated from the here and now. There are abundant examples in Canada of all religious organizations (sects as well as churches) denouncing those habits and values of the people which were felt to counter God's commandments and His purpose for the nation. The long history of both Catholic and Protestant campaigns against alcohol abuse and their disapproval of inhumanity in the working place around the turn of the nineteenth century are cases in point. The same scholars and theologians who in our "priestly section" stressed integration, reconciliation, and God's care for the nation, almost in the same breath attack unsafe working conditions (Hutchinson 1977, 210), demonic nationalism (Gualtieri 1977, 517), and manipulations and compromises in political life (Despland 1977, 536). And they can do so because in Christianity there is equal room for legitimation and critique, love and judgment, the priest and the prophet.

The Canadian churches also counter their endorsement of national loyalty with rejection of those commitments (such as aid to and even trade with, countries which have a poor human rights record) it regards as unethical. "My country right or wrong" is a slogan Canadian churches disown unless it means nothing more than loving one's country as parents love their children. Whitewashing is less and less part of the churches' vocabulary. If patriotism means being soft on the nation's shortcomings, most Canadian churches nowadays want nothing to do with it. They are happy to strip patriotic attachments when they stand in the way of the Christian vision of justice and incorruptibility in the same way as they perpetually loosen commitments to the kind of individualism which neglects the common good. Yet they tread too gingerly sometimes when denominational loyalty is at stake. In a pluralistic situation, they become used to bolstering boundaries, with the result that financial giving to the denomination is occasionally identified with giving to God and, correspondingly, less effort is put in advancing national causes.

The rites and prayers of the Canadian churches reflect the ongoing vision of their God-given task. Standards of unselfish dedication, unwavering responsibility, altruistic service, steady reliability, and sterling character are articulated regularly as values to be expected from local, provincial or national leaders. If these leaders do not live up to these expectations, lie too much, behave too mechanically, like weathervanes, they stand condemned. And although Christianity is more prone than the population at large to forgive, it is also adamant that these standards are too important to be dismissed out of hand. Sunday after Sunday the prayers in the churches reflect concretely what the social order is supposed to be all about. Even prayers which at first sight seem exclusively personal are, in actual fact, often astute reminders of which behaviour serves the common good and which does not, which perspective is approved and which is not. One can think about these implicit blueprints for acting and believing as constant legitimators. Yet in actual fact they are just as often incisive critiques in that they also articulate the negative side of the same coin (evil versus good, unbelief versus belief, disloyalty versus loyalty, irresponsibility versus responsibility, lying versus honesty, selfishness versus altruism, self-affirmation versus self-denial, etc.).

This brings us to the last point: the dramatization of the churches' critique of nationalism. In the same way as love and judgment, acceptance and rejection, legitimation and critique are reflected in beliefs, commitment, and rituals, so these opposites are dramatized when attitudes towards the social order or the national good are the subject of discussion or preaching. The nation as both loved and judged by God is a recurring theme in much ecclesiastical writing and speaking, as we have already noted. The theme is archetypical in that it connects with the essence of the socialization process. Both the child who is only loved and not judged and the child who is only judged and not loved are deemed to be actual or potential misfits in Canadian society. To extend the entire realm of childhood experiences and parental strategies to other forms of social organization (the nation or society as compared with the family) integrates these forms through the common basic impulse and dialectic. Yet judgment and insistence on standards goes essentially counter to love and insistence on acceptance, no matter what. In Canada the population and the churches can be as harshly critical of the power-wielders as they are because they also deeply respect the holders of power (the Crown and the Queen who guarantee the democratic form of government). The same holds true in Christianity, which can hold love and judgment in an uneasy balance because they both meet in God. Yet the efficacy of the dramatization lies less in the articulation of this one essential point than in the innovative variety with which it is presented.

SUMMARY

Canadian identity or national solidarity has been strengthened at various times by actual or perceived threats from the outside. The War of 1812 and fear of invasions from the south bolstered patriotic sentiments throughout the nineteenth century, so did the Boer War, World War I, and World War II. A sense of belonging together was further advanced by participation in the federal political machinery, by having to defend one's culture against newcomers, by federal social and economic initiatives, by the mass media, by charismatic leadership in Ottawa, and by common values of egalitarianism and restraint.

Yet, during most of Canada's history, the weakening factors seemed to have been almost as strong. Foremost among them were and are the rivaling English and French cultures, the first one having numbers, the second one, primogeniture on its side. Other regional and ethnic loyalties often vie successfully with national ones. Powerful unions and corporations can usually assume with impunity that their constituents will support them against the common good whenever loyalties collide.

Christianity has, as often as not, consciously or unconsciously reinforced each of the contending ethnic groups; French Catholicism did for Francophone culture what Anglicanism and the United Church did for the Anglophone equivalent. Yet the split between church and culture has widened of late. Religious organizations in Canada tend to take advantage of their separateness and hoe closely to the long Judaeo-Christian tradition of stressing both God's care for, and God's judgment of, the nation.

The priestly and prophetic, or the loving and the critical, modes find their equivalent in the ways Canadian national sentiments hatch their sacralizations. The symbol of the Crown and its personification in the Queen, the national anthem and the national flag are from the sociological point of view, ever so many factors strengthening or sacralizing the national fabric and the preferred democratic form of government. By contrast, the almost perverse and constant carping of Canadians at their local, provincial and federal governments (and its obvious de-sacralizing or stripping effect) can only take place within the context of a secure and stable sense of democratic nationhood with all its secular and religious accoutrements.

CHAPTER 16

EDUCATION AND LITERATURE

EDUCATION

In the first settlements of Canada (whether French or English), education, together with care for the sick and indigent, was the prerogative of the Church. As early as 1616 Récollet priests taught reading and writing. In the new parishes the priest often began schools where he gave instruction in religion as well as in reading and writing. Secondary education was begun by the Jesuits in Quebec in 1636 when they opened a college where Greek, Latin, philosophy, and theology were taught to students with professional aspirations. Bishop Laval opened a Petit Séminaire in 1668, also in Quebec, for the training of priests who would take some courses at the college. All schools were based on models existing in France at the time.

The British conquests of 1760 disrupted whatever school system there was in New France. For several generations learning fell so much into disrepute that by 1827 hardly 10% of the French population could sign its name. In the second quarter of the nineteenth century the government began to finance elementary education, but the 1,282 schools existing in 1832 began to languish when the Legislative Council disapproved the appropriate Education Act in 1836 (Audet 1970, 159). Yet in the eastern townships of Quebec, English-speaking immigrants from the United States had taken matters into their own hands and had opened schools at the initiative of their various town meetings. In 1846 a new school act established the principle (still existing in Quebec) whereby separate school commissions for Catholics and Protestants collect funds in proportion to the number of their adherents; but particularly in rural areas, a land tax for schools proved to be unpopular (Johnson 1968, 34).

In the first quarter of the nineteenth century the small population of Upper Canada (now southern Ontario) had a number of elementary and grammar schools at its disposal. The latter received some governnment assistance, but the bulk of the cost fell on local individuals who had taken the initiative. John Strachan, who had come to Kingston in 1799 to take charge of an academy (he subsequently became first Anglican bishop of Upper Canada, from 1839 to 1867), attempted to make the Church of England the educational arm of the state. He did not succeed, although the school laws of 1846 and 1850 (based on the recommendations of Egerton Ryerson, a Methodist minister) required that religion be taught as part of the curriculum. In the next decade, separate school supporters were exempted from paying rates for the common schools and could raise taxes for their own schools. Yet "as late as 1865 three-quarters of the Roman Catholic children were attending the public schools" (Ibid., 41). Until 1985 the province of Ontario supported the Catholic school system only up to and including grade 10, but since then it has also begun to fund grades 11 and 12.

In Newfoundland the first missionaries (whether Anglican, Catholic, or Methodist) usually taught schools too, and if they did not, the schoolmasters were supported by the various ecclesiastical organizations. This denominational system of education became reflected in the Education Act of 1874, which provided a division of grants for Protestant and Roman Catholic schools according to population. This system prevails until the present day. The provincial government pays salaries of the teachers and pays 90% of the school costs, yet the schools are owned and controlled by the churches which must raise the additional 10% of the costs.

Before Nova Scotia became an English preserve, French Capuchin missionaries, who called it Acadia, established schools on the south shore as early as 1630. For most of the seventeenth century the Récollets and a convent maintained schools in Port Royal. The Congrégation de Notre Dame conducted a convent school for girls in Louisburg from 1727 to 1758, when the fortress was destroyed. The first English schools in the area were established by two schoolmasters sent out by the Society for the Propagation of the Gospel after the founding of Halifax in 1749. The first School Act passed by the Assembly in 1766 linked schools with the Church of England, but in the second quarter of the nineteenth century, many voices were heard favouring free education for the large number of children who did not attend school. The appropriate legislation to make this possible was passed in 1864. To accommodate schemes for separate schools, Catholic schools were rented as part of the public school system, "formal religious instruction being conducted after school hours" (Hamilton 1970, 105).

The pattern repeats itself in western Canada. The first schools were invariably attached to mission posts, whether Anglican, Catholic, Methodist, or Presbyterian. Also, funding for these missions and schools usually came from the Hudson's Bay Company. And so Father Joseph Provencher established the first Catholic mission school at St. Boniface in 1818, and Father Albert Lacombe began his school at Fort Edmonton in 1860. The Rev. John West of the Church of England established the first school in what is now Winnipeg in 1820. The Rev. and Mrs. Robert Staines of the Church of England began the first school at Fort Victoria on Vancouver Island in 1849, the Hudson's Bay Company paying £100 for his chaplaincy and £340 for his schoolmaster's duties (Johnson 1968, 62). The Methodist missionary James Evans established the first Protestant Indian mission and school near Norway House in 1840. The Hudson's Bay Company was rather unhappy about some of the clergy (it did not hide its anger about Evans' interference with their trade on Sunday), but it felt that the nuisance they created was outweighed by the contribution they made to law and order, or, as Governor George Simpson had it, by the fact that the Church was "an excellent institution for teaching the lower orders to respect and obey their superiors" (Lupul 1970, 247).

However, there was no holding back the growing conviction that education should be available to all, free of cost, and that schools should be non-sectarian. In 1869 British Columbia issued the Common School Ordinance centralizing and secularizing education. The spirit of that ordinance still prevails in that, presently (1985), British Columbia does not provide aid to any of its 100 or so religious schools, the vast majority of which is Catholic. The School Act of Alberta, on the other hand, allows for the creation of separate school districts so that Catholic or Protestant minorities can receive the same funds as the public schools. Saskatchewan also equally supports a Catholic and a public school system. By contrast, Manitoba refuses to pay the salaries of teachers in the Catholic separate schools, although it does provide grants for textbooks.

In Canada, education has moved from control by religion in the early beginnings to considerable emancipation at the end of the twentieth century. If that emancipation is incomplete, it is not because the major Protestant denominations have their doubts about the separation (they do not), but because the Catholic Church, ever since Pius IX (pope from 1846 to 1878), has harboured the suspicion that secular education had its own implicit philosophy not necessarily congruent with a Christian one. Some of the smaller Christian sects (for instance, the Seventh Day Adventists and the Christian Reformed) share this Catholic view and have translated the conviction into a financially burdensome system of schools in which they insist on socializing their children according to a Christian view of the world.

In tertiary education, emancipation from ecclesiastical ties has also made great strides. Almost all Canadian universities in the nineteenth century originated from denominational initiatives, whether Jesuit, Anglican, Presbyterian, Methodist, Baptist or Lutheran. In the first decade of the twentieth century things began to change when, in western Canada, the provinces themselves took initiatives for the establishment of tertiary education. Mushrooming enrollment after World War II widened the influence of government on university financing and curtailed whatever sectarian authority remained.

Yet the present equal access of the population to secular, tertiary education does not mean that the highly educated (those with a university degree)

are now evenly spread over the entire denominational spectrum. Nor are
they equally represented in all age groups: in the 1971 census the percentage
of individuals with a university degree among those who were 25-44 years
old (6.77%) was twice as high as among those 45 and over (3.36%).

Table 16.1 shows the percentages of individuals 15 years and over who
mentioned on the 1971 census forms that they had a university degree. Jews
(13.23% and 25.34%) and those with no religion (12.47% and 14.64%) had a
higher percentage of university graduates than the population at large
(4.66% and 8.20%). There are a number of reasons for this overrepresentation. The Jews have traditionally stressed higher education, it being one of
few opportunities for upward mobility and security. Both for them and for
immigrants from the Asian mainland, chances for immigration to Canada
improved vastly if they had the education necessary for the various new
positions created in industry and academia after World War II. The overrepresentation of university graduates among those who put "no religion"
on the census form can be partly attributed to individuals with higher
education feeling less compelled to adhere to any religious tradition, partly
to the larger number of atheists and agnostics in this category.

Table 16.1

Percentage of individuals 15 years and over, not attending school full time, who possessed a
university degree at the time of the 1971 and 1981 census in Canada, by denomination.

	1971	1982
Total Population	4.66	8.20
Anglicans	4.98	8.76
Baptist	3.35	6.48
Greek Orthodox	3.58	7.25
Jewish	13.23	25.34
Lutheran	3.38	6.26
Mennonite-Hutterite	3.21	6.12
Pentecostal	1.14	2.87
Presbyterian	4.41	7.70
Roman Catholic	3.51	6.46
Salvation Army	.91	2.56
United Church	5.22	8.65
No Religion	12.47	14.64

Table 16.1 also shows that the major Protestant denominations (United,
5.22%, and 8.65%; Anglican 4.98%, and 8.76%; Presbyterian 4.41%, and
7.70%) have valued a university education slightly more than Catholics
(3.51%, and 6.46%) or, probably more correctly, have had more opportunity to go to university. The differences between Catholics and Protestants
are particularly great in Quebec where the latter form a small minority. In
this province 8.53% in 1971; 11.82% in 1981 of Presbyterians, 7.50% in
1971; 10.82% in 1981 of Anglicans, and 7.46% in 1971; 10.08% in 1981 of

United Church adherents have a university degree as compared with 3.65% in 1971; 6.16% in 1981 of Catholics.

By far the lowest percentage of university graduates are found among the sectarian groups in Canada: Pentecostals (1.14% in 1971; 2.87% in 1981) and Salvation Army (.91% in 1971; 2.56% in 1981). It is also true for other countries, such as the United States, that the appeal of the evangelical sects is greatest among the uneducated. In Canada this observation holds for all age groups. By contrast, the youngest members of some of the ethnic groups (Ukrainian Catholics 15-24 years of age, for instance) had, in 1971, a larger percentage of university graduates (3.45%) than the national average (2.88%), even though their parents and particularly their grandparents had, and still have, less than their national share. This seems to show that among at least some immigrant groups, parents strongly encourage their children to use advanced education to move up the social ladder.

LITERATURE

Religious themes permeate some of the best-known Canadian novels. However critical the authors may be about the provincialism, the dreariness, and the conservatism of local parishes, priests and ministers, they often use biblical archetypes and religious symbols to considerable advantage. The growing understanding of the Christian view of salvation, sin, crucifixion and resurrection is sometimes traced through the life history of an individual. I would like to clarify this point through a summary of some of these major novels.

Morley Callaghan

In 1933 Morley Callaghan wrote *Such is my Beloved*, the story of an eager young priest, Father Stephen Dowling, serving the cathedral in a large Canadian town during the depression. Father Dowling's sermons reflected strong convictions about the social problems of the day, to the considerable discomfort of older colleagues and the well-to-do of the parish.

One winter evening, Father Dowling is accosted near the cathedral by two prostitutes. He befriends them and vainly attempts to find jobs for them so that they do not have to walk the streets. In his efforts he gets no support from the powerful and instead is reported to the bishop. He is transferred, and the prostitutes are quietly deported by the police.

In this story Callaghan is trying to say that the Church has two faces. On the one hand, it reinforces existing morality and existing power. It sternly rebukes those who overstep the boundaries between appropriate and inappropriate behaviour and it tacitly maintains the status quo. If it deals with the poor, the outcasts, the lame, the sick, and the orphans, it does so within the existing framework of charity, thereby encouraging society to proceed as usual. This face is represented by the bishop, the older clergy, and the rich parishioners.

The other face of the Church is its identification with (and love for) the disprivileged - the prostitutes in the book. It suspends the rules of stern morality, freely forgives, and restores the forgiven to its bosom. Yet by doing so, it relativizes with the left hand what it defends with the right. This revolutionary stance, represented by the Christ of the Gospels and by Father Dowling, differs from the revolutionary ideas of Dowling's communist friend, Charles Stewart, who pins all hopes for the perfect society on the overthrow of the present one. Callaghan infers that violent eradication does not solve much of anything. Its replacements will soon suffer from the same injustices, inequalities, and rigidities of the old one. By contrast, Christ keeps alive the tension between established morality and forgiveness of sinners, sameness and change, without allowing the one to surrender to the other.

To Callaghan, the Catholic Church is the Body of Christ, broken on the cross (Dowling's defeat and madness at the end of the book), yet also restored and risen (Dowling's love and integrity). The Church is in the world and yet not of the world, in the same way as flesh and spirit are opposites, Callaghan seems to say. Towards the end of the book (p.136), Father Dowling is preparing for mass on Easter Sunday and he suddenly wonders "if it could be that the bodies of Midge and Ronnie (the prostitutes) were being destroyed as the bread and the wine would be destroyed, so that God could enter in the mystery of transubstantiation. 'The death of Christ, the life of souls,' he thought, and was full of hope as he passed through to the altar."

It is on a similar note of sacrifice turning into salvation that Callaghan finishes the book. Dowling is described as follows:

> There was a peace within him as he watched the calm,
> eternal waters swelling darkly against the one faint streak
> of light, the cold night light on the skyline. High in the sky
> three stars were out. His love seemed suddenly to be as
> steadfast as those stars, as wide as the water, and still
> flowing within him like the cold smooth waves still rolling
> on the shore (p.144).

Hugh MacLennan

In *Two Solitudes* (first published in 1945) MacLennan describes the frailty of the bonds between English-speaking and French-speaking Canada (the two solitudes of the title). The novel begins in the French parish of Saint-Marc-des-Erables in Quebec in 1917 where, at the instigation of a Protestant financier from Montréal, the seigneur, or large property-owner, Athanase Tallard (who also represents the district in the House of Commons in Ottawa) decides to begin a factory using the falls in the area for hydroelectric power. He is strongly opposed in this by Father Emile Beaubien, a farmboy who experienced the devastations of industrialization in a previous parish. The priest now preaches ceaselessly against the evil of industry and the cities. They produce godlessness, illegitimacy, and workers who are nothing but helpless pawns in the schemes of the English managers who enrich themselves at their expense, he says.

Father Beaubien is a strong leader who keeps a tight hold on the people. "Too tight," says Athanase Tallard, who then adds

> Here the Church and the people are almost one and the same thing, and the Church is more than any individual priest's idea of it. You will never understand Quebec until you know that. The Church, the people and the land. Don't expect anything else in a rural parish (p.28).

By contrast, Tallard is an enlightened, well-read man of the world, anti-clerical but in sympathy with the higher clergy. He has begun a book about religion which he thinks "must rest on fear if it is to exist at all" (p.34). By hammering on their imperfect patriotism and their lack of purity, the guilt feelings of the masses can be kept alive and the iron grip of religion maintained, he muses in the book.

Yet all his enlightenment and learning has not made Athanase Tallard a happy man. In Parliament he has vainly attempted to bridge the gap between the English pro-conscription forces and the French anti-conscription sentiments, making him a lone figure, unpopular with both sides. He has a vision about the new factory providing employment for the underemployed and impoverished farmers of Saint-Marc-des-Erables, but all he gets for his efforts is mounting antagonism from the very people who stand to profit from his policies.

The plans for the factory are destroyed when Father Beaubien turns the parish against Tallard. Even the latter's servants leave because "this isn't a Christian house. I can't work here anymore" (p.195). Athanase Tallard dies broken and bankrupt. It is as though MacLennan is saying that the two solitudes of English and French culture, Protestantism and French Catholicism are irreconcilable and will remain so. But then the book also has other figures, such as John Yardley, a retired Nova Scotia sea captain, who seems to be capable of bridging the gap between the two cultures through humanity and common sense, and Athanase's son, Paul, who falls in love with and marries a girl from the English aristocracy of Montréal. In other words, the quote from Rainer Maria Rilke ("Love consists in this, that two solitudes protect, and touch, and greet each other") at the beginning of the book illustrates not only the actual polarities within Canadian society, but also the ties of love, common sense, and humanity which bind them together.

In Hugh MacLennan's *The Watch that Ends the Night*, religious symbolism is more prominent than in the *Two Solitudes* where religion is portrayed as the reinforcer of two separate traditions. In *The Watch that Ends the Night* (first published in 1958), the three main characters all struggle with a faith they have lost, to regain it in different form later in life. The narrator, George Stewart, is a teacher who has become known in Montreal for his radio commentaries. He used to believe that God cared for him personally but had then fallen in love with Catherine, and she became his rock (p.8). Catherine, a painter who later marries George, has a rheumatic heart, all the more reason for George to suspend belief in a just God. She, too, feels that her wretched heart makes faith very difficult, although she wishes she could believe (p.294).

Jerome Martell believed in God until World War I when he had to kill eleven Germans with a bayonet and when in the military hospital he met a Jewish boy from Oshawa who blamed capitalism for the atrocities. Jerome was brought up in a lumbercamp in New Brunswick from which he escapes in a tiny canoe from the murderer of his unmarried mother. He is then adopted by a Baptist minister in Halifax ("probably the only genuine Christian I'll ever meet in my life," p.250) who only felt close to God when he was drunk. Jerome Martell reminds one of Norman Bethune. He also becomes a surgeon, serves in the Spanish war and ends up in China. Here, however, similarities end. Martell survives the ordeal in China and returns to Canada, where he has been given up for dead for almost a decade, and where his wife (Catherine) is now married to George Stewart.

However, in China where he was left to die of amoebic dysentery, something strange had happened. Slowly recuperating, he passes the time recalling the gospels and psalms, and then one day Jesus seems to appear to him. "He wasn't anyone I had ever known before. He wasn't the Jesus of the churches. He wasn't the Jesus who had died for our sins. He was simply a man who had died and risen again. Who had died outwardly as I had died inwardly" (p.308). Catherine to whom he tells the story has had a similiar experience more than once, she says.

However, to George Stewart who has never been close to death, God is like a cat with a bird in its claw prolonging the fun (p.319), as He allows Catherine to survive another embolism, further weakening her heart. Yet, during the torment of his beloved, suspended between life and death for days on end, a subtle change comes over Stewart. It slowly dawns on him that making gods out of political systems, authority, reason, success, or one's wife and children is shortchanging life.

> Then a man discovers in dismay that what he believed to be his identity is no more than a tiny canoe at the mercy of an ocean. Sharkfilled, plankton-filled, refractor of light, terrible and mysterious, for years this ocean has seemed to slumber beneath the tiny identity it received from the dark river.

> Now the ocean rises and the things within it become
> visible. Little man, what now? The ocean rises, all frames
> disappear from around the pictures, there is no form, no
> sense, nothing but chaos in the darkness.... (p.321).

At this point Stewart remembers the first verses of the Bible:

> And the earth was without form, and void; and darkness
> was on the face of the deep.... And the spirit of God moved
> upon the face of the waters. And God said: Let there be
> light: And there was light.
> Here, I found at last, is the nature of the final human
> struggle (p.321).

The conflict between dark and light, fissioning and fusing, destruction and creation, fear and courage, hate and love, terror and defiance, shame and honour, despair and hope - all resolve in God who laid the foundation of the earth, Stewart discovers. And the chaos which had been within him for days "disappeared and my soul was like a landscape with water when the fog goes" (p. 346). It is on this note of accepting both life and death and of experiencing 'the joy of the Lord' that the book ends.

Sinclair Ross

The title of *As For Me and My House* is taken from the first sermon which the Rev. Philip Bentley preached in the little prairie town of Horizon. He has been in the ministry for twelve years and this is his fourth parish. He always preaches on this text from Joshua 24:15 (As for me and my house we will serve the Lord) for his first Sunday.

> It nails his colours to the mast. It declares to the town his
> creed, lets them know what they may expect. The Word of
> God as revealed in Holy Writ - Christ Crucified - salvation
> through His Grace - those are the things that Philip stands
> for (p.3).

The story of Bentley's year in Horizon (before he leaves the ministry) is told by his wife in the form of diary entries. She describes him as strong, virile, handsome, but also aloof and appearing tired. His good looks rather than his sermons make him popular initially, but after a few years the congregation grows tired of him, his troublemaking wife, and his sermons (they always revolve around the theme of "a watchful Almighty who plans for and leads us and lets nothing go astray" p.182) and then "we crate our furniture again and go" (p.14).

The church is the only church in Horizon and reflects its environment. It is the time of the depression and drought on the prairies. The roof of the parsonage leaks, but there is hardly enough money to pay the minister his meagre ($1000 per year) salary, leave alone to do major repairs. There are dark days of dust when everything is gritty and when the sand manages to work its way even through the rags around the window frame. During the church service, the membership is listening "to the wind, not Philip, the whimpering and strumming through the eaves, and the dry hard crackle of sand against the window" (p.63). People's minds become gritty and irritable. Petty jealousies and frictions penetrate the relations in the choir, the Ladies Aid, and the board. Tumbleweeds bounce up the street. There is fickleness, unpredictability, in events.

Main street has many false-fronted stores. It is as though they want to prettify what is irredeemably ugly and futile. There is a pretense in appearing to be a large shop when, in actual fact, there is only one floor. The narrator thinks how ridiculous all this is, but her husband looks at it with the eyes of an artist. He draws the little false-fronted stores as he sketches his congregation the way he sees it from the pulpit.

> Seven faces in the first row - ugly wretched faces, big-mouthed, mean-eyed - alike, yet each with a sharp, aggressive individuality - the caricature of a pew, and the likenesses of seven people (p.26).

Yet, of late, his drawing has changed from a defiance of his subject matter (Bentley grew up in a town like Horizon) to a sullen, hopeless acceptance, as though those tumbledown shabby prairie towns have now become his prison, the scaffolding of his life. There is also an increasing awareness in the book of the minister's hypocrisy. At first it was only smoking late at night when church members were not likely to drop by. However, now it has become Philip preaching what he does not believe himself, but saying it because his bread and butter depend on it. He rationalizes that

> religion and art are almost the same thing anyway. Just different ways of taking a man out of himself, bringing him to the emotional pitch that we call ecstasy or rapture. They're both a rejection of the material, common-sense world for one that's illusory, yet somehow more important. Now it's always when a man turns away from this common-sense world around him that he begins to create, when he looks into a void, and has to give it life and form …. if man can lose himself in religion, he can lose himself just as easily in art (pp.199-200).

Yet, as his wife realizes, he is a failure in the ministry. Religion cannot be used as a vehicle to escape from suffocating provincialism, and so, at the end of the book, soon after a big windstorm when chimneys and most of false fronts are blown down, Philip crates his furniture again to start a secondhand bookstore in a small city.

Margaret Laurence

In *The Stone Angel*, religion is seen through the eyes of a ninety-year-old, saucy, steely, self-willed woman, Hagar Shipley. Like her father, a self-made Scottish merchant, one of the pioneers of Manawaka (Manitoba), her stare "could meet anyone's without blinking an eyelash" p.8. The father, Jason Currie, never missed a service of the local Presbyterian Church and was one of the biggest contributors when the new church was erected. Hagar is disinherited when she marries a good-looking, virile, ne'er-do-well farmer, Brampton Shipley. Bram usually says the wrong things. When the new minister preached his first sermon on the ephemeral nature of earthly joys, Bram "whispered in a gruff voice that must have carried at least as far as three pews ahead and three behind: 'Won't the saintly bastard ever shut his trap?'"(p.89). Hagar never went to church again after that, isolating herself from the respectable citizens of Manawaka.

Yet the unrespectable had their own religion. Murray Lees, Hagar's drinking companion in a derelict cannery to which she has fled to escape the nursing home which her family is prodding her to enter, used to sing with great abandon about being saved by the Blood of the Lamb in his grandfather's Larkspur Street Tabernacle in Blackfly. Here he also attended vigils about the end of the world, although his mother had forbade him to go. "She was an Anglican and she worried about the possibility of any other Anglican seeing me sauntering into the Tabernacle," p.226.

To Hagar, worrying about what people are thinking shows weakness of character (p.227). She has little respect for the minister, The Rev. Troy, a plump and pink little man whom the family has lured into persuading Hagar to enter the nursing home.

> "A person needs contemporaries", he says, "to talk with, and remember." He says no more. He speaks of prayer and comfort, all in a breath, as though God were a kind of feather bed or spring-filled mattress. I nod and nod and nod. Easier to agree, now, hoping he will soon go. He prays a little prayer, and I bow my head, a feather in his cap or in the eiderdown of God. Then mercifully he leaves (p.53).

Religion, to Hagar, represents conforming and comforting, neither of which her indomitable spirit finds easy to do or surrender to. And although Mr. Troy's voice may be leaping like a spawning salmon (p.41) she is not easily persuaded. She is like her father who was said to be a God-fearing man but actually feared no one, God included, she is convinced. Therefore, she does not have much use for praying: "Nothing I prayed for came to anything" (p.119). Yet her adversary does not give up easily.

> "Don't you believe," Mr. Troy inquires politely, ear-
> nestly, "in God's infinite mercy?" I blurt a reply without
> thinking. "What's so merciful about Him I'd like to
> know?" (p.120)

Yet sometimes Hagar is not so sure. "What if it matters to Him after all, what happens to us?" (p.90). But then she abandons the thought. "Can God be One and watching .... focussing His cosmic and comic glass eye on this or that, as the fancy takes Him? Or no - He's many-headed, and all the heads argue at once, a squabbling committee...." (p.93), she muses irreverently. It is more in character for her to observe: "There we sat, among the doilies and the teacups, two fat old women, no longer haggling with one another, but only with fate, pitting our wits against God's" (p.212).

The Old Testament image of Jacob wrestling with the angel appeals to her. When her son John restores the heavy marble angel which has fallen off its pedestal on her father's grave, it reminds her of the story (p.179). Similarly, at the end of the book (p.304) her other son, Marvin, asks for her forgiveness, tightly holding her hands.

> Now it seems to me that he is truly Jacob, gripping with all
> his strength, and bargaining. I will not let Thee go, unless
> Thou bless me. And I see I am thus strangely cast, and
> perhaps have been so from the beginning, and can only
> release myself, by releasing him.

Yet all the wrestling with God, the church and ministers comes to an end just before Hagar's death. She asks Mr. Troy to sing Psalm 100 for her (All people that on earth do dwell, Sing to the Lord with joyful voice). He does so and she realizes forcefully and shatteringly that this is what she always wanted simply to rejoice in God (p.292). But the wilderness of pride and the demon of fear shackled her and all she touched, she realizes. She is unregenerate, and yet for the first time in life she has caught a glimpse of the salvation which lies behind the confession, and the blessing which follows the wrestling. And this is what the stone angel represents: wholeness beyond the grave of stress and struggle.

Religion in the narrow sense of religious organization, or even in the sense of Christian symbolism, figures much less prominently in Margaret Laurence's later book, *The Diviners*. True, the diviner, Royland, from whom the book derives its title, has also been a "ripsnortin Biblepuncher." But his divining is only used by Laurence as a symbol for Morag Gunn's search for the hidden depth of her being.

Morag became an orphan when she was five. She blames God for the death of her parents and thinks that He is mean. Jesus, on the other hand, has her genuine affection. He is cool as a cucumber, she feels (p.78). She is adopted by Manawaka's garbage collector, Christie Logan and his wife Prin.

The Logans are not exactly high society. Prin and Morag attend the United Church, but the stepmother is like "a barrel of lard with legs" (p.108) and therefore sits self-consciously in the back of the church. On a particular Sunday, when Morag is 14, one of the hymns they sing is 'In Christ there is no East or West, in Him no North or South." But after the service no one will say "Good Morning," and Morag decides then and there not to attend church anymore.

Morag loses herself in writing and so compensates for her social marginality and loneliness. She also loses herself in the physical act of lovemaking, and this too appears to be an avenue for coming to terms with her essential selfhood. In spite of sexual compatibility, however, her marriage to a much older professor of English at the University of Toronto fails. She wants to be someone in her own right rather than a wife-child. She flees far from Manawaka (the location of her social marginality) and Toronto (the location of her dependence) to Vancouver. But here, too, she

> no longer feels certain of anything. There is no fixed centre. Except, of course, that there *is* a fixed centre, and furthermore is rapidly expanding inside her own flesh (p.295).

She is expecting (out of wedlock) the child of a Métis singer whom she does not want to marry (he is 'moving through the world like a dandelion seed carried by the wind" (p.272). The child (a girl) is born, grows up and throughout the book is the subject of Morag's perpetual fussing and worry. Obviously, motherhood is not a fixed centre either.

At the end of the book Morag has a conversation with Royland, who confesses that one does not need God for divining. Wanting to explain it is an obstacle to becoming a diviner. What matters is doing it. Self-expression rather than self-analysis, Margaret Laurence appears to conclude, is what life is all about. Yet the conclusion has the feeble ring of futility. After all, self-expression is only relative and must be experienced in the larger context of selflessness as religious symbolism appears to hint.

Gabrielle Roy

Religion is deeply, yet unobtrusively, woven into the major characters in Roy's *The Tin Flute*. Rose-Anna Lacasse, the matriarch who has borne eleven children in abject poverty in depression-struck Montréal, is associated with the lithograph of Our Lady of Sorrows at the foot of her bed, "offering her bleeding heart to a pale ray of light from between the window curtains" (p.48). She does not demand much love but gives it in magnanimous portions. Usually she unburdens her daily problems of making ends meet to the saints because she cannot form a picture of God ("all that came to her was a vision of cottonwool clouds, with a dove flying over them" (p.66). She prefers the intercession of the saints whose pictures and statues she can see. Yet, when it is very urgent and her family is involved, she prays directly to God. Even so, her devotions sometimes turn involuntarily into a vision of dollar bills flowing "off into the air, whirling and falling through the night, driven by the wind" (p.48).

Yvonne is one of the younger children. She is a religious fanatic and sobs when she has to miss mass. If

> she missed one mass she would be deserting Our Lord in his torments. Rose-Anna has understood the simple story: in Yvonne's classroom at the convent there was a heart pierced with thorns, and every little girl who went to mass had the right to pull one out as she came to school. With tears streaming down her white face Yvonne had said: "Oh Mamma, there are so many wicked people who put thorns in the heart of Jesus every day. Let me go to mass" (p.61).

Yvonne comforts her dying little brother Daniel, who so badly wanted a tin flute, with a vision of heaven where the Holy Virgin will be holding "you in her arms. You'll be like the infant Jesus in her arms" (p.255). Yet Rose-Anna does not care much for what she regards as the unhealthy piety of her younger daughter who, like her husband, has her head in the clouds and escapes reality (p.112).

No, Rose-Anna expects more from her oldest child, her daughter Florentine, a waitress in the five-and-ten, around whom the story line of the book is woven. She thinks that Florentine will "be her salvation. The girl has so much assurance and resourcefulness" (p.113). However, the girl falls head over heels in love with an ambitious drifter, Jean, who is both attracted and disturbed by the Madonna and the Infant Jesus over the buffet in the Lacasse house. It evoked his unhappy childhood in an orphanage and reminds him of the taciturn and bitter woman who had raised him after she "had made a vow to adopt a child if her only daughter was restored to health. Thus he had served as a bargaining point in a trade with the saints, but the girl had died all the same, later on" (p.141). Florentine becomes pregnant by him, but he disappears.

Yet Jean's friend, Emmanuel Létourneau, has long been deeply in love with Florentine. He is like Rose-Anna, compassionate and self-giving. He is impressed by a patriotic speech (World War II has now broken out) made by Rose-Anne's husband, Azarius Lacasse. It is the kind of speech that makes people swell with the same kind of pride they feel on Saint-Jean-Baptiste day (the 24th of June) when Québec celebrates the feast day of its patron

saint with parades, pageants and much oratory and singing (p.210). Yet, the
Lacasse family is much below the Létourneaus. Emmanuel's father is a
dealer in religious objects, ornaments, and church wines and has acquired
the same unctuous way of speaking as his clients. He associates

> almost exclusively with people of Traditionalist views, and
> occupied a post of honor in several religious and patriotic
> societies. His reverence for the past made him reject at
> once anything that seemed tainted with modern ideas or
> foreign elements (pp.86-7).

Consequently the father scorns his son. He is a fool, he says, "who will
never stick to his own class" (p.89). Yet, at the end of the book, Emmanuel,
who is now enlisted, marries Florentine on his furlough and thereby saves
her from both disgrace and grinding poverty.

Gabrielle Roy seems to say in *The Tin Flute* that real salvation comes
from Christ's spirit of self-denial and compassion rather than from over-
heated piety, unrealistic illusions, class-bound conservatism and ecclesiastical bargains with morality.

Marie-Claire Blais

There is a melancholy streak running through many of the best Canadian novels. Yet, in Marie-Claire Blais' *A Season in the Life of Emmanuel*, it
is more than a streak: despair and dynamism intermingle absurdly throughout the novel. The book opens with the birth of Emmanuel, the sixteenth
child of a Québec farmer and his wife in an era when electricity and
telephone are still novelties. Birth is part of the day's work, and the mother
is milking the cows that same night. "God's blessing is upon large families,"
says Monsieur le Curé. However, Emmanuel (the book describes only the
winter he is born), the father, and particularly the mother remain shadowy
figures. Centre-stage is occupied by Grand-mère Antoinette. She is the
matriarch imperiously and grudgingly ruling the unruly mob of children
and animals. Her affection is always hidden. The squalor of poverty and
perversity does not permit lowering one's armour. She goes to Mass every
morning at 5 a.m. and prevents the escape of the children to the outhouse at
the time of evening prayers when everyone obediently kneels on the cold
floor of the living room.

Yet the effect of this high level of religious involvement is limited.
Jean-Le Maigre (the brightest and most creative of all children; he writes
exercise books full of beautiful poetry and prose) and his teenaged brother
land in reform school for setting the school on fire. The Reformatory is a
jungle and they are rescued from it by the village priest, just before Easter.
All the priest's preaching and all his stern warnings against the large variety
of sins seems to have little effect. Before he and his brother engage in sexual

play, Jean-Le Maigre coolly suggests that they must confess this to the priest the next morning, "his mouth already watering at the idea of telling the Curé his sins" (p.39). There is no sense of being burdened by guilt, and therefore delinquent acts take place without much hesitation.

Brother Théophile, a rank pervert preying upon young teenaged boys in the Noviciat where Jean-Le Maigre has been sent, confesses and goes in peace,

> then began doing it again next day, or given the chance, the very same day of his confession. But he was still filled with a great hope as he felt that God was waiting for him in every church, that he would go on receiving His forgiveness like a special food containing the precious energy he needed to accomplish evil - the moment he had received benison (p.107).

Not only that morality and forgiveness can work against one another, and that piety and perversity coexist under the same roof of the Noviciat, but there is only a hairbreadth difference between convent and brothel, Blais suggests. Father Moisan may fulminate against Madame Octavie, owner of the brothel, but she and most of her girls were originally zealous nuns and at least one of them, Héloise (Emmanuel's older sister), had her sensuality and ecstasies awakened in the convent (p.29). On her wall Héloise combines lewd pictures and a crucifix, and she compares her past duties in the convent with the present ones in the brothel as "slipping from one form of contentedness to another" (p.126).

Death, suffering, and suicide (Emmanuel's older brother, a student in his final seminary year, hangs himself on Good Friday) are familiar companions all through the book, though the warlike spirit of Emmanuel and his grandmother (p.101) are equal to it. Although the many funerals she has attended in her life have been a nuisance, Grand-mère consoles herself through the memory of heaven and by remembering the good meals afterwards, generously provided by Monsieur le Curé (p.21). When Jean-Le Maigre is buried, Blais describes Antoinette as follows:

> Her tears having at last succeeded in putting out the red-hot coals of hell, Grand-mère Antoinette was forced to blow her nose with considerable violence as she passed from the Mass to the burial itself, as though from one spectacle of suffering to the next (pp.92-3).

SUMMARY

On all levels (primary, secondary, tertiary) education in Canada was begun by religious organizations. Even after a public school system was started around the middle of last century to provide free education for everyone, the Catholic Church and some of the smaller sects refused to surrender what they perceived to be the Christian purpose of education to the secular spirit pervading other schools. Right up to the present day, separation has been rather costly in that, at least in some provinces, the financial burden of denominational schooling revolved on those churches which insisted on maintaining it.

In Canada, the highly educated (those with a university degree), are anything but evenly spread over the denominational spectrum. The percentage of Jews and those without religion who have a university degree is almost three times as great as the percentage in the population at large. At the other pole, Pentecostals and Salvation Army adherents have less than a third of the national percentage of individuals with tertiary education (2.87% and 2.56% as compared with 8.20% of the population, according to the 1981 census).

Religion figures prominently in some of the major Canadian novels. Often the mainline religious organizations are portrayed as conservative, bought off by the respectable, caught up in their own structural webs. By contrast, the sects are seen as havens for the emotionally exuberant, less than respectable, and underprivileged. Remarkably often, outlines are informed by religious symbolism: death versus life, sin versus salvation, crucifixion versus resurrection, hell versus heaven.

CHAPTER 17

POLITICS AND SECULARISM

Education is not the only subsystem of Canadian society which has come out from under the religious umbrella. The influence of religion on the political arena has similarly waned considerably, even though it is still visible in voting patterns and in the less organizational guise of militant political commitments. This emancipation has meant that channels of commitment are not any more flowing exclusively from Christian organizations, but can also well up from various secular causes and crusades.

POLITICS

There is no need to elaborate the points made in previous chapters that in Quebec, French Catholicism and government leaned heavily on one another at various times and places, or that in the first half of the nineteenth century the Anglican Church influenced many political issues in what is now Ontario, or, for that matter, that one of three major parties in Canada (the New Democratic Party) had its origins in the social gospel. Here it will be argued that religious belonging, more than ethnic or class membership, affects the way people have voted and still vote.

There is abundant and early evidence for the argument. Alford (1963, 276) analyzed nine public opinion surveys in Canada and found that "the differences between the religions within similar strata were consistently larger than the differences between classes within the same religion." Meisel (1956, 486) drew a sample of voters in Kingston, Ontario, in 1953 and found that 83% of Catholics had voted Liberal and 2% Conservative, whereas the percentage of United Church adherents was 35% Liberal and 46% Conservative. Fifteen years later Meisel (1975, 264) concluded from the 1968 national election study that "class factors do not wash out the effects of religion on voting." Irvine (1974, 560) concluded that the voting differences between Catholics and non-Catholics in Canada were "approximately three times as strong as ethnic ones."

Being an active (churchgoing) or inactive Catholic or Protestant does not seem to make much difference. Meisel (1956, 494) noted that in 1955, in Kingston, those close to the Catholic Church (the occupants of a convent) tended to vote less for the Liberals in the provincial elections of that year than Catholic laymen. As table 10.7 in chapter 10 of this book shows, nationally, the voting behaviour of regular church attenders does not differ significantly from those who go to church irregularly or not at all. The exception is the New Democratic Party, which seems to attract a greater proportion of the non-churchgoers in Canada than the other political parties.

Although the figures about Catholics voting Liberal and Protestants, Conservative, are beyond dispute, it would be wrong to conclude that there is a venerable tradition linking party and denomination, or that all provinces show the same pattern. Catholics on the Prairies in the 1968 election tended to be less interested in the Liberal party than in the other provinces (Meisel 1975, 3,263). Also, the stronghold of Liberalism (Catholic Quebec) was just as strongly Conservative in the last third of the nineteenth century until, in 1896, Wilfrid Laurier took advantage of the troubles besetting the Conservatives (Meisel 1975, 256) and turned the tables. Similarly, in 1951 the Liberals in Newfoundland held all the Protestant seats and the Progressive Conservatives the Catholic ones (Rothney 1962, 564-5).

The pattern is also blurred by the tendency of the younger, well-educated, urban Protestants to vote Liberal (Meisel 1975, 270). More recently, the economic recession of 1982/83, corruption scandals in the Liberal party in Quebec, and the rise of the Parti Québecois in that province seem to have considerably weakened the hold of the Liberal party on Catholics and Protestants alike, so that western-Canadian Liberals have almost completely disappeared in provincial and federal parliaments.

The question remains why, however blurred, the pattern persists that Catholics align themselves with the Liberal party and Protestants with the Conservative one. Have religious organizations tended to divide the labour amongst themselves by "sacralizing" separate political constituencies? The answer to that question must be ambivalent. Our dialectical frame of reference leads us to expect both alliances and conflicts between major subsystems, in our case, the political and religious. What seems to be clear is that those parties, such as the New Democratic Party (or the Labor Party in Australia, Mol 1971, 300), which stress commitment to unifying political platforms tend to lose active churchmembers to parties with more flexible, almost opportunistic, programmes. It is as though, at least in Australia and Canada, church attenders feel uncomfortable in militant political movements, possibly because they usurp the place of Christian loyalites.

McDonald (1969, 130) tests the hypothesis that Catholics in Ontario vote Liberal because, at the time, the Conservatives refused to financially support Catholic schools beyond grade 10. As education in Canada is a provincial issue, one could reasonably expect this Conservative policy to affect provincial rather than federal voting patterns. Yet McDonald (1969,138) finds that "the relationship of provincial voting choices and attitudes on separate schools was in fact no greater than at the federal (level)."

Would Catholics be more likely to vote for a Liberal candidate when he also happens to be Catholic? Laponce (1958, 256) shows that from 1911 to 1953 (and other data show the same pattern after 1953), on average, 50% of Liberal M.P.s, but only 11% of Conservative M.P.s were Catholic. By contrast, during that same period, on average, only 6% of the Liberal M.P.s were Anglicans, but of the Conservative M.P.s, as many as 29%. Meisel, in his analysis of the 1957 federal election (1969,139ff) also found that Catholic candidates running as Liberals did better than Catholics running as Conservatives. Although religious affiliation is rarely mentioned in campaign literature and is played down by the party officials (they want to appeal to as broad a constituency as possible), the voter may actually be guided by his religious preference. Yet McDonald (1969, 143) dismisses this possiblity:

> The religion of the candidate showed some influence, however only in a hypothetical municipal election. The religion of the candidates in the 1968 federal election appeared to have had no effect. The candidate's religion is not strong enough an inducement to break the effect of party identification.

Where does this leave us? If neither issues such as Catholic school support nor affiliation of candidates makes much difference, why does the pattern persist? Meisel (1975, 270) mentions *verzuiling* (a Dutch word for pillarization, the phenomenon of political, trade union, broadcasting, and newspaper organizations, converging along religious lines, as is typical for some European countries) as a possible explanation. Although in Canada, Meisel says, the relationship is less formal (and I may add, less inclusive) than in Europe, there is a stable support system for the Liberal party by impressive majorities of French Canadians and English Catholics. In other words, in most Catholic homes, the habit to vote Liberal at election time may not be "venerable," yet is relatively consistent. Similarly, Protestants may tend to vote Conservative at election time, provided there is no compelling reason to break with the family tradition.

It is to the political advantage of candidates to deny, or ignore, anti-Catholic or anti-Protestant sentiments in their constituencies. Yet they did exist in the past and were even openly acknowledged in such organizations as the Protestant Defense League and the Orange Order. Similarly, anti-French attitudes amongst Anglophone voters may have had more effect than Canadians are prepared to admit. McDonald (1971, 178) provides evidence that in the 1968 election, those with high anti-French and anti-Catholic attitudes were more inclined to vote Conservative. And this leads

us back to the consolidating effect of religion for functionally separate
sub-systems: national divisions and prejudices may be potentially dangerous for any party with national aspirations, and yet if it has been associated
in the minds of the voters with some of these divisions, the party is not likely
to overtly dissociate itself from an important source of electoral support.
The major parties are therefore likely to covertly encourage the stable
support of ethnic, class, and religious segments of the population, while
overtly appealing to other ethnic, class, and religious groups as well.

It is because of this broad support that Meisel (1975, 273) regards the
long-term prospects of the Liberal party as excellent in contrast with the
Progressive Conservatives, who lack a traditional constituency of this kind.
Yet the continuing secularization and diversification of the Catholic Church
in Canada begun in the 1960s and its lessening political influence may also
erode the stable Catholic support for the Liberal party. Certainly the
resounding defeat of the Liberal party in the 1984 Federal elections showed
that many Catholics have abandoned traditional political allegiances.

So far we have only discussed the relationship between the mainline
churches in Canada and the major political parties. However, our frame of
reference also draws attention to possible sacralization patterns outside
mainstream Christianity and within the political arena as such. We began to
detect some of these when we touched on the militancy of some of the
left-wing parties in Australia and Canada. These sacralization patterns are
more clearly visible in the small Marxist parties in the Toronto area which
were described by Roger O'Toole. Their members ardently believe that
capitalism is doomed and that the proletariat will inaugurate a golden age of
justice. They live by these beliefs and are prepared not only to witness to the
vision but also to make sacrifices, if necessary (O'Toole 1977, 19,54,63).
They insist on total dedication to their programmes. The Internationalists
(a Maoist organization) highlight conversions "from a life of selfishness,
idleness, debauchery and parasitism to a new, meaningful conscious existence in the sect" (p.38). These Marxist parties form exclusive shelters for
the like-minded and reinforce the boundaries around the group through
chanting, banner-waving, and repetition of slogans. Their myths and beliefs contrast the darkness, alienation, and misery of the present age with a
bright, fulfilling, and wholesome future. Although at least one of these
organizations (The Socialist Labour Party, founded by Daniel De Leon) is
now almost a century old, and the membership has aged with it, the beliefs
of these groups are as strong as ever.

SECULARISM

If I were asked by some stranger to North American
culture to show him the most important religious building
in Canada, I would take him to Toronto's Maple Leaf
Gardens. Unlike most religious buildings, it is not dedi-

cated to the worship of one sect or church, but with
marvellous openjawed gluttony and Hindu profusion, it
engulfs the myriad rites and servants of many gods ....
(Here) is the religious cult that celebrates the Garden's
reason for being - Hockey Night in Canada (Kilbourn
1968, 6).

It is not accidental that many Canadians, like Kilbourn, think of religion
when they watch enthusiastic spectators and hero worshippers in sport
arenas. Neither is it accidental that other Canadians, such as the Rev. Philip
Bentley in *As For Me and My House* by Sinclair Ross identify religion and
art. Sport, art, play, and religion all have expression and dramatization in
common, and it is therefore understandable that they are associated in
people's minds. Yet association does not mean equivalence, and we have
been careful to distinguish the particular contribution which religion makes
to expressing existence by limiting ourselves to the four categories of
sacralization: transcendental ordering, emotional anchoring, sameness
enacting and dialectic dramatization.

Nevertheless, it is inevitable that at least some of these categories also
emerge in the other expressive spheres. We have seen how sacralization
patterns can arise outside the bounds of religious organizations, and one can
therefore expect that they do so particularly in those areas of existence
which similarly attempt to delineate and order through expression. Emotional anchoring or unification through commitment, in particular, seem to
often turn up outside religious organizations.

SPORTS

Competitive sports enact the interplay between pandemonium and
order, the unpredictable and the predictable. It is the latter (the predictable
and the orderly) which is usually latent, yet celebrated through the all-
pervasiveness of rules and the final authority of referees. They remain firm
whatever the outcome of the game. Yet, because of the stable context,
aggression and competition can be given comparatively free rein. Players
and (more vicariously) spectators act out these basic interactions of social
life.

Individual, non-competitive sports also have their integrative effects,
although they are on the personal rather than the social level. For the
devotees of jogging and swimming, physical exertion enhances mental
well-being. Exercise, they say, produces endorphins and affects the activities of the right-brain, emotional health, and sense of integrity. Sport
enthusiasts maintain that their occupational performance and their relations
with others improve through the daily jolt they give their bodies, allowing
concerns and preoccupations to fall into appropriate patterns, as in dreams.
Slusher (1967, 128) refers to the unification of body, mind, and spirit
through athletic activities.

Yet jogging and fitness can become a cult, so much so that for some athletes, running the marathon in less than three hours has become an obsession. In Canadian hockey there is a special name for wives of such fanatics: "hockey-widow." For those who succeed, glorification of performances may end up in disillusionment. Paul Henderson of Kincardine, Ontario, scored the winning goals in the 1972 Canada-Soviet Union hockey series and found himself unable to handle the adulation heaped upon him by the public. He turned into a recluse and began to re-assess life. Commitment to Christ followed, and he formed a study group for Canadian athletes wanting to link faith and sports (The Hamilton *Spectator*, July 19, 1975, p.29). For Henderson, glorification of performance and success lacked the more comprehensive sets of meaning and security of traditional Christianity.

In *The Sun also Rises*, Ernest Hemingway discusses the bullfight as an enactment of the contest between chaos and order; and Johan Huizinga (1970, 29) similarly thinks of play in general as the creation of order in a confused and imperfect world. Teamsports, in particular, teach players the values of both cooperation and aggression. For cooperation it is necessary to control the individual's aggressive bent and to discipline it sufficiently so that it can serve the common good. Passing the ball or the puck to someone in a better position to score is a form of self-denial (denying oneself the glory of making a goal) and is approved and encouraged. Yet fierce attack on the opposition and cunning penetration of the defense are also exalted.

Self-discipline and ascetic behaviour (abstaining from drinking, heavy eating and sex before a big game) are mutually sustaining values of sports and religion; or, as Badertscher (1977, 407) has it for hockey: "Both morally and mentally, then, hockey is a school for life in the inner-worldly ascetic mode." Practising sacrifice of appetites for the sake of the larger goal strengthens the commitment to these goals. A community instinctively approves a well-developed capacity for self-denial. It assures the members of such a community that individuals can cope with potentially disruptive experiences of humiliation, indignity, defeat or pride, arrogance, victory. If Canadians in the 1980s have made a hero of Wayne Gretzky (of Brantford, Ontario, but playing for the Edmonton Oilers) it is not only because he is the highest scorer in the National Hockey League, but also because he exemplifies humility in spite of fame, common sense in spite of adulation, and team spirit in spite of individual competence. Both sports and religion encourage the higher loyalties and commitments which guarantee the control of potentially harmful feelings of revenge or overbearingness on the part of the members of any given community. As a footnote, Gretzky's teammates attribute his phenomenal success also to an uncanny ability to envision where the puck will go and of being there when it does, as though he is looking at the play from a distance, from the stands.

There is more. Communal spectator games and religious services take place regularly, and therefore they continuously reinforce sentiments of common belonging and common adherence to beliefs and values which control and balance aggression/self-assertion/sin with big-heartedness/altruism/compliance. Rites reinforce sameness and continuity and thereby prevent important beliefs and values from being lost out of sight. A community suffers together with the local team when it loses a game, and it exults when the team wins; or, as Al Purdy (1956, 60; also Sinclair-Faulkner 1977, 384) has it: "I've seen the aching glory of a resurrection in their eyes if they score, but crucifixion's agony" if they lose. The loss, as much as the victory, can draw communities, ethnic groups, or nations together through common suffering or rejoicing.

There are interesting examples of soccer rousing the sentiments of ethnic groups even more than religion can. Wherever the Serbs and the Croats have immigrated after World War II, they have perpetuated their traditional animosity for one another. Although they are also separated by religion (the Croats are primarily Catholic, the Serbs Orthodox), they express their separate nationhood on the soccerfield: each nation feels that it has conquered the other when it wins a game. Similarly, in 1972, and to a lesser extend in 1984 when the Canada Cup had become a tradition, Canadians felt that their national identity was a stake when the Soviet Union seemed to be on the verge of winning the hockey series. The myth of the invincibility of Canada in ice hockey (Hoppener 1972, 1) was in grave danger, and so Canadians, at the time, regarded defeat as national humiliation and victory (when it came) as vindication of the national honour. Sport events can strongly raise commitment to communal, ethnic, or national integrity. Internationally, the Olympics allow for the free flow of national pride when various teams and individuals compete for the honour of getting the gold medal. Yet the solemn spectacle of the opening and closing ceremonies, the torch-bearing, the parades, the oaths, and the unfolding of the Olympic flag provide a stable, awe-inspiring context for the national competitions.

Like religion, sport does not just promote and cultivate the integrity of various other levels of social organization. It often reinforces its own organization through sacralizing mechanisms. Edwards (1973, 261-2) gives some examples. He points to "saints" (e.g., Babe Ruth in baseball) who have become immortal through their triumphs on the playing fields and "gods," the superstars, whose charisma enthused millions. "Scribes" (sports reporters and telecasters) similarly enhance the reputation and standing of the organization in the eyes of the public. "Seekers of the Kingdom" (the true believers, devotees, fanatics and converts) reinforce loyalty and commitment to the club, which keeps cups and other trophies in those places where religious organizations have their "shrines." It is because of strong loyalties to sports organizations and adulation of god-like superstars that one can encounter Canadian clergymen who privately (or sometimes even publicly) denounce these commitments as idolatry (trespass on their terrain). The fact that nowadays they tend to do this privately shows a change in public opinion. About the turn of the century (when the Lord's Day Alliance was at the height of its power), scheduling training sessions in sports on Sunday mornings would have been out of the question. They now occur fairly frequently.

ALCOHOLICS ANONYMOUS

Although there are many secular organizations in Canada which exhibit at least some of what we have called sacralization mechanisms (usually commitment and ritual), Alcoholic Anonymous tends to have all of them. A.A. is the most successful fellowship of recovered alcoholics. The success rate of all other rehabilitative methods is, by common consensus, much less impressive (Vaillant 1983). A.A. provides alcoholics intending to overcome their addiction with a support group of people with similar problems. These groups are ready at any time of the night or day to rush to the aid of a member who is on the verge of a relapse, and it stages celebrations for those who have managed to stay sober for a particular length of time (3 months, 6 months, a year, etc.).

A.A. comes rather close to what we have called "objectification," or transcendental ordering, typical for religious organizations. Although it allows the widest possible interpretation of who God is (if a member wants to define God as a rather vague power of some kind that is fine with A.A.), it also insists in its twelve steps of recovery that members acknowledge that only a power greater than themselves can restore them to sanity and that only by turning their will "over to the care of God as we understand him" can they get well again. A.A. members are convinced that recognizing their powerlessness over alcohol and believing in a power beyond themselves (and submitting to this power with trust) are central to a successful recovery.

Prayerful surrender and commitment, however, are not sufficient in themselves. Members of Alcoholics Anonymous believe that only commitment to groups of recovering alcoholics can sustain the resolve to refrain from alcohol. To an outsider, A.A. gatherings resemble nothing so much as public confessions at a revival meeting. Members take their turn to embarrassingly relate the damage they have done to their families, spouses, employers, and friends while enslaved to alcohol. Then they describe how they were saved through the support they received from specific A.A. members who stood by them on their first day without a drink. It is this responsibility for other ex-alcoholics which stiffens the resolve of individual members to do without alcohol, even when their craving seems intolerable.

Faithful attendance at A.A. meetings (there are roughly three to four thousand of these weekly gatherings all over Canada) bolsters the now re-born ex-alcoholic in his endeavour to stay away from the bottle. Too much self-reliance and not enough dependence on the fellowship of recovering drunks (A.A. carefully insists that full recovery is unlikely) often causes a relapse. Active participation in the ritual of welcome, recitation, meditation and discussion adds to the newly found integrity of a member and to the viability of the group. Without the meetings and their strictly followed programmes (each item having its own specific function), the influence of A.A. would be very minor and insignificant.

A.A. has a well-defined set of beliefs regarding existence. It maintains that the stress of modern societies, the alienation of individuals from an impersonal culture, the achievement and success orientation of modern man, all require a toll in the form of alcoholism. A.A. believes that alcohol has become, for many, an outlet and pacifier for such deep-seated problems as meaninglessness and powerlessness. Yet it is realistic enough not to attempt a wholesale onslaught on the ills of the times. It confines its efforts to providing an antidote only to those who have succumbed to the strain by alcohol addiction. It does so by insisting on a simple transcendental belief, surrender to God's care and the fellowship of other ex-alcoholics, a strong programme of mutual help, and a world- wide system of weekly meetings. At its meetings it uses the prayer of St. Francis of Assisi contrasting hatred and love, wrong and forgiveness, discord and harmony, error and truth, despair and hope, shadow and light, sadness and joy (Csicsai 1983).

OTHER SECULAR CAUSES, IDEOLOGIES AND PROPS

In Brian Moore's *The Luck of Ginger Coffey* (1972, 70), a fellow proof-reader at the Montreal *Tribune* feels that he must acquaint Ginger (a newcomer from Ireland) with the major Canadian values: "Money is the Canadian way to immortality...Money is the root of all good here, One nation, indivisible, under Mammon that's our heritage." In Margaret Atwood's *Surfacing* (1973, 42), the heroine, reminiscing about her youth, says that glamour to her was "a kind of religion," and that the pictures of fashion models on her bedroom walls were the corresponding "icons." What both authors mean is that the prime motivating forces, the unifying commitments, can be quite different from the source of salvation in organized Christianity or Christian theology. Preoccupation with health, power, and fame are other commitments which the Canadian public at large associates with religious feeling.

Free enterprise and business success comprise the theology of George A. Cohon who in a decade amassed a personal fortune of $50 million by peppering Canada with 400 McDonald hamburger outlets. Peter Newman (1981, 175-6) describes his commercial commitments as "born-again evangelism" and his personnel as "smiling, smiling not for Jesus, but for Big Mac." Cohon's chief operating officer, who left to start his own hamburger chain, has become a heretic, a non-person ("....in my religion I forgot his name," said Cohon). Cohon actually admits "McDonald's is a religion with me."

The Canadian public at large often associates militancy with religion. A good example is the Women's Liberation Movement. Particularly in the early stages of the movement, its fervency (Stephenson, 1977, 116) was its most conspicuous characteristic. It wanted to unite all women against oppression and discrimination. In the 1980s it began to mellow, while maintaining its beliefs in the necessity for greater equality and justice for women. It also continues to keep these goals in the forefront of attention through a strategy of conscious-raising and the ritual encouragement of feelings and emotions aroused by actual wrongs.

Another source of beliefs and commitments bypassing organized Christianity has to do with horoscopes, palmreading, witchcraft, black magic, etc. Palmreaders sometimes have offices in shopping malls. Bibby (1979, table A4) shows that as much as 15% of his Canadian sample read the horoscope daily; 62% percent consult it occasionally. The percentage of individuals who read their horoscope regularly goes up among Protestants who are not members, but affiliates (not formal members of a denomination): 22% for United Church affiliates as against 13% for members, 23% for Conservatives affiliates as against 10% for members (Conservatives in Bibby's survey are Protestants belonging to the smaller, often evangelical denominations such as Baptist, Brethren, Pentecostal, Salvation Army). Unfortunately, from the data published in Bibby (1979), it is not possible to discover more about the kind of people who consult their horoscope daily, but if Australian data are any indication, they tend to be the irregular churchgoers, the insecure, and the frightened (Mol 1971, 43).

In all societies individuals search for patterns and structure when integrity is felt to be in jeopardy. Reading one's horoscope in the daily newspaper is a way to anticipate (and therefore, in some measure, to control) future events. The sense of being at the mercy of the unknown lessens when the future can be ordered or structured, even when this structuring is obviously unreliable and tentative. Those, who at crucial turning points in life have their cards read, hope to receive the same benefit as Indians who read the cracks in the scorched shoulderbone of the caribou in order to get guidance for action when the choices and options are wide open. Those who read cards (often Tarot cards) for clients begin by shuffling the cards (thereby recreating the primal situation of randomness and chaos) and then interpret the symbols of the cards in such a way that they become relevant for the questions asked. Of necessity, the symbols are rather abstract (for instance, a card numbered one represents the archetype of an element, card number two, its opposite; and number three, the harmonization of one and two), thereby allowing a wide application. The vagueness and the comprehension of the symbol make it possible for the diviner to suggest that an important relationship for the client is likely to deteriorate when a card with a two appears and improve when a card with a three turns up.

SUMMARY

In Canada organized religion used to be more strongly intertwined with voting patterns than class or ethnicity: French Canadians and English-speaking Catholics tended to vote Liberal and Protestants preferred the Progressive Conservatives. Yet the pattern is not immutable, as the 1984

Federal election showed. There have been earlier periods in history when French and Newfoundland Catholics massively supported the Conservatives. Also, in western Canada the pattern was usually more blurred than in other parts of the country.

The vernacular often uses the adjective "religious" when a political party (particularly a Marxist one), or social movement (such as Women's Liberation), or a sport event (the play-offs for the Stanley Cup in ice hockey) strongly arouses the loyalties of members, participants, and spectators. Sports clubs often have their own saints, gods, and shrines. Yet these unifying commitments are usually not transcendental in the sense that they are relevant for a wide range of existential experiences. Alcoholics Anonymous is one of the few secular organizations which professes to rely on a transcendental power for personal restoration.

Money, free enterprise, democracy, and objectivity have all been suggested as quasi-religious sources of motivation for large numbers of Canadians. If they have in no way eclipsed Christianity, it is partly because the inclusive relevance of the latter has been a suitable counterbalance to the restrictive concerns of the former. Yet also on a more cosmic level, meaningful structuring of crisis events and future uncertainties takes place in areas which to Christians are downright superstitious and idolatrous: horoscopes, card readings and other methods of divining. In canada, as in all pluralistic, modern societies, religious organizations and religious symbolism have to compete with patterns of sacralization arising from within secular structures.

CONCLUSION

This book has looked at religion in Canada from the social- scientific point of view. It has analysed and described the most diverse religious phenomena (traditional Indian practices, mainline Christian beliefs, sectarian exclusiveness, ethnic religious culture, commitments to hockey) using a dialectical model. The model and the underlying classifications regard society as a field of cooperating (the aspect stressed by the functional school in sociology) and contending (the aspect stressed by the conflict school in sociology) units of social organization (systems, subsystems). It is dialectical, not only because it pays equal attention to the forces which cooperate/integrate and the forces which contend/fragment, but also because it assumes that the pull and counterpull of progress and order are essentially what survival and evolution are about. Both seem to oppose and to need each other.

How did this show? The Hutterite chapter describes the tug-of- war between community and the larger, Canadian society. It also describes the ways in which the boundaries between these two contending units of social organization are strengthened. Yet Hutterite values of hard work, frugality, and honesty accord with some of the ideals of the surrounding Canadian culture and therefore soften the same boundaries through mutual appreciation. Another example: the mainline Canadian churches and denominations (units of social organizations in their own right) pray for Queen and "those in authority over us," interpret national events in the light of their respective traditions and thereby reinforce the national identity. Yet they also draw the line between themselves and the nation when they are convinced that injustice is done to the natives (the primate of the Anglican Church, Archbishop Edward W. Scott, 1981) or to the unemployed (The Canadian Catholic bishops in 1983).

The advantage of our scheme of reference and the questions it promotes (It always asks: "To which units of social organization [system, sub-system] does the material or situation under investigation refer and do these units contend or cooperate with one another?") is that one can detect what otherwise would remain hidden. An example: the material on the native religions of Canada showed that it was not sufficient to think in terms of

296

person, family, clan, tribe, but that the (to moderns, rather foreign) category of ecosystem (the unity of self and physical environment) had to be
introduced to make sense of the data.

The model has, of course, also a religious component. By this I mean
that, over and above questions dealing with religious organizations, other
questions dealing with non-organizational, typically "religious" issues, are
asked. These questions can be best put as follows: "In which ways do
transcendentalization (cosmic ordering), commitment (emotional unification), ritual (sameness enacting) and myth (dialectic dramatization) affect
the integrity or fragmentation of these units or systems?" The assumption
behind the question is that, however arbitrary or controversial definitions
are, religion can be summed up or defined by these four subcomponents of
transcendental ordering, emotional anchoring, sameness enacting, and
dialectic dramatization, all of which (or at least the majority of which) must
be present for a phenomenon to be called "religious." The advantage of this
definition is that it conforms to common parlance. It is not too all-
encompassing, yet, on the other hand, it is wide enough to incorporate what
functionalists call "functional alternatives" to religion. An example: When,
both in common and scholarly language, ice hockey in Canada is called a
religious phenomenon, our scheme of reference allows us to investigate in
which of the four subcomponents hockey actually resembles religion and
can become a substitute for it (in this instance, the answer being that it is
mainly the second and fourth component which make it "religious," as is
shown in the last chapter).

How then does religion, in the sense we have defined it, affect "the
cooperating, but also contending field of units of social organization" in
Canada? A global, first order, answer is contained in the title of this book.
Faith has an integrative, whole-making, quality which stands over against
the precarious, fragile nature of social structures. In other words, in the
push and pull of units of social organization religion functions as the arbiter,
peacemaker, restorer and healer, mitigating conflict and fragmentation,
reinforcing buttresses. Examples: faith shores the confidence of countless
individuals and checks meaninglessness and alienation. Another: in 1837
the Catholic Church of Quebec sided with the established British order
when Louis-Joseph Papineau led a rebellion against the chateau clique. In
the same year it also had *To Deums* sung when Queen Victoria succeeded to
the throne. By doing so, it put oil on troubled waters.

Yet a dialectical approach to religion cannot be satisfied with simple
answers of this kind. True, God saves more often than He destroys and
religion generally restores rather than weakens boundaries. But then, God
punished Israel by allowing the Assyrians to overrun the country, and, at
the time, the Catholic Church of Quebec dealt a blow to French ethnic
cohesion by backing the British oppressors. In other words, by reinforcing
one unit of social organization (national order), it weakens another one
(ethnic identity). To give the opposite example: during the First World War
the Ukrainian Greek Catholic and the Ukrainian Greek Orthodox churches

fought tooth and nail for Ukrainian ethnic identity against a government which forbade the teaching of Ukrainian in public schools in order to bolster national unity. In other words, by reinforcing one unit of social organization (ethnic identity) it weakened another one (national identity).

The dialectic in which religion is entangled goes beyond the units of social organization, the boundaries of which are subject to both positive (boundary maintaining) and negative (boundary challenging) forces. The four mechanisms of sacralization by which we have subdivided religious phenomena each have their own internal dialectic. Each of these sacralizing forces contains within itself de-sacralizing possiblities. I would like to illustrate this observation from the Canadian materials of this book.

First, transcendentalization. Through belief in God the pain of individuals can be relieved, social action can be legitimated and unified, and disorder can be placed in a context of order. In other words, through making order into an object and summing up that order in God (Who is love, all-knowing, all-powerful, eternal, all-ordering), the strains and stresses of living are relativized - they are related to a meaningful context. Yet relativization can also do the opposite. It can and does diminish the importance and even "holiness" of man's attachments to his family, community, tribe, nation, etc. Rather than increase the reverence for Canada as it was, the Social Gospellers at the beginning of the twentieth century pointed to its inadequacies. Adopting standards of justice, love, and self-denial in God's Kingdom, they judged the actual Canadian society as being much in need of improvement and they set out to improve it. In other words, transcendentalization can sacralize/legitimate but also de-sacralize/censure.

The same with commitment. Undoubtedly, feelings of loyalty and dedication have strengthened all major Canadian institutions and units of social organization. Yet these very emotional attachments were a hindrance when change became the order of the day. On the Canadian frontier, the values of thriftlessness, gambling, drinking, and irresponsibility to which the riffraff were committed became a disadvantage for the building of families and communities. The revival meetings of Henry Alline and the Salvation Army, among others, stripped individuals from these attachments and welded (converted) them to a new life of frugality, reliability, and care. Shamans and other charismatic leaders decommitted members of their tribes from neglect of taboos or from maladaptive traditions and recommitted them to a renewed acceptance of rules or welded them to more adaptive views of existence.

The same with ritual. The simple *sobranya* ceremony of the Doukhobors unified the membership and made its opposition to outside influences all the more formidable. Yet the changes brought about by a child being born or entering adulthood or a father dying made rituals of detachment from previous identities (rites of passage) as necessary as the subsequent rituals of attachment. As a matter of fact what is true for the Doukhobors is true for all of Canada: however secular Canadian society may have become, the rites dealing with birth, marriage, and death remain ubiquitous. All of them go through phases of separation/stripping as well as phases of attachment/welding.

We have translated myth as dialectic dramatization and thereby assumed that it (as well as theology and ideology) acts out basic disparities within a particular society. In Canada this is true for both native, Christian, and "secular" religion. The contrast between chaos and order in Kwakiutl society was the basic principle behind the taming of the man-eating monster in the winter dances. In Christianity, similiar disparities are represented in the Sunday morning sermons in which themes of order versus chaos, evil versus good, sin versus salvation, freedom versus constraint, crucifixion versus resurrection, integrity versus fragmentation are nearly always present. In modern secular Canada, games and play act out the chaotic potential of aggression, attack, and defense in a context of stable order (rules and impartial refereeing). Television dramas and novels similarly enact themes of good versus evil and order versus change in detailed and in variegated ways.

The social-scientific model and the classifications of religion which form the warp and woof of this study have not always been obvious - even when it was there in the choices of presentation. The secondary sources upon which I had to rely were often silent on the information I needed for a full account. For instance, the Catholic capacity to juggle the contrasting demands of ethnic, national and church/organizational identities was poorly documented and there was no time to go to the primary sources, which, I am sure, would contain the full story. Yet I hope that this study will be complemented and surpassed by more detailed investigations of the available primary sources in the not too distant future. I believe that the dialectical model has the potential for much exciting and innovative analysis of religion in Canada.

BIBLIOGRAPHY

Acquaviva, Sabino. "Italy", in (eds.) Mol, Hans; Hetherton, Margaret; Henty, Margaret, *Western Religion*. The Hague: Mouton, 1972, pp. 305-324.

Alford, Robert R. *Party and Society: The Anglo-American Democracies*. Chicago: Rand McNally, 1963.

Alford, Robert R. "The Social Bases of Political Cleavage in 1962", in Meisel, John (ed.), *Papers on the 1962 Election*. Toronto: University of Toronto Press, 1964, pp. 203-234.

l'Allemant, Charles. *Rélation de ce qui s'est passé en La Nouvelle France 1626*. Montreal: Editions du jour, 1972.

Allen, Richard. *The Social Passion (Religion and Social Reform in Canada)* Toronto: University of Toronto Press, 1971.

Alline, Henry. *Life and Journal of the Rev. Mr. Henry Alline*. Boston: Gilbert and Dean, 1806.

Allingham, J.D. *Religious Affiliation and Social Class in Ontario*. Unpublished M.A. thesis. Hamilton, Ontario: McMaster University, 1962.

Almerich, Paulina "Spain" in (eds.) Mol, Hans; Hetherton, Margaret; Henty, Margaret. *Western Religion*, The Hague: Mouton, 1972, pp. 459-477.

Alston, John P. "Social Variables Associated With Church Attendance, 1965 and 1969: Evidence From National Polls." *Journal for the Scientific Study of Religion*, Vol. 10, No. 3 (Fall 1971), pp. 233-236.

Ambert, Ann-Marie   *Divorce in Canada*. Don Mills, Ontario: Academic Press, 1980.

Anderson, Grace M.   "Voting Behaviour and the Ethnic-Religious Variable: a Study of a Federal Election in Hamilton, Ontario." In *Canadian Journal of Economics and Political Science*, Vol. XXXII, 1966, pp. 27-37.

Anderson, Kevin Victor   *Report of the Board of Enquiry into Scientology*. Melbourne: Government Printer, 1965.

Antliff, J. Cooper   "Historical Sketch of the Primitive Methodist Church in Canada" *Centennial of Canadian Methodism*. Toronto: William Briggs, 1981 pp. 181-204.

Archibald, W. Peter   *Social Psychology as Political Economy*. Toronto: McGraw-Hill Ryerson, 1978.

Armstrong, Maurice W.   *The Great Awakening in Nova Scotia 1776-1809*. Hartford, Connecticut: The American Society of Church History, 1948.

Atwood, Margaret   *Surfacing*. Don Mills, Ontario: General Publishing Co., 1973.

Audet, Louis-Phillippe   "Attempts to Develop a School System for Lower Canada: 1760-1840" in (Eds.) Wilson, J. Donald; Stamp, Robert M.; Audet, Louis-Philippe, *Canadian Education: a History* Scarborough, Ontario: Prentice Hall, 1970, pp. 145-166.

Bader, Edward L.   "New Approaches to Interfaith Marriage: A Report." In *The Ecumenist*, 6, no. 5 (July-August 1968), pp. 172-4.

Badertscher, John.   "Response to Sinclair-Faulkner" in (Ed.) Slater, Peter *Religion and Culture in Canada*. Waterloo, Ontario: Wilfrid Laurier University Press, 1977.

Bailey, Alfred Goldsworthy.   *The Conflict of European and Eastern Algonkian Cultures 1504-1700*. Toronto: University of Toronto Press, 1969. (First published 1937).

Bainbridge, William Sims.   *Satan's Power (A Deviant Psycho-therapy Cult)*. Berkeley, California: University of California Press, 1978.

Balikci, Asen.   "The Netsilik Eskimo" in (Editors) Crysdale, Steward and Wheatcroft, Les *Religion in Canadian Society*: Toronto: Macmillan 1976, pp.86-99.

Barbier, Louis P. *The Story of First Lutheran Church Toronto, 1851-1976.* Toronto: Privately Produced, 1976.

Barbier, Louis P. *Follow the Footsteps of your Forefathers (1898-1978, 80th Anniversary of First Lutheran in Toronto).* Toronto: Privately Published, 1978.

Barnes, Samuel H. "Quebec Catholicism and Social Change." *Review of Politics*, 23, no. 1 (1961), pp. 52-76.

Baum, Gregory. *Catholics and Canadian Socialism: Political Thought in the Thirties and Forties.* Toronto, Ontario: Lorimer, 1980.

Beaulieu, Maurice, and André Normandeau. "Le Role de la Réligion a Travers l'Histoire du Canada Francais." *Cité Libre*, 16, no. 71 (1964), pp. 15-24.

Beckford, James A. *The Trumpet of Prophecy: A Sociological Study of Jehovah's Witnesses.* Oxford: Basil Blackwell, 1975.

Belkin, Simon. *Through Narrow Gates: A Review of Jewish Immigration, Colonization and Immigrant Aid Work in Canada, 1840-1940.* Montreal: Canadian Jewish Congress, 1966.

Bender, H.S. "Amish Division." *The Mennonite Encyclopedia I*, 1955.

Bennett, John W. *Hutterian Brethren.* Stanford, California: Stanford University Press, 1967.

Bennett, John W. "The Hutterites: A Communal Sect" in (eds.) Crysdale, Stewart and Wheatcroft, Les, *Religion in Canadian Society*, Toronto: Macmillan, 1976, pp. 256-267.

Berton, Pierre. *The Comfortable Pew: A Critical Look at the Church in the New Age.* Toronto: McClelland and Stewart, 1965.

Beverley, James, A. "National Survey of Baptist Ministers" in (Editor) Zeman, Jarold K. *Baptists in Canada (Search for Identity Amidst Diversity)* Burlington, Ontario: Welch, 1980 pp. 267-276.

Bibby, Reginald W. "Religiosity in Canada: a National Survey" in (eds.) Beattie, Christopher and Crysdale, Stewart. *Sociology Canada: Readings* (2nd edition). Toronto: Butterworth, 1977.

Bibby, Reginald W. "The State of Collective Religiosity in Canada." *Canadian Review of Sociology and Anthropology*, 16, no. 1, 1979, pp. 105-116.

Bibby, Reginald W. *Canadian Commitment*. Toronto: United Church Research Office, 1979.

Bibby, Reginald W. "Religion and Modernity: The Canadian Case." *Journal for the Scientific Study of Religion*, 18, no. 1 (March 1979a), pp. 1-17.

Bilby, Julian William. *Among unknown Eskimos: Twelve years in Baffin Island*. London: S. Service, 1923.

Birket-Smith, Kaj. *Eskimos*. New York: Crown Publishers, 1972.

Blais, Marie-Claire. *A Season in the Life of Emmanuel*. New York: Grosset and Dunlop, 1969.

Bloch-Hoell, Nils. *The Pentecostal Movement*. Oslo: Universitetsforlaget, 1964.

Boas, Franz. *The Central Eskimos*. Sixth Annual Report of the Bureau of American Ethnology (1888), pp. 399-669.

Boas, Franz. "The Eskimo of Baffin Land and Hudson Bay." *Bulletin American Museum of Natural History*, 15 (1907).

Boas, Franz. *Tsimshian Mythology*. Washington: Annual Reports of the Bureau of American Ethnology, 1916.

Boas, Franz. *The Religion of the Kwakiutl Indians* (Part II - translations). New York: Columbia University Press, 1930.

Boas, Franz. *Kwakiutl Ethnography*. Chicago: University of Chicago Press, 1966.

Boas, Franz. *The Social Organization and the Secret Societies of the Kwakiutl Indians*. (First published in 1897). New York: Johnson Reprint Corporation, 1970.

Bock, Philip K. "The Religion of the Micmac Indians of Restigouche" in (eds.) Crysdale, Stewart and Wheatcroft, Les. *Religion in Canadian Society*, Toronto: Macmillan, 1976, pp. 141-150.

Bodsworth, Fred. *The Sparrow's Fall*. Scarborough, Ontario: New American Library of Canada Limited, 1968.

Bogensberger, Hugo and Paul Zulehner. "Austria" in (editors) Mol, Hans; Hetherton, Margaret; Henty, Margaret, *Western Religion*. The Hague: Mouton, 1972, pp. 47-66.

Boon, T.C.B. *The Anglican Church from the Bay to the Rockies*. Toronto: The Ryerson Press, 1962.

Bowles, Richard P., and others. *The Indian: Assimilation, Integration or Separation*. Scarborough, Ontario: Prentice-Hall, 1972.

Brady, Alexander. *Democracy in the Dominion*, Toronto: University of Toronto Press, 1958.

Brébeuf, Jean de. *Rélation de ce qui s'est passé dans le pays des Hurons, 1636*. Tome 1. Montreal: Editions du Jour, 1972.

Brown, Arnold. *What Hath God Wrought (The History of the Salvation Army in Canada: 1882-1914)*. Toronto: Salvation Army Printing and Publishing House, 1952.

Buliard, R.P. *Inuk*. New York: Farrar, Straus and Young, 1951.

Callaghan, Morley. *Such is my Beloved*. Toronto: McClelland and Stewart, 1957.

Campbell, Douglas F., and David C. Neice. *Ties that bind: Structure and Marriage in Nova Scotia*. Port Credit, Ontario: The Scribblers Press, 1979.

Campiche, Roland J. "Switzerland" in (editors) Mol, Hans; Hetherton, Margaret; Henty, Margaret, *Western Religion*. The Hague: Mouton, 1972, pp. 511-528.

Canada's Religious Composition. (Profile Study of the 1971 Census of Canada). Bulletin 5.1-10, May 1976. (Catalogue 99-710, Vol. V - part 1).

Cardinal, Harold. *The Unjust Society: The Tragedy of Canada's Indians*. Edmonton: Hurtig, 1969.

Cardinal Harold. *The Rebirth of Canada's Indians*. Edmonton: Hurtig, 1977.

Carrington, Philip. *The Anglican Church in Canada*. Toronto: Collins, 1963.

Carroll, John. *Salvation! O the Joyful Sound*. Toronto: Oxford University Press, 1967.

Chamberlin, J.E. *The Harrowing of Eden*. New York: Seabury Press, 1975.

Chapin, Miriam. *Quebec Now*. Toronto: Ryerson Press, 1955.

Chown, S.D. *The Story of Church Union in Canada*. Toronto: Ryerson Press, 1930.

Christian, William A., Jr. *Person and God in a Spanish Valley*. New York: Seminar Press, 1972.

Clark, S.D. *Church and Sect in Canada*. Toronto: University of Toronto Press, 1948.

Clark S.D. *The Developing Canadian Community*. Toronto: University of Toronto Press, 1968.

Clarke, Harold D.M., Jane Jenson, Lawrence LeDuc, Jon H. Pammett. *Political Choice in Canada*. Toronto: McGraw-Hill Ryerson, 1979.

Clement, Wallace. *The Canadian Corporate Elite*. Toronto: McClelland and Stewart, 1975.

Clifford, Keith N. "His Dominion: A Vision in Crisis." in (editor) Slater, Peter *Religion and Culture in Canada*. Waterloo, Ontario: Wilfrid Laurier University Press, 1977, pp. 23-42.

Codere, Helen. "Kwakiutl" in (ed.) Spicer, Edward H., *Perspectives in American Indian Culture Change*. Chicago: University of Chicago Press, 1969. pp. 431-516.

Comer, George. "A Geographical Description of Southampton Island and notes on the Eskimo." *Bulletin of the American Geographical Society*, 42 (1910), pp. 84-90.

Connor, Ralph [The Rev. C.W. Gordon, a Presbyterian minister in Winnipeg]. *Glencarry School Days*. Toronto: McClelland and Stewart, 1975 (originally published in 1902).

Conway, Flo, and Jim Siegelman. *Snapping*. Philadelphia: J.B. Lippincott, 1978.

Cooper, A.I.H. *The Role of Conjuring in Saulteaux Society*. New York: Octagon Books, 1971.

Corlett, William Thomas. *The Medicine Man of the American Indian and his Cultural Background*. Springfield, Illinois: Charles C. Thomas, 1935.

Cronmiller, Carl Raymond. *A History of The Lutheran Church in Canada*. Toronto: The Evangelical Lutheran Synod of Canada, 1961.

Crowe, Keith J. *A History of the Original Peoples of Northern Canada*. Montreal: McGill University Press, 1974.

Crysdale, Stewart. *The Industrial Struggle and Protestant Ethic in Canada*. Toronto: Ryerson Press, 1961.

Crysdale, Stewart. *The Changing Church in Canada: Beliefs and Social Attitude of United Church People*. Toronto: United Church of Canada, Board of Evangelism and Social Service, 1965.

Crysdale, Stewart. "The Sociology of the Social Gospel: Quest for a Modern Ideology" in (Eds.) Crysdale. Stewart and Wheatcroft, Les Toronto: *Religion in Canadian Society*, MacMillan, 1976, pp. 423-433.

Crysdale, Stewart. "Social Awakening among Protestants, 1872 to 1918" in (eds.) Crysdale, Stewart and Wheatcroft, Les *Religion in Canadian Society*. Toronto: Macmillan, 1976, pp. 191-206.

Csicsai, Rose. *From Alienation to Integration in Alcoholics Anonymous: A Descriptive Analysis Using Dialectical Sociology of Religion*. Hamilton, Ontario: McMaster University, unpublished M.A. thesis, 1983.

Daly, George Thomas. *Catholic Problems in Western Canada*, Toronto: The MacMillan Company of Canada Ltd., 1921.

Daner, Francine. *The American Children of KRSNA*. New York: Holt, Rinehart and Winston, 1976.

Darcovich, William, and Paul Yuzik. *A Statistical Compendium on the Ukrainians in Canada*, Ottawa: University of Ottawa Press, 1980.

Darroll, Bryant M. (ed.). *Religious Liberty in Canada: Deprogramming and Media Coverage of New Religions*. Toronto: Canadians for the Protection of Religious Liberty, 1979.

Darroll, Bryant M., and Herbert W. Richardson, (eds.). *A Time for Consideration: A Scholarly Appraisal of the Unification Church*. New York: Edwin Mellen Press, 1978.

Davies, Blowden. *A String of Amber: the Heritage of the Mennonites*. Vancouver: Mitchell Press, 1973.

Davis, Kenneth, R. "The Struggle for a United Evangelical Fellowship, 1953-1965" in (editor) Zeman, Jarold K. *Baptists in Canada (Search for Identity Amidst Diversity)*. Burlington, Ontario: Welch, 1980, pp. 237-265.

Davis, Morris and Joseph Krauter. *The Other Canadians: Profiles of Six Minorities*. Toronto: Methuen, 1971.

Dawson, C.A. *Group Settlement: Ethnic Communities in Western Canada*. Toronto, Ontario: The MacMillan Company of Canada Ltd., 1936.

Dawson, C.A. and E.R. Younge. *Pioneering in the Prairie Provinces: The Social Side of the Settlement Process*. Toronto: Macmillan, 1940.

Despland, Michel. "Religion and the Quest for a National Identity: Problems and Perspectives" in (editor) Slater, Peter, *Religion and Culture in Canada/Religion et Culture au Canada*, Waterloo, Ontario: Wilfrid Laurier University Press, 1977, pp. 525-551.

Deweese, Charles W. "Church Covenants and Church Discipline among Baptists in the Maritime Provinces" in (editor) Moody, Barry M. *Repent and Believe (The Baptist Experience in Maritime Canada)*. Hantsport, Nova Scotia: Lancelot Press, 1980, pp. 27-45.

Dixon, William G. "Public Administration and the Community" in (ed.) Hawthorn, Harry B. *The Doukhobors of British Columbia*. Vancouver: The University of British Columbia, 1955, pp. 184-220.

Dominic of Saint-Denis, Capuchin. *l'Église Catholique au Canada*. Montréal: Les Éditions Thau, 1956.

Donohue, Patrick. "Pressure Points in the Catholic Church." *Today Magazine* 10 April 1982, pp. 10-16.

Driedger, Leo. "Impelled Migration: Minority Struggle to Maintain Institutional Completeness." *International Migration Review*, 1973, Vol. 7, pp. 257-67.

Driedger, Leo. "Jewish Identity: the Maintenance of Urban Religious and Ethnic Boundaries." *Ethnic and Racial Studies*, 3, no. 1, (January 1980), pp. 67-88.

Driedger, Leo, and Glenn Church. "Residential Segregation and Institutional Completeness: A Comparison of Ethnic Minorities", *Canadian Review of Sociology and Anthropology*, 11 (1974), pp. 30-52.

Driedger, Leo, and Jacob Peters. "Characteristics of Mennonite Identity: A Comparison of Mennonite and Other German Students." *Mennonite Quarterly Review*, 47 (July 1973), pp. 225-44.

Dumont, Fernand. "Sur Notre Situation Réligieuse." *Rélations*, 25, issue 302 (1966), pp. 36-38.

Dumont, Fernand, and Gerald Fortin. "Un sondage de pratique réligieuse en milieu urbain." *Recherches Sociographiques*, 1, (4), 1960, pp. 500-02.

Durasoff, Steve. *Bright Wind of the Spirit*. London: Hodder and Stoughton, 1972.

Edwards, Christopher. *Crazy for God*. Englewoods Cliffs, N.J.: Prentice Hall, 1979.

Edwards, Harry. *Sociology of Sports*. Homewood, Ill.: Dorsey Press, 1973.

Eggan, Fred. *The American Indian, Perspectives for the Study of Social Change*. Chicago: Aldine, 1966

Elkin, Frederick. *The Family in Canada*. Ottawa: Canadian Conference on the Family, 1964.

Elliott, David R. "The Devil and William Aberhart: The Nature and Function of his Eschatology." *Studies in Religion*, 9, no. 3 (1980), pp. 325-337.

Ellis, Walter E. "Baptists and Radical Politics in Western Canada, 1920-1950" in (Editor) Zeman, Jarold K. *Baptist in Canada (Search for Identity amidst Diversity)*. Burlington, Ontario: Welch, 1980, pp. 27-45.

Ellwood, Robert S. Jr. *Religious and Spiritual Groups in Modern America*. Englewoods Cliffs, N.J.: Prentice Hall, 1973.

Engelmann, F.C., and M.A. Schwartz. *Political Parties and the Canadian Social Structure*. Scarborough, Ont.: Prentice-Hall, 1971.

Enroth, Ronald M. *Youth, Brainwashing and the Extremist Cults*. Grand Rapids, Michigan: Zondervan, 1977.

Epp, Frank H. *Mennonites in Canada, 1786-1920: the History of a Separate People*. Toronto: Macmillan, 1974.

Epp, Frank H. *Mennonite Peoplehood: a Plea for New Initiatives*. Waterloo, Ontario: Conrad Press, 1977.

Epp, Frank H. "The Mennonite Experience in Canada" in (Eds.) Coward, Harold and Kawamura, Leslie. *Religion and Ethnicity*. Waterloo, Ontario: Wilfrid Laurier University Press, 1978, pp. 21-36.

Ethnic Origins of Canadians. (Profile Study of the 1971 Census of Canada). Bulletin 5.1-9, May 1977. (Catalogue 99-709, Vol. V - part 1).

Evans, Christopher. *Cults of Unreason*. New York: Farrar, Strauss and Giroux, 1973.

Evenson, G.O. *Adventuring for Christ: The Story of the Evangelical Lutheran Church of Canada*. Calgary: Foothills Lutheran Press, 1974.

Eylands, Valdimer J. *Lutherans in Canada*. Winnipeg, Manitoba: The Icelandic Evangelical Lutheran Synod in North America, 1945.

Falardeau, Jean-Charles. "The Role and Importance of the Church in French Canada" in (Eds. Rioux, Marcel and Martin, Yves), *French-Canadian Society*, Vol. I., Toronto: McClelland and Stewart, 1971, pp. 342-357.

Falardeau, Jean-Charles. "The Seventeenth-Century Parish in French Canada" in (eds.) Crysdale, Stewart and Wheatcroft, Les. *Religion in Canadian Society*. Toronto: Macmillan, 1976, pp. 101-112.

Farris, Allan L. "The Presbyterian Church in Canada: 1600-1850" in (eds.) Smith, Neil G.; Farris, Allan L.: Markell, H. Keith *A Short History of the Presbyterian Church in Canada* Toronto: Presbyterian Publications, n.d. pp. 19-49.

Faulds, James. *Our Doctrinal Heritage: A Study of the Articles of Doctrines in the Basis of Union of the United Church of Canada*. N.p., n.d.

Fitch, E.R., ed. *The Baptists of Canada*. Toronto : The Standard Publishing Co., 1911.

Flanagan, Thomas. *Louis 'David' Riel: 'Prophet of the New World'*. Toronto: University of Toronto Press, 1979.

Flint, David. *The Hutterites: A Study in Prejudice*. Toronto: Oxford University Press, 1975.

Foster, William A. *Canada First*. Toronto: Hunter Rose, 1890.

Francis, E.K. *In Search of Utopia: The Mennonites in Manitoba*. Altona, Manitoba: D.W. Friesen and Son, 1955.

Freed, Josh. "The Moon Stalkers," a six-part series in the *Hamilton Spectator*. February 11, 13-17, 1978.

Freed, Josh.   *Moonwebs: Journey into the Mind of a Cult*. Toronto: Dorset Publishing, 1980.

Friedman, Robert   *Hutterite Studies*. Goshen, Indiana: Mennonite Historical Society, 1961.

Friedmann, Wolfgang G.   *German Immigration into Canada*. Toronto: Ryerson Press, 1952.

Frijda, N.H.   *Emigranten, niet-emigranten*. The Hague: Staatsdrukkerij, 1960.

Frodsham, Stanley Howard.   *With Signs Following: The Story of the Pentecostal Revival in the Twentieth Century*. Springfield, Missouri: Gospel Publishing House, 1946.

Fumoleau, Réné.   *As Long as this Land Shall Last*. Toronto: McClelland and Stewart, 1977(?).

Garigue, Philippe.   *La vie familiale des Canadiens Francais*. Montréal: Les Press de l'Université de Montréal, 1962.

Garrison, Omar V.   *The Hidden Story of Scientology*. London: Arlington Books, 1974.

Gaver, Jessyca Russell.   *Pentecostalism*. New York: Award Books, 1971.

Giddings, J. Louis.   *Ancient Men of the Arctic*. New York: Knopf, 1971.

Gilmour, J.L.   "The Baptists in Canada" in (eds.) Shortt, Adam and Doughty, Arthur G. *Canada and its Provinces (A History of the Canadian People and their Institutions)* Volume XI. Toronto: Glasgow, Brook and Co., 1914, pp. 345-377.

Gingerich, Orland.   *The Amish of Canada*. Waterloo, Ontario: Conrad Press, 1972.

Glock, Charles, and Robert Bellah, eds.   *The New Religious Consiousness*. Berkeley, California: University of California Press, 1976.

Goa, David.   "Secularization Among Ethnic Communities in Western Canada" in (eds.) Coward, Harold and Kawamura, Leslie *Religion and Ethnicity*. Waterloo, Ontario: Wilfrid Laurier University Press, 1978.

Goldman, Irving.   *The Mouth of Heaven: An Introduction to Kwakiutl Religious Thought*. New York: Wiley, 1975.

Gosling, W.G.   *Labrador: its Discovery, Exploration and Development*. Toronto: Musson, n.d.

Gosselin, A.-H.   *L'Église du Canada depuis Monseigneur de Laval jusqu'a la Conquète*. Quebec: Laflamme et Proulx, 1911.

Grant, George.   *Lament for a Nation*. Toronto: McClelland and Stewart, 1970.

Grant, John Webster.   *Canadian Experience of Church Union*. Richmond, Virginia: John Knox Press, 1967.

Grant, John Webster.   *The Church in the Canadian Era: The First Century of Confederation*. Toronto: McGraw Hill Ryerson, 1972.

Grant, John Webster.   "A Decade of Ferment: Canadian Churches in the 1960s" in (eds.) Crysdale, Stewart and Wheatcroft, Les *Religion in Canadian Society*. Toronto: Macmillan, 1976, pp. 207-218.

Grant, John Webster.   "Religion and the Quest for a National Identity: the Background in Canadian History?" in (editor) Slater, Peter *Religion and Culture in Canada*. Waterloo, Ontario: Wilfrid Laurier University Press, 1977, pp. 7-21.

Grant, John Webster.   "Missionaries and Messiahs in the Northwest." In *Studies in Religion*, 9, no. 2 (Spring 1980), pp. 125-36.

Grayston, Donald.   "Marriage as a Way of the Spirit" (Paper given for the interchurch consultation on marriage, divorce and re- marriage). Aylmer, Quebec, 1981.

Greeley, Andrew M., and Peter H. Rossi.   *The Education of Catholic Americans*. Chicago: Aldine, 1966.

Gregg, William.   *Short History of the Presbyterian Church in the Dominion of Canada*. Toronto: Printed by the author, 1892.

Grenfell, Wilfred T., and others.   *Labrador*. New York: Macmillan, 1922.

Gualtieri, Antonio R.   "Towards a Theological Perspective on Nationalism" in (editor) Slater Peter, *Religion and Culture in Canada / Religion et Culture au Canada*. Waterloo, Ont.: Wilfrid University Press, 1977, pp. 507-524.

Gustafsson, Berndt.   "Sweden" in (editors) Mol, Hans; Hetherton, Margaret; Henty, Margaret, *Western Religion*. The Hague: Mouton, 1972, pp. 479-510.

Hall, Charles Francis. *Life with the Esquimaux*. London: S. Low, Son and Marston, 1864.

Hall, Douglas. *The Canada Crisis: A Christian Perspective*, Toronto: The Anglican Book Centre, 1980.

Hallowell, A. Irving. "Ojibwa Ontology, Behaviour and World View" in (ed.) Diamond, S. *Culture in History*. New York: Columbia University Press, 1960, pp. 19-52.

Hallowell, A. Irving. *The Role of Conjuring in Saulteaux Society*. New York: Octagon, 1971 (First published in 1942).

Hamilton, William B. "Society and Schools in Nova Scotia" in (eds.) Wilson, J. Donald; Stamp, Robert M.; Audet, Louis-Philippe. *Canadian Education: a History*, Scarborough, Ontario: Prentice-Hall, 1970, pp. 86-105.

Hamm, Peter Martin. *Continuity and Change among Canadian Mennonite Brethren, 1925-1975: a Study of Sacralization and Secularization in Sectarianism*. Unpublished Ph.D. dissertation. Hamilton, Ontario: McMaster University, 1978.

Handy, Robert T. *A History of the Churches in the United States and Canada*. Oxford: Clarendon Press, 1976.

Harney, Robert E. *Italians in Canada*. Toronto: The Multicultural History Society of Ontario, 1978.

Harney, Robert, and Harold Troper. *Immigrants: A Portrait of the Urban Experience, 1980-1930*. Toronto: Van Nostrand, 1975.

Harris, W.R. *History of the Early Missions in Western Canada*. Toronto: Hunter, Rose and Co., 1893.

Hawkes, Ernest W. *The Labrador Eskimo*. Memoir 91 of the Geological Survey of Canada, Anthropological Series No. 14, Government Printing Bureau, Ottawa, 1916. Reprint New York: Johnson Reprint Corp., 1970.

Hawthorn, Harry Bertrand (ed.). *The Doukhobors of British Columbia*. Vancouver: Dent and Sons, 1955.

Hébert, Gerard. "Ou en sont les Temoins de Jehovah?" *Relations*, No. 273 (1963), pp. 263-6.

Heer, David M., and Charles A. Hubay Jr. "The Trend of Interfaith Marriages in Canada, 1922-72." in Ishwaran, K. (editor) *The Canadian Family Revised*. Toronto: Holt, Rinehart and Winston, 1976, pp. 408-17.

Hellson, John C. "The Pigeons, a Society of the Blackfoot Indians" in (eds.) Waugh, Earle H. and Prithipaul, K. Dad, *Native Religious Traditions*. Waterloo, Ontario: Wilfrid Laurier University Press, 1979, pp. 181-220.

Henderson, J.L.H. *John Strachan 1778-1867*. Toronto: University of Toronto Press, 1969.

Herbison, Herb. "Doukhobor Religion" in (eds.) Blishen, Jones, Naegele and Porter. *Canadian Society*, Toronto: MacMillan, 1968, pp. 539-562.

Herstein, H.H., L.J. Hughes, and R.C. Kirbyson. *Challenge and Survival: The History of Canada*. Scarborough: Prentice-Hall, 1970.

Higgins, Edward. "South Africa" in (editors) Mol, Hans; Hetherton, Margaret; Henty, Margaret, *Western Religion*. The Hague: Mouton, 1972, pp. 437-458.

Hill, Daniel G. *Study of Mind Development Groups, Sects and Cults in Ontario* (A Report to the Ontario Government). Toronto: Ontario Government Publications, 1980.

Hiller, Harry H. *A Critical Analysis of the Role of Religion in a Canadian Populist Movement: The Emergence and Dominance of the Social Credit Party in Alberta*. Unpublished Ph.D. Dissertation. Hamilton: McMaster University, 1972.

Hiller, Harry H. *Canadian Society: A Sociological Analysis*. Scarborough, Ontario: Prentice-Hall, 1976.

Hill-Tout, Charles. *The Native Races of the British Empire*. Vol. 1, *North America, the Far West*, London: Archibald Constable, 1907.

Hill-Tout, Charles. *The Salish People*. Vancouver: Talon Books, 1978.

Hine, Virginia. "Pentecostal Glossolalia: Toward a Functional Interpretation." *Journal for the Scientific Study of Religion*, 8, (1969), pp. 211-26.

Hodge, Frederick Webb. *Handbook of Indians in Canada*. New York: Kraus Reprint Co., 1969 (First published 1913).

Hollenweger, Walter J. *The Pentecostals*. London: S.C.M., 1972.

Holt, Simma. *Terror in the Name of God: The Story of the Sons of Freedom Doukhobors*. New York: Crown, 1964.

Hoppener, Hank. *Death of a Legend*. Toronto, Copp Clark, 1972.

Horner, Ralph G. *Ralph C. Horner, Evangelist: Reminiscences from His Own Pen*. Brockville, Ontario: Mrs. A.E. Horner, publisher, n.d.

Horowitz, Aron. *Striking Roots: Reflections on Five Decades of Jewish Life*. Oakville, Ontario: Mosaic Press, 1979.

Horsch, John. *The Hutterian Brethren 1528-1931 (A Story of Martyrdom and Loyalty)*, Cayley, Alberta: Macmillan Colony, 1974.

Hostetler, John A. *Amish Society*. Baltimore: The Johns Hopkins University Press, 1963.

Hostetler, John A. *Hutterite Society*. Baltimore: The Johns Hopkins University Press, 1975.

Hostetler, John A. *Hutterite Life*. Scottsdale, Penn.: Herald Press, 1976.

Hostetler, John A., and Gertrude Enders Huntington. *The Hutterites in North America*. New York: Holt, Rinehart and Winston, 1967.

Houtart, Francois. "Belgium" in (editors) Mol, Hans; Hetherton, Margaret; Henty, Margaret, *Western Religion*. The Hague: Mouton, 1972, pp. 67-82.

Hubbard, L. Ron. *Scientology: A New Slant on Life*. Los Angeles, California: The Church of Scientology Publications, 1976.

Hubbard, L. Ron. *What is Scientology?* Los Angeles: The Church of Scientology Publications, 1978.

Huel, Raymond. "The Irish French Conflict on Catholic Episcopal Nominations: The Western Sees and the Struggle for Domination Within the Church." *Sessions d'Étude 1975*, Ottawa: The Canadian Catholic Historical Association, 1976, pp. 50-70.

Hughes, Everett C. "Action Catholique and Nationalism: a Memorandum on the Church and Society in French Canada, 1942" in (Eds.) Crysdale, Stewart and Wheatcroft, Les. *Religion in Canadian Society*. Toronto: Macmillan, 1976, pp. 172-189.

Huizinga, Johan. *Homo Ludens*. London: Temple Smith, 1970.

Hultkrantz, Ake. *Conceptions of the Soul among North American Indians*. Stockholm: The Ethnographical Museum of Sweden, 1953.

Hultkrantz, Ake. "Ritual in Native North American Religions", in (eds.) Waugh, Earle, H. and Prithipaul K. Dad. *Native Religious Traditions*. Waterloo, Ontario: Wilfrid Laurier University Press, 1979, pp. 135-147.

Hultkrantz, Ake. "The Problem of Christian Influence on Northern Algonkian Eschatology". *Studies in Religion*, 9, no. 2 (1980), pp. 161-183.

Hunt, Richard A. and Morton B. King. "Religiosity and Marriage." *Journal for the Scientific Study of Religion*, 17 (December 1978) pp. 399-406.

Hutch, Richard A. "The Personal Ritual of Glossolalia". *Journal for the Scientific Study of Religion*, 19, no. 3 (September 1980), pp. 255-266.

Hutchinson, Roger. "Religion, Ethnicity and Public Policy", in (eds.) Coward, Harold and Kawamura, Leslie. *Religion and Ethnicity*. Waterloo, Ontario: Wilfrid Laurier University Press, 1978, pp. 135-150.

Hutchison, Bruce. *Canada, Tomorrow's Giant*. Toronto: Longmans, Green and Co., 1957.

l'Incarnation, Marie de. *Word from New France (Selected Letters)*. Toronto: Oxford University Press, 1967.

Irvine, William P. "Explaining the Religious Basis of the Canadian Partisan Identity: Success on the Third Try." *Canadian Journal of Political Science*, 7, no. 3 (September 1974), pp. 560-564.(&

Isambert, Francois A. "France" in (editors) Mol, Hans; Hetherton, Margaret; Henty, Margaret, *Western Religion*. The Hague: Mouton, 1972, pp. 175-187.

Ishwaran, K. "Family and Community among the Dutch Canadians" in (Editor) Ishwaran, K. *The Canadian Family*, Toronto: Holt, Rinehart and Winston, 1971, pp. 225-47.

Ishwaran, K. "Calvinism and Social Behaviour in a Dutch-Canadian Community", in (Editor) Ishwaran, K. *The Canadian Family*, Toronto: Holt, Rinehart and Winston, 1971, pp. 297-314.

Ishwaran, K. *The Canadian Family Revised*, Toronto: Holt, Rinhart and Winston, 1976.

Ishwaran, K. *Family, Kinship and Community*. Toronto: McGraw-Hill Ryerson Ltd., 1977.

Jacek, Henry, John McDonough, Ronald Shimizu, Patrick Smith. "The Congruence of Federal-Provincial Campaign Activity in Party Organizations: The Influence of Recruitment Patterns in Three Hamilton Ridings." *Canadian Journal of Political Science*, 5, no. 2 (June 1972), pp. 190-205.

Jacquet, Constant H. *Yearbook of American and Canadian Churches*. Nashville, Tenn.: Abingdon, 1980.

Jaenen, Cornelius J. *The Role of the Church in New France*. Toronto: McGraw-Hill Ryerson, 1976.

Jaggs, W. Kenneth. *A Survey of the Upsurge in the Development of New Religious Movements with Particular Reference to the Movement Known as Scientology*. Toronto: Addiction Research Foundation, Substudy No. 790, 1976.

James, William C. "The Canoe Trip as a Religious Quest." *Studies in Religion*, 10, no. 2 (1981), pp. 151-167.

Jamieson, Stuart. "Economic and Social Life" in (editor) Hawthorn, Harry B. *The Doukhobors of British Columbia*. Vancouver: The University of British Columbia, 1955. pp. 44-96.

Jenness, Diamond. *The Life of the Copper Eskimo*. Report of the Canadian Arctic Expedition, 1913-18, XII. Ottawa: F.A. Acland, 1922.

Jenness, Diamond. *The Ojibway Indians of Parry Island, Their Social Religious Life*. Ottawa: National Museum of Canada, 1935.

Jenness, Diamond. *The Carrier Indians of the Bulkley River*. Washington: Bulletin 133 of the Bureau of American Ethnology, 1943.

Jenness, Diamond. *The People of the Twilight*. Chicago: University of Chicago Press, 1970. (First published 1928).

Jenness, Diamond. "Canadian Indian Religion" in (eds.) Crysdale, Stewart and Wheatcroft, Les. *Religion in Canadian Society*. Toronto Macmillan, 1976, pp. 71-78.

Jenness, Eileen. *The Indian Tribes of Canada*. Toronto: Ryerson Press, 1966, (First published 1933).

The Jesuit Rélations and Allied Documents. Vol. 8, *Quebec, Hurons, Cape Breton, 1634-1636*. Vol. 9, *Quebec, 1636*. Vol. 18, *Hurons and Quebec, 1640*. Vol. 36, *Lower Canada, Abenakis, 1650-1651*. Vol. 60, *Lower Canada 1675-1677*. Cleveland: Burrows Brothers, 1897-99.

Johnson, F. Henry. *A Brief History of Canadian Education*. Toronto: McGraw-Hill, 1968.

Johnson, L.P.V., and Ola J. MacNutt. *Aberhart of Alberta*. Edmonton, Alberta: Institute of Applied Art, 1970.

Jolicoeur, Catherine. "La Vie Religieuse des Acadiens a travers leur Croyances Traditionnelles." *Sessions d'Étude (La Societé Canadienne d'Histoire de l'Église Catholique)*, 1981, pp. 79-87.

Judah, J. Stillson. *Hare Krishna and the Counter-Culture*. New York: John Wiley and Sons, 1974.

Kage, Joseph. *The Dynamics of Economic Adjustment of Canadian Jewry*. Montreal: Jewish Immigrant Aid Services of Canada, 1970.

Kaill, Robert G. "The Impact of Clerical Attitudes and Liberalism on Ecumenism" in (eds.) Crysdale, Stewart and Wheatcroft, Les *Religion in Canadian Society*. Toronto: Macmillan, 1976, pp. 398-410.

Kalbach, Warren E., and W.W. McVey. "Religious Composition of the Canadian Population" in (eds.) Crysdale, Stewart and Wheatcroft, Les. *Religion in Canadian Society*. Toronto: Macmillan, 1976, pp. 221-240.

Kalbach, Warren E., and Madeline H. Richard. "Differential Effects of Ethno-Religious Structure on Linguistic Trends and Economic Achievements of Ukranian Canadians" in (Eds.) Petryshyn, W.R. *Changing Realities: Social Trends Among Ukrainian Canadians*. Edmonton: The Canadian Institute of Ukrainian Studies, 1980.

Kallen, Evelyn. *Spanning the Generations: A Study in Jewish Identity*. Don Mills, Ontario: Longman, Canada, 1977.

Kaplan, Bert, and Thomas F.A. Plaut. *Personality in a Communal Society: An Analysis of the Mental Health of the Hutterites*. Lawrence, Kansas: University of Kansas Publications, 1956.

Kauffman, J. Howard, and Leland Harder. *Anabaptists four centuries later*. Kitchener: Herald Press, 1975.

Kaufman, Robert. *Inside Scientology*. London: Olympia Press, 1972.

Kehrer, Gunter. "Germany: Federal Republic" in (editors) Mol, Hans; Hetherton, Margaret; Henty, Margaret. *Western Religion*. The Hague: Mouton, 1972, pp. 189-212.

Kerans, Patrick. "Punishment vs. Reconciliation: Retributive Justice and Social Justice in the Light of Social Ethics in Canada" in (editor) Slater, Peter, *Religion and Culture in Canada / Religion et Culture au Canada*, Waterloo, Ont.: Wilfrid Laurier University Press, 1977, pp. 225-269.

Kertzer, Morris N. *What is a Jew?* New York: Macmillan, 1974.

Kilbourn, William. "Prologue" in Kilbourn, William (editor). *Religion in Canada*. Toronto: McClelland and Stewart, 1968, pp. 6-24.

Kildahl, John P. *The Psychology of Speaking in Tongues*. New York: Harper and Row, 1972.

Kildahl, John P. "Psychological Observations" in (editor) Michael P. Hamilton, *The Charismatic Movement*. Grand Rapids, Michigan: Eerdmans, 1975, pp. 124-142.

Klassen, William. "Two men from the West" in (ed.) Slater, Peter, *Religion and Culture in Canada*. Waterloo, Ontario: Wilfrid Laurier University Press, 1977, pp. 271-288.

Kuhring, Mrs. G.A. *The Church and the Newcomer* (issued by the Joint Committee on Education of the Church of England in Canada). Toronto: The Church House, n.d.

Kulbeck, Gloria Grace. *What God hath Wrought: A History of the Pentecostal Assemblies of Canada*. Toronto: Pentecostal Assemblies of Canada, 1958.

Kurelek, William, and Abraham Arnold. *Jewish Life in Canada*. Hurtig Publishers; Edmonton, 1976.

Laeyendecker, Leo. "The Netherlands" in (editors) Mol, Hans; Hetherton, Margaret; Henty, Margaret. *Western Religion*. The Hague: Mouton, 1972, pp. 325-363.

Laflèche, Guy. "La Chamanism des Amerindiens et des Missionnaires de la Nouvelle-France." *Studies in Religion*, 9, no. 2 (1980), pp. 137-160.

Lahontan, Louis Armand de Lom d'Arce, baron de. *New Voyages to North America*. Vols. 1 and 2. New York: Franklin, 1970 (First published 1703).

Lalive d'Épinay, Christian. *Haven of the Masses: A Study of the Pentecostal Movement in Chile*. London: Lutterworth, 1969.

Landes, Ruth. *Ojibwa Religion and the Midewiwin*. Madison: University of Wisconsin Press, 1968.

Landes, Ruth. *The Ojibwa Woman*. New York: Norton, 1971.

Langtry, J. *History of the Church in Eastern Canada and Newfoundland*. London: Society for the Promoting of Christian Knowledge, 1892.

Laponce, J.A. "The Religious Background of Canadian M.P.'s." *Political Studies*, 6, no. 3 (1958) pp. 253-258.

Laurence, Margaret. *The Stone Angel*. Toronto: McClelland and Stewart, 1968.

Laurence, Margaret. *The Diviners*. Toronto: Bantam Books, 1978.

Lazerwitz, Bernard. "Religion and Social Structure in the United States" in Schneider, Louis, editor, *Religion, Culture and Society*. New York: Wiley, 1964, pp. 426-439.

Le Clercq, Chrétien. *New Relation of Gaspesia*. Toronto: The Champlain Society, 1910 (First published 1691).

Le Jeune, Paul. *Rélation de ce qui s'est passé en la Nouvelle France, 1626*. Tome 1. Montréal: Éditions du Jour, 1972.

Le Jeune, Paul. *Rélation de ce qui s'est passé en la Nouvelle France, 1634*. Tome 1. Montréal: Éditions du Jour, 1972.

Le Jeune, Paul. *Rélations des Jesuites 1637-1641*. Tome 2. Montréal: Éditions du Jour, 1972.

Lee, John A. *Sectarian Healers and Hypnotherapy* (Report to the Committee on the Healing Arts, Toronto, December 1967). Toronto: Queen's Printer, 1970.

Leland, C. Charles Godfrey. *The Algonquin Legends of New England, or Myths and Folklore of the Micmac, Passamaquoddy and Penobscot Tribes*. London: Sampson Low, Marston, Searle, and Rivington, 1884.

Levine, Saul V.   "Adolescents, Believing and Belonging." *Annals of the Society for Adolescent Psychiatry*, 7 (1979).

Levine, Saul V.   "The Role of Psychiatry in the Phenomenon of Cults." *Canadian Journal of Psychiatry*, 24 (November 1979).

Levine, Saul V.   "The Physical and Mental Health Aspects of Religious Cults and Mind Development Groups." Appendix in Hill, Daniel G., *Study of Mind Development Groups, Sects and Cults in Ontario* (A Report to the Ontario Government). Toronto: Government Publications, 1980, pp. 665-717.

Levine, Saul V., and Nancy E. Salter   "Youth and Contemporary Religious Movements: Psychosocial Findings." *Canadian Psychiatric Association Journal*, 21 (1976).

Levitt, Joseph.   "The Birth of the Nationalist League" in (eds.) Clark, Samuel D.; Grayson, Paul J. and Grayson, Linda M. *Prophecy and Protest: Social Movements in Twentieth-Century Canada*, Toronto: Gage, 1975, pp. 317-321.

Lifton, Robert Jay.   *Thought Reform and the Psychology of Totalism*. New York: Norton, 1961.

Lipset, Seymour M.   "Revolution and Counter-Revolution: The United States and Canada." Berkeley, California: Institute of International Studies, University of California, n.d.

Locher, G.W.   *The Serpent in Kwakiutl Religion*. Leyden, The Netherlands: Brill, 1932.

Loken, Gulbrand.   *From Fjord to Frontier: A History of the Norwegians in Canada*. Toronto: McClelland and Stewart, 1980.

Lottes, Klaus V.   *Jehovah's Witnesses: a Contemporary Sectarian Community*. Unpublished M.A. Thesis, Hamilton, Ontario: McMaster University, 1972.

Lower, Arthur R.M.   *Colony to Nation: A History of Canada*, Toronto, Longmans, Green, 1946.

Loy, John W., Barry D. McPherson, and Gerald Kenyon   *Sports and Social Systems*. Reading, Mass.: Addison-Wesley, 1978.

Lucas, Henry S.   *Netherlanders in America: Dutch Immigration in the United States and Canada, 1789-1950*. Ann Arbor: The University of Michigan Press, 1955.

Lupul, Manoly R. "Education in Western Canada Before 1873" in (Eds.) Wilson, J. Donald; Stamp, Robert M.; Audet, Louis-Philip, *Canadian Education: a History*. Scarborough, Ontario: Prentice-Hall, 1970.

Lurie, Nancy Oestreich. "The Contemporary American Indian Scene" in (eds.) Leacock, Eleanor Burke and Lurie, Nancy Oestreich, *North American Indians in Historical Perspective*. New York: Random, 1971. 418-480.

Lüschen, G. "The Interdependence of Sport and Culture" in Sage, G. (Ed.) *Sport and American Society*, Don Mills: Wesley Publishing Co., 1974.

Lussier, Antoine S. "The Métis" in (eds.) Sealey, D. Bruce and Kirness, Verna J., *Indians Without Tipis*. Agincourt, Ontario: The Book Society of Canada, 1974, pp. 39-52.

Lynch, Charles. "His Grace Pleads against Caesar on new BNA ACT." *The Spectator* (Hamilton, Ontario), 8 January 1981, p. 2.

Lyon, George Fr. *The Private Journal of Captain G.F. Lyon of H.M.S. Hecla, during the recent Voyage of Discovery under Captain Parry*. London, 1824. Also Boston, 1824. Barre, Massachusetts: Imprint Society, 1970.

MacCormac, J. *Canada, America's Problem*. New York: Viking Press, 1940, pp. 61-71.

MacInnes, Daniel William. *Clerics, Fishermen, Farmers and Workers: the Antigonish Movement and Identity in Eastern Nova Scotia, 1928 - 1939* (Unpublished Ph.D. thesis). Hamilton, Ontario: McMaster University, 1978.

MacKinnon, Frank. *The Crown in Canada*. Calgary, Alberta: McClelland and Stewart West, 1977.

MacKinnon, Ian F. *Settlements and Churches in Nova Scotia, 1749-1776*. Halifax: T.C. Allen & Co., 1930.

MacLean, John. *The Indians: their Manners and Customs*. Toronto: Briggs, 1889.

MacLean, John. *Canadian Savage Folk*. Toronto: William Briggs, 1896.

MacLennan, Hugh. *Two Solitudes*. Toronto: Macmillan, 1957.

MacLennan, Hugh. *The Watch that Ends the Night*. Scarborough, Ontario: The New American Library, 1958.

MacQueen, Angus James. "Coming out of the Clerical Cocoon." *MacLean's Magazine*, 26 April 1982, p. 10.

MacRae, Peter H. *The Anglican Church and the Ecumenical Movement in New Brunswick* (Unpublished M.A. thesis). University of New Brunswick, 1969.

Malcolm, Andrew. *The Tyranny of the Group*. Totowa, New Jersey: Littlefield, Adams and Co., 1975.

Mandelbaum, David G. *The Plains Cree*. Regina: Canadian Plains Research Center, 1979 (First published, partly in 1940).

Mann, W.E. *Sect, Cult and Church in Alberta*. Toronto: University of Toronto Press, 1955.

Mann, W.E. "The Canadian Church Union, 1925" in (Eds.) Crysdale, Stewart and Wheatcroft, Les. *Religion in Canadian Society*. Toronto: Macmillan, 1976, pp. 385-397.

Markell, H. Keith. "The Presbyterian Church in Canada: 1850-1925" in (eds.) Smith, Neil G.; Farris, Allen L.; Markell, H. Keith, *A Short History of the Presbyterian Church in Canada*. Toronto : Presbyterian Publications, n.d., pp. 50-73.

Marquis, Thomas Guthrie. *The Jesuit Missions*. (Vol. 4 of Chronicles of Canada) Toronto: Glasgow, Brook & Co., 1920.

Marsden, Lorna R., and Edward B. Harvey. *Fragile Federation: Social Change in Canada*, Toronto: McGraw-Hill Ryerson, 1979.

Martin, David. "Great Britain: England" in (editors) Mol, Hans; Hetherton, Margaret; Henty, Margaret. *Western Religion*. The Hague: Mouton, 1972, pp. 229-247.

Martin, Walter. *The Kingdom of the Cults*. Minneapolis: Bethany Fellowship, 1977.

Marunchak, Michael H. *The Ukrainian Canadians*. Winnipeg: Ukrainian Free Academy of Sciences, 1970.

Masters, D.C. *The Coming of Age*. Toronto: C.B.C. Publications, 1967.

Maude, Aylmer. *A Peculiar People (The Doukhobors)*. New York: AMS Press, 1970 (First published in 1904).

McDonald, Lynn. "Religion and Voting: A Study of the 1968 Canadian Federal Election in Ontario." *Canadian Review of Sociology and Anthropology*, 6, no. 3 (1969), pp. 129-144.

McDonald, Lynn. "Attitude Organization and Voting Behaviour in Canada." *Canadian Review of Sociology and Anthropology*, 8, no. 3 (August 1971), pp. 164-184.

McDonald, Michael. *Bibliography on the Family from the Fields of Theology and Philosophy*. Ottawa: Vanier Institute, 1964.

McDonnell, Killian. *Charismatic Renewal and the Churches*. New York: Seabury Press, 1976.

McGee, Thomas D'Arcy. *Speeches and Addresses*. London: Chapman and Hall, 1865.

McIlwraith, T.F. *The Bella Coola Indians*. Vols. 1 & 2. Toronto: University of Toronto Press, 1948.

McLelland, Joseph C. "Walter Bryden" in (editor) Reid, W. Stanford *Called to Witness (Profiles of Canadian Presbyterians)*. Hamilton, Ontario: Committee on History (Presbyterian Church of Canada), 1980, pp. 119-127.

McNaught, Kenneth. "The National Outlook of English-Speaking Canadians" in (Editor), Russell, Peter, *Nationalism in Canada*, Toronto: McGraw-Hill Ryerson, 1966.

McPherson, Aimee Semple. *This is That*. Los Angeles: Echo Park Evangelistic Association, 1923.

McWhinney, Edward. *Canada and the Constitution 1979-1982: Patriotism and the Charter of Rights*. Toronto: University of Toronto Press, 1982.

Mealing, F. Mark. "The Doukhobors: Family and Rites of Passage" in (ed.) K. Ishwaran, *Canadian Families: Ethnic Variations*. Toronto: McGraw-Hill Ryerson, 1980, pp. 181-197.

Meisel, John. "Religious Affiliation and Electoral Behaviour: a Case Study." *Canadian Journal of Economics and Political Science*, 22, no. 4, (November 1956), pp. 481-496.

Meisel, John. *The Canadian Federal Election of 1957*. Toronto: University of Toronto Press, 1969.

Meisel, John. *Working Papers on Canandian Politics*. Montreal: McGill-Queen's University Press, 1975.

Mikolaski, Samuel J. "Baptists on the March" *The Canadian Baptist*, 128, no. 7, (July/August 1982), pp. 4-5.

Millett, David. "A Typology of Religious Organizations Suggested by the Canadian Census." *Sociological Analysis*, 30, (1969), pp. 108-19.

Milner, Sheilagh H., and Henry Milner. "Authoritarianism and Sellout in Quebec in the 1930s" in (Eds.) Crysdale, Stewart and Wheatcroft, Les. *Religion in Canadian Society*. Toronto: Macmillan, 1976, pp. 161-172.

Miner, Horace. *St. Denis - A French Canadian Parish*. Chicago: University of Chicago Press, 1939.

Mladenovic, M. "Orthodoxy in Canada and Vatican II." *The New Review*. 6(4); 1-19, 1966.

Moir, John S. *Church and State in Canada, 1627-1867* (Basic Documents). Toronto: McClelland and Stewart, 1967.

Moir, John S. *The Church in the British Era: From the British Conquest to Confederation*. Toronto: McGraw-Hill Ryerson, 1972.

Moir, John S. *Enduring Witness: A History of the Presbyterian Church in Canada*. Presbyterian Publications, n.d. (about 1975).

Moir, John S. "Canadian Protestant Reaction to the Ne Temere Decree," *Sessions d'Etude (La Société Canadienne d'Histoire de l'Eglise Catholique)* 1981, pp. 78-90.

Mol, Johannis (Hans) J. *Churches and Immigrants*. The Hague: Research Group for European Migration Problems, 1961.

Mol, Johannis (Hans) J. *Christianity in Chains*. Melbourne: Nelson, 1969.

Mol, Johannis (Hans) J. "Secularization and Cohesion." *Review of Religious Research*, 2, no. 3 (Spring 1970), pp. 183-191.

Mol, Johannis (Hans) J. *Religion in Australia*. Melbourne: Nelson, 1971.

Mol, Johannis (Hans) J. "New Zealand" in (editors) Mol, Hans; Hetherton, Margaret; Henty, Margaret. *Western Religion*. The Hague: Mouton, 1972, pp. 365-379.

Mol, Johannis (Hans) J. "Marginality and Commitment as Hidden Variables in the Jellinek/Weber/Merton Theses on the Calvinist Ethic." *Current Sociology*, No. 22, 1974, no. 1-3, pp. 279-297.

Mol, Johannis (Hans) J. "Major Correlates of Churchgoing in Canada" in (eds.) Crysdale, Stewart and Wheatcroft, Les. *Religion in Canadian Society*, Toronto: Macmillan, 1976, pp. 241-254.

Mol, Johannis (Hans) J. *Identity and the Sacred*. Oxford: Blackwell, 1976; or New York: Free Press, 1977.

Mol, Johannis (Hans) J. "Introduction" in (ed.) Mol, Hans *Identity and Religion*, London, Sage, 1978, pp. 1-17.

Mol, Johannis (Hans) J. *Wholeness and Breakdown: A Model for the Interpretation of Nature and Society*. Madras: The Dr. S. Radhakrishnan Institute for Advanced Study in Philosophy, University of Madras, 1978a.

Mol, Johannis (Hans) J. "Theory and Data on the Religious Behaviour of Migrants." *Social Compass*, 26, no. 1 (1979a), pp. 31-39.

Mol, Johannis (Hans) J. "The Identity Model of Religion: How It Compares with Nine Other Theories of Religion and How It Might Apply to Japan" (Opening address of the International conference of the Sociology of Religion, Tokyo, 1978). *Japanese Journal of Religious Studies*, 6, no. 1 & 2 (March-April-June 1979b), pp. 11-38.

Mol, Johannis (Hans) J. "The Origin and Function of Religion: A Critique of, and Alternative to, Durkheim's Interpretation of the Religion of Australian Aborigines." *Journal for the Scientific Study of Religion*, 18, no. 4 (December 1979c), pp. 379-389.

Mol, Johannis (Hans) J. "Belief: its Contribution to Whole-making." *Religious Traditions* (A Journal in the Study of Religion), 2, no. 2 (October 1979d), pp. 6-23.

Mol, Johannis (Hans) J. *The Fixed and the Fickle: Religion and Identity in New Zealand*. Waterloo, Ontario: Wilfrid Laurier University Press, 1982a.

Mol, Johannis (Hans) J. *The Firm and the Formless: Religion and Identity in Aboriginal Australia*. Waterloo, Ontario: Wilfrid Laurier University Press, 1982b.

Mol, Johannis (Hans) J. "Time and Transcendence in a Dialectical Sociology of Religion" *Sociological Analysis*, 42, no.4 (1982c), pp.317-324

Mol, Johannis (Hans) J. *Meaning and Place: An Introduction to the Social Scientific Study of Religion*. New York: Pilgrims Press, 1983.

Moody, Barry M. "The Maritime Baptists and Higher Education in the Early Nineteenth Century" in (Editor) Moody, Barry M. *Repent and Believe (The Baptist Experience in Maritime Canada)*. Hantsport, N.S.: Lancelot Press, 1980 pp. 88-102.

Moore, Brian *The Luck of Ginger Coffey*. Toronto: McClelland and Stewart, 1972.

Morgan, Lewis Henry. *League of the Iroquois*. Secaucus, New Jersey: Citadel Press, 1972 (First published 1851).

Morice, A.G. "The Roman Catholic Church West of the Great Lakes." In (eds.) Shortt, Adam, and Doughty, Arthur G. *Canada and its Provinces (A History of the Canadian People and their Institutions by one Hundred Associates)*, Vol. 11, Toronto: Glasgow, Brook and Co., 1914.

Morton, W.L. *The Canadian Identity*, Toronto: University of Toronto Press, 1975.

Mowat, Farley. *People of the Deer*. Boston: Little, Brown and Co., 1955.

Moyles, R.G. *The Blood and Fire in Canada: A History of the Salvation Army in the Dominion 1882-1976*. Toronto: Peter Martin, 1977.

Muller, Werner. "North America" in Krickeberg, Walter; Trimborn, Hermann; Muller, Werner; Zerries, Otto, *Pre-Columbian American Religions*. London: Weidenfeld and Nicolson, 1968, pp. 147-229.

Muller, Werner. "The Kwakiutl of British Columbia." In (eds.) Crysdale, Stewart and Wheatcroft, Les. *Religion in Canadian Society*, Toronto: Macmillan, 1976, pp. 79-85.

Murphy, Terrence. -"James Jones and the Establishment of Roman Catholic Church Government in the Maritime Provinces." *Sessions d'Etude (La Société Canadienne d'Histoire de L'Église Catholique)* 1981, pp. 26-42.

Nansen, Fridtjof. *Eskimo Life*. London: Longmans, Green and Co., 1894.

Needleman, Jacob, and George Baker, (eds.). *Understanding the New Religions*. New York: Seabury Press, 1978.

Nelles, Viv, and Abraham Rotstein (eds.). *Nationalism or Local Control: Responses to George Woodcock*, Toronto: New Press, 1973.

Newbery, J.W.E. "The Universe at Prayer." In (eds.) Waugh, Earl H., and Prithipaul, K. Dad, *Native Religious Traditions*, Waterloo, Ontario: Wilfrid Laurier University Press, 1979, pp. 165-178.

Newman, Peter, C. *The Acquisitors (The Canadian Establishment, Vol. 2)*. Toronto, Ont.: McClelland and Stewart, 1981.

Nichol, John Thomas. *The Pentecostals*. Plainfield, New Jersey: Logos International, 1966.

Nock, David. "Anglican Bishops and Indigenity: John Porter revisited." *Studies in Religion*, 8, no. 1 (Winter 1979), pp. 47-55.

Noonan, Brian. "The Contribution of Separate Schools to the Development of Saskatchewan: 1870 to the Present." *Sessions d'Etude (La Société Canadienne d'Histoire de l'Èglise Catholique)* 1979, pp. 71-81.

Oliver, Edmund H. *His Dominion of Canada*. Toronto: Board of Home Missions of the United Church of Canada, 1932.

O'Toole, Roger. "Sectarianism in Politics: The Internationalists and the Socialist Labour Party." In (eds.) Crysdale, Stewart and Wheatcroft, Les., *Religion in Canadian Society*, Toronto, MacMillan, 1976, pp. 321-334.

O'Toole, Roger. *The Precipitous Path: Studies in Political Sects*. Toronto: Peter Martin Associates, 1977.

Painchaud, Robert. "Les Éxigences Linguistiques dans le Récrutement d'un clergé pour l'Ouest Canadian, 1818-1920." *Session d'Étude (La Société Canadienne de l'Église Catholique)* 1975, pp. 43-64.

Paris, Erna. *Jews: an Account of their Experience in Canada*. Toronto: Macmillan, 1980.

Parkman, Francis. *The Jesuits in North America*. Boston: Little, Brown and Company, 1963 (First published 1867).

Patrick, Ted. *Let our Children Go*. New York: Dutton, 1976.

Patterson, E. Palmer II. *The Canadian Indian: A History since 1500*. Don Mills, Ontario: Collier Macmillan, 1972.

Penton, M. James. *Jehovah's Witnesses in Canada: Champions of Freedom of Speech and Worship*. Toronto: Macmillan, 1976.

Peron, Father Francois du. "Letter to Father Joseph Imbert du Peron" (27 April 1639), in (ed.) Kenton, Edna, *The Indians of North America*, Vol. 1, New York: Harcourt, Brace & Co., 1927, pp. 368-375.

Perspective Canada II (A Compendium of Social Statistics 1977). Ottawa: Ministry of Supply and Services, 1977.

Peter, Karl. "The Dynamics of Open Social Systems." In (eds.) Gallagher, and Lambert, *Social Process and Institution: The Canadian Case*, Toronto: Holt, Rinehart and Winston, 1971, pp. 164-172.

Peter, Karl. "The Dialectic of Family and Community in the Social History of Hutterites." In (ed.) Larson, Lyle E., *The Canadian Family in Comparative Perspective*, Scarborough, Ontario: Prentice Hall, 1976, pp. 337-350.

Peter, Karl. "The Hutterite Family." In (ed.) K. Ishwaran, *The Canadian Family Revised*, Toronto: Holt, Rinehart and Winston, 1976a, pp. 289-303.

Peter, Karl. "Problems in the Family, Community and Culture of Hutterites." In (ed.) Ishwaran, K., *Canadian Families: Ethnic Variations*, Toronto: McGraw-Hill Ryerson, 1980, pp. 221-236.

Peters, Victor. *All Things Common: The Hutterian Way of Life*. Minneapolis: The University of Minnesota Press, 1967.

Petersen, William. *Planned Migration: The Social Determinants of the Dutch-Canadian Movement*. Berkeley: University of California Press, 1955.

Petryshyn, W. Roman. "The Ukrainian Canadians in Social Transition." In (ed.) Lupul, Manoly, *Ukrainian Canadians, Multiculturalism and Separatism: an Assessment*, Edmonton: University of Alberta Press, 1978.

Pickering, W.S.F., and J.L. Blanchard. *Taken for Granted: A Survey of the Parish Clergy of the Anglican Church of Canada*. Anglican Church of Canada, 1967, n.p.

Pope, Liston. *Millhands and Preachers*. New Haven: Yale University Press, 1942.

Porter, John. "Higher Public Servants and the Bureaucratic Elite of Canada." *The Canadian Journal for Economics and Political Science*, 24 (1958), pp. 483-501.

Porter, John. *The Vertical Mosaic: an Analysis of Social Class and Power in Canada*. Toronto: University of Toronto Press, 1966.

Porter, John. "Canadian Character in the Twentieth Century." in (ed.) Mann, W.E. *Canada: a Sociological Profile*, Toronto: Copp Clark, 1971, pp. 1.

Preston, Richard J. *Cree Narrative: Expressing the Personal Meanings of Events*. Ottawa: National Museum of Canada, 1975.

Provost, H. "La Régime des curés au Canada francais." *Canadian Catholic Historical Association*, 1955 Report, pp. 85-103.

Purdy, Alfred. *The Caribou Horses*. Toronto: McClelland and Stewart, 1965.

Querido, Augusto. "Portugal." In (eds.) Mol, Hans; Hetherton, Margaret; Henty, Margaret. *Western Religion*, The Hague: Mouton, 1972, pp. 427-436.

Raddall, Thomas H. *His Majesty's Yankee*. Toronto: McClelland and Stewart, 1977 (First published 1942).

Radecki, Henry. *Ethnic Organizational Dynamics: the Polish Group in Canada*. Waterloo, Ontario: Wilfrid Laurier University Press, 1979.

Radecki, Henry, with Benedykt Heydenkorn. *A Member of a Distinguished Family: The Polish Group in Canada*. Toronto: McClelland and Stewart Ltd., 1976.

Ramirez, Bruno, and Michael Del Baso. *The Italians of Montréal: From Sojourning to Settlement*. Montreal: Les Éditions du Courant Inc., 1980.

Ramsey, Bruce. *A History of the German-Canadians in British Columbia*. Winnipeg, Manitoba: National Publishers, 1958.

Rasmussen, Knud Johan Victor. *Across Arctic America*. New York: Putnam, 1927.

Rasmussen, Knud Johan Victor. *Intellectual Culture of the Iglulik Eskimos*. Report of the Fifth Thule Expedition, 1921-24, 7, no.1. Copenhagen: Gyldendalske Boghandel, 1929.

Rasmussen, Knud Johan Victor. *The Netsilik Eskimos*. (Social Life and Spiritual Culture) Report of the Fifth Thule Expedition, 1921-24, 8, no. 1 & 2. Copenhagen: Nordisk Forlag, 1931 (Reprinted New York: AMS Press, 1976).

Rasmussen, Knud Johan Victor. *Intellectual Culture of the Copper Eskimos*. Report of the Fifth Thule Expedition, 1921-24, 9. Copenhagen: Nordisk Forlag, 1932 (Reprinted New York: AMS Press, 1976).

Rawlyk, George A. "From New Light to Baptist: Harris Harding and the Second Great Awakening in Nova Scotia." In (Editor) Moody, Barry M. *Repent and Believe (The Baptist Experience in Maritime Canada*, Hantsport, Nova Scotia: Lancelot Press, 1980 pp. 1-26.

Redekop, Calvin W. *The Old Colony Mennonites: Dilemmas of Minority Life*. Baltimore: Johns Hopkins University Press, 1969.

Reid, Raymond (ed.). *The Canadian Style*. Toronto: Fitzhenry and Whiteside, 1973.

Richert, Jean Pierre. "The Impact of Ethnicity on the Perception of Heroes and Historical Symbols." *Canadian Review of Sociology and Anthropology*, 11 (May 1974), pp. 156-163.

Riddell, Walter Alexander. *The Rise of Ecclesiastical Control in Quebec*. New York: Longmans, Green & Co., 1916.

Rideman, Peter (anglicized name for Riedemann). *Account of our Religion, Doctrine and Faith* (Hutterians). London: Hodder and Stoughton, 1950 (First published in Germany in 1565).

Ringuet. *Thirty Acres*. Toronto: McClelland and Stewart, 1968 (First published in 1938).

Rioux, Marcel. *Quebec in Question*. Toronto: James Lewis and Samuel, 1971.

Rioux, Marcel, and Y. Martin. *French Canadian Society*. Toronto: McClelland and Stewart, 1964.

Robertson, Heather. *Reservations are for Indians*. Toronto: James Lewis & Samuel, 1970.

Roche, Anne. "Love Among the Ruins." *Today Magazine*, 10 April 1982, pp. 8-16.

Rohner, Ronald P., and Evelyn C. Rohner. "The Kwakiutl: Indians of British Columbia." In (ed.) Elliott, Jean Leonard. *Native Peoples*, (Vol. I of *Minority Canadians*), Scarborough, Ontario: Prentice-Hall, 1971, pp. 116-133).

Rohold, S.B. *The Jews in Canada*. Toronto: Board of Home Missions of the Presbyterian Church of Canada, 1913.

Rome, David. *Canadian Jewish Archives*. Montreal: Canadian Jewish Congress, 1976.

Rome, David. *Clouds in the Thirties (on Anti-Semitism in Canada, 1929-1939)*, Section 3. Montreal: n.p., 1977.

Rome, David. *Clouds in the Thirties (on Anti-Semitism in Canada, 1929-1939)*, Section 4. Montreal: n.p., 1978.

Rosenberg, Stuart E. *The Jewish Community in Canada*, Volume I (A History). Toronto: McClelland and Stewart, 1970.

Rosenberg, Stuart E. *The Jewish Community in Canada*, Volume II (In the Midst of Freedom). Toronto: McClelland and Stewart, 1971.

Rosenberg, Stuart E. "Canada's Jews: an Overview." *Judaism*, 20 (Fall 1971a), pp. 476-489.

Ross, John Arthur. *Regionalism, Nationalism and Social Gospel Support in the Ecumenical Movement of Canadian Presbyterianism*, Hamilton, Ontario: McMaster University, 1973.

Ross, Sinclair. *As For Me and My House*. New York: Reynal and Hitchcock, 1941.

Rothney, Gordon O. "The Denominational Basis of Representation in the Newfoundland Assembly, 1919 - 1962." *Journal of Economics and Political Science*, 28 (1962), pp. 557-570.

Roy, Gabrielle. *The Tin Flute*. Toronto: McClelland and Stewart, 1969 (Originally published in 1949).

Russell, Kenneth C. "God and Church in the Fiction of Margaret Laurence." *Studies in Religion*, 7, no. 4 (Fall 1978) pp. 435-446.

Ryan, William F. *The Clergy and Economic Growth in Quebec*. Quebec: Les Presses de l'Université Laval, 1966.

Ryan, William F. "The Church's Contribution to Progress, 1896-1914." In (eds.) LaBlanc, Philip, and Arnold Edinborough, Arnold. *One Church, Two Nations*, Don Mills, Ontario: Longmans, 1968, pp. 82-95.

Sack, Benjamin G. *History of the Jews in Canada*. Montreal: Harvest House, 1965.

Samarin, William J. *Tongues of Men and Angels: The Religious Language of Pentecostalism*. New York: Macmillan, 1972.

Samarin, William J. "Making Sense of Glossolalic Nonsense." *Social Research*, 46, no. 1 (Spring 1979), pp. 88-105.

Sandall, Robert. *The History of the Salvation Army*, Vol. 3, 1883-1953 (Social Reform and Welfare Work). London: Thomas Nelson, 1966.

Sanderson, J.E. *The First Century of Methodism in Canada*, Vol. 1, 1775-1839. Toronto: William Briggs, 1908.

Sanderson, J.E. *The First Century of Methodism in Canada*, Vol. 2, 1840-1883. Toronto: William Briggs, 1910.

Schoolcraft, Henry R. *History, Condition and Prospects of the Indian Tribes of the United States*, Vol. 5. New York: Paladin Press, 1969, (First published 1855).

Schwartz, Gary. *Sect Ideologies and Social Status*. Chicago: University of Chicago Press, 1970.

Schwartz, Mildred A. *Public Opinion and Canadian Identity*. Berkeley: University of California Press, 1967.

Scott, Gini Graham. *Cult and Countercult*. Westport, Conn.: Greenwood Press, 1980.

Scott, H.A. "The Roman Catholic Church East of the Great Lakes, 1760-1912." In (eds.) Shortt, Adam, and Arthur G. Doughty. *Canada and its Provinces: A History of the Canadian People and their Institutions by one Hundred Associates*, Vol. 11, Toronto: Glascow, Brook and Co., 1914, pp. 11-112.

Scott, Jamie S. Scott. "Redemptive Imagination in Margaret Laurence's Manawaka Fiction." *Studies in Religion*, 9, no. 4 (Fall 1980), pp. 427-440.

Seeley, John R., Alexander R. Sim, and E.W. Loosley, E.W. *Crestwood Heights: A Study of the Culture of Suburban Life*. Toronto: University of Toronto Press, 1974 (First published in 1956).

Seppanen, Paavo. "Finland." In (eds.) Mol, Hans; Hetherton, Margaret; Henty, Margaret. *Western Religion*, The Hague: Mouton, 1972, pp. 143-173.

Shaffir, William. *Life in a Religious Community: the Lubavitcher Chassidim in Montreal*. Toronto: Holt, Rinehart and Winston, 1974.

Shimpo, Mitsuru. "Native Religion in Sociocultural Change: the Cree and Saulteaux in Southern Saskatchewan, 1830-1900." In (eds.) Crysdale, Stewart and Les Wheatcroft. *Religion in Canadian Society*, Toronto: Macmillan, 1976, pp. 128-140.

Shulman, Alfred. "Personality Characteristics and Psychological Problems." In (ed.) Hawthorn, Harry B. *The Doukhobors of British Columbia*, Vancouver: The University of British Columbia, 1955, pp. 122-160.

Siegfried, André. *Canada*, London: Jonathan Cape, 1937.

Silcox, Charles Edwin. *Church Union in Canada*. New York: Institute of Social and Religious Research, 1933.

Silver, A.I. "Introduction" in Tardivel, Jules-Paul, *For My Country*. Toronto: University of Toronto Press, 1975, pp. vi-xl.

Sinclair-Faulkner, Tom. "Hockey in Canada." In (ed.) Slater, Peter. *Religion and Culture in Canada*, Waterloo, Ontario: Wilfrid Laurier University Press, 1977, pp. 383-405.

Skelton, O.D. *Life and Letters of Sir Wilfrid Laurier*, Toronto: J.M. Dent, 1919.

Skinner, Alanson. *Material Culture of the Menonimi*. New York: Indian Notes and Monographs, Museum of the American Indian, Heye Foundation, 1921.

Smiley, Donald, V. "Federalism, Nationalism, and the Scope of Public Activity in Canada." In (ed.) Russell, Peter. *Nationalism in Canada*, Toronto: McGraw-Hill Ryerson, 1966, pp. 95-111.

Smiley, Donald, V. *Canada in Question: Federalism in the Eighties*. Toronto: McGraw-Hill Ryerson, 1980.

Slusher, Howard S. *Man, Sport and Existence*. Philadelphia: Lea and Febiger, 1967.

Sontag, Frederick. *Sun Myung Moon*. Nashville, Tenn.: Abingdon, 1977.

Spada, A.V. *The Italians in Canada*. Montreal: Riviera, 1969.

Sparks, Jack. *The Mindbenders*. New York: Nelson, 1977.

Speck, F.G. *Naskapi* (The Savage Hunters of the Labrador Peninsula). Norman: University of Oklahoma Press, 1977 (First published 1935).

Stefansson, Vilhjalmur. *My Life with the Eskimos*. New York: Macmillan, 1951 (First published 1913).

Steinsaltz, Adin. *The Essential Talmud*. New York: Bantam Books, 1977.

Stephenson, Marylee. "Housewives in Women's Liberation." In (ed.) Stephenson, Marylee. *Woman in Canada*, Toronto: General Publishing Co., 1977, pp. 109-125.

Sterling, Chandler W. *The Witnesses: One God, One Victory*. Chicago: Henry Regnery Co., 1975.

Stevenson, W.C. *The Inside Story of Jehovah's Witnesses*. New York: Hart Publishing, 1968.

Stewart, Gordon, and George Rawlyk. *A People Highly Favoured of God: The Nova Scotia Yankees and the American Revolution*. Toronto: Macmillan, 1972.

Stolee, H.J. *Speaking in Tongues*. Minneapolis, Minnesota: Augsburg Publishing, 1963.

Stoner, Carroll, and Jo Anne Parker. *All God's Children*. Radner, Pa.: Chilton, 1977.

Sutherland, Alexander. *Methodism in Canada: Its Work and its Story*. London: Kelly, 1903.

Tarasoff, Koozma. *A Pictorial History of the Doukhobors*. Saskatoon: Prairie Books Department, 1969.

Tardivel, Jules-Paul. *For My Country/Pour la Patrie*. (An 1895 Religious and Separatist Vision of Quebec set in the Mid-Twentieth Century). Toronto: University of Toronto Press, 1975.

Tarr, Leslie K. *This Dominion His Dominion: The Story of Evangelical Baptist Endeavour in Canada*. Willowdale, Ontario: Fellowship of Evangelical Baptist Churches in Canada, 1968.

Testa, Bart. "Bearing Witness to a Mass Exodus." *MacLean's* magazine, 16 March 1981, pp. 47-9.

Thompson, David. *Travels in Western North America 1784-1812*. Toronto: Macmillan, 1971.

Thompson, Margaret E. *The Baptist Story in Western Canada*. Calgary, Alberta: The Baptist Union of Western Canada, 1974.

Thomson, W. Nelson. "Witness in French Canada." In (ed.) Zeman, Jarold K. *Baptists in Canada: Search for Identity amidst Diversity*, Burlington, Ontario: G.R. Welch, 1980 pp. 45-65.

Thorgaard, Jorgen. "Denmark." In (ed.) Mol, Hans; Hetherton, Margaret; Henty, Margaret. *Western Religion*, The Hague: Mouton, 1972, pp. 135-141.

Threinen, Norman J. *In Search of Identity: A Look at Lutheran Identity in Canada*, Winnipeg: Lutheran Council in Canada, 1977.

Trudeau, Pierre Elliott (ed.). *La Grève de l'Amiante*. Québec: Université Laval Press, 1954.

Turner, Lucien McShan. *Ethnology of the Ungava district, Hudson Bay territory*. Bureau of American Ethnology, 11th Annual Report, 1889-90. Washington, 1894.

Upton, L.F.S. *Micmacs and Colonists* (Indian-white relations in the Maritimes 1713-1867). Vancouver: University of British Columbia Press, 1979.

Vaillant, George. *The Natural History of Alcoholism: Causes, Patterns, and Paths to Recovery*. Cambridge, Massachusetts; Harvard University Press, 1983.

Vallee, Frank, G. *Kabloona and Eskimo in the Central Keewatin*. Ottawa: The Canadian Research Centre for Anthropology, St. Paul University, 1967.

Vallee, Frank G. "Religion of the Kabloona and Eskimo." In (Eds.) Crysdale, Stewart and Wheatcroft, Les. *Religion in Canadian Society*, Toronto: Macmillan, 1976, pp. 151-160.

Vernon, C.W. *The Old Church in the New Dominion: The Story of the Anglican Church in Canada*. London: The Society of Promoting Christian Knowledge, 1929.

Vogt, Edward D. "Norway." In (eds. Mol, Hans; Hetherton, Margaret; Henty, Margaret. *Western Religion*, The Hague: Mouton, 1972, pp. 381-401.

Vosper, Cyril. *The Mind Benders*. London: Neville Spearman, 1971.

Wade, Mason. *The French Canadians 1760-1967*. Volume 1 (1760-1911), Volume II (1911-1967). Toronto: Macmillan of Canada, 1968.

Walens, Stanley. *Feasting with Cannibals: An Essay in Kwakiutl Cosmology*, Princeton, N.J.: Princeton University Press, 1981.

Wallis, Roy. *Sectarianism: Analyses of Religious and Non-religious Sects*. London: Owen, 1975.

Wallis, Roy. *The Road to Total Freedom* (A Sociological Analysis of Scientology). London: Heinemann, 1976.

Wallis, Roy. *Salvation and Protest* (Studies of Social and Religious Movements). New York: St. Martin's Press, 1979.

Wallot, Jean-Pierre. "Religion and French-Canadian Mores in the early Nineteenth Century." *Canadian Historical Review*, March 1971, pp. 51-95.

Walsh, H.H. *The Christian Church in Canada*. Toronto: Ryerson Press, 1956.

Walsh, H.H. *The Church in the French Era* (From Colonization to the British Conquest). Toronto: Ryerson Press, 1966.

Ward, Conor K. "Ireland." In (eds.) Mol, Hans; Hetherton, Margaret; Henty, Margaret. *Western Religion*, The Hague: Mouton, 1972, pp. 295-303.

Watkins, Melville. "Technology and Nationalism." In (ed.) Russell, Peter. *Nationalism in Canada*, Toronto: McGraw-Hill Ryerson, 1966, pp. 284-302.

Watt, Frank. "Nationalism in Canadian Literature." In (ed.) Russell, Peter. *Nationalism in Canada*, Toronto: McGraw-Hill Ryerson, 1966, pp. 235-251.

Waugh, Earle H., and K. Dad Prithipaul. *Native Religious Traditions*, Waterloo, Ontario: Wilfrid Laurier University Press, 1979.

West, J.A., and J. Cr. Toonder. *The Case for Astrology*. New York, Coward-McCann, 1970.

Weyer, Edward Moffat. *The Eskimos: Their Environment and Folkways*, New Haven, Connecticut: Yale University Press, 1969 (First published in 1932).

Whyte, Donald R. "Religion and the Rural Church." In (eds.) Blishen, Jones, Naegele, Porter. *Canadian Society*, Toronto: Macmillan, 1968, pp. 574-589.

Wilson, Bryan R. *Sects and Society*. London: Heinemann, 1961.

Wilson, Douglas J. *The Church Grows in Canada*. Toronto: Ryerson Press, 1966.

Wilson, Robert S. "British Influence in the Nineteenth Century." In (ed.) Zeman, Jarold K. *Baptists in Canada (Search for Identity Amidst Diversity)*, Burlington, Ontario: G.R. Welch, 1980 pp. 21-43.

Withrow, W.H. *The Native Races of North America*, Toronto: Methodist Mission Rooms, 1895.

Wolkan, Rudolf. *Die Hutterer*, Nieuwkoop: DeGraaf, 1965.

Wood, William W. *Culture and Personality Aspects of the Pentecostal Holiness Religion*, The Hague: Mouton, 1965.

Woodcock, George, and Ivan Avakumovic. *The Doukhobors*, Toronto: McClelland and Stewart, 1977.

Woodsworth, J.S. *My Neighbour*, Toronto: Methodist Church, 1911.

Woycenko, Ol'ha. *The Ukrainians in Canada*, Winnipeg: Trident Press, 1967.

Young, Egerton Ryerson. *Stories from Indian Wigwams and Northern Campfires*, London: Charles H. Kelly, 1893.

Young, Egerton Ryerson. *By Canoe and Dog-train among the Cree and Salteaux Indians*, London: Charles Kelly, 1894.

Zeman, Jarold K. (ed.). *Baptists in Canada: Search for Identity Amidst Diversity*, Burlington, Ontario: G.R. Welch, 1980.

INDEX